Joyce and the Law

The Florida James Joyce Series

UNIVERSITY PRESS OF FLORIDA

Florida A&M University, Tallahassee
Florida Atlantic University, Boca Raton
Florida Gulf Coast University, Ft. Myers
Florida International University, Miami
Florida State University, Tallahassee
New College of Florida, Sarasota
University of Central Florida, Orlando
University of Florida, Gainesville
University of North Florida, Jacksonville
University of South Florida, Tampa
University of West Florida, Pensacola

JOYCE
AND THE
LAW

EDITED BY JONATHAN GOLDMAN

UNIVERSITY PRESS OF FLORIDA
Gainesville / Tallahassee / Tampa / Boca Raton
Pensacola / Orlando / Miami / Jacksonville / Ft. Myers / Sarasota

Copyright 2017 by Jonathan Goldman
All rights reserved
Published in the United States of America

This book may be available in an electronic edition.

First cloth printing, 2017
First paperback printing, 2020

25 24 23 22 21 20   6 5 4 3 2 1

Library of Congress Cataloging-in-Publication Data
Names: Goldman, Jonathan (Jonathan E.), editor.
Title: Joyce and the law / edited by Jonathan Goldman.
Other titles: Florida James Joyce series.
Description: Gainesville : University Press of Florida, 2017. | Series: The Florida James Joyce series | Includes bibliographical references and index.
Identifiers: LCCN 2017018508 | ISBN 9780813054742 (cloth)
ISBN 9780813064475 (pbk.)
Subjects: LCSH: Joyce, James, 1882–1941—Criticism and interpretation. | Authors, Irish—Criticism and interpretation. | Law and literature—History. | Joyce, James, 1882–1941—Characters. | Law—Ireland—History.
Classification: LCC PR6019.O9 Z64734 2017 | DDC 823/.912—dc23
LC record available at https://lccn.loc.gov/2017018508

The University Press of Florida is the scholarly publishing agency for the State University System of Florida, comprising Florida A&M University, Florida Atlantic University, Florida Gulf Coast University, Florida International University, Florida State University, New College of Florida, University of Central Florida, University of Florida, University of North Florida, University of South Florida, and University of West Florida.

University Press of Florida
2046 NE Waldo Road
Suite 2100
Gainesville, FL 32609
http://upress.ufl.edu

CONTENTS

Foreword vii
Acknowledgments ix

Introduction: James Joyce and the Law 1
Jonathan Goldman

PART I. LEGAL LIVES OF JOYCE'S CHARACTERS

1. Criminal Conversation: Marriage, Adultery, and the Law in Joyce's Work 15
   Janine Utell

2. Joyce and British Finance Law: Adrift on the Waters of International Investment 31
   Carey Mickalites

3. Joyce, the Aliens Act, and Immigration 47
   Steven Morrison

PART II. LEGAL REGIMES OF JOYCE'S SPACES AND PLACES

4. National Languages and Neutral Idioms: Joyce among the Language Laws 63
   Tekla Mecsnóber

5. Rights and Losses: The Ends of Minority Recognition in Joyce and International Law 84
   Rich Cole

6. Dublin Inc.: Municipal Corporation Reform in "Ivy Day in the Committee Room" 105
   Celia Marshik

7. "Nobody Owns": *Ulysses*, Tenancy, and Property Law   122
   Andrew Gibson

8. *Pro Bono Publico*: Urban Space in "Cyclops"   135
   Robert Brazeau

   PART III. JOYCE'S LEGAL LANGUAGES AND SOURCES

9. "Eating orangepeels in the park": Largesse, Libel, and Public Action in *Ulysses*   157
   Anne Marie D'Arcy

10. The Law in/of *Finnegans Wake*: A Starchamber Quiry   179
    Terence Killeen

11. The Logos of Trademark: Joyce, Bass Ale, and Brand Insignias   193
    Jonathan Goldman

    PART IV. CIRCULATION AND ITS LEGALITIES

12. Literature Meets Law in Court: The Trials of *Ulysses*   213
    Joseph M. Hassett

13. The Prestige of the Law: Revisiting Obscenity Law and Judge Woolsey's *Ulysses* Decision   228
    Kevin Birmingham

14. *Ulysses* as Deodand: Books, Automobiles, and the Law of Forfeiture   246
    Robert Spoo

15. The Past and Future of Joycean Copyright   262
    Amanda Golden

    List of Contributors   277
    Index   279

FOREWORD

Call it *CSI Joyce*: admirable forensic skill has been displayed in Goldman's star chamber inquiry. Uncovering the importance of an actual murder case from October 1922 from its presence in the *Finnegans Wake* notebooks, Terence Killeen uses the perfect analogy of the bloodhound: "they do leave the particular scent of their legal origins on the text, and it is possible for a skilled reader to, as it were, sniff them out." Joyce is our fox, and all after. Stephen's fox, "red reek of rapine in his fur" (2.148), has left his scent, and it is up to us to track the quarry down. To be "at fault" is neither a legal nor a moral term: it is a term originally taken from foxhunting meaning "to overrun the line of scent." Stephen is "at fault" because he has let the fox of his riddle escape; Bloom is "at fault" (15.633) in "Circe" because he has lost his way. The characters lose the scent: this is what it means to be literally at fault. So we are all at fault, according to Joyce: all of us have lost the scent. The bloodhounds in *Joyce and the Law* have picked up the trail, and now we can follow their way.

The 1898 Local Government Act, the Licensing Act of 1902, the state of Irish Land Law in 1903, the Aliens Act of 1905: all these old statutes come alive in this book and are given meaning for Joyce and for today. By taking the "bloody big books" (12.254) that Denis Breen has tucked under his armpit and actually reading them, these writers have done us all a tremendous service. Celia Marshik shows how a municipal statute opens the door to a new reading of "Ivy Day in the Committee Room," Robert Brazeau gives us the unintended consequences of legal attempts to limit alcohol consumption in Dublin, and Andrew Gibson turns the thickets of property law into a compelling meditation on the nature of ownership. Steven Morrison shows that the rhetoric leading up to the Aliens Act was equally toxic on both sides of the Irish Channel: "So far as Ireland is concerned, she sees the Jews swarming in while her children are going out" (*United Irishman*); "There is hardly an Englishman in this room who does not live under the constant danger of being driven from his home . . . by the off-scum of Europe" (British Brothers League). This is hard but necessary reading in 2016, as waves of migrants land on European shores. The legal concerns in this volume are still topical in the twenty-first century: Janine Utell's study of divorce law takes us to gay marriage, Carey Mickalites's reading of Limited Liability looks ahead to the Celtic Tiger's real estate bubble, and Morrison makes clear that Bloom is by birth an anchor baby. These are issues that simply won't go away.

Joseph M. Hassett is revelatory on Quinn's incompetence as a legal advocate for Anderson and Heap; Quinn defended *Ulysses* on the grounds that the book was too difficult to understand, and thus could not appeal to the baser instincts. A more compelling argument, as Hassett points out, is that Joyce's work has a "terrible veracity," a defense first suggested by John Yeats and followed by Judges Woolsey and Augustus Hand, who were willing to allow that the sexual urges felt by the characters in *Ulysses* were expressions of a natural idea. Again, we are all at fault in Joyce's universe: Judge Learned Hand went further to argue that the free expression of truth and beauty could not be restricted, for to do so would be a mutilation that would actually encourage perversion. Learned Hand, besides having the all-time best name in legal history, turns out to have been a model reader of literary criticism: corruptible people, he says, are precisely those who will read only excerpts. Truer words were never spoken . . .

Sebastian D. G. Knowles
Series Editor

ACKNOWLEDGMENTS

This collection is the result of collaboration not just between authors and editors but also among institutions and colleagues. At the University Press of Florida, series editor Sebastian Knowles offered support and suggestions, a sharp eye and a sharp wit, from the proposal stage to his intense reader report. Every chapter here is better for his incisive yet entertaining commentary. Editors Michele Fiyak-Burkley, Sian Hunter, and Shannon McCarthy have been enthusiastic and communicative as they helped usher the book toward publication. Ann Marlowe's copyedits were vigilant and keen. I understand how the series maintains its standards and continues its success against the odds of the current publishing climate.

At New York Institute of Technology's Manhattan campus, the English Department has, led by Chair Katherine Williams, supported my work on Joyce and the law as it has all of my research and writing. I am continually grateful to my colleagues there: Cathy Bernard, Mike Gamble, Aiping Gao, Jennifer Griffiths, Lori Jirousek-Falls, Lissi Krikelis, Michael Schiavi, and Gary Stephens. This project benefited from internal NYIT grants that sponsored release time, research materials, and conference funding and provided me with an adroit editorial assistant, Luisa Uribe. I thank particularly Dean James Simon, Provost Rahmat Shoureshi, and retired president Edward Giuliano. NYIT's Office of Sponsored Research (especially Allison Andors) and Center for Teaching and Learning (Francine Glazer) have provided myriad forms of support. The NYIT librarians always have my back.

As a fellow of the New York Public Library's Wertheim Study, I have been helped immeasurably by library staff, including Jay Barksdale, Carolyn Broomhead, and Melanie Locay. The International James Joyce Foundation supported this project by allowing contributors to hone their arguments at panels held at the 2015 Modern Language Association Convention in Chicago and the 2016 International James Joyce Symposium in London.

The history of *Joyce and the Law* begins at the 2012 Joyce Symposium in Dublin, where *James Joyce Quarterly* editor Sean Latham and I took a few minutes to sit down together at Duke's. Our conversation there set in motion my guest-edited special issue of *JJQ* (50.4, "Legal Joyce") that evolved and expanded into this volume. Sean merits my endless gratitude, as does *JJQ* managing editor Carol Kealiher. Thanks also go to Peter Murray for his editorial assistance on that issue. *Joyce and the Law* contains revisions of *JJQ* "Legal Joyce" articles by Kevin Birmingham, Robert Brazeau, Andrew Gibson, and Celia Marshik and a thoroughly overhauled version of my introductory essay. It also contains a revision of my work on trademark published in *JJQ* 51.1. I am indebted to the journal for allowing these essays to appear here, and to its staff for the contributions from which this volume benefits.

It has been an honor to work with my fourteen fellow *Joyce and the Law* authors. They produced exceptionally well-researched and well-wrought work; all were responsive, diligent, and cheerful throughout the editorial process. Some went beyond their purview to help with editorial matters, including constructive critiques of my own essays here and connecting me with other potential contributors. I wish to thank them particularly: Bob Spoo, Rob Brazeau, Amanda Golden, Anne Marie D'Arcy, Janine Utell, and Rich Cole. My longtime colleagues Alisa Hartz and Jason Solinger also provided feedback along the way.

I may never write an entire book devoted to Joyce, so I wish to take this moment to thank John Bishop, whose mentoring during my undergraduate days drove my interest in Joyce studies. (It's his fault.)

I wish to thank my parents and sister: Kathi, Larry, and Carolyn Goldman, none of whom ever expected I would have anything to do professionally with the law. Lastly, all possible gratitude goes to Jamie Favaro, whose aid, tangible and intangible, has been essential to any project I have engaged in over the last six years.

Introduction

James Joyce and the Law

JONATHAN GOLDMAN

In the works of James Joyce, the law is flush with contradictions, confusions, ambiguities, and absurdities. It penetrates every aspect of the social world, much as in the writings of Joyce's contemporary Franz Kafka, whose fictions are, more than Joyce's, associated with the shadows cast by legal regimes. In Joyce's work the law is rarely the authoritarian obstacle we often think of as Kafkaesque. To Joyce the law is a set of languages that can create a world, an intricate system that acts as a shaper of events, absorbed and deployed by the godlike author whose godlike presence it mirrors. Like that author, it does not have to be announced by name to make its presence felt in the text; it can sit back and pare its nails, silent, invisible. Legality arises in Joyce's texts as negotiable in life and in print. The law is finally a discourse—a set of social signs and codes—as is clear from many moments of Joyce's writing: Farrington's legal copy-work in *Dubliners*'s "Counterparts," the parodies of legalese of "Cyclops" and the trial scenes of "Circe" in *Ulysses*, and the myriad passages of *Finnegans Wake* that pick up the law where the earlier works leave off.

Joyce's view of that discourse's power and its parallels to literary production invite our critical attention. Paul J. Heald writes of scholarship that assumes that "law and literature serve very similar functions in society," as each "is a language—a system of signs around which we constitute ourselves as a community" (6). For readers who argue that literature inflects, rather than reflects, how a culture thinks—that narrative works have mutually influential relationships with their historical contexts—the point of contact between literature and legal discourse constitutes an exhilarating object. The law literalizes these critical premises while throwing the power of literary language—less tangible, more affective—into relief. Ravit Reichman, writing of law and literary modernism, argues that these two seemingly disparate idioms "exist in a *contingent* relationship ... one of mutual implication" where ethical matters of literature are in dialogue with legal doctrine (2).

Such understandings animate *Joyce and the Law*, in which an international cohort of fifteen critics seizes upon the opportunity to analyze Joyce and the law together. The volume treats Joyce's works from *Dubliners* to the *Wake* (including some surprising stops en route) alongside legal statutes, documents, and cases; in the context of law enforcement, government mandate, and international agreement; and against a backdrop of legal rhetoric and legal theory. These essays illustrate how legal research elucidates the movements and motivations of Joyce's characters and the language and shape of his narratives—including both his fictional works and his biography.

The volume demonstrates that the law is an underexplored archive. We are a century removed from Joyce, and the Dublin of 1904 has long disappeared. Joyce's narratives are set in basic material conditions different from ours, in buildings and streets that have since been redeveloped and redesigned, in a time before generations of development in technology, media, and of course the law. Readers know that Joyce's characters travel by tram, horse carriage, bicycle, and occasionally motorcar but not by airplane, and that they read newspapers and send telegrams but have no Internet access. The legal statutes that govern the world of early twentieth-century Dublin and Europe, the differences between the law then and the law now, may be less obvious, even to longtime scholars—and have certainly been less accessible. While its specifics are not at the forefront of the collective conscious of the Joyce community, the law is everywhere in Joyce's omnivorous text. His works are saturated with legal rhetoric and situations of questionable legality.

For example, issues of marriage and marital infidelity, meaning the particular legal regime that governed matrimony and divorce in nineteenth- to early twentieth-century Great Britain and its colonies, dominate much of Joyce's writing. As Janine Utell shows in her essay "Criminal

Conversation: Marriage, Adultery, and the Law in Joyce's Work," marital law hangs over the heads of characters such as Mrs. Sinico and Mr. Duffy of "A Painful Case" from *Dubliners*. Utell explains that extramarital sexual congress—legally codified as "criminal conversation"—was grounds not only for a divorce suit but for a tort action as a property crime. Mere suspicion of adultery could be devastating, and the knowledge indelibly colored relations between the sexes. Utell, playing with the trope of "conversation," examines how Joyce deploys dialogue between men and women in *Giacomo Joyce*, *Exiles*, *Dubliners*, and *Ulysses* to portray his countrymen (and by implication himself) "caught up in a legal discourse that denied them the autonomy to shape their private lives."

Utell's piece inaugurates *Joyce and the Law* and establishes its scholarly strategy, thus signaling a divergence from much prior criticism treating Joyce and law. Because Joyce's works from *Dubliners* onward have been the subject of legal wrangles, scholars have long taken interest in the famous brushes with the law checkering Joyce's career. That is, Joyce/law criticism has often addressed the regimes of censorship, obscenity, and copyright—the legal whether, what, and who of Joyce's publishing history. Richard Ellmann's biography *James Joyce* narrated Joyce's entanglements with the law: the struggles to publish *Dubliners* amid concerns about libel actions and to publish *Ulysses* amid concerns about obscenity, the imbroglios over piracy with Samuel Roth and over pants with Henry Carr of the English Players.[1] Closer and more sustained looks at such matters began to appear in the 1990s and continued through the early years of this century in a spate of critical treatments of Joyce's various battles over state suppression and intellectual property. Joseph Kelly, Celia Marshik, and Paul Vanderham scrutinized censorship and the fights to publish Joyce's works despite charges of obscenity; Sean Latham examined Joyce through the prism of libel law; and Paul K. Saint-Amour and Robert Spoo wrote extensively about copyright issues (encouraging a trend of copyright criticism in modernist studies).[2]

In the midst of this scholarly flurry, Spoo and Joseph Valente edited a special Summer 2000 issue of *James Joyce Quarterly* titled "Joyce and the Law," which collected scholarship largely explicating the legal concerns of Joyce's career. It featured, for example, United States Court of Appeals judge Conrad Rushing's article "The English Players Incident: What Really Happened," which corroborates Joyce's reputation for being "litigious," and

Carol Shloss chronicling her own wrangle over legal permissions with the Joyce estate (with Spoo serving as her counsel) in "Privacy and Piracy in the Joyce Trade: James Joyce and *le droit moral*." These articles do much to situate Joyce's career in the legal histories pertinent to literary circulation, that is, freedom of expression and intellectual property. The context of legal battles between scholars and the Joyce estate made such writings particularly timely.

Joyce and the Law is in dialogue with that history. Spoo and Valente's theme was reprised fifteen years after their collection when I guest-edited the *JJQ* special issue "Legal Joyce," dated Spring 2013 but published in early 2015. A reboot of sorts, "Legal Joyce" with its connections to and departures from the Spoo and Valente *JJQ* sketched a new moment in Joyce/law studies, showing that reading Joyce through legal concerns can speak to critical approaches organized around structures of class and nationhood and incorporating postcolonial and feminist views of Joyce. The essay by Utell described above demonstrates such possibilities. The contents of the special issue only began to explore this potential, however; *Joyce and the Law* continues the work, reprinting, in slightly revised versions, essays by Kevin Birmingham, Robert Brazeau, Andrew Gibson, and Marshik, with Spoo contributing an essay that springboards from his *JJQ* piece on Judge John Woolsey. The present volume treats a wider range of legal matters and devotes the first three sections to the kind of work that researches the legal regimes inflecting Joyce's narratives rather than those affecting his publication and dissemination, as characterized much previous criticism.

The first section, "Legal Lives of Joyce's Characters," focuses on laws that cast a shadow over the private actions of Joyce's protagonists. Following Utell's chapter, Carey Mickalites reads Joyce through the legal regime of British and international finance circa 1900. "Joyce and British Finance Law: Adrift on the Waters of International Investment" addresses both the *Dubliners* story "After the Race" and Leopold Bloom's version of financial planning in *Ulysses*. Mickalites argues that Joyce's work critically reflects Anglo-Irish anxieties over speculation and legal regulation of investments, and that the movement from *Dubliners* to *Ulysses* navigates between existing finance laws and laissez-faire British policy in order to imagine real social improvement for the Irish. Bloom, he writes, is "constantly negotiating the contingent world of finance and seeking to balance the risks of speculation with prudent calculation." That is, Bloom's plans are based on his striving to turn finance law and its limitations to his advantage.

Utell and Mickalites represent a central aim of *Joyce and the Law*: to offer research into the law and use it to understand the legal circumstances, the constraints and parameters, of Joyce's characters—the personal and societal implications of their choices. The subsequent contribution, Steven Morrison's "Joyce, the Aliens Act, and Immigration," follows suit, using immigration law to offer a revealing context for Bloom's family history, and for the anti-Semitic and xenophobic language of Haines, Mr. Deasy, the Citizen, and others in the novel. Morrison argues that *Ulysses* imagines a revised ethics of citizenship and immigration; it negotiates not only with laws governing 1904 Dublin but also with those of the time and place in which Joyce and his writings circulate, most saliently the debates about immigration in the United Kingdom that came to a head with the passing of the Aliens Act of 1905. The terms of this debate over British immigration law also help Morrison claim that the perhaps curiously disproportionate number of non-Irish nationals that populate Joyce's works is a function of his legal critique.

While the first section concentrates on laws that color the private motivations and dilemmas of Joyce's characters, the essays in part II, "Legal Regimes of Joyce's Spaces and Places," treat regimes governing public spaces in Ireland and Joyce's Europe. Tekla Mecsnóber in "National Languages and Neutral Idioms: Joyce among the Language Laws" argues that much of the *Wake*, specifically the passages that showcase the contrasting language politics of the brothers Shem and Shaun, responds to the "legislative frenzy for defining and enforcing new official languages in numerous, often new, nation-states." That is, she reads Joyce's polyglot book as reflecting societal concerns about language purity. Rich Cole parallels this approach in his "Rights and Losses: The Ends of Minority Recognition in Joyce and International Law." Cole reads "Cyclops" alongside legal regimes governing international statehood, showing that the episode's language is shaped by Joyce's interest in the movement, represented by the League of Nations accord, that systematically suppressed the rights of smaller populations in the race to national sovereignty. Cole's and Mecsnóber's essays, with their focus on governance and the legal inequities for minority populations, connect logically to Marshik's "Dublin Inc.: Municipal Corporation Reform in 'Ivy Day in the Committee Room.'" This piece recontextualizes the *Dubliners* story as highlighting Joyce's strong interest in municipal self-government, his casting nationalist agendas as inadequate to Dublin's needs as a sovereign legal entity. Marshik explains the legal purview of the Dublin Corporation, established to manage the affairs of the metropolis, and concludes that Joyce is at least as interested in the Corporation's Committee Room as he is in the Ivy Day that celebrates and laments Charles Stewart Parnell. This is quite a different understanding of the story than is often taught.

The section's last two essays concentrate on the legislation of Dublin spaces, public and private respectively. Gibson, in "'Nobody Owns': *Ulysses*, Tenancy, and Property Law," analyzes scenes from *Ulysses* alongside the legal regime governing tenancy in 1904 Ireland: "the site par excellence," as he calls it, "of the intractable colonial face-off." Summarizing the historical conflict between colonial versions of tenancy and those of the traditional and local Brehon law, he shows Joyce's ambivalence about both, and argues that *Ulysses* exposes the rentier culture in Dublin of the early twentieth century as a social and economic disaster. Brazeau's "*Pro Bono Publico*: Urban Space in 'Cyclops'" addresses laws governing alcohol in public space. It treats "Cyclops"—giving a nod to Fritz Senn, who addressed the legal language of the episode for the Spoo-Valente issue—in the context of the Inebriates Act of 1898 and the Licensing Act of 1902, which sought to restrict the clustering of pubs. Brazeau argues that Joyce uses the law to theorize and depict space as constructed through language and codes. His essay concludes the two sections of *Joyce and the Law* that explicate laws governing individuals and collectives to understand how specific legal regimes inflect plots in Joyce's work.

The following section, "Joyce's Legal Languages and Sources," uses specific legal histories and documents to parse Joyce's texts. Anne Marie D'Arcy's "'Eating orangepeels in the park': Largesse, Libel, and Public Action in *Ulysses*," addresses legal battles fomented by Queen Victoria's controversial Ireland visit in 1900, an event parodied in the "Circe" episode of *Ulysses*. As D'Arcy recounts, Maud Gonne wrote a scathing article about the royal visit, "The Famine Queen," for the *United Irishmen*, which was immediately suppressed over concerns of sedition. This in turn led to Gonne's criminal libel case, for which Arthur Griffith's testimony against Ramsay Colles, publisher and editor of the *Irish Figaro*, was crucial. D'Arcy locates hitherto overlooked references to these developments all over *Ulysses* and the *Wake*. Taking a wider angle, Terence Killeen's "The Law in/of *Finnegans Wake*: A Starchamber Quiry" argues that the *Wake* serves as a filter of legal language and history. Killeen scours Joyce's notebooks and drafts to identify numerous places where Joyce makes use of his notes on legal sources, specifically the Bywaters-Thompson case and the Maamtrasna murder trial. More generally, he identifies the book's debt to the notion of legal inquiry, a mode he asserts is fundamental to its structure and technique. Killeen's view that legal inquiry helps shape Joyce's text prefigures how I see trademark law in my own entry, "The Logos of Trademark: Joyce, Bass Ale, and Brand Insignias," reprised and revised from *JJQ* 51.1. This essay reads Joyce through the prism of trademark law of the late 1800s and early 1900s, finding parallels between trademark registration and Joyce's specific self-construction as authorial brand, legible in *Ulysses*.

The final section of *Joyce and the Law* returns critical attention to the legal contexts of Joyce's literary life, contributing new research and commenting on the critical history of reading the laws governing the movements of Joyce and his books. Part IV, "Circulation and Its Legalities," starts with two essays that treat principal figures in the twelve-year legal battle over the U.S. publication of *Ulysses*. Joseph M. Hassett's "Literature Meets Law in Court: The Trials of *Ulysses*" critiques John Quinn's failed defense of a portion of *Ulysses* that appeared in the *Little Review* in 1920, and lauds the work of the judges John Woolsey and Augustus and Learned Hand in *Ulysses*'s court victories of the next decade. The subsequent essay, Birmingham's "The Prestige of the Law: Revisiting Obscenity Law and Judge Woolsey's *Ulysses* Decision," is part biographical sketch, part literary analysis of a legal tract; it reassesses the unusual features of Woolsey's ruling, such as his sparse use of case history and his famous but eccentric forays into modernist-style prose, by deploying new archival research and interviews with surviving acquaintances of Woolsey. The suppressions of *Ulysses* also undergird Spoo's essay, "*Ulysses* as Deodand: Books, Automobiles, and the Law of Forfeiture," which, departing from critical predecessors, presents *Ulysses* as a protagonist in Joyce's battles against suppression. Spoo writes that the material book "stood accused as a sort of dangerous instrumentality, a *res* or thing subject to the strictures of civil forfeiture" and observes *Ulysses* as a "defendant" and a "deodand"—an object removed from its context and put on trial. Like

Hassett, Spoo valorizes the judicial daring that resisted and reversed such treatment.

Spoo then emerges as scholarly object himself in the volume's last essay. Amanda Golden's "The Past and Future of Joycean Copyright" chronicles how copyright has affected the publication of Joyce's work and the scholarly and aesthetic use of Joyce's words, and how the legal regime has been used in criticism. She also offers prognosticatory thoughts on the outcomes of recent technological developments and copyright changes, writing that "critics can quote more liberally and editions can speak to the changing scope of Joyce scholarship in the twenty-first century." While research continues in the history of Joyce and copyright, Golden's essay gives an overview of how this legal regime has inflected Joyce studies thus far. Like those of Hassett, Birmingham, and Spoo, moreover, it continues the important work of noting that Joyce's writing is inextricable from the changing legal contexts, claims, challenges, and rulings that affected its circulation and those that continue to do so.

Absent from *Joyce and the Law* is one essay that would have fit perfectly into the book's third section: a contribution planned by the late, lamented Supreme Court justice of Ireland, Adrian Hardiman, who passed away suddenly in early 2015. Some months earlier, I had the honor of reading an incomplete draft of Judge Hardiman's essay about "the Cornwall Case," mentioned in the "Eumaeus" chapter of *Ulysses* (16.1201–1205). Judge Hardiman intended to offer a new reading of this reference, whose source, he would show, critics have incorrectly identified. I mention Judge Hardiman's absent essay here to pay tribute to his scholarship and to note that the topic of Joyce and law is resonant enough with our own moment to attract the attention of a judge in Ireland's highest court.

. . .

Joyce and the Law mirrors much recent Joyce scholarship, which, swept up in the wave of what is sometimes called materialist modernism, has paid renewed attention to the cultural discourses of Joyce's moment, viewing literature as participating in the cultural sea changes identified with technological, mass-reproducible society, and approaching Joyce more than ever as a participant in and shaper of early twentieth-century mass society. Indeed, the materialist turn in modernist scholarship, a mode of criticism indebted to both poststructuralist theory and archival gruntwork, seems to invite a new look at legal regimes based on the not-so-simple fact that laws are composed of text, text that determines decisions and guides movements of individuals and societies. As Kevin Dettmar and Mark Wollaeger put it, "The law courts, we have come recently to recognize, are among those institutions of modernism that were too long effaced from our official histories, and need to be restored" (viii). This volume puts their observation into practice and extends it beyond the courts to the offices, texts, and languages of the law and their relation to Joyce's work. The volume shows two forms of cultural production working in tandem—seeing Joyce and his culture thinking through and revising legal discourse through narrative.

The exegetical work contained herein is often used to argue that Joyce's engagement with the law constitutes a kind of activism. A current running through the volume is a citizen's (not the Citizen's) relation to civic society. Joyce interrogates the laws of marriage, citizenship, municipal governance, tenancy, inebriation, in order to offer a better way, a better world. To Utell, reading the law in tandem with Joyce "reveals the possibly progressive thinking at the foundation of his representation of sexual and domestic relationships." That is to say, the legalities that Joyce negotiates clarify the attitudes that underlie his depictions of marital strain. To Mickalites, Bloom is a vehicle by which Joyce strives for a "future for Ireland that works within existing finance laws but that might also transfer the terms of British colonial control to practical Irish social reform and economic security"—a pragmatic but politicized figure through which to imagine Irish financial stability. These are merely examples from the first two essays; other authors here, such as Morrison, Mecsnóber, and Cole, depict Joyce's texts as deeply critiquing existing laws and imagining better versions, thus illuminating Joyce's oppositional political ethics. These contributors see Joyce's narratives as incubators, his characters as case studies for imagining new approaches to legal issues. Joyce's is an activist stance, and by highlighting it, the authors here further this activist work. In some cases their analyses reflect on contemporary circumstances, like Utell's ruminations on single-sex marriage, and Gibson's promoting radical political options as having potential to assuage inequalities in the law. They are paralleled by the critiques (Spoo, Hassett) of legal work by Joyce's advocates in the legal histories of his publications. It seems that scholarship in law and literature lends itself to recognizing an activist position, and taking one.

. . .

Though united by some shared scholarly concerns, the essays here are certainly not of a piece. They vary tremendously in their emphases on close reading, theorization, and historical narration. These divergences reflect the variety of professional situations of the authors. In reaching out to potential contributors, my curatorial goals included enlisting not only academic scholars but also legal professionals (represented here by Hassett, a litigator in private practice, and Spoo) and authors who publish for audiences beyond academe (such as Birmingham and Killeen). The contributors also write from a range of positions on their career timelines and from a range of professional engagements with Joyce, from graduate student to established medieval scholar to Joyce-studies royalty. These factors reflect in the stylistic variety of the essays. They also allow for the volume's wide purview: among us we address legal regimes of marriage/divorce, investment, citizenship, language use, national minority rights, municipal sovereignty, tenancy, alcohol, libel, sedition, murder, trademark, and the old warhorses of obscenity and copyright—each either at length or by the way.

My introduction to the *JJQ* "Legal Joyce" ended by suggesting the issue as a springboard for future scholarship. I see the present volume the same way. I wonder how Joyce might be productively read alongside other legal regimes. How might we use research regarding labor law to better understand moments such as the death of Michael Furey in "The Dead"? How might we consider the implications of truancy law in our reading of "An Encounter" and *A Portrait of the Artist as a Young Man*, petty larceny in "Two Gallants," contract law in "Counterparts"? How could legal research illuminate *Ulysses* by examining the vagrancy of Corliss and the complaint of Denis Breen, the *Wake* by looking at the defense of HCE? What about laws regarding gambling, prostitution, public urination, even expectoration, which might be applied all over Joyce's oeuvre? And indeed, the 2016 symposium saw Katherine Ebury addressing the death penalty and Jaya Savige unveiling his revelatory research into Joyce's notes on banking and insurance law—both presentations part of work in progress for publication. Scholarship in this vein and further research into legal materials should open up Joyce anew.

Notes

This introduction draws from my introductory essay, "The Legal Fictions of James Joyce," in "Legal Joyce," the special issue of *James Joyce Quarterly* (Spring 2013). Mostly new writing, it incorporates passages from that piece—as I have not revised everything simply for the sake of paraphrase—and reprises its ideas.

1. About *Dubliners*, see pages 329–32; about Carr, 427–28, 440–47; about *Ulysses*, 497, 502–4, 666–67, 678–79, 691n; about Roth, 585–87, 604.

2. See, for example, Latham, *The Art of Scandal*; Marshik, *British Modernism and Censorship*; Saint-Amour, *The Copywrights*; Spoo, "Copyright Protectionism and Its Discontents: The Case of James Joyce's *Ulysses*" and *Without Copyrights*.

Works Cited

Dettmar, Kevin, and Mark Wollaeger. Foreword to Latham, *The Art of Scandal*, iii–xviii.
Ellmann, Richard. *James Joyce*. Rev. ed. Oxford: Oxford University Press, 1982.
Heald, Paul J. *A Guide to Law and Literature for Teachers, Students, and Researchers*. Durham, NC: Carolina Academic Press, 1998.
Kelly, Joseph. *Our Joyce: From Outcast to Icon*. Austin: University of Texas Press, 1998.
Latham, Sean. *The Art of Scandal: Modernism, Libel Law, and the Roman à Clef*. Oxford: Oxford University Press, 2009.
Marshik, Celia. *British Modernism and Censorship*. Cambridge: Cambridge University Press, 2006.
Reichman, Ravit. *The Affective Life of Law: Legal Modernism and the Literary Imagination*. Stanford, CA: Stanford University Press, 2009.
Saint-Amour, Paul K. *The Copywrights: Intellectual Property and the Literary Imagination*. Ithaca, NY: Cornell University Press, 2003.
Spoo, Robert. "Copyright Protectionism and Its Discontents: The Case of James Joyce's *Ulysses* in America." *Yale Law Journal* 108.3 (December 1998): 633–67.
———. *Without Copyrights: Piracy, Publishing, and the Public Domain*. New York: Oxford University Press, 2013.
Vanderham, Paul. *James Joyce and Censorship: The Trials of "Ulysses."* New York: New York University Press, 1998.

PART I

Legal Lives of Joyce's Characters

1

Criminal Conversation

Marriage, Adultery, and the Law in Joyce's Work

JANINE UTELL

This chapter turns a suspicious glance on men and women in Joyce's work who disrupt the legal regime governing sexual relations. In a reading attentive to the ever-present possibility of adultery, the intimate space between men and women in Joyce's work becomes suspect, and adultery becomes a politically and socially transgressive act. What we mean by love and trust, how we define female subjectivity, the pursuit of autonomy in intimate life under a sexually repressive legal regime: these are all called into question throughout Joyce's texts. A number of Joyceans, as well as legal scholars including Richard Posner and Ravit Reichman, have noted Joyce's attention to the construction of public and private lives, the fault lines between the two realms, the ways individuals can get caught in the gaps, and the implications for personal and political autonomy. I use the representation of intimate scenes in *Giacomo Joyce*, *Exiles*, *Dubliners*, and *Ulysses*, particularly conversations between men and women that have the potential to tip over into the illicit, to build on these general themes in order to consider how the legal space of marriage becomes a site where sociosexual power is interrogated.

Through analyzing these moments in Joyce's texts and reading them in the context of turn-of-the-century law regarding marriage and adultery, we can examine discursive moves that echo the codification of intimacy and companionship; they do so by using similar language and tropes to those processes of codification, thereby illuminating the extent to which such awareness of legal norms infiltrates intimate life. Yet we also see Joyce resisting that codification, pushing back against legal structures that overdetermine intimate relationships. Reading Joyce's work through the lens of law reveals the possibly progressive thinking at the foundation of his representation of sexual and domestic relationships. What occurs between erotic partners in private was of the utmost importance to Joyce, because that private space is one where autonomy and self-efficacy is possible. At the same time, that space is constructed and constrained by laws that restrict the fullest expression of human intimacy in all its disorder. For Joyce, until marriage, that very public statement of private connection, could be undone, until it could be seen as something other than demeaning, it was not worth doing at all; and he devoted much of his writing to exploring alternatives.

In Joyce's time "criminal conversation," or extramarital sexual congress, was still the basis for tort actions in Ireland: under a law in effect since the eighteenth century, a husband could sue the "seducer" of his wife for damages. The grounds were twofold: first, the other man had essentially "damaged" the husband's "property," and second, by seducing the wife away from her husband, the seducer had broken the "consortium" of the marriage, thereby depriving the husband of the society and services of his wife. Criminal conversation, then, was a crime of property. Moreover, because a wife had neither property nor legal personhood, the criminal conversation suit could not be brought against her. In fact, she was not allowed to offer evidence on her own behalf, take the stand, or even be present in the courtroom. A criminal conversation case was a matter for the two men involved, husband and lover.

So let's say it's turn-of-the-century Dublin and you want a divorce. If you're a man, you bring a criminal conversation suit against your wife's alleged lover. Your wife might actually be committing adultery. You might suspect as much and find ways to make the available evidence as suggestive as possible: seeking out impressionable chambermaids, for instance, or friends who might have incriminating letters. On the other hand, your wife might not be committing adultery at all. You would just like a divorce. You might pay a "seducer" to play the role—in either case. Of course, you have to be careful, for if the jury suspects you of "negligence," meaning complaisance or inattentiveness in the marriage, you will lose. (Would Leopold Bloom have won a criminal conversation suit against Blazes Boylan? Would Martha Clifford's husband—if there was one—

have won such a suit against Bloom? More on that in a moment.) You conjure up enough evidence to be convincing, you bring a criminal conversation suit, you are awarded a handsome sum—damages in criminal conversation cases could range up to more than £10,000—and then you move on to the next step: petitioning Parliament to bring a bill forward on your behalf, because the only way to get a divorce is by special private act of Parliament, a privilege that costs upwards of £500. If all of this is the result of collusion with your wife's "seducer," you might never bother to collect the damages at all, or collect just for appearances' sake and then give the money back. If collusion is suspected, though, the jury will not find in your favor. All the while, every salacious detail is being reported in a highly sensationalist press, consumed hungrily by readers looking for something "spicy," in the words of one amused 1909 judge (quoted in Stone 225).

Victorian debates around marriage and divorce, and what was seen as a desperate need for reform, came to a head with the Matrimonial Causes Act of 1857.[1] Irish MPs participated in the debates, but ultimately the 1857 act never applied to Ireland. A taste of some of those debates can actually be found in the pages of Leopold Bloom's own newspaper, the *Freeman's Journal*, which criticized those who would make divorce cheaper and easier because of the effect this would have on public morals (Urquhart 302). From here on out, I would like to take up the notion of "criminal conversation," and the availability—or impossibility—of divorce in Joyce's work. I play with the trope of conversation; while "criminal conversation" in the legal sense means adulterous sexual congress, I contend that Joyce uses the device of scenes of conversation—represented and reported dialogue between men and women—to gesture toward the possibilities of illicit intimacy, adultery, and divorce. Scenes of seemingly innocuous "conversation" have the potential to become "criminal," to lead to adultery or the suspicion thereof. At the end of this essay, I suggest that Joyce viewed men and women as caught up in a legal discourse that denied them the autonomy to shape their private lives the way they chose. Joyce was interested in pushing up against the legal boundaries that seek to contain desire, showing that those boundaries stifle whatever ideals of love and companionship we may possess. Ultimately, for Joyce, an irregular relationship, beyond the bounds of marriage, is preferable to participating in the regulatory mechanisms of marriage.[2]

Giacomo Joyce and *Exiles*

The trope of conversation metonymizes sexual desire in *Giacomo Joyce* and *Exiles*, even if it never becomes "criminal"; such discourse generates an intimacy that must be regarded with suspicion. *Giacomo Joyce* plays with the idea of "criminal conversation": instances of erotic contact with the unnamed girl, a student, take place through conversation.[3] An outsider to this dyad might not see it as suspicious, as sexual, but as our speaker allows us into the world of his desire, we come to see moments of voice, of listening, of talk as highly charged.

The speaker of *Giacomo Joyce* does not necessarily see himself as dynamic or seductive. Moments of conversation are charged because of the context, not because of what is being said. Early on he narrates, "I launch forth on an easy wave of tepid speech.... The wave is spent" (*GJ* 1). There is a feel of the detumescent here, as all erotic energy is expended, a bit weakly, in talk. In the next fragment, he places himself in a subservient position to the paramour, again through talk: "There is one below would speak to your ladyship" (*GJ* 1). The relationship of teacher and student creates a natural context for talk, for conversation, and these instances shape the fragments and the speaker's desire: "I rush out of the tobacco-shop and call her name. She turns and halts to hear my jumbled words of lessons, hours, lessons, hours" (*GJ* 4). Even when there is nothing specific to say, conversation becomes an opportunity for erotic connection, at least on the part of the speaker.

After the girl undergoes some kind of unspecified operation, her besotted teacher visits her, and this is one of the few moments we see *her* talking: "Once more in her chair by the window, happy words on her tongue" (*GJ* 11). The fragment immediately before depicts the speaker simultaneously fearing for the girl's life and conscious, in a sexual manner that is more than hinting of erotic jealousy and violence, of her body being cut open: "The surgeon's knife has probed in her entrails and withdrawn, leaving the raw jagged gash of its passage on her belly" (*GJ* 11). The mental activity of thinking about her body is quickly replaced by the safer move toward conversation. Finally, conversation, mere conversation, is shown to be sterile: "My words in her mind: cold polished stones sinking through a quagmire.... My voice, dying in the echoes of its words" (*GJ* 13–14). Conversation is a conduit to intimacy, but it must remain coded; it is subject to constraints on individual freedom, sexual and otherwise.

Giacomo Joyce also sees Joyce using a technique that reoccurs throughout his fiction: the indirect reporting of women's voices, thoughts, and mental activity. The speaker of *Giacomo Joyce* informs us of the "happy words on her tongue"; he presumes to represent for us the fact of his "words in her mind." As we shall see in our discussion of "A Painful Case," the male narrator or speaker often takes it upon himself to tell us what the female member of the conversing pair might be thinking, feeling, or saying. Even *Ulysses*, which concludes with one of the most famous instances of a woman's inner voice in all of literature, is composed of seventeen other episodes in which that woman's thoughts, memories, and words are reported to the reader by a male. Via this technique, Joyce interrogates the nature of female subjecthood in a world where women do not exist as legal beings. He pursues this line of questioning more explicitly in one of the rarer instances where we have the direct representation of female thinking and voice: *Exiles*, his only play.

The question of individual freedom in matters of love and sexuality is the major preoccupation of *Exiles*, which begins with conversation and then pursues the consequences of suspicion, deception, and freedom in love. Richard Rowan, a writer, has what amounts to an open relationship with his romantic partner, Bertha. They have eloped (much as Joyce himself did with Nora Barnacle), and he considers her his wife. Another pair, Beatrice Justice and Robert Hand, are intertwined with Bertha and Richard: Robert professes himself in love with Bertha, while Richard is interested in Beatrice, who claims to be attracted to him as well.

Exiles opens with a scene of conversation between Richard and Beatrice, alone; Bertha is away, due back any moment. Beatrice confesses that she visits the house, ostensibly to give Richard's son Archie piano lessons, because "otherwise I could not see you" (*E* 19). (Because Richard and Bertha have a common-law arrangement, Archie is illegitimate, a fact Richard refers to with bitterness when he talks of his mother consequently rejecting him [*E* 24]). Richard acknowledges he too feels something for Beatrice, but has held back because of Robert: "It was that that made me so reserved with you—then—even though I felt your interest in me, even though I felt that I too was something in your life" (*E* 20). When Robert enters the scene, Richard leaves, and Robert and Beatrice converse. Robert and Beatrice are joined by Bertha and Archie, Beatrice and the boy leave for his lesson, and Robert and Bertha are now alone. They have a conversation, and Robert confesses "that I have a deep liking for you" (*E* 31). Robert and Bertha talk, and much of their talk is about how people who like each other talk, the ways conversation between people attracted to each other can conduce to illicit desire. Robert demands, "Did you not like me to speak to you in that way?" and Bertha says, "I think men speak like that to all women whom they like or admire" (*E* 32–33). The subject of the conversation is conversation itself, and their talk ends with a passionate kiss. Act 1 concludes with Bertha telling all to Richard.

What is striking about *Exiles* is that there is no deception on the part of the possibly—or potentially—adulterous pair Robert and Bertha. Bertha tells Richard everything, because according to the rules of their relationship, she is "free." He has no legal hold over her. In return, Bertha accuses Richard of deceiving her, in his interest in Beatrice. Bertha likewise has no legal hold over Richard, but even if she did, she would be powerless to do anything about his interest in another woman. She is not legally his wife, and there can be no adultery without marriage. And, of course, women could not sue husbands for criminal conversation anyway because, obviously, husbands were not their wives' property.

Bertha knows that for all of Richard's fine talk about "liberty," he is still subject to the same jealousies and the same double standard as any other man. Richard claims to not want to possess Bertha legally, but he cannot help feeling jealous over another man wanting to possess her sexually; this becomes clear in act 2, when Bertha arrives at Robert's home for a tryst. Act 2 ends with Bertha and Robert together, Robert kissing her hair, and with our uncertainty over whether sexual congress takes place. The next day, Richard suspects: "You will tell me. But I will never know. Never in this world ... The truth! But I will never know, I tell you" (*E* 102). There is no clear evidence, no possibility of truly knowing, despite Richard engaging in an almost legalistic process of interrogation and evidence gathering. Evidence is sought, reflecting a kind of absorbing of certain ways of legal thinking; yet at the same time, Richard sees the inadequacy of such processes. He wants to resist the impulse but cannot, while simultaneously resigning himself to the hopelessness of doubt. In act 3, Robert tells all: that Bertha still "belongs" to Richard. He says, "I failed.... She is yours" (*E* 107). As Robert recounts his encounter with Bertha, is he easing his friend's mind or coming up with an alibi? Despite all his principles, Richard feels he must possess Bertha, but that their relationship can only be riven by doubt.

Richard and Bertha more or less come back together at the end of the play. Richard claims to grant Bertha complete freedom to pursue her own desires; he does not exactly encourage her to have an affair with Robert, but he does not discourage her either, saying to her only that she is "free" (*E* 56) and has "complete liberty" (*E* 52). Richard's attempts to create a space outside the law, where they are each free and granted sexual autonomy, are compromised by his own jealousy. Bertha never deceives him, but the knowing actually turns out to be worse. At the end, Robert leaves and Bertha and Richard are left to figure out how to overcome what Richard calls a "restless living wounding doubt" (*E* 112). Richard's doubt is not whether Bertha has had an affair with Robert, but whether she truly loves Richard at all.

The play calls for resistance to sexual and marital norms, while also acknowledging the difficulty of that resistance because these human, private relations have been shaped, determined, by legal structures. The characters see the ways in which legal thinking and legal discourse make true freedom in intimacy impossible, but they struggle to escape such logic. Joyce makes this clear in his notes to the play: he writes, "Robert wishes Richard to use against him the weapons which social conventions and morals put in the hands of the husband. Richard refuses. Bertha wishes Richard to use these weapons also in her defense. Richard refuses also" (*E* 113). Husbands have weapons in their arsenals to defend what is theirs, granted them by laws and social norms, but this is an impossible approach to human relationships. At the same time, individuals cannot help but feel desire and jealousy; this is "nature's law," according to Robert (*E* 63). The legal regime within which Joyce's characters reside can never wholly contain the disruptive force of desire, nor can it mitigate the doubt engendered by love.

Dubliners

Throughout *Dubliners*, married characters hint at the desire for options to escape marriage. Chandler in "A Little Cloud" fantasizes about leaving his wife and child after a night out drinking with Gallaher: "A dull resentment against his life awoke within him. Could he not escape from his little house? . . . Could he go to London?" (*D* 68). Separations were not unheard of. Mrs. Mooney in "The Boarding House" is described as having one, which a woman could do, as she does, in the case of cruelty; in fact, the number of women achieving separations like this in Ireland increased dramatically after 1857 (Urquhart 313). What is striking about Chandler's thinking in "A Little Cloud" is that it takes him to London. Certainly London would be a cosmopolitan adventure of the type Chandler craves. But London is also the location of the Divorce Court. Is Chandler thinking about taking up residence in London and ending his marriage (something that would have been difficult for an Irish citizen but not completely impossible)?

The representation of marriage as limiting freedom and generating bitterness due to failed expectations exemplifies Joyce's attitudes toward sociosexual norms. Chandler's marriage is characterized by a relentless banality, an absence of true companionship. Why should the law bind two people together in such stale misery? Is such a structure limiting individuals' ability to achieve happiness and fulfillment? It is these questions, I think, that underlie Joyce's interrogations and investigations into the nature of marriage. They are also what prompt his sympathy toward those who would seem to compromise said sociosexual norms by making legally risky moves. Joyce evinces sympathy toward the Blooms, and we can see similar sympathy toward other couples caught in transgressive moments. Take "A Painful Case." This story, too, has Joyce using the trope of conversation to create instances where talk between a man and a woman takes on a suspicious cast, suggesting the possibility of illicit desire. In this story Mrs. Emily Sinico has no remedy for her loveless marriage. The negligence on the part of her husband, which makes her unhappy and lonely, prefigures Molly Bloom's feelings about her marriage in *Ulysses*.

In "A Painful Case" Mr. Duffy, a bachelor of highly regular habits, meets Mrs. Sinico at a concert. The story is focalized through Mr. Duffy, so we have no evidence for how Mrs. Sinico might feel about her husband, her relationship with Mr. Duffy, or the manner in which he ends it. We can only make a guess based on his representation to himself and us of her marriage: Captain Sinico commands a merchant ship; he seems somewhat oblivious to his wife; he never seems to mind Mr. Duffy's visits, imagining him to be a possible suitor for the Sinico daughter. Mrs. Sinico remains a cipher, as everything about her is reported, with questionable reliability, by Mr. Duffy: her gestures, what she says (we never hear her actual words save for one instance, when she comments on the poor audience at the concert), and the story of her final end, falling in front of train while probably drunk. As in many narratives of suspected criminal conversation, we are not always entirely sure how to take the evidence presented to us: Is it adultery, or isn't it? What do we know, and how do we know it?

What we do know is that Mr. Duffy presents his relationship with Mrs. Sinico as consisting entirely of conversation, and that he is quite cagey about what he thinks he is doing with her. After an evening of intimate talk, she "caught up his hand passionately and pressed it to her cheek" (*D* 93). The reader is not surprised by this action, and perhaps has come all along to regard the development of "conversation" between Mr. Duffy and Mrs. Sinico as suspicious. Moreover, we greet Mr. Duffy's astonishment and dismay with a certain suspicion: how has he not seen how she felt? From the moment of their first encounter he has seemed to recognize something in her, and something in his feelings: "He tried to fix her permanently in his memory"; "Her face, which must have been handsome, had remained intelligent"; he spends a great deal of time noticing her eyes and does not neglect to notice her figure (*D* 91–92). He sees their thoughts as "entangled" and their relationship as an "adventure," even as he claims to not be doing anything "incongruous" or "stealthy" (*D* 92). The indirect reporting of all the facts of the "painful case," including Mr. Duffy's understanding of Captain Sinico, who "had dismissed his wife so sincerely from his gallery of pleasures that he did not suspect anyone else would take an interest in her" (*D* 92), evokes the idea of testimony, as if Mr. Duffy imagines recounting the story of their would-be affair to a reader/jury.

The tone shifts once Mr. Duffy reads of Mrs. Sinico's death in the paper. The article is offered in full, and Mr. Duffy notes the clichés and tropes: "The threadbare phrases, the inane expressions of sympathy, the cautious words of a reporter" (*D* 97). What is striking is that the story of Mr. Duffy and Mrs. Sinico ends with a newspaper account not of a criminal conversation case but of a sordid death, possibly suicide. Perhaps the story could only end with either of these two resolutions: these are the options available to men and women caught in unhappy private lives, especially neglected and lonely wives trapped in miserable and dissatisfying marriages. After Mr. Duffy takes in the news, he turns his interrogation on himself. He places *himself* on trial, for *not* taking the opportunity to pursue passion:

"He asked himself what else could he have done. He could not have carried on a comedy of deception with her; he could not have lived with her openly" (*D* 98). In these moments, bordering on despair, he considers the possible avenues for the two of them, and sees the ways they were trapped. Gone is his initial response to the news article, which was revulsion, his sense of sociosexual norms activated to render a judgment upon her born of convention and moralism. Instead he sees them both as deeply lonely, deeply unfree.

Ulysses

Criminal conversation cases resonated with the public because they highlighted already existing anxieties about the nature of female sexuality, the changing social role of marriage, and the boundaries between public and private life as well as the capacity of the law to monitor those boundaries. Reporting on criminal conversation and divorce cases became a kind of subgenre of melodrama, where cuckolded husbands were cast as victims of sexually aggressive "new women." This victimhood was often viewed askance, however, and did not necessarily prompt sympathy on the part of those in the courtroom or the newspaper-reading public, who came to see the husbands bringing the cases as weak and ineffectual, even effeminate (Savage 524).[4] Republishing criminal conversation and divorce cases as books was common practice; much of the reporting in the London press before and after the Matrimonial Causes Act was reprinted in Irish newspapers; and the civil courts of Dublin charged with hearing criminal conversation cases in the late nineteenth century were the source of a great deal of salacious reading material themselves. You couldn't get a divorce in Ireland, but you could certainly read all about it.

Bloom might have read such tales and transcripts in the *Freeman's Journal* and elsewhere. In the "Circe" episode of *Ulysses*, it seems as though he himself might be participating in a criminal conversation case. In *Ulysses* the idea of criminal conversation is useful to Joyce in several ways, all of which speak to how legal frameworks shape public and private lives: public spectacle, discursive performance, private space. While many have noted the ways Joyce is drawing on the spectacle of the trial, the public drama of the courtroom, in "Circe" the suggestion is often that Bloom himself is on trial for assorted crimes having to do with some kind of deviance or perversion.[5] It strikes me as possible that in "Circe" Joyce is drawing on tropes and narrative elements that were part of the representation of criminal conversation cases.

Early in "Circe," Bloom finds himself entangled in conversation with Mrs. Breen (U 15.390–576). The two use a suggestive code to discern whether there might be mutual sexual interest:

> BLOOM (*meaningfully dropping his voice*) I confess I'm teapot with curiosity to find out whether some person's something is a little teapot at present.
> MRS BREEN (*gushing*) Tremendously teapot! London's teapot and I'm simply teapot all over me (*she rubs sides with him*) (U 15.456–460)

The "meaningful" inflection, the confession, the curiosity—these all cue the reader to find this exchange slightly heated, to perceive the innuendo. It appears to be lifted directly out of the sordid gossip of illicit liaisons, and Mrs. Breen herself seems able and willing to decipher Bloom's charged code.[6]

This moment occurs shortly after Bloom encounters Molly, who is depicted as sexually aggressive as well as patronizing to her husband: "Mrs. Marion from this out, my dear man, when you speak to me. (*satirically*) Has poor little hubby cold feet waiting so long?" (U 15.307–308). "Mrs. Marion" is an echo of Bloom's discovery of Blazes Boylan's letter to Molly in "Calypso" as he thinks, "Bold hand. Mrs. Marion" (U 4.244–245), but it is also Bloom imagining Molly erasing her marriage. She publicly questions his masculinity and flaunts her sexual power, thereby tapping into the sociosexual anxieties activated by criminal conversation cases. We might read Bloom's innuendo and encoded engagement with Mrs. Breen as a response, one that he deploys in order to place himself outside the possibility of legal retribution—Molly certainly could not sue him—but which also nevertheless places Mrs. Breen in a certain amount of jeopardy.

This danger for the woman is revealed by the appearance of Martha Clifford shortly thereafter: she is caught in Nighttown by the First Watch and begs Bloom to clear her name (U 15.54–55). It is never clear whether Martha Clifford is married, but she is led through Nighttown with a crimson halter around her neck, not unlike how a wife might be brought to the cattle market and sold as one of the few alternatives to divorce available to rural and working people in the eighteenth century (C. Gibson 51). The depiction of Martha in "Circe" reveals the danger she has put herself in by corresponding with Bloom, sending him the erotic letter shown in the "Lotus-Eaters" episode (*U* 5.240–260). Such a letter could serve as evidence in a criminal conversation case. Packets of love letters presented in court often found their way into newspaper stories and books, as in the case of *Grady v. Grady*, heard at the Matrimony and Probate Court in Dublin in November 1880; its subsequent publication included copies of the love letters submitted as evidence.

In "Calypso," Bloom finds the letter from Blazes Boylan inviting Molly to a tryst—or so we suspect, following the lead of the suspicious husband. He thinks "Bold hand" throughout the episode, suspicion reverberating in his mind. In "Circe," the suspicious husband who has found the lover's letter in the doorway becomes the servant who lets the lover in and then spies on the tryst through a keyhole. In this guise he also colludes with the lover to facilitate the adulterous rendezvous. Evidence provided by servants was often essential to criminal conversation cases, not only for their centrality to the proceedings but also for their entertainment value. They provided the low comedy and melodrama for which readers turned to such stories. Here Joyce draws upon this common motif, conflating it with the unfortunate and ludicrous figure of the cuckold. Bloom is dressed in "flunkey's prune plush coat and kneebreeches, buff stockings and powdered wig," and as he lets Boylan in he says, "Madam Tweedy is in her bath, sir." Boylan heads in the direction of Molly, offering to Bloom, "You can apply your eye to the keyhole and play with yourself while I just go through her a few times" (*U* 15.3760–3790). It would not be wrong to read this scene, as many have done, as an indictment of Bloom's voyeuristic tendencies. Yet we can also read it as an almost archetypal moment out of representations of adulterous trysts facilitated and witnessed by servants, many of which appeared as testimony in criminal conversation cases. Furthermore, it amplifies a signal we receive throughout *Ulysses*: Bloom is a cuckold because he goes along with Molly's adultery. The evidence presented of Bloom's facilitation of his wife's affair—rendered comically but no less radically in this moment in "Circe"—means that Bloom loses any legal grounds he might have to seek "restitution" for the "loss" of his "wife's society and services." What we see here is a form of collusion with Blazes Boylan. In this scene we might be looking at clear evidence of the criminal conversation of Molly and Blazes. However, if the two men are in it together, Bloom cannot claim to be wronged.

But, ladies and gentlemen, I put it to you: What if the Blooms themselves were put on trial for criminal conversation? If Bloom were indeed to wake up on 17 June and answer the question posed in "Ithaca"—"Divorce, not now.... Suit for damages... not impossibly" (*U* 17.2200–2205)—with "yes," an entirely different "yes" from the one we get at the end of "Penelope," what would that look like? What evidence might be brought to bear on the charges at hand?

According to Molly, the meeting suggested in the letter delivered in "Calypso" is simply to "organize" the program for her upcoming concert, to be managed by Boylan (*U* 4.310–313). We never see the letter, unlike the missive sent by Martha Clifford, so we do not know if she is lying. As Barbara Leckie argues, this lack of knowing, this fundamental uncertainty, is at the heart of adultery cases: Is it adultery? Is it not? How do we know? (106). "Ithaca" reveals several clues—bits of Plumtree's Potted Meat, some rearranged furniture—but is it conclusive? Does Bloom, in fact, have enough to pursue any of the lines of retribution open to him: "Duel by combat, no. Divorce, not now.... Suit for damages... not impossibly" (*U* 17.2200–2205)? Even if he did, "Penelope" provides Molly's confession and defense: "what else were we given all those desires for Id like to know I cant help it if Im young still can I its a wonder Im not an old shrivelled hag before my time living with him so cold never embracing me... serve him right its all his own fault if I am an adulteress" (*U* 18.1397–1400, 1516). Bloom's negligence as a husband would be enough to get his case thrown out of court.

Furthermore: Molly cannot bring a criminal conversation case against her husband, despite "several highly respectable Dublin ladies hold[ing] up improper letters received from Bloom" (*U* 15.1078–1079), although there might be some man out there inclined to name Bloom in a suit. But even when the Jurors are presented with evidence that "Gob, he organized her" (*U* 15.1145), they suspect Molly is not entirely in the wrong in her liaison with Boylan, and not only for Bloom's negligence and possible collusion. The Crier tell us that Bloom is a "wellknown... bigamist, bawd, and cuckold" (*U* 15.1158–1159). Bloom has his sexual transgressions made public, announced by the Crier, parsed by the Jurors; his shame is brought out for all to see. And if such charges were true, Molly herself might have a case against him.

We can look at *Ulysses* for what is not present just as much as we can take account of what is. For instance, given all of the reminiscences we have revealed to us through Bloom, why do we never see him having a memory of his wedding day? The encounter at Howth is certainly a kind of marriage, with the sensual sharing of seedcake taking the place of a civil ceremony or a joining at the altar. It is these kinds of intimate moments, outside the realm of legal discourse, that Joyce privileges. They serve as an alternative to conventional, legally defined and determined unions. Furthermore, they open up to a vision, not only of what can be done, but of what can be undone. If the erotic impulse that led to the moment of sharing the seedcake disappears, shouldn't the individuals involved have the autonomy to then dissolve the union? Bloom grants Molly a great deal of autonomy in the intimate, private life of their marriage—autonomy she is denied in the legal realm.

This concern with autonomy, with individual rights to privacy and personal fulfillment, led Joyce to hold what we might venture to call "progressive" views on marriage. Again and again in his work, we see instances where marriage is not a space for personal fulfillment, where autonomy and individual and shared flourishing are denied, where escape would almost certainly be welcome and is impossible. In "The Boarding House," for example, marriage is the means by which two individuals are deprived of their autonomy: "Once you are married you are done for" (*D* 54). Mr. Doran is trapped into marrying Polly Mooney, and we watch his slow and inexorable realization of what is to come. Yet the depiction of Polly in the final paragraphs of the story serves as an equal challenge to marriage and women's role within it. All she can do is look in the mirror, waiting, gazing. Whatever thoughts she might be having—"hopes and visions" (*D* 56)—in contrast to the detailed reporting of Mr. Doran's panicked mindwork, are held back from the reader, if they are really there at all. She is seemingly emptied of thought, of will. *Ulysses* provides us the epilogue to the story of Bob Doran and Polly Mooney in "Cyclops," where Bloom runs into Mr. Doran drinking away his sorrows for having had to "patch up the pot" (*U* 12.816). A more ambiguous representation of the husband-wife relationship might be seen in "The Dead," where intimate conversation between Gabriel and Gretta has the potential to lead to a deeper connection—or may instead serve to show how the gap between a man and a woman, even in (or possibly especially in) marriage, is unbridgeable.

Ultimately, how two people choose to join their lives, for Joyce, is really nobody's business but the two people involved. Furthermore, erotic fulfillment should be part of a general project of autonomy, and we cannot imagine true freedom until individuals have the right, equally, to pursue such fulfillment. What would Joyce have made of recent developments around gay marriage in the United States and Ireland? He might have seen these as positive moves precisely because of his progressive political commitment to personal autonomy and self-flourishing.[7] On the other hand, he might have turned that same suspicious glance on the whole endeavor. If the very institution of marriage is a set of legal chains, what is the good of giving more people the right to place themselves in those chains?

Notes

1. This law abolished divorce by special private act of Parliament, established the Divorce Court in London, and did away with criminal conversation tort cases as separate proceedings. After 1857, husbands had to make adultery part of divorce proceedings and couldn't pursue separate tort cases on the grounds of criminal conversation. The law, however, applied only to England, not Ireland, where things proceeded as they always had until the creation of the Free State in 1922, at which point divorce became impossible because Irish citizens could no longer petition Parliament. The 1937 constitution prohibited divorce entirely, and so it remained until 1997. See Lawrence Stone on divorce reform in England, and Michele Dillon on the same (or lack thereof) in Ireland.

2. Something we, of course, see in Joyce's own life, in his elopement with Nora Barnacle. Interestingly, Joyce did not "regularize" this union until 1931, in a civil ceremony in London; in addition to further reforms passed in the mid-1920s (including those permitting women to bring divorce cases against their husbands on the grounds of adultery, and the opening of divorce to grounds other than adultery), the Joyce marriage would have been affected by the 1926 Legitimacy Act, which allowed for the legitimization by the marriage of their parents of children born in irregular relationships. The last was important to Joyce, who said he finally married Nora so that their children, Giorgio and Lucia, would be able to inherit his estate (*JJII* 637–39).

3. Vicki Mahaffey has considered the identity of the unnamed girl in *Giacomo Joyce*, and my own reading of this text elsewhere is indebted to her work.

4. Gail Savage's discussion of *Russell v. Russell* (June 1922, several months after the publication of *Ulysses*) illuminates many of these currents. Barbara Leckie has traced the importance of journalism related to adultery and divorce not only in shaping ideas about gender but also for narrative (92, 106). I have written elsewhere on the importance of the Charles Parnell–Katharine O'Shea adultery and divorce case for Joyce's thinking on these issues, and the ways the representation of the case both in the newspapers and in Katharine O'Shea Parnell's memoir is mined by Joyce for his fiction. Christine Froula calls Parnell a "fractal reflection" throughout his work of Joyce's interest in sexual love and freedom, an assessment I share (370).

5. Such scenes are echoed in *Finnegans Wake* and the unspoken/unspeakable crimes of HCE; for example, Wolfgang Streit details the possible readings of HCE's crimes, especially in the context of the rhetorical and psychosexual need for confession (146–47). Streit's theorization of confession, indebted to Michel Foucault, offers a helpful nuance here as we consider the role confession plays in the social and legal ritual of the trial.

6. I am indebted to my anonymous readers for suggesting this intriguing reading of Bloom's exchange with Mrs. Breen. Feedback on the concluding paragraphs of this essay is acknowledged as well.

7. I direct readers particularly to Andrew Gibson's recent work on Joyce's progressive politics, especially on the subject of personal autonomy.

Works Cited

Dillon, Michele. *Debating Divorce: Moral Conflict in Ireland*. Lexington: University of Kentucky Press, 1993.

Ellmann, Richard. *James Joyce*. Rev. ed. New York: Oxford University Press, 1982.

Froula, Christine. "Sex." In *James Joyce in Context*, edited by John McCourt, 366–77. 2009. Reprint, New York: Cambridge University Press, 2014.

Gibson, Andrew. *The Strong Spirit: History, Politics, and Aesthetics in the Writings of James Joyce, 1898–1915*. New York: Oxford University Press, 2013.

Gibson, Colin S. *Dissolving Wedlock*. New York: Routledge, 1994.

Joyce, James. *Dubliners*. 1914. New York: W. W. Norton, 2006.

———. *Exiles*. New York: Viking, 1951.

———. *Giacomo Joyce*. London: Faber and Faber, 1968.

———. *Ulysses*. 1922. New York: Vintage, 1986.

Leckie, Barbara. *Culture and Adultery: The Novel, the Newspaper, and the Law, 1857–1914*. Philadelphia: University of Pennsylvania Press, 1999.

Mahaffey, Vicki. "'Giacomo Joyce.'" In *"Giacomo Joyce": Envoys of the Other*, edited by Louis Armand and Clare Wallace, 22–55. Bethesda, MD: Academica Press, 2002.

Posner, Richard A. *Law and Literature*. 3rd ed. Cambridge, MA: Harvard University Press, 2009.

Reichman, Ravit. *The Affective Life of Law: Legal Modernism and the Literary Imagination*. Stanford, CA: Stanford University Press, 2009.

Savage, Gail. "Erotic Stories and Public Decency: Newspaper Reporting of Divorce Proceedings in England." *Historical Journal* 41 (1998): 511–28.

Stone, Lawrence. *Road to Divorce: England, 1530–1987*. New York: Oxford University Press, 1990.

Streit, Wolfgang. *Joyce/Foucault: Sexual Confessions*. Ann Arbor: University of Michigan Press, 2004.

Urquhart, Diane. "Ireland and the Divorce and Matrimonial Causes Act of 1857." *Journal of Family History* 38 (2013): 301–20.

Utell, Janine. *James Joyce and the Revolt of Love: Marriage, Adultery, Desire*. New York: Palgrave Macmillan, 2010.

2

Joyce and British Finance Law

Adrift on the Waters of International Investment

CAREY MICKALITES

From the mid-nineteenth through the early twentieth century, British finance—in the areas of banking, company formation, stock valuation, and foreign investments—functioned according to a deeply entrenched laissez-faire policy of unfettered markets. At the same time, waves of fraud and failed businesses throughout the period prompted the formulation of new legal measures to regulate company formation and promotion, to impose tighter restrictions on securities, and to legally distinguish between unsecured speculation and rational investment practices. Financial policy in Britain and Ireland up to 1914 thus operated within a highly ambiguous and dramatically charged discursive space between the laissez-faire ethos of financial practice and Parliamentary efforts to control its potential excesses.

This essay reads select moments in *Dubliners* and *Ulysses* to show how James Joyce's fiction critically treats the shady definitions of British finance law from a distinctly Irish perspective. While it has long been a critical commonplace that Joyce portrays a woefully stunted Irish economy under English colonial rule, little has been written about how his work negotiates realistically and imaginatively with the often legally nebulous nature of British financial systems. For example, "After the Race" depicts the exuberant young Jimmy Doyle as a reckless and feckless Irish newcomer to international company finance, virtually equating Doyle's investment in a French auto firm under limited liability law with excessive gambling. But Joyce would radically alter this picture in *Ulysses*. If we attend to the legal implications of Leopold Bloom's financial schemes, we see that he continually attempts to balance the conflicting impulses of investment fantasies that would capitalize on the vague nature of British finance law and a practical bourgeois realism associated with prudent participation in domestic and international finance. Bloom is a model for a new *Homo economicus*, one who seeks to balance moderation and financial risk and to imagine ways to translate the nebulous nature of British financial policy into the social good of Ireland. In thus contrasting his depictions of Irish participation in domestic and international finance—from risky speculation to prudent investment in the public good—we see how Joyce critically negotiates with existing finance laws and laissez-faire British policy in order to imagine real social improvement for the citizens of "dear, dirty Dublin."

Fraud and Finance Law (A Brief History)

Modern British finance laws sporadically stumbled into being, emerging in response to waves of crisis and financial fraud from the middle of the nineteenth century on. They simultaneously register urgent needs to prevent fraudulent economic practices, to protect investors from excessive losses and thereby to grow the economy, and to uphold a specifically British devotion to laissez-faire ideology and free trade policies. Here I focus particularly on the inception of limited liability law, the changing policies affecting company prospectuses, the increasing dependence of the British economy on largely unregulated international investment, and a widespread cultural anxiety stemming from the close association between financial speculation and illicit gambling in this laissez-faire environment.

Passed in 1855, the Limited Liability Act had wide support among pro-business free trade advocates who saw it as a means of expanding investments toward domestic growth, while more conservative types feared it would encourage unbridled speculation. This divergence of views makes a certain sense: prior to liability law, shareholders in public companies were liable for the full extent of company losses, discouraging the prudent from buying shares, while conservative economists like J. R. McCulloch complained that the lack of legal consequences for risky financial behavior would promote dangerous speculation (Robb 25). That latter concern, however, became increasingly outmoded after the passage of the Limited Liability Act and, the following year, the Companies Act, which further loosened requirements on company incorporation, including as it did the elimination of stipulations on minimum paid-up capital for newly registered companies (Robb 25–26). These legal changes in favor of free trade allowed for significantly greater risk, since company organizers, shareholders, and small investors were no longer liable for losses beyond their initial investment.

Several additional factors helped shape this laissez-faire economic environment. From the 1850s to 1914 more and more of Britain's real wealth became tied up with foreign investments, such that by 1913 "sixty percent of the quoted value of the London Stock Exchange was in foreign stocks" (Delany 127), often based on little capital security. During the same period, moreover, the laws affecting company prospectuses were so vague as to allow for utter deception. As David Itzkowitz argues, by the 1870s the lack of clear legal regulation of company prospectuses and similar financial documents prompted anxieties about the distinction between sound rational investment and "extravagant speculation." If a speculative impulse was understood to be at the heart of all investment, then what, specifically, would distinguish it from illicit gambling? Brokers in particular, operating outside the scanty rules of the Stock Exchange that prohibited advertising, were free to promote shares with the most favorable of promises, and often adopted the rhetoric of professional bookies. Speculation understood as risky investment thus contributed to the view of participants as simultaneously "sporting 'men of the world' and as rational, calculating capitalists" (Itzkowitz 111). This is not to say that such practices were not fraudulent; numerous trials in which deception could be proved resulted in waves of high-profile convictions across the late nineteenth and early twentieth century. But the point is that with limited legal oversight and stipulations on investment, the distinctions between legitimate investment, wild speculation, and immoral gambling became harder to draw. Finally, this laissez-faire legal climate especially affected foreign investments, on which the financial security of the British increasingly depended. The limited regulations on the communication of financial data found a haven for fraud in promoting shares in overseas companies and development loans with only the most superficial signs of government securities on investments, especially when companies claimed to deal in more remote locations. This drama of shady legal regulations on financial operations, from the inception of Limited Liability Law and the Companies Acts through the turn of the century, led the finance writer Anthony Pulbrook to conclude in 1906 that "shares on the Stock Exchange are not guided by their intrinsic value but by the law of supply and demand and that for all practical purposes shares may be regarded as counters for gambling purposes" (quoted in Robb 91). In the light of this brief historical drama, we can turn to Joyce's fictional deployments of the nebulous nature of British finance law within the Irish and international context.

Racy Investments: Irish Gambling and International Finance

"After the Race" focuses on middle-class Irish merchant-investors represented by Mr. Doyle and his son Jimmy. More accurately, the father and son reveal a fissure between conservative practices of capital accumulation and rational investment on the one hand and speculative impulses often associated with gambling on the other. Mr. Doyle begins his career as a butcher, saves and reinvests his capital by opening multiple butcher shops, and through financial diligence earns "his money many times over" (*D* 43). Jimmy, born into relative privilege, recklessly runs up bills his father must pay. But he also forms a business acquaintance with Charles Ségouin, owner of a race car and of a new French auto-production firm, suggesting an analogous relation between fast cars and international finance at the beginning of the twentieth century.

Jimmy's investment in the new firm not only motivates his friendship with Ségouin but serves as the basis for the story's dramatic plotting within the hazy distinctions between the careful accumulation of real money and the immaterial promises of future returns on investments. Seamus Deane has suggested that Jimmy and other Dubliners are all too willing to subsume the squalid reality of their lives in the illusory glamour of Continental cosmopolitanism (23), a point that we might tweak here to say that Jimmy's attraction to international investment reflects a speculative ethos made possible by limited regulations on company formation and financial disclosure. The story's first mention of Jimmy, as he's riding in the back of the French car near the end of the 1903 Gordon Bennett Cup, describes him as being "too excited to be genuinely happy" (*D* 43), and this excitement comes largely from his association with Continental capital and the hazy promise of turning his inherited reserves into future gains.

While Jimmy thinks that "he really had a great sum under his control," that control is then immediately qualified by the investment risk in which "he was about to stake the greater part of his substance!" (*D* 44). "Substance" here names the Doyles' accumulated capital that Jimmy hopes to invest toward future returns. At the same time, the word's connotations include his "character" or even his material body, and thus Joyce, in yoking together these implications, suggests that the very substance of Jimmy's existence as a character depends on future returns on his investment. In other words, it is not merely that Jimmy's middle-class identity is defined by his material property, but that his very being is constituted in the purely abstract possibility of future capital gains dependent on market fluctuations.

But Jimmy's financial being also depends on knowledge of the market, knowledge often rendered dubious by the limited regulations affecting company prospectuses. Since the middle of the nineteenth century, and as a corollary to Limited Liability and similar acts, loose regulations meant company prospectuses frequently "contained lurid promises of success rather than substantial financial data" and could mask insolvency with outlandish promises of future returns and overvalued assets (Robb 96–97). Joyce's narrative, by withholding the details of the investment, suggests that Jimmy might fall prey to just such "lurid promises." Urged by his father to undertake the investment, Jimmy thinks, "Of course, the investment was a good one" (*D* 44). But the "substance" of the company's assets and values on shares rests only on favorable impressions. Thus "Ségouin had managed to give the impression that it was by a favour of friendship that the mite of Irish money was to be included in the capital of the concern," and, "Moreover, Ségouin had the unmistakable air of wealth" (*D* 44–45).

Even Jimmy's calculating father seems impressed by the force of rumor and public confidence as measures of share values: observing his son preparing for the dinner to celebrate the investment and "giving a last equation" to his tie knot, Jimmy's father "felt even commercially satisfied at having secured for his son qualities often unpurchasable" (*D* 45). Finally, in contrast to Mr. Doyle's careful accumulation of capital reserves, at the party comprised of the company's owner and international investors, the young men talk "volubly and with little reserve" (*D* 46), their boisterous excitement suggesting the practice of floating a company's assets and shares with equally little capital reserve. Thus, while Mr. Doyle's new money respectability is grounded in the careful "equation" of all values, the language in the passage slides seamlessly into the "unpurchasable" realm of rumor and financial speculation that, like unrestrained conversation, can float free from clear requirements on company reserves.

All of these suggestions of the exciting risk of international investment in the face of unregulated finance point to the story's concluding gambling scene in which the Irish Jimmy loses heavily to his fellow investors from France and England. In the most general sense, the scene reflects the widespread anxieties associated with the close links between legal investment and reckless gambling. If Joyce's prose to this point in the story suggestively buries solid financial information under favorable impressions and the "air of wealth," the drunken Jimmy becomes totally intoxicated by the sheer excitement of fast-paced betting: "Play ran very high and paper began to pass. Jimmy did not know who exactly was winning but he knew that he was losing. But it was his own fault for he frequently mistook his cards and the other men had to calculate his I.O.U.s for him. They were devils of fellows but he wished they would stop" (D 48). Losing at the card table presages the likely losses he's to face on investing his substantial sum in the French firm. Driven by the manic thrill of risk and returns, and in the absence of clear regulations on company prospectuses and share values, Joyce correlates IOUs with company shares, gambling and investment, in a way that echoes the sentiments of financial observers like Pulbrook who equated company shares with gambling tokens.[1]

More specifically, Joyce positions Jimmy as an unwitting Irish speculator who, with "little reserve," can only lose in the game of international finance. It is not insignificant in Joyce's volume about the paralysis of colonial Ireland that Jimmy is the biggest loser while Routh, a young Englishman, ultimately wins the pot. Many of the other characters in *Dubliners* are paralyzed by their compliance with a stunted Irish economy under colonial control, and in "After the Race" Joyce reproduces the familiar stereotype of an Irish tendency to reckless and irrational economic behavior. We can draw two further, related conclusions from this. The easy reproduction of that Irish cultural stereotype, for one, betrays a certain laissez-faire attitude on the part of Joyce's narrator. But as part of his attempt to give his fellow Dubliners a look at themselves in his "nicely polished looking glass," Joyce's stereotypical depiction of Irish irrationality might be thought of as its own literary risk, one that hopes to capitalize on laissez-faire British finance laws that in many cases favored the tricks of company deception, unsecured speculation, and financial fraud.[2]

Bloom: Ireland's New *Homo economicus*

The stereotype of Irish financial imprudence featured in "After the Race" threads throughout Joyce's later works. While I focus on Leopold Bloom's approaches to risk and financial management in this section, I would like, as a brief transition, to consider Stephen Dedalus as a kind of interim figure linking *Dubliners* and *Ulysses*. Upon receipt of his essay prize money in *Portrait*, Stephen alternately squanders his liquid assets and balances his capital investments, both motivated by a desire to offset his father's embarrassing losses witnessed on their trip to Cork to sell off family property. On the one hand we have Stephen the spendthrift: "For a swift season of merrymaking the money of his prizes ran through Stephen's fingers," and he buys great quantities of "delicacies and dried fruits" for his family, takes them to the theater each night, and regularly shares Vienna chocolates with his guests (*P* 97). On the other, he sets up his own domestic lending institution: he "drew up a form of commonwealth for the household by which every member of it held some office, opened a loan bank for his family and pressed loans on willing borrowers so that he might have the pleasure of making out receipts and reckoning the interests on the sums lent" (*P* 98). Mimicking the imperial commonwealth on the domestic level, Stephen establishes a small Bank of Ireland whose loans might improve the family finances. But Stephen also mimics Simon Dedalus's spendthrift habits and accumulation of debts, as well as Jimmy's Continental pleasure seeking, and he soon runs out of money.[3] By 16 June 1904 Stephen has become the prodigal son. And by the time he leaves Bella Cohen's at the end of "Circe" he is, like Jimmy Doyle, doubly liquidated: dead drunk and near penniless, the fetishized "dancing coins" (*U* 2.449) paid by Deasy that morning having magically disappeared. From his portrait of the irrational investor to that of the artist as a young man, Joyce continues to figure an Irish ineptitude for finance. But he significantly balances that figure in the dense economic imaginary of *Ulysses*. Enter Bloom.

As an ad canvasser, Bloom deals daily with the appeals to public wish fulfillment in the economic sphere, as others have discussed at length.[4] But we might also note that his prudently managed private assets and bourgeois conceptions of social change position him as a comic ideal of rational economic man. Bloom seeks to counter the appeals of private speculation under laissez-faire British financial policy with social welfare schemes that might both capitalize on the nebulous nature of British investment and finance law and secure a better economic future for colonial Ireland. We can begin with his critical reflections on an unsecured foreign investment opportunity before turning to his ideas for socially investing in the future of Ireland.

In the "Calypso" chapter of *Ulysses*, whose art is economics according to the Gilbert schema, Bloom skims a newspaper ad for Agendath Netaim, an investment scheme sponsored by the Turkish government with a company address in Berlin to purchase land in Palestine which would then be planted with a choice of olives, citrus fruits, or almonds. "Every year you get a sending of the crop," Bloom reads, and investors "Can pay ten down [on the eighty-mark investment] and the balance in yearly instalments" (*U* 4.191–199). While the company prospectus doesn't offer capital returns on investments, instead promising a crop yield, its payment system and its multinational operations reflect real-world foreign investments whose securities were often dubious. Bloom's response to the lush detail is ambivalent, thinking "Nothing doing. Still an idea behind it" (*U* 4.200), before dismissing the exotic appeal of the whole enterprise, thinking of the Palestinian landscape as "a barren land" burdened by the "dead names" of the Old Testament, "the grey sunken cunt of the world" (*U* 4.219, 228).

Dismissing the scheme as the stuff of financial fraud, Bloom seems aware of the false promises and inflated company values that loose restrictions on prospectuses allowed, particularly in the area of foreign investments and loans requiring only the scantiest indications of legal oversight or solid government securities. The prospectus and Bloom's dismissal thus tacitly and critically reflect the delicate nature of British foreign finance policy during the period. Within the Ottoman Empire, the Palestinian land is under Turkish authority. Early in the nineteenth century Britain enjoyed a free trade agreement with Turkey, and its ongoing diplomatic aid sought to maintain political stability in the region favorable to investment and trade, rather than promoting British finance directly (Platt 184, 205). By the turn of the century, however, German competition, supported by Deutsche Bank and the German government, had squeezed British wool and other exports out of the Turkish market. British diplomats sought to secure more protection for and promotion of British commercial interests in the region, a move the government repeatedly refused to take (189). The English public was accordingly reluctant to risk heavy investments in Turkish securities, since they couldn't be secured on the London market, a position summed up by Sir Edward Grey in 1908 when, addressing the Turkish government, he stated that while "H.M. Government was 'most anxious to attract British capital into Turkey for *bona fide* concessions and commercial enterprises, and . . . sincerely desirous that . . . the entry of British capital into Turkey should not be greatly delayed,' there was no prospect of a London flotation at the present time" (Platt 193).

In light of Britain's long-standing commercial interests in Turkish economic development and its laissez-faire approach to securing those investments, Bloom's wariness regarding the fantastical Agendath Netaim makes sense. Were he to buy shares, his investment would likely be secured by German banks and a politically precarious Turkish government overseeing an undeveloped infrastructure. As an Irish citizen, subject to British law, Bloom prudently decides against what thus appears an investment lacking British security. Rather than risk his capital on exotic foreign returns, Bloom looks to Ireland's domestic economy, imagining ways to negotiate and capitalize on the nebulous system of British finance in order to counter a colonially stunted Irish economy.

Throughout *Ulysses* Bloom entertains various social improvement schemes that often veer between his bourgeois financial prudence and his socialistic, even utopian, aspirations. Those schemes, as we'll see, alternately seek to exploit British laissez-faire financial policy for the economic benefit of the colony and to counter the ongoing British exploitation of Ireland in the form of export control and uneven taxation to limit competition. But in order to better gauge the legal implications and economic viability of those moderate financial schemes, we need to visit Barney Kiernan's pub and Bloom's counterpart and nemesis, the violently nationalist "citizen."

Partly modeled on Michael Cusack, Sinn Feiner and extoller of traditional Irish sport and manliness, the citizen in the "Cyclops" chapter is a comic figure of nationalist excess, a blowhard who scapegoats England and Bloom's Jewishness alike for Ireland's economic woes. The episode as a whole contains a series of stylistic parodies that range from ancient Irish legal practices to contemporary sports reporting. A major target of the chapter's parodic thrust is the nationalist rhetoric of English colonial exploitation of Irish resources and exports voiced by the citizen, whose monologues on the subject alternate between accuracy and hyperbole, providing, as we'll see, a foil for Bloom's moderate approach to legal economic reform. The citizen loudly laments the demise, partly due to taxation and control of export markets favorable to the English, of Irish "potteries and textiles, the finest in the whole world! And our wool that was sold in Rome in the time of Juvenal," as well as flax, damask, and Limerick lace, before concluding his windy diatribe with the rhetorical question "What do the yellowjohns of Anglia owe us for our ruined trade and our ruined hearths?" (U 12.1241–1244, 1254–1255). As L. M. Cullen argues, "Large [Irish] firms were as a rule export-oriented" and "It was only by the development of export markets that industrial firms could reach a scale of production" that would allow them to compete internationally (157). According to Don Gifford's annotations, Irish wool and flax industries had long been subject to English taxation and other measures to suppress competition, contributing to the demise of those export markets (350). Historians have found similar evidence that such restrictions partly "ruined" Ireland's economy and place in international trade (Fetter 81). These restrictive policies on Irish exports and finance, and the citizen's complaints against them, are echoed a few chapters later by the alleged Skin-the-Goat in the cabman's shelter in "Eumaeus": "airing his grievances . . . anent the natural resources of Ireland . . . and all the riches drained out of it by England levying taxes on the poor people that paid through the nose and always gobbling up the best meat in the market and a lot more surplus steam in the same vein" (U 16.986–993). Note here how the narrator's language is exhausted, reflecting the late-night setting of the chapter, and infused with ambiguity: the keeper's complaint about the English appropriations of the best Irish produce slides into the narrator's dismissive comment, intimating that the English colonial demands and the Irish complaints about them are both full of "surplus steam." This also explains the rumor that the keeper is Skin-the-Goat Fitzharris, sentenced as an accessory to the Phoenix Park murders, as it suggests an assimilation of violent nationalism and skinning, a faint allusion to the wool industry. Joyce parodies the excessive nature of nationalist rhetoric on Irish export policy, and such inflated speech corresponds to the rigid version of nationalism taking hold in Ireland from the days of Parnell through the Easter Uprising, with which Joyce was thoroughly familiar. As Cullen suggests, members of the Irish trading classes, like their English counterparts, were often wary of protective tariffs, while those in favor of more radical political measures—a category that would include Joyce's fictional citizen—"tended to overestimate Ireland's natural advantages and resources" and "assumed optimistically that under altered political arrangements much of the country's industrial recovery would be spontaneous" (164).

In contrast, Bloom's financial schemes for social reform generally speak for more moderate measures, and his approach, even when socialistic or wildly utopian, often seeks to counter Irish economic stagnation in the colonial system in terms compatible with already existing finance laws and policy.[5] Even though the citizen and the narrator repeatedly castigate Bloom as a Jew and an ad salesman—viewing him as a usurious moneylender guilty of "swindling the peasants" (*U* 12.1150)—he's also mockingly conflated with Arthur Griffith, the narrator reporting on gossip that Bloom gave Griffith the ideas for Sinn Fein that include "swindling the taxes off of the government and appointing consuls all over the world to walk about selling Irish industries" (*U* 12.1574–1577). This contradictory perception of Bloom is crucial, for it indexes how he alternates between, and sometimes intertwines, the radical visions of nationalist resistance and the realities of British finance policy.

His welfare scheme in "Lestrygonians" imagines a way for Ireland to capitalize on its future through a combination of saving and a state-sponsored system of investment and interest, a plan to counter Ireland's staggering overpopulation and unemployment. In Bloom's imaginary proposal, for each newborn child £5 would be invested out of Irish taxes paid to Britain at 5 percent compound interest up to the age of twenty-one. In Bloom's reckoning, this would amount to a return of a "hundred and ten and a bit" for a total of £10 10s (*U* 8.382–386). As Mark Osteen points out, Bloom forgets to compound the interest annually, which would bring the total to almost £14, close to the amount of Bloom's savings (105). Bloom's plan yokes the seductions of speculation in a laissez-faire financial climate to an ethical investment that might help to alleviate Ireland's dire poverty and unemployment, modeling something like the "revolution . . . on the due instalments plan" that he sleepily advocates later in "Eumaeus" (*U* 16.1101). And as Jaya Savige has shown, Bloom here draws on his knowledge of the evolving life insurance industry in Britain and Ireland: his proposal for managing risk (of poverty, accident, unemployment) "would make him a kind of actuarial father of his race," and even "foreshadows both Arthur Griffith's proposal for an Irish national insurance scheme (made at the inaugural meeting of Sinn Fein the following November), and the British Parliament's decision under David Lloyd George... to pass the National Insurance Act of 1911" (85). Bloom models a comically ideal *Homo economicus* for Ireland, balancing bourgeois prudence and a socially ethical approach to speculation and risk management through which English laissez-faire financial policy might be exploited in overcoming Irish economic and social paralysis.

We might think of such schemes as the practical realization of the comic references to Bloom as "the new Messiah for Ireland," first voiced sarcastically by the citizen in "Cyclops" (*U* 12.1642). In light of that comic-messianic association, we can focus here on his utopian fantasy for social reform before turning to the practical measures underlying it. Just before his imaginative rise to leader of the new "Bloomusalem" in the hallucinatory "Circe" chapter—in which he speaks for a socialist utopia—Bloom's first initiative as the new Lord Mayor of Dublin invokes a practical plan to channel funds from private finance to public works: "run a tramline, I say, from the cattlemarket to the river. That's the music of the future. . . . But our bucaneering Vanderdeckens in their phantom ship of finance . . ." (*U* 15.1367–1370). The charge against the phantom control of financiers trails off, but Bloom continues to decry the various "hobgoblins produced by a horde of capitalistic lusts upon our prostituted labour" (*U* 15.1393–1394). That pronouncement finds its culmination in a socialist utopia as alternative to the violently exclusive aspirations for economic independence of a narrow nationalism. In reply to the Home Rule question, "When will we have our own house of keys?" Bloom speaks for "the reform of municipal morals" corresponding to shared manual labor and public spaces and, in a final thrust at the citizen's hyper-nationalist and inflated hopes for Irish exports, proclaims "No more patriotism of barspongers and dropsical imposters. Free money, free rent, free love and a free lay church in a free lay state" (*U* 15.1683–1693).

These passages in "Circe," then, are as inflated as the nationalist rhetoric about financing Irish independence through control of natural resources and exports that we hear from the citizen and others. But I mention them because their optimistic aims also anticipate Bloom's ideas for a kind of home rule that would join private investment and interest to Irish public improvement, thus imagining ways to translate the risks and gains entailed by loose legal regulations on speculative finance and company securities into a system that might secure better social conditions in the blighted colony. First, as a version of his bourgeois "revolution . . . on the due installments plan," Bloom imagines acquiring his suburban dream home, dubbed Flowerville, according to standard loan and accounting principles. The property, valued at £1,200, would be financed by "the Industrious Foreign Acclimatised Nationalized Friendly Stateaided Building Society" (*U* 17.1658–1659) providing capital "derived from giltedged securities" at 5 percent interest, and following a £400 down payment Bloom would pay £60 per year plus 2½ percent interest over a twenty-year period (*U* 17.1658–1665). He then imagines a series of get-rich-quick schemes that might expedite the purchase, each of which involves an extraordinary stroke of luck and shows Bloom's occasional seductions by high-risk investments. Offsetting such gambles, he subsequently considers a range of schemes for investing in Irish public works like hydroelectric production, public transportation, and a better infrastructure for the transport of cattle. These latter approaches to public improvement and social reform are to be partly financed by donations from "eminent financiers" such that by "joining capital with opportunity the thing required was done" (*U* 17.1710–1751).

As Mark Osteen has pointed out, Bloom's plan for financing his home is beyond his current means and is thus "implausible" (415), as are his other plans for financing infrastructure improvement, since they depend on gifts and donations from the wealthy with no stated system of returns with which to solicit their investment. But Bloom's close attention to investment, interest, and requirements on capital securities does reflect commercial development and finance policies in early twentieth-century Dublin. Indeed, the period between the late 1870s and 1914 witnessed waves of attempts in and around Dublin to improve infrastructure and housing conditions, involving the city Corporation, building and loan societies, and combinations of commercial investment and public spending. Joyce's fictional and parodically named "stateaided" building society, to whom Bloom thinks of applying for a secured loan, both reflects the aims of historically specific organizations then in operation and mocks the limited success of their development initiatives, mostly due to a dependence on an uncertain money market and poor city management. Joseph O'Brien provides something of a case study we can use for comparison. O'Brien describes how the Dublin Artisans' Dwellings Company, a private building organization, undertook development projects around the turn of the century to improve housing for both working- and middle-class citizens, but did so mostly outside the city's central sections of dire poverty, building cottages that "only the well-paid tradesman and skilled worker could afford" (127). Strictly not a charitable institution, the company assured purchasers of its shares a 5 percent commercial dividend that attracted private speculators and large investors including the Guinness family of stout fame. By 1907, however, the company ceased operations, "victim to the uncertainty of the money market" on which its finances depended (127).

With the objectives of improving housing conditions for employed citizens, and stimulating investment and economic growth, and doing so along strictly commercial, and not charitable, lines, the activities of building societies like the Dwellings Company provide some historical grounding for Bloom's plans for financing his dream cottage. As a middle-class Dubliner with respectable but moderate assets, the £400 down payment is clearly beyond Bloom's current means. But his imaginary scheme, including the 5 percent interest to be paid to investors in the fictional building society, reflects the financing practices of the real Artisans' Dwellings Company. So his domestic dream, while beyond his financial means, is in line with existing laws and finance practices in colonial Dublin's struggle to alleviate poverty and help citizens acquire property. At the same time, though, the comically inflated possibilities that Bloom entertains for acquiring capital, such as "the independent discovery of a goldseam of inexhaustible ore" (U 17.1753), are the stuff of pure fantasy. Bloom's imaginary prospectus, then, reflects the real-world terms for financing new development projects, but in the passage's comic inflation of those terms—simply "joining capital with opportunity"—Joyce critically exposes the limits of applying capitalist principles to social improvement within a volatile market and in the absence of viable legal protection. Through Bloom's late-night reverie, Joyce forges a tension that pits the realism of Bloom's calculations and the commercial financing of adequate living conditions against the equally real threat that a volatile money market and questionable securities pose to those practices.

I'd like to conclude on that tension. As Andrew Gibson argues in another context, I think this tension between historical reality and Bloom's financial fantasies exemplifies how Bloom "represents possibilities, possible change, even a possible future," and that while he is at times a "utopian figure," Joyce "also presents the possibilities in question as compatible with a determinate set of historical realities" (Gibson 59). So on the one hand, Joyce's fiction often reveals an Irish fixation on scarcity that reflects laissez-faire British financial policy and imbalanced colonial management of trade and investment. If "After the Race" figures Irish foreign investment according to conventional stereotypes of reckless speculation, that image also captures something of the anxiety associated with financial speculation under limited legal regulations. And if the citizen mirrors an overzealous nationalist approach to righting domestic finance through recourse to a magically infinite supply of resources and export goods, his violent protestations still index the ways in which British colonial legislation and trade policy weakened Ireland's economic standing in international trade. Between these extremes, on the other hand, Bloom may not be the "new Messiah for Ireland," but rather its new *Homo economicus*, a comically rational economic man constantly negotiating the contingent world of finance and seeking to balance the risks of speculation with prudent calculation. As such, Bloom's elaborate scheming in "Ithaca" imagines an alternative future for Ireland that works within existing finance laws but that might also transfer the terms of British colonial control to practical Irish social reform and economic security.

Notes

1. Joyce's notes on commercial law offer suggestive parallels with the fictional Jimmy's investment. Under "essential conditions" for fraud, Joyce includes "false representation," "turpitude or recklessness" on the part of company promoters, and, most important, the "intention that deceived party should act on fraud. (A man buying shares in open market cannot sue Co[mpany] for fraudulent misrepresentation in a prospectus.)" While the story gives no indication that Ségouin is guilty of fraud, it does suggest that even if Jimmy falls victim to misrepresentation, he will still be liable for his own losses (Groden 3: 507).

2. I thank the anonymous reader of the manuscript for this suggestion about the story's laissez-faire risk.

3. Stephen's spendthrift habits reflect Joyce's own which, as Mark Osteen points out, he inherited from his father. See *The Economy of "Ulysses,"* 7–9.

4. See Osteen, *The Economy of "Ulysses,"* especially chapter 4. For a detailed Lacanian reading of the role of advertising across a range of Joyce's work, see Leonard, *Advertising and Commodity Culture in Joyce*.

5. In perhaps a similar vein, Emer Nolan notes that, in light of the nationalist interest in fostering international capitalism, "the cosmopolitan Bloom and his Gaelicist antagonist represent two sides of the same coin. For all his patriotic bluster, the citizen wants Ireland to enter the capitalist world; but Bloom is already an apologist for that 'music of the future' (15.1368)" (91).

Works Cited

Attridge, Derek, and Marjorie Howes, eds. *Semicolonial Joyce*. Cambridge: Cambridge University Press, 2000.

Cullen, L. M. *An Economic History of Ireland since 1660*. London: Batsford, 1972.

Deane, Seamus. "Dead Ends: Joyce's Finest Moments." In Attridge and Howes, *Semicolonial Joyce*, 21–36.

Delany, Paul. *Literature, Money, and the Market: From Trollope to Amis*. Basingstoke, Hants.: Palgrave, 2002.

Fetter, Frank W., and Derek Gregory. *Monetary and Financial Policy*. Dublin: Irish University Press, 1973.

Gibson, Andrew. *Joyce's Revenge: History, Politics, and Aesthetics in "Ulysses."* Oxford: Oxford University Press, 2002.

Gifford, Don. *"Ulysses" Annotated: Notes for James Joyce's "Ulysses."* With Robert Seidman. Berkeley: University of California Press, 1989.

Groden, Michael, et al., eds. *The James Joyce Archive*. 63 vols. New York: Garland, 1978.

Itzkowitz, David C. "Fair Enterprise or Extravagant Speculation: Investment, Speculation, and Gambling in Victorian England." In *Victorian Investments: New Perspectives on Finance and Culture*, edited by Nancy Henry and Cannon Schmitt, 98–119. Bloomington: Indiana University Press, 2009.

Joyce, James. *Dubliners*. 1914. New York: Viking, 1962.

———. *A Portrait of the Artist as a Young Man*. 1916. New York: Viking, 1964.

———. *Ulysses: The Corrected Text*. Edited by Hans Walter Gabler et al. New York: Random House, 1986.

Leonard, Garry. *Advertising and Commodity Culture in Joyce*. Gainesville: University Press of Florida, 1998.

Nolan, Emer. "State of the Art: Joyce and Postcolonialism." In Attridge and Howes, *Semicolonial Joyce*, 78–95.

O'Brien, Joseph V. *"Dear, Dirty Dublin": A City in Distress, 1899–1916*. Berkeley: University of California Press, 1982.

Osteen, Mark. *The Economy of "Ulysses": Making Both Ends Meet*. Syracuse, NY: Syracuse University Press, 1995.

Platt, D.C.M. *Finance, Trade, and Politics in British Foreign Policy, 1815–1914*. London: Oxford University Press, 1968.

Robb, George. *White-Collar Crime in Modern England: Financial Fraud and Business Morality, 1845–1929*. Cambridge: Cambridge University Press, 1992.

Savige, Jaya. "Underwriting *Ulysses*: Bloom, Risk and Life Insurance in the Nineteenth Century." In *James Joyce in the Nineteenth Century*, edited by John Nash, 77–94. Cambridge: Cambridge University Press, 2013.

3

Joyce, the Aliens Act, and Immigration

STEVEN MORRISON

James Joyce was born a British subject and he died in that same condition. Joyce retained a United Kingdom passport throughout his life, which has been taken either to suggest some form of ambivalence about British rule or, more plausibly, as a token of his many reservations about the Irish Free State. In fact, Joyce's legal status after 1922, certainly while resident in France, would have been largely unaffected if he had elected to swap passports. The new green Irish passports were issued with Saorstát Éireann emblazoned on the cover, but the request page inside, originally appearing over the signature of the Governor General, still required free passage for the bearer in the name of His Britannic Majesty. Successive Irish governments, though conscious of the costs defrayed by having "Britain effectively carr[y] out most of Ireland's immigration control" (O'Halpin 105), nevertheless wrestled with the notion that it was possible to be entirely Irish only while resident in Ireland. After 1939 reference to the king was dropped from the passports, but for as long as Ireland remained, no matter how unenthusiastically, a member of the Commonwealth, the British government regarded soi-disant Irish citizens as de facto British subjects, especially once they were outside the Free State. The dispute remained unresolved until the passing of the British Nationality Act of 1948 and the Ireland Act of 1949. It may be that, as Louis Gillet claimed, Joyce retained a British passport in the belief that his own freedom was "better off in the large unity of the *Commonwealth* than in the limits of an intolerant and annoying fatherland" (185), but the difficulty in finally separating the second from the first "rendered all animated greatbritish and Irish objects" (*FW* 403.23) legally indistinguishable throughout his lifetime in any case.

It seems altogether more probable that, like most Irish people of his age and background, Joyce regarded national identity as falling outside the purview of the law. That the Irish were British in a legal sense and in no other was very much the point at issue. The accommodation of four nations within one state had always required a degree of flexibility, and the first attempts to clarify the legal status of the British subject were of relatively recent date. British subject status was acquired through being born almost anywhere in the British Empire or, outside it, to a British father. The Irish-born son of Rudolf Virag qualifies without ambiguity only by birth—"Ireland, says Bloom. I was born here" (*U* 12.1431)—whereas the Gibraltar-born daughter of Major Tweedy actually qualifies on both counts. To be born within the British monarch's domains was to be presumed a loyal subject until death, as Irish emigrants returning home as United States citizens occasionally discovered.

As for the distinction between native and foreigner, to be English in Ireland was to be foreign, "strangers to our shore" (*U* 2.392–393)—and vice versa, as Irish migrants to Britain from the 1840s onward could testify—but not to be a foreign national. For those born outside the Empire who wished to become British, nineteenth-century reforms had started to replace the ancient and costly mechanism of denization with a more modern process of naturalization, but it remained a complex business. The right of entry into the United Kingdom, however, was relatively straightforward. Such controls as there were on immigration, vestigial remnants of the Napoleonic Wars, were rarely invoked and impossible to enforce, allowing what was in effect an open border policy to prevail. The state of Bloom's father's right of residence is a matter that *Ulysses* leaves entirely open to speculation—thus the significance to Bloom of his having been born in Ireland—but it is entirely possible that he would have landed in Britain and made his way to Ireland without encountering a single legal check. A belief in the economic benefits of the free movement of labor, along with pride, in both Britain and Ireland, in the tradition of acting as safe haven for those fleeing persecution abroad, from the Huguenots to Karl Marx, set the tone for a longstanding laissez-faire attitude toward immigration. In 1904, however, this was about to change. The Aliens Act of 1905 was "the first recognisably modern law that sought permanently to restrict immigration into Britain according to systematic bureaucratic criteria" (Glover 1), and it had implications, in the opinion of its many critics, not just for the traditions of asylum, but for the traditional concept of British nationality itself. The debate surrounding the Aliens Act is equally crucial when considering immigration and nationality in Joyce's work, since it permeated the contemporary context in which that work is so thoroughly saturated.

The Alien Question

As can be seen from the responses in "Cyclops" to Bloom's identification of his nation, the legal right of residence in the United Kingdom was hardly the determining factor with regard to nationality. As Vincent Cheng points out, national identity was near universally understood at the time in terms of race (17): if *jus soli* was the basis of the law, *jus sanguinis* always trumped it in the popular imagination, not even excluding Bloom's own imagination. "Strange he never saw his real country" (*U* 7.87), he thinks, as he stands behind the supposedly Italian councillor Nannetti, who is, in terms of the law and by birth, exactly as British a subject as is Bloom himself. In "Oxen of the Sun," Bloom's silent thoughts on the frivolity of the medical students having been communicated to the reader, the narrative abruptly switches to the trenchant style of the eighteenth-century polemicist Junius and responds as if those thoughts constituted considerable affront:

> But with what fitness, let it be asked of the noble lord, his patron, has this alien, whom the concession of a gracious prince has admitted to civic rights, constituted himself the lord paramount of our internal polity? Where is now that gratitude which loyalty should have counselled? During the recent war whenever the enemy had a temporary advantage with his granados did this traitor to his kind not seize that moment to discharge his piece against the empire of which he is a tenant at will while he trembled for the security of his four per cents? Has he forgotten this as he forgets all benefits received? (*U* 14.905–913)[1]

If British nationality had a working definition in advance of any developed legal formulation, it largely consisted of this: to be native was not to be alien. The word "alien," deriving from feudal law and entailing the suspension of many "civic rights," had by 1904 acquired a distinct new resonance, through its constant application, in both Parliament and the press, to a particular immigrant group: "From the 1880s onwards, the word 'alien' . . . had become a popular synonym for East European Jews, and everyone was aware of this deadly chain of racialising equivalences. . . . in everyday parlance, 'aliens' simply *were* indigent Jews" (Glover 4).

If the migration of East European Jews fleeing persecution dated back to the 1880s—much the same time at which the word "anti-Semitism," of German extraction, itself began appearing in English—the debate surrounding immigration came to a head around 1904, a year described by David Glover as constituting "a pivotal moment in the history of anti-Semitism in Britain" (119). A Royal Commission of 1903 had looked to address the concerns of more than two decades regarding an influx of Jewish migrants to the poorest parts of London and other British cities, while the consequent Aliens Act, eventually passed in August 1905, imposed new controls on immigration, applying specifically to "alien steerage passengers" traveling on board ships in numbers greater than twenty (tellingly, those who could afford their own cabins were not considered part of the problem). The establishment of such controls faced formidable resistance, and the Aliens Bill had a tortuous passage through Parliament as a result. The country's foremost authority on constitutional law, A. V. Dicey, considered it an unparalleled danger to individual liberty, while Herbert Asquith, whose Liberal government would subsequently encourage leniency in the application of the new law, thought it to be "setting at defiance one of the noblest and one of the most beneficent traditions of British policy" (Gainer 150). Social campaigners such as Beatrice Webb contested the widespread derogatory views of the immigrants, the Booth Report of 1889 declaring the refugee Jews "the most law-abiding inhabitants of East London. They keep the peace, they pay their debts, and they abide by their contracts; practices in which they are undoubtedly superior to the English and Irish labourers among whom they dwell" (Winder 186). Nor was basic sympathy with the plight of the refugees lacking. When, in "Circe," J. J. O'Molloy includes as part of his defense of Bloom the idea of his client as "a poor foreign immigrant who started scratch as a stowaway and is now trying to turn an honest penny" (*U* 15.942–944), it is as if he stands before one of the future immigration boards attempting to play on such sympathies.

But in spite of the quality of the opposition to it, the Aliens Act undoubtedly enjoyed a greater quantity of support, nourished by a relentless campaign against the immigrants in "the old sniggering publicking press" (*FW* 229.08). To anyone paying attention to British and Irish newspapers during these years—and Joyce was paying closer attention than most—the so-called Alien Question was unignorable, a constant feature of reports, editorials and letters. If the debate in Parliament and in the papers often flew in the face of the social, economic, and statistical realities, it would hardly be the last time this would apply where immigration was the subject.[2] The same is true of the fact that alarm about the immigrants was often at its highest precisely where the effects of actual immigration were at their most negligible. Neil R. Davison claims of Ireland that "Dublin, and to a lesser degree Cork, received their share of [the] immigrants" (20), but the numbers contradict this: of the 150,000 or so Jewish immigrants to the United Kingdom between 1881 and 1911, fewer than 5,000 made their way to Ireland, less than half the number received by Liverpool alone. Nor is this surprising, given that the opportunities for work presented by London or Manchester had as much of a draw on young Irish people as on Jewish immigrants at the time.

Ireland, Immigration, and Anti-Semitism

Cormac Ó Gráda's recent account of post-1880 Jewish immigration into Ireland confirms what Louis Hyman first proposed in the 1970s, that the Jewish Dubliners of *Ulysses* are all drawn from or are the descendants of the small number of Jews who, like Bloom's father, entered Ireland sometime before the new arrivals. Almost entirely "middle class and English speaking, its workplaces and residences well dispersed across the city," this informal community "was inconspicuous and bent on integration" (*Jewish Ireland* 95). Having only recently been "admitted to" almost the full range of "civic rights" by nineteenth-century reforms, the older Jewish Dublin treated the Lithuanian newcomers—a more homogeneous, possibly more religiously observant, and certainly more cohesive group, resident in a part of Dublin that became known as Little Jerusalem—with anxiety and suspicion. This was generally the response of established Jewish communities in Britain as well, and it is worth noting that the settled Jewish residents of Dublin, to whom Bloom is obviously related, were commonly distinguished from the Lithuanian newcomers by being referred to as "English Jews." Their not ungrounded fears were that an unprecedentedly large influx of Jewish immigrants would lead to a resurgence of anti-Jewish sentiment.

As it happened, the new anti-Semitism of the 1880s differed from and even directly inverted some of the ancient prejudices, though both, significantly, are brought to bear on Leopold Bloom. The new immigrants were inaccurately characterized as unskilled and uneducated; they were presented as, paradoxically, a feckless burden on poor relief and, simultaneously, maniacally industrious to the point of depriving all others of work; and in moving to the most crowded parts of the cities, they came to be associated with the crime, deprivation, and disease—"coming over here to Ireland filling the country with bugs" (*U* 12.1141–42)—which obviously long predated their arrival. These prejudices had found a new target, but they were not in themselves new, of course, since they were identical to those that had met Irish migrants to Britain earlier in the century. Nor were the traditional and more recent forms of anti-Jewish resentment finally incompatible. Possibly planted there by such British conspiracy theorists of the time as Arnold White or Leo Maxse, the "German jews" of Haines's imagination (*U* 1.667), architects of global financial dominance, were deemed to be making deliberate use of the East European refugees as foot soldiers in their plans, driving down wages and fomenting civil unrest.

The passage of the Aliens Bill through Parliament and the press commentary that surrounded it offer a context in which to treat much of the anti-Semitism represented in *Ulysses*. Mr. Deasy's views seem partly informed by the new racial anti-Semitism of the 1880s and afterward—"England is in the hands of the jews . . . her finance, her press" (*U* 2.346–347)—and partly informed by more ancient forms of religious prejudice: "They sinned against the light" (*U* 2.361). But his final, celebrated remark to Stephen Dedalus arises directly out of this contemporary antialien moment, couched though it is in historical terms. The proud boast of having "never persecuted the jews" (*U* 2.438) was referred to by both sides in the debate in Ireland during 1904, but was not the timeless claim it was made to seem. It appears to have achieved currency only when the Chief Rabbi of London visited Dublin in 1892 and—as instanced by Michael Davitt in a letter to the *Freeman's Journal* of the eighteenth of January, 1904—"declared that when he set foot on Irish soil he was in the only land in Europe in which his race had never suffered persecution" (5). When Deasy proceeds to deliver his punchline—"Because she never let them in" (*U* 2.442)—this is no less firmly planted in the grounds of the contemporary debate. Arnold White, prolific proponent of the need for immigration controls and "veteran of many battles with official statisticians" (Gainer 7), managed the trick of being nakedly anti-Semitic, as the modern reader would understand that term, while deploring contemporary anti-Semitism itself as an un-British import. Michael Davitt, in early 1904 the boaster-in-chief on this issue of Ireland's proud history of tolerance and recently returned from reporting on the persecutions in the Jewish Pale in Russia for W. R. Hearst's *Journal-American*, managed to be, if anything, even more equivocal on the matter:

> Where anti-Semitism stands, in fair political combat, in opposition to the foes of nationality, or against the engineers of a sordid war in South Africa, or as the assailant of the economic evils of unscrupulous capitalism anywhere, I am resolutely in line with its spirit and programme. Where, however, it only speaks and acts in a cowardly racial warfare . . . it becomes a thing deserving of no more toleration from right-minded men than do the germs of some malady laden with the poison of a malignant disease. (ix–x)

Yet both men, seemingly on opposite sides of the debate over the Alien Question, equally deploring the anti-Semitism that had created a "state of hostility in Great Britain which runs into many channels of our national life" (White 201), drew the same conclusion: the necessary response to the rise of anti-Semitism was to restrict the number of Jews who might provoke it, whether by draconian and targeted restrictions on immigration or—the preferred solution of Davitt, a committed Zionist—finding somewhere else for them to go.

Mr. Deasy is of course technically correct in saying that Ireland "never let them in." Britain let them in and, with the passing of the Aliens Act, would now exercise unprecedented control over keeping them out, control extended still further by the 1914 British Nationality and Status of Aliens Act (although, by that time, the aliens of primary concern were Germans). Of the fourteen ports of entry established by the 1905 Act, newly endowed with immigration officers and boards, none was in Ireland. Nor, in spite of the hysteria evident in some parts of the Irish press, was there any need for such controls in Ireland, given the relatively small numbers who made their way there. That Dublin's small community of Lithuanian Jews is nowhere clearly in evidence in Joyce's work effectively contests the idea that prejudice atrophies where the objects of that prejudice are absent. On the contrary, in *Ulysses* some of the most overtly anti-Semitic rhetoric, first in "Hades" and then again in "Cyclops," is reserved for Reuben J. Dodd who, as Robert Boyle established in the 1960s, wasn't even Jewish.

Strangers to Our Shore

That the missing Jewish immigrants, economically proximate to those working classes also largely missing from *Ulysses*, are not absent from Joyce's work as a result of any unwillingness to depict immigrant communities can be seen by the representation, indeed *over*-representation, of Italians in *Ulysses*. Originally treated by sections of the British press, like the Irish before them and the East European Jews after them, as a disturbing new threat to law, order and the traditional way of life, the Italians of *Ulysses* cover the full social range and are in various stages of assimilation, from Nannetti, Member of Parliament and future Lord Mayor, all the way through to the group arguing in Italian around the ice-cream car in "Eumaeus" (*U* 16.309–319), from Cuprani the printer (*U* 7.99–100) and the stout-trousered Almidoni Artifoni (*U* 10.364) to the unnamed organ grinders (*U* 8.721, 17.2137) and Rabaiotti with his *"ice gondola"* (*U* 15.5), earning a living on the streets. That the small number of Jews in Dublin still dwarfed the number of Italians, by a factor of about seven to one, is in no way reflected in *Ulysses* and it is at least some of the Italians who play the role of immigrant proper, as opposed to naturalized or Irish-born British subject. Earlier in Joyce's work, in "Eveline," the account of an abandoned attempt at emigration contains within it the figure of the immigrant Italian street-organ player, sent away with sixpence and Eveline's father's curse of "Damned Italians! coming over here!" (*D* 40).[3]

The idea of a new wave of anti-Semitism and a resentment of foreigners whipped up purely by the debate surrounding the Aliens Act in England cannot efface entirely certain genuine particularities of the Irish situation. Ireland's 5,000 Jews still represented a tenfold increase during a period in which its overall population fell by around half a million. The disturbances in Limerick in January 1904, instigated by Father John Creagh and perpetrated by violent mobs, took place in a city that until the 1880s had a Jewish population measurable on the fingers of one hand. Opponents of the Aliens Act in England could correctly point out that immigration and emigration were roughly in balance, but emigration was not a matter for such dispassionate analysis in Ireland. As the *United Irishman* put it on the twenty-third of January, 1904,

> The stalwart men and bright-eyed women of our race pass from our land in a never-ending stream, and in their place we are getting strange people, alien to us in thought, alien to us in sympathy, from Russia, Poland, Germany, and Austria—people who come to live amongst us, but who never become of us. (5)

But if attitudes toward the effects of emigration were poles apart between Ireland and England, attitudes toward the supposed dangers of immigration were often barely separable and shared by highly unlikely bedfellows, providing an almost unique instance in which Irish Nationalist papers like Arthur Griffith's *United Irishman* and D. P. Moran's *Leader* were of one voice with Nora Joyce's favorite, the *Daily Mail* (Maddox 72) and other strongly Unionist papers in England. If one reads this, as Ira Nadel and Neil Davison both do, as local instances of a broader European anti-Semitism, with the Dreyfus Affair—of great interest to the *United Irishman*, as Nadel has demonstrated (64–66)—as its principal focus, then the harmony is perhaps unremarkable. On the other hand, if one takes contemporary relations between Britain and Ireland more fully into account, with the Aliens Act serving as the focal point, the extent of the tacit agreement between British and Irish nationalists is extraordinary. The *Leader*, in its pro-Creagh coverage of the Limerick disturbances, made a point of including material drawn directly from the English press, as if to suggest that Limerick and the East End of London were of a piece and equally overrun with foreign Jews. An editorial of June 1904 proudly directed its readers to an advertisement for a firm of Dublin house furnishers which included the words "No connection with Jews," while it mocked moderate nationalist papers such as the *Evening Telegraph* for having refused to carry it. That the faultlines ran through Britain and Ireland, rather than between them, was not acknowledged directly, but it did lead to occasional difficulty in maintaining a clear editorial line. On the twenty-eighth of May, 1904, responding to Frederick Ryan's argument in *Dana* that setting the mob on immigrant Jews was a capitalist ploy to keep the masses downtrodden, the *United Irishman* attempted to square the circle:

> We cannot, nor can Mr. Ryan, view without apprehension the power wielded in Europe by the Jewish financiers. A world ruled by the Jewish capitalist would eventually invite the destruction which an oppressed and brutalised proletariat wreaks upon a debauched civilisation. So far as Ireland is concerned, she sees the Jews swarming in while her children are going out. The fault lies in the fact that we are ruled not by ourselves but by foreigners, to whom our interests are diametrically opposed. (1)

Opposed in all respects save this, it would seem, where Irish native and English foreigner found themselves, not of one mind on the Alien Question, but of shared "twosome twiminds" (*FW* 188.14), with liberal protestors issuing calls for tolerance from either side of the Irish Sea and tub-thumping nationalists in Dublin and London finding uniquely common cause in a fear and resentment of the alien. If, in "Cyclops," many of the Citizen's more bigoted views are scarcely separable from those of contemporary English nationalism, it is a discomfiting commonality rooted in the context of the Aliens Act of 1905. When the leader of the antialien British Brothers League addressed a meeting of the time with these words: "There is hardly an Englishman in this room who does not live under the constant danger of being driven from his home, pushed out into the streets, not by the natural increase of our own population, but by the off-scum of Europe" (Gainer 36), it is rhetoric of a kind that might have appeared in the *United Irishman* or issued from the mouth of the Citizen with no further adjustment, other than to that fifth word.

A Convenient Fiction

In his lecture of 1907, "Ireland, Island of Saints and Sages," the legally British Joyce told his technically Austrian audience:

> Nationality (if it really is not a convenient fiction like so many others to which the scalpels of present-day scientists have given the coup de grâce) must find its reason for being rooted in something that surpasses and transcends and informs changing things like blood and the human word. (*CW* 166)

It is presumably this unspecifiable "something" with which Joyce sought to endow Leopold Bloom, Irish by birth, British in law, both of these and other things besides by blood and the evidence of his own words. To look beyond *Ulysses*, if nationality is, often unconsciously, the product of an opposition of supposed binaries—be these, in the case of the "benighted queendom" (*FW* 241.22) of 1904, Irish and English or native and alien—then *Finnegans Wake* is founded on the splitting, merging, and splitting again of such binaries, in a book that maintains its own open border policy. Nevertheless, when Joyce puts forward the concept of "an Irish emigrant the wrong way out" becoming in time a "Europasianised Afferyank!" (*FW* 190.36, 191.04), in a paragraph from I.vii where there is a significant clustering of the word "nation," it is hard not to see his imagination, appealing as it may be to modern sensibilities, running far ahead of the national reality. Genuine aliens are thin on the ground in Joyce's work primarily because they were thin on the ground in Dublin, and those Jews in Ireland who were the greatest exception to this in 1904, two decades later the majority of them British subjects, dwindled rapidly in number after 1922. To return to Michael Davitt's words, it was as though the debate around the Aliens Act, "the germs of some malady" in Britain, had indeed left the "poison of a malignant disease" in Ireland, productive of a governmental response to immigration between the wars that displayed "an exaggerated fear that admission of aliens would cause political difficulties, giving rise to prejudice and tension, as if Jews themselves were responsible for their persecution" (Wills 395). As noted above, this logic, victim blaming *avant la lettre*, actually dates from the time of the first Aliens Act, but in Ireland in the 1930s it led to a policy toward the newest generation of Jewish refugees that was at best "illiberal and ungenerous" (Wills 396). In Britain, the East European immigrants and their descendants left a mark on every sphere of public life over the course of the twentieth century. By contrast, Ó Gráda notes the "unimportance of immigration in modern Irish history, at least before the era of the Celtic Tiger in the 1990s" (*Jewish Ireland* 1–2).

The figure of the alien, however, as revivified by the debates leading up to the Aliens Act of 1905, was of clear significance to Joyce, a British subject for all of his life but simultaneously an alien in Austria, Switzerland, and France for the greater part of it. This was precisely because the alien was, in much political and nationalist discourse of the time, a creature of the imagination, fantastical inhabitant of "the kongdomain of the Alieni, an accorsaired race" (*FW* 600.10–11). In Ireland, where immigrants were too few to present a meaningful check to such fantasies, the disparity between the imaginary and the actual alien was especially great. The imbalance is reflected in Joyce's work, but not simply in deference to the historical reality. By largely occluding the real immigrant in favor of the unreal alien, Joyce's writing foregrounds the key figure in contradistinction to which the "legal fiction" (*U* 9.844) of nationality was being devised at the time. By virtue of the chimerical nature of the alien, Joyce was simultaneously presented with a figure through which the convenient fiction of nationality might be reimagined and rewritten.

Notes

1. Though Junius never uses the word "alien," both the North American colonies and Ireland are described as "alienated" more than once in the *Letters*. The reference in this passage to "the recent war" plays on the anti-Semitic allegation that the Boer War had been instigated by Jewish profiteers. The Lithuanian Jews who came to Dublin did have links with South Africa, and some who had made their way there fleeing persecution in Russia found themselves seeking temporary refuge in Ireland during the war (Ó Gráda, *Jewish Ireland* 12).

2. During the 2016 referendum on Britain's membership of the European Union, many of these same phenomena were certainly apparent: anti-immigrant hysteria in the popular press; a political campaign to leave the E.U. which pandered to and stoked that hysteria in complete disregard of the facts; and some of the highest proportions of leave voters to be found in those areas least affected by immigration (whereas in London, one of the world's great immigrant cities, nearly two-thirds voted to remain). Whether "taking back control" of the nation's borders will prove any more practicable in the coming years than it was in 1905 remains to be seen.

3. In 1911 there were twelve Italian-born organ grinders and street musicians at work in Dublin. A report in the *Irish Times* of January 1904, some months before "Eveline" was written, told "of two Casalatticans, Carmano Nardone and Giovanni Capeldi, who were charged . . . with annoying the well-known writer George Moore by playing outside his house in up-market Ely Place, 'and refusing to desist when asked to do so.' Moore complained that the noise was intolerable but Capeldi protested that he left when he had finished the tune, and promised not to play outside Moore's house any more" (Ó Gráda, "Because" 11).

Works Cited

Boyle, Robert. "A Note on Reuben J. Dodd as 'a dirty Jew.'" *James Joyce Quarterly* 3 (1965): 64–66.

Cheng, Vincent J. *Joyce, Race, and Empire*. Cambridge: Cambridge University Press, 1995.
Davison, Neil R. *James Joyce, "Ulysses," and the Construction of Jewish Identity*. Cambridge: Cambridge University Press, 1996.
Davitt, Michael. *Within the Pale: The True Story of Anti-Semitic Persecutions in Russia*. London: Hurst and Blackett, 1903.
Gainer, Bernard. *The Alien Invasion: The Origins of the Aliens Act of 1905*. London: Heinemann Educational Books, 1972.
Gillet, Louis. "The Living Joyce." In *Portraits of the Artist in Exile: Recollections of James Joyce by Europeans*, edited by Willard Potts, 170–204. Portmarnock: Wolfhound Press, 1979.
Glover, David. *Literature, Immigration and Diaspora in Fin-de-Siècle England: A Cultural History of the 1905 Aliens Act*. Cambridge: Cambridge University Press, 2012.
Hyman, Louis. *The Jews of Ireland from Earliest Times to the Year 1910*. Shannon: Irish University Press, 1972.
Maddox, Brenda. *Nora: A Biography of Nora Joyce*. London: Hamish Hamilton, 1988.
Nadel, Ira B. *Joyce and the Jews: Culture and Texts*. Basingstoke, Hants.: Macmillan, 1989.
Ó Gráda, Cormac. "'Because She Never Let Them In': Irish Immigration a Century Ago and Today." UCD Centre for Economic Research Working Paper Series, University College Dublin, December 2013.
———. *Jewish Ireland in the Age of Joyce: A Socioeconomic History*. Princeton: Princeton University Press, 2006.
O'Halpin, Eunan. "Politics and the State, 1922–32." In *A New History of Ireland*, edited by J. R. Hill, vol. 7, *Ireland 1921–1984*, 86–126. Oxford: Oxford University Press, 2003.
White, Arnold. *The Modern Jew*. London: William Heinemann, 1899.
Wills, Clair. *That Neutral Island: A History of Ireland During the Second World War*. London: Faber and Faber, 2008.
Winder, Robert. *Bloody Foreigners: The Story of Immigration to Britain*. London: Little, Brown, 2004.

PART II

Legal Regimes of
Joyce's Spaces and Places

4

National Languages and Neutral Idioms

Joyce among the Language Laws

TEKLA MECSNÓBER

With the "general lack of interest in Joyce's politics" firmly behind us (MacCabe 139), recent years have seen various historically and politically informed ways of interpreting Joyce's linguistic practices in *Ulysses* (1922) and *Finnegans Wake* (1939). Most of them are concerned with Joyce's relationship with the main constituents of the Irish linguistic complex: Standard English, Hiberno-English, and Irish Gaelic. Andrew Gibson, for instance, convincingly situates the language(s) of *Ulysses* as part of a semicolonial revenge on Standard English as the language of the colonists (13–15). Somewhat more generally, Giorgio Melchiori sees "Joyce's politics of language" as "the politics of revolution" that involves "the subversion of English itself" (12, 15). Focusing on specifically Irish varieties, Katie Wales regards the language of *Finnegans Wake* as a "universalised Hiberno-English" in which Joyce could "most feel at home" and resolve the "lifelong tension" of "an Irish writer who did not write in Irish" (33), whereas Tim Conley suggests that Joyce countered "nationalist 'gibberish'" such as the artificial Irish of the Gaelic League "with an international gibberish" (317). Using Hiberno-English as their reference point, Erika Rosiers and Wim Van Mierlo conclude that *Finnegans Wake* is an exercise in creating a universal language as hybrid as Anglo-Irish (68). Laurent Milesi combines the three perspectives by claiming that Joyce's "linguistic politics" involved using Hiberno-English as a tool—"a middle course of literary action between the imposed rigours of an English tradition and the artificially revived nationalist orthodoxies of Irish Gaelic"—as well as a model of a hybrid or creolized idiom that can, more generally, "question . . . the analogy between the national and the natural" ("Difference" 4, 5–6).

While it would be difficult to deny the explanatory value of these views, focusing on the importance of the Irish context can leave other contexts—such as a broader European one—unduly neglected. In contradistinction, my goal here is to show that the language issue, including questions pertaining to the right or injunction to use specific languages in specific situations as defined by international, national, or local regulations, was at least as contentious and complex an issue in Joyce's time in the rest of Europe as well, and that such regulations can be seen as relevant in interpreting Joyce's late work. I agree with Tim Conley's insight that Joyce's "sundering of linguistic borders" is profitably considered in the context of international modernism (317, 316), but I argue that this contextualization should also take into account concrete European political issues such as the sundering of state borders and the imposition of (new) official language policies. I also agree with Rosiers and Van Mierlo that the presence of various universal languages in the text of the *Wake* is most likely due to the fact that "international languages were part of the real world [Joyce] tried to incorporate in his book," but not with the qualification "at least as pre-existing permutations of natural language" (66). Rather, I would argue that Joyce's use of and references to, for instance, international auxiliary languages in the *Wake* (and in fact in *Ulysses*) are part of his politically informed response to, and critique of, the spread of what Yasemin Yildiz has recently termed the "monolingual paradigm": the idea that "having one language was the natural norm, and that multiple languages constituted a threat to the cohesion of individuals and societies," an idea centering on and reinforced by the insistence on "the gendered and affectively charged kinship concept of the 'unique mother tongue'" (6). In contrast to many previous accounts, Joyce's subversion of such a normative monolingual "analogy between the national and the natural" will be situated in the context of the language-related legislation of the wider European scene, rather than solely the Irish one.

In particular, this essay wishes to investigate a specific tension encoded in Joyce's *Finnegans Wake* in the divergent linguistic politics of the two rival brothers, Shaun and Shem: the tension between languages perfected, promoted, and prescribed as "official" or even "national" by various institutions on the one hand and, on the other, languages that are not marked by a single political bias and are thus seen as neutral, including international languages of mixed origins. It will argue that although Joyce's use of language in general and in *Finnegans Wake* in particular can rightly be seen as a response to the Irish situation, a compelling case can be made for Joyce responding also to the European situation. More specifically, this situation can be seen as involving two rival trends: a legislative frenzy for defining and enforcing new official languages in numerous, often new, nation-states, set against repeated efforts to surpass the hardening linguistic compartmentalization by introducing an auxiliary language to serve the cause of international communication and peace.

National Languages and Neutral Idioms in the *Wake*

Some of the most memorable passages in *Finnegans Wake* refer to the contrasting language politics of twin brothers Shaun and Shem. A self-professed "mailman of peace" (*FW* 408.10), Shaun is happy enough to "pass [his] opinions, properly spewing, into impulsory irelitz" (421.26–27), reinforcing apparently impulsive as well as irate claims for compulsory Irish. This is not so surprising if one remembers that "the voce of Shaun" was a few pages earlier equated with the "vote of the Irish" and emerged "through deafths of durkness greengrown" (407.12–14), suggesting that "dear dogmestic Shaun" (411.23) is as potentially limited (deaf, dark, and dogmatic) as he is patriotic (sharing the national color green). He answers the question posed by the Czech national anthem, "Where is my home?" (*Kde domov můj*), with a confident "here/this" (*hic/haec*) in "Hek domov muy" (411.18), although "Hek" also resonates with overtones of a rather more mixed nature: those of the fallen father figure HCE, defiance in the English "heck," but also retreat in the German *Heck* (rear) and limitation in the Dutch *hek* (fence). Despite his politically rather ambiguous description as an Irish "paykelt" with a stable "selary" (413.1) "on his [British] majesty's service" (408.14), "decent Lettrechaun" (419.17; Shaun as a literate and quintessentially Irish leprechaun) is a staunch defender of purity, linguistic and visual: he admits to having demonstrated his loyalty to the Irish national idea of "Down with the Saozon Ruze!" (411.30; cf. Saxon rule; ruse; Breton *saoz*, "English," and *ruz*, "red") by having "painted our town a wearing greenridinghued" (411.24). This is of course a purity questioned as easily by the polyglot associations that his very words evoke as by any etymological dictionary or cultural encyclopaedia.

The rival brother Shem infuriates Shaun by the impurity of his letter ("the fuellest filth ever fired," 419.35), multiply mixed identity ("Shem Skrivenitch," 423.15, with Semitic, Irish, Latin/Italian, and Slavic associations; see McCourt 208), and the linguistic ambiguity of his "bilingual head" (424.2). Shaun characteristically distrusts Shem's interest in Europe ("europicolas") as an infectious disease that, once "caught," got Shem into the dubious international brotherhood of "Bro Cahlls and Fran Czeschs and Bruda Pszths and Brat Slavos" (423.35–424.1). Shem does not, indeed, appear to share Shaun's linguistic purism, and his being a "freak" (424.2) and a "hybrid" (169.9) is paralleled by his "artificial tongue with a natural curl" (169.15–16). While he does go so far as to boast that "he would wipe alley english spooker . . . off the face of the erse," he would do this act of revenge metaphorically and in many voices, "multiphoniaksically spuking" (178.6–7), relying on "different foreign parts of speech he misused" (173.35–36). Composed "in universal, in polygluttural, in each auxiliary neutral idiom, sordomutics, florilingua, sheltafocal, flayflutter, a con's cubane, a pro's tutute, strassarab, ereperse and anythongue athall" (117.13–16), his whole letter—as introduced in book I chapter 5 (I.5) of the *Wake*—reflects his "mixed racings" (117.22) as well as his liberal interest in every language variant that is not singled out and made compulsory as a national language: low-prestige variants spoken by social outcasts (like the sociolect of Irish travelers, concubines, prostitutes, or homeless children) and international languages (like Universal or Idiom Neutral) and other, often mixed (polyglot) auxiliary languages, as well as the sign language of deaf-mutes ("sordomutics") or the traditional language of flowers ("florilingua").

John Nash has recently demonstrated that Joyce's decision to employ the emphatically but not unquestionably patriotic brother Shaun as a postman is highly appropriate in the context of the contested allegiances of the postal service of the Irish Free State (152–59). My point here is that if Joyce remained faithful to his 1924 note that "postman & style of narration [are] symbolical of our time" (*JJA* 57:5),[1] this symbolism can be true in a broader European context as well. The years that followed the First World War were troubled times for postal workers in many European countries, in which individual and collective linguistic habits were closely monitored and were regarded as symbolic of political loyalties. Thus, German-speaking postal workers—as well as railway workers, teachers, and civil servants—were dismissed and replaced by Slovene speakers in South Styria only a few days after their native region was proclaimed on 20 October 1918 to be part of the State of Slovenes, Croats and Serbs, newly seceded from a defeated and disintegrating Austro-Hungary (Judson 241). Some five hundred kilometers to the north, in the small German-speaking town of Höritz (Hořice), German-speaking postal workers (as well as railway workers, gendarmes, and many teachers) were replaced by Czech-speaking ones in 1919, a few months after they found themselves in the new Czechoslovak state, formed by declaring independence on 28 October 1918 (Judson 247–48). A month after the Anglo-Irish Treaty was ratified by the Dáil Éireann on 7 January 1922, the new postmaster-general was reported by the *Irish Times*—a paper Joyce regularly read and took notes from—to be considering ways of making sure that "the staff generally now employed in the Post Office would make themselves conversant with Gaelic without losing any more time" ("Gaelic in the Post Office"), and a knowledge of Gaelic was reported to be made mandatory for new appointments in Gaelic-speaking areas from April 1923 ("Gaelic Compulsory").

It is easy to see why the postal service, with its crucial practical function as facilitator of national and international communication and its highly symbolic function as the carrier of language made visible, was seen in various newly formed nation-states as one of the first areas where the linguistic preferences of the new state could be demonstrated, often in anticipation of their codification in one of the numerous laws and statutes regulating the use of languages in Europe. Thus the radical reshaping of the identity of the postal services happened before "Czechoslovak" was made the official language on 29 February 1920 by a language rights act passed in parallel with the constitution of the newly established Czechoslovakia (*Constitution* 47), before "Serbocroatoslovenian"—itself, just like "the Czechoslovak language," a political product of the monolingual paradigm—was made the official language in 1921 by the constitution of what was by now the Kingdom of Serbs, Croats and Slovenes (Kamusella 228), and before Irish was made the "National language of the Irish Free State (Saorstát Eireann)," with "the English language ... equally recognised as an official language" in the Constitution of the Irish Free State, which became effective on 6 December 1922 ("Constitution").

In the postal service, the demonstration of official language preferences was achieved by a number of measures. The spoken presence of the new national language was ensured through employing postal workers—often newly appointed—with sufficient linguistic proficiency. The written presence was guaranteed through, for instance, new stamps that carried the name as well as the language of the new state into all corners of the world. Indeed, the *Irish Times* called 1919 the *annus mirabilis* of stamp collectors, with more than 2,500 new issues, a record number due largely to the enthusiasm of "the new States of Europe—Czecho-Slovakia, Poland, Yugo-Slavia, and the rest" ("Feast"). Not to be outdone, the Irish Free State announced a competition for new stamps on 3 February 1922, issuing the previously used British stamps with overprints that claimed these stamps—in Gaelic and with distinctive Gaelic lettering—for the Provisional Government of Ireland in late February 1922 and, after the Free State constitution came into effect, for the Irish Free State on 12 December 1922 ("Irish Free State Stamps"; "Irish Free State Stamps: The New Overprints"). The first newly designed Irish stamp was issued on 6 December 1922, the exact day on which the Free State was legally established. Ambitiously, it bore not only the name, again in Gaelic and in Gaelic lettering, but also the map of an undivided Ireland (Éire), somewhat contradicting its description in the *Irish Times* as "a quiet stamp" ("Free State Stamp").

There is positive evidence in Buffalo Notebook VI.B.10 (cf. *JJA* 46:49) that Joyce read this last article and took note of the phrase "quiet stamp" from it, inserting it into the first draft of book I chapter 4 (I.4) of what was to become *Finnegans Wake* as part of an appropriately conflicted description: "such various venom a quiet stamp could cover!"[2] Likewise, Shaun's painting the city a patriotic green in the *Wake* was most likely modeled on another prompt act of Irish postal symbolism: the repainting, as early as April 1922, of the traditional red pillar boxes to give them, in the words of a contemporary comic reaction in the *Irish Times*, "a grand coat of emerald green" ("Murty's Letter").[3] More important than the symbolism of stamps or letter boxes is, however, the fact that Joyce seems also to have been aware of the heated public discourse surrounding the more fundamental issue of "compulsory Irish" at the postal service and elsewhere. As a search of the *Irish Times* reveals, this was a question discussed in almost six hundred articles and letters published on the topic between 1921 and 1929 in that newspaper alone, providing news and opinions on proposed and actual regulations in the postal service, elementary and intermediate schools, the National University, the armed forces, civil servants, municipal boards, the churches, the legal profession, and the reestablished and symbolically renamed national legislative body, the Dáil itself. There are at least two points worth noting here. First, it seems very appropriate that Joyce incorporated the phrase "compulsory Irish" in a crucial chapter that, as we have seen, also comments on the general and linguistic politics of the two rival brothers of the *Wake*, Shem the penman and Shaun the postman. Second, Joyce inserted this phrase into the section (which he began drafting in 1924) most probably in early 1928,[4] after a period of heated debates about the introduction of compulsory Irish in various segments of the life of the new Irish state.

National Languages in Joyce's Europe

Although Joyce grew up in an Ireland where no constitution or overarching law defined an "official" or "national" language, legislation on language use in specific situations went back to the second century following the arrival in 1169 of the Anglo-Normans in Ireland. Until 1878 all of this legislation, beginning with article 3 of the Statutes of Kilkenny in 1366/67, was aimed at promoting the use of English and limiting the use of Gaelic (Crowley 9, 12, 13). In 1878, more than four decades after the establishment in 1831 of the national school system, where even the marginal use of the Irish language was often actively discouraged by both teachers and parents (Crowley 121), Irish appeared in the official school system of modern Ireland for the first time. Thanks to the efforts of the Society for the Preservation of the Irish Language, "Celtic" was now "given the status of a marginal extra subject" (Crowley 135). Further efforts by the Gaelic League resulted in the enhancement of the status of Irish in intermediate schools in 1901, the ordaining of bilingual programs for Irish-speaking and bilingual districts in 1904, and the introduction of Irish as a matriculation requirement at the National University of Ireland in 1909 (Crowley 143–45). Despite these concessions, Joyce's official education—like that of the majority of his peers—was conducted entirely in English, with no option of Gaelic as part of the official curricula. Likewise, the linguistic landscape of Dublin was dominated by official and unofficial signage in English, including legends on coins and banknotes.[5] However, as the Gaelic League was successful in its campaign for street signage in Gaelic during and after the municipal elections in 1901 (see "Irish Language"; "Dublin Corporation"), Irish street name plates began to appear in the last few years of Joyce's residence in Dublin, soon giving rise to disagreements about the wording and spelling of the inscriptions (see "Celtic Association"). Predictably, street name changes received a boost as Ireland came closer to independence: a few days before the signing of the Anglo-Irish Treaty, a special committee of the Dublin Corporation proposed "drastic changes" to the names of a number of Dublin streets and bridges "with the least possible delay" ("Dublin Street Names").

Settling in Austrian Pola (Pula) in 1904 and Trieste in 1905, Joyce could observe a rather different linguistic dispensation. Apart from the superficial similarity between the circumstances of the Irish living in Dublin under English rule and Italians living in Trieste under Austrian rule, the linguistic situation was much less hegemonistic and more diverse in the Adriatic city. In terms of public display, the language with the highest visibility in multilingual Trieste itself appears to have been Italian rather than German. The multilingual character of the Austro-Hungarian Empire was also manifested on Austrian banknotes, which spelled out the denomination in all ten recognized languages of the dual empire—German, Hungarian, Polish, Czech, Italian, Slovene, Croatian, Ruthenian (Ukrainian), Serbian, and Romanian—while most Austrian coins carried inscriptions in nearly neutral Latin (Cuhaj, *Paper Money* 84–86; *Coins* 149–51). These banknotes can, in fact, be seen as visible encapsulations of the rather liberal Austrian constitution of 1867, which guaranteed widespread linguistic rights to all recognized nationalities under the Austrian umbrella. Specifically, article 19 granted that "All the races of the state shall have equal rights, and each race shall have the inviolable right of maintaining and cultivating its nationality and language," recognized "the equality of the various languages in the schools, public offices, and in public life," and ordained that "In the countries populated by several races, the institutions of public instruction shall be so organized that each race may receive the necessary instruction in its own language, without being obliged to learn a second language" ("Austrian Constitution"). While the languages so recognized were limited to ten, and while the practical implementation of such rights was often imperfect and even impossible, by the turn of the century all of these recognized nationalities managed to achieve the establishment of not only state-supported elementary schools but also state-supported secondary schools and often university faculties with instruction in their respective languages (Judson 13). If in November 1904, shortly after Joyce's arrival in Pola, the Italian nationalists of Trieste and Pola rioted over the establishment of an Italian-speaking faculty of law, it was not because it did not happen at all, but because it happened in Innsbruck rather than in Trieste (McCourt 16).

Teaching English in Italian-speaking commercial schools and at the Italian Università Popolare must have made Joyce aware of the linguistic contrast with Ireland (McCourt 172–73, 207–8), which, as he wrote in the 1910 article "The Home Rule Comet" for the Triestine Italian paper *Il Piccolo della Sera*, "almost entirely abandoned its language and accepted the language of the conqueror without being able to assimilate its culture or adapt itself to the mentality of which this language is the vehicle" (159). The Austrian situation may also have helped Joyce to put the failure of the Irish legal system to cater for Irish speakers into sharper perspective. His 1907 article "L'Irlanda alla sbarra" ("Ireland at the Bar") is a savagely indignant portrayal of the case of Myles Joyce, who was convicted of murder and executed in 1882 after a trial in which the work of the interpreter for the Irish-speaking defendants was fatally inadequate. Although Joyce interprets the story more generally, saying, "The figure of this bewildered old man, left over from a culture which is not ours, a deaf-mute before his judge, is a symbol of the Irish nation at the bar of public opinion" (146), the specific cause of the problem was the legal system of Ireland: the Administration of Justice (Language) Act (Ireland) of 1737 prescribed that "all Proceedings in Courts of Justice within this Kingdom shall be in the English Language," without guaranteeing adequate provisions for nonspeakers of English.

Although Zurich, where Joyce took shelter between late June 1915 and October 1919, was dominated by speakers of the local version of German, Switzerland provided Joyce with a linguistic environment where multilingualism was recognized and protected, as Italian, German, and French had been recognized as official languages since 1798 (Kamusella 40). This was evident on Swiss currency as well: while coins shunned the language question by using abbreviations or neutral Latin inscriptions, all banknotes of the Swiss National Bank were trilingual (Cuhaj, *Paper Money* 1120–21). Linguistically tolerant Zurich also provided a contrast to news about the growing linguistic intolerance in Europe during the First World War: news about the German occupiers replacing Flemish street names with German ones in the Belgian Knokke in April 1915 ("Germanising Knocke"), about the Austrian occupiers introducing compulsory German into Serbian primary schools and banning the Cyrillic script in April 1916 ("Germanising Serbia"), or about Austria preparing to make German the official language throughout the country in March 1917.[6] It is tempting to conjecture that these experiences lent added impetus to the exploration of linguistic intolerance in two episodes of *Ulysses* that Joyce was composing at the time: "Aeolus," finished by August 1918, and "Cyclops," composed between June and October 1919 (cf. *Letters* 2:455).

The Trieste that Joyce saw on his return from Zurich in October 1919 was very different from the one that he left. The Italian occupation of Trieste was sanctioned by the Treaty of Saint-Germain-en-Laye, signed on 10 September 1919, as well as the subsequent Treaty of Rapallo on 19 November 1920, but in contrast to most states, Italy was not obliged to give legal guarantees for the protection of minority rights in exchange for its territorial gains. This made it easier for the country to set forth an administrative Italianization of the civil service, courts, and school system. By March 1920, Trieste became the scene of anti-Slovene riots, and the fascist movement soon became a major political factor in the area (Judson 243–44; MacCabe 159).

Having decided to leave Trieste, Joyce arrived in Paris in early July 1920 with the plan to stay three months and write "Circe" and "Eumaeus" "in peace" (*Letters* 1:265). The linguistic landscape of Paris was, of course, predominantly French: after the Revolution of 1789, France was one of the first countries to insist on linguistic unity as a prerequisite for the ideological unity of the state, and had enforced standard French from the 1790s as the language of education, administration, and public life in general in the entire country (Weber 67–94; Kamusella 40). This did, of course, not prevent Paris from being the city where the post–World War I peace treaties, with their elaborate provisions for the protection of linguistic minorities of other countries, were negotiated and signed. Joyce arrived there in early July 1920, about six months after the Treaty of Versailles with Germany came into effect on 10 January, a month after the Treaty of Trianon was signed with Hungary on 4 June, a few days before the Treaty of Saint-Germain with Austria came into effect on 16 July, and about six weeks before the abortive Treaty of Sèvres was signed with Turkey on 20 August. Under the aegis of the League of Nations, these treaties put the seal on the breaking up of the multiethnic and multilingual German, Austrian, and Ottoman Empires, redefined the remnants as nation-states, and gave international recognition to a number of new nation-states, including Poland, Czechoslovakia, and the Kingdom of Serbs, Croats and Slovenes, which was formed by the merging of the short-lived State of Slovenes, Croats and Serbs with the Kingdom of Serbia.

I have argued elsewhere that the late insertion, in October 1921, into the text of the "Cyclops" episode of what look like a Polish and a composite Czech-Slovak-Serb-Croat-Slovene member of the "Friends of the Emerald Island" can be seen as a comic retrospective post-Versailles registering of the claims of these nationalities to independent nationhood (Mecsnóber 33). The Paris peace treaties can, however, also be seen to have had a more general and less obvious effect on Joyce's art, by highlighting the flaws of the conflation of language use, national identity, and political nationhood. In most cases the language provisions of these treaties—modeled on articles 7, 8, and 9 of the minorities treaty with Poland—guaranteed that members of ethnic minorities would have the right to "the free use . . . of any language in private intercourse, in commerce, in religion, in the press or in publications of any kind, or at public meetings," to "adequate facilities . . . for the use of their language before the courts," and, in areas where a "considerable proportion" of them were residents, to "adequate facilities for ensuring that in the primary schools the instruction shall be given to [their] children . . . through the medium of their own language" ("Minorities Treaty"). In return, states were allowed to—and mostly did—establish official languages and make them a compulsory subject in all schools (articles 7 and 9). Enlightened as these provisions were, they did not, as we have seen, prevent nation-states from promoting the official language with more fervor than they had for the accommodation of minority languages, and press reports soon appeared about alleged violations of minority rights.[7] While trying to solve the "nationality question," the Paris treaties highlighted and reinforced the crucial importance of language in European nationalisms: they served to strengthen the idea of the identification of language use and nationality, as well as nationality and nationhood, and, in the long run, promoted the monolingual paradigm. In many ways, the increasing nationalism of the 1930s in several European states was an unintended outcome of this paradigm. Slovak plans to make Slovak (as opposed to Czechoslovak) the sole official language of Slovakia ("Czech-German Talks") and Sudeten German plans to make German an official language ("Towards Settlement") in 1938 turned out to be language-political preludes to the next world war.

Neutral and Mixed Idioms

In the years following the First World War, however, a contrary drive was also discernible in Europe and America: a drive for a neutral language that could facilitate international communication. There had been several proposals for such languages since the late nineteenth century, but it was Esperanto, an auxiliary language launched by L. L. Zamenhof in 1887 and featuring a simple and regular grammar and a vocabulary based on the three main European language families, Romance, Germanic, and Slavic, that came closest to becoming an official means of communication.[8] In June 1919, a petition was sent by the British Esperanto Association to the League of Nations for the adoption of Esperanto ("News in Brief"). In December 1920, delegates of eleven countries including Czecho-Slovakia, Belgium, and Italy proposed a draft resolution declaring the League of Nations's interest in making the teaching of Esperanto general in schools ("League of Nations Flag"). In September 1921 and 1922, the League of Nations discussed the possibility of promoting Esperanto worldwide as an "easy means of international intercourse" ("League and Esperanto"),[9] and the issue was revived in June 1926, when the British League of Nations Union "invited" the League to encourage the teaching of Esperanto as the most suitable international auxiliary language ("League of Nations Union"). The Irish press also reflected the increased concern with Esperanto: the *Irish Times*, for instance, published about two hundred items related to the topic between its first mention in 1901 and 1940, with the most mentions in 1925 and 1926. It seems clear from these articles that the feature that Irish advocates of Esperanto found most important was, in addition to its practical qualities, its political neutrality: this perspective was brought up repeatedly between 1905 and the 1930s.[10]

Joyce seems to have shared this increased interest in universal languages, as suggested by his reading of Otto Jespersen's 1928 book *An International Language* in the late 1930s,[11] and by his repeated exploitation of Esperanto, Volapük, and other auxiliary languages between 1921 and 1938. In Joyce's work, the earliest references to Esperanto are in "Circe," the *Ulysses* episode that engages most obviously with universal alternatives to national languages. The first mention of Esperanto happens in the curious context that seems to link the international language to Gaelic. Having asked an unknown for the name of the street in Spanish, Bloom is given the street name in Gaelic, "*Sraid Mabbot*" (*U* 15.218). Bloom's polyglot response—"Haha. *Merci.* Esperanto. *Slan leath.* (*he mutters*) Gaelic league spy, sent by that fireeater"—may imply that he regards Gaelic and Esperanto as similarly utopian in their hope of becoming as widely used as French. (This exchange may also be read as Joyce's comment on the language competence of Gaelic Leaguers or on the League's promotion of Gaelic street names, which—here—does not go further than turning Mabbot Street into Sráid Mabbot.) The second reference takes place in the even more hallucinatory context of the Messianic Scene and fits more obviously into the theme of universal languages that keeps surfacing in the episode. At the beginning, having sung in ecclesiastic Latin, the long-standing European "universal" language, an elated Stephen advocates a characteristic philosophico-poetic vision of a salvation accompanied by the universal pentecostal language of gestures: "So that gesture, not music not odours, would be a universal language, the gift of tongues rendering visible not the lay sense but the first entelechy, the structural rhythm" (15.105–107). At the end of the episode, Lynch, who had his reservations about Stephen's theories, seems to accuse Stephen of getting into fights because "He likes dialectic, the universal language" (15.4726). Typically, Bloom takes a more practical view. In the Messianic Scene itself, having tried to make himself understood in a range of living languages including Spanish, Gaelic, and German/Yiddish, he recommends not only the "Union of all, jew, moslem and gentile" but also "esperanto the universal language with universal brotherhood" (15.1686–1692). In this Bloom is well informed: brotherhood (*frateco*) having been one of the rallying cries of the Esperanto movement (in addition to peace and goodwill), "universal brotherhood" is a phrase that, following Zamenhof, Esperantists were fond of using in the early 1900s.[12] What is especially interesting for us, in addition to Joyce's familiarity with the ideology of the Esperanto movement, is the timing. He wrote the largest part of "Circe," with the first Esperanto reference, in the second half of 1920, and he added the Messianic Scene in the summer of 1921 (*JJA* 15:303, viii). As we have seen, by this time there had been several initiatives to make Esperanto an officially recognized auxiliary language through the League of Nations.

Joyce returned to Esperanto in October–November 1925 as he was composing the first draft of what became book III chapter 4 (III.4) of *Finnegans Wake*. At this time he inserted a brief conversation in (almost correct) Esperanto (*FW* 565.25-28) into a context otherwise dominated by echoes of Gaelic phrases from the song "Siúil a Rún," or "Shule Aroon."[13] Further strings of Esperanto were added to I.3 (*FW* 52.14-16) and I.6 (*FW* 160:29-32) at galley stage during the final revisions in 1938 (*JJA* 50:76, 1; *JJA* 50:206). Laurent Milesi has argued that Joyce's use of Esperanto in 1925 is "astonishing since it would push the earliest draft usage of foreign units, unconnected to motifs, back to late 1925" ("Dream" 18), and it would therefore provide a turning point in the composition history of the *Wake*: from this point on, the text was more definitely a multilingual project. Whether it is possible to identify such a linguistic turning point or not—Rosiers and Van Mierlo suggest 1928 (58); Crispi, Slote, and van Hulle propose 1926 (22)—it appears that self-referential reflections on the multilingualism of Shem and his letter ran in many ways parallel to the use of Esperanto in the composition process. The idea that the *Wake* was conceived from a very early stage as a polyglot project is supported by the fact that Shem is described as "explaining the meanings of all the other foreign words he used" already in the first draft of I.7 (Hayman 110). Still, by 1925 Shem's reliance on foreign linguistic material has become more diverse as well as perverse, as evidenced by the changes in "all the *different* foreign parts of speech he *misused*."[14] A significant surge in the theme of multilingualism and artificiality can be seen in 1927-28, when Joyce reworked and extended previously drafted sections of the *Wake*, some of them already published, for serialization in Eugene Jolas's newly established magazine *transition*. It was at this stage in 1927 that Joyce inserted the phrase "artificial tongue with a natural curl" into Shem's description ("Continuation ... [7]" 34; cf. "Extract" 108) and the anticolonial threat that "he would wipe alley English spooker ... off the face of the erse" into Shem's drunken boasting ("Continuation ... [7]" 42; cf. "Extract" 113). At the same time as he added "impulsory irelitz" to Shaun's description of his linguistic activities in III.1, Joyce also inserted references to Shem's suspect multilingual contacts and language use: his immersion in European cultures when "he caught the europicolas and went into the society of jewses,"[15] his "bilingual head,"[16] and his inventing his own "idioglossary" (*FW* 423.9).[17]

The most significant reinforcement of the theme of multilingualism seems to have happened, however, during Joyce's final revisions between 1936 and 1938, at a time when he is known to have concentrated on a conscious extension of "foreign" linguistic elements in the text (Rosiers and Van Mierlo 58, 65–68). In addition to inserting further phrases taken from Esperanto and other international and national languages, Joyce now specified the source of Shem's infection with "europicolas" as a multiethnic Breton, French, Czech, German, Hungarian, Slovakian, and (generic) Slav fraternity—"Bro Cahlls and Fran Czeschs and Bruda Pszths and Brat Slavos" (*FW* 423.36–424.1)—and in early 1938 added the explicit multilingual reference "multiphoniaksically spuking" to Shem's boastful threat (*JJA* 50:226; cf. *FW* 178.6–7). Most crucially, it was at this stage, in early 1938, that, having just read Otto Jespersen's account of auxiliary languages such as Esperanto and Idiom Neutral in *An International Language* (1928), Joyce inserted into the description of Shem's letter the long list of international and nonstandard idioms—"in universal, in polygluttural, in each auxiliary neutral idiom, sordomutics, florilingua, sheltafocal, flayflutter, a con's cubane, a pro's tutute, strassarab, ereperse and anythongue athall" (*JJA* 50:158; cf. *FW* 117.13–16)—which was discussed at the beginning of this essay.

This passage can, in fact, be seen as a revisiting of some of Joyce's earlier writings on language use. "Universal" can remind us of the various potentially universal languages that were discussed in "Circe," and "florilingua" echoes the "language of flowers" (*U* 5.261) that Bloom contemplated, appropriately enough, in "Lotus Eaters." "Sordomutics," or deaf-and-dumb language, can recall Joyce's long-standing interest in French Jesuit Marcel Jousse's and British philologist Sir Richard Paget's gesture-based theories of linguistic evolution—or indeed those of Italian philosopher Giambattista Vico (Jolas 168; McMillan 195–96). It can, however, also be seen as a more specific reference to an international sign language for the deaf and dumb, which received some publicity in the 1920s and 1930s as a result of being used at a series of international sports events for the deaf ("Deaf Mutes' Sports"; "Silent Service") and of being ingeniously promoted by Sir Richard Paget in live demonstrations ("Sign Language"). In this sense, the Wakean reference to potentially universal "sordomutics" can also be seen as a redeeming of the linguistic disempowerment of Myles Joyce, who, like Ireland itself, was described by Joyce in "L'Irlanda alla sbarra" as standing "sordomuto" or "deaf and dumb" before the judge ("L'Irlanda" 218; "Ireland" 146). One could read this reiteration of the old phrase as

Joyce suggesting that the *Wake* wants to break out of the paradigm of language domination, of the radical inequality between fully empowered native speakers and disenfranchised others: nobody is a native speaker of Wakese, and all readers are to some extent rendered challengingly or even uncomfortably deaf and dumb by its "sordomutics."

Multiphoniaksically spuking: The *Wake* among the Language Laws

It is striking how insistently Joyce returned to the question of artificial languages during and even before the writing of *Finnegans Wake*, especially if Eugene Jolas was right in asserting that the Irish writer otherwise—like Jolas himself—"spoke ... with a certain derision of such auxiliary languages as Esperanto and Ido [a derivative of Esperanto], which seemed to him to be without possibilities of any kind" (168).[18] Joyce's interest surely had to do with the fact that the ambitions, if not the tools, of constructed languages were not unlike his own. In fact, the rather striking parallel between the universal aspirations of Wakese and auxiliary languages and the possible contrast between their actual strategies was noted a long time ago. Writing at the instigation of Joyce, Robert McAlmon, for instance, began his 1929 essay "Mr Joyce Directs an Irish Word Ballet" with a metaphoric parallel between Esperanto as a universal language and the gesture-based language that he later identifies with the idiom of the *Wake*: "Had the inhabitants of the tower of Babel sought for an esperanto language, their gropings would have been, to be successful, into some composite subconscious of individual and race types; the language emerging might readily have been a dance or a symphony of music" (105). Having evoked what he sees as the universal nature of music, dance, and sign language, McAlmon goes on to elaborate the comparison of Joyce's text with auxiliary languages, stating that Joyce "does not intend to create a new literary esperanto, but he wishes to originate a flexible language that might be an esperanto of the subconscious and he wishes to believe that anybody reading his work gets a sensation of understanding, which is the understanding which music is allowed without too much explanation" (110–11). Without putting overmuch emphasis on the use of and parallels with actual auxiliary languages, one can usefully place claims for the universal aspirations of Joyce's language in the context of a disenchantment with the monolingual paradigm in the 1920s and 1930s. Indeed, one can argue that Joyce seems to have shared this disenchantment with a number of avant-garde artists who were keen to explore multilingualism and Esperanto in their writing at precisely the same time.[19]

In this essay I have argued that the resolute and increasing multilingualism of Joyce's *Finnegans Wake* can be meaningfully related to a number of widely reported changes in European linguistic policies and practices during the period stretching from the Paris Peace Conference to the crumbling, in the late 1930s, of the system of nation-states that the conference established. In fact, Joyce's multilingualism is difficult to account for solely on the basis of the Anglo-Irish context: it appears that for a Joyce who once complained about not being able to "express [himself] in English without enclosing [himself] in a tradition" (*Letters* 2:397), only a medium that relied on a multiplicity of sources could seem like an "auxiliary neutral idiom," an idiom free from a limiting national tradition. If a language is indeed a national construct, "a dialect with an army and navy" in the often quoted words of Max Weinreich, then the unruly and transnational dialect—or rather idiolect—of the *Wake* is indeed "nat language at any sinse of the world" (*FW* 83.12).

Notes

1. The note was "penned in at the bottom" of the earliest sketch of III.1–2 in January 1924 (BL 47471 f.42; *JJA* 57:5); see Van Mierlo 350. The note was also published by David Hayman in *A First-Draft Version* (91). Responding to the same note, Ingeborg Landuyt quotes Hayman to suggest that Joyce's reliance on postal symbolism was related to the general prominence of communication technology in the modern age (21). Landuyt also provides a detailed overview of Joyce's use of one of his most important sources regarding general postal history, Eugène Gallois's 1894 book *La Poste et les moyens de communication*. For Joyce's other sources on the same topic, see Vincent Deane, introduction to *VI.B.16*, 7–9.

2. Deane, introduction to *VI.B.10*, 12–13. Joyce ended up refining the phrase out of recognition, if not existence, by the final text, lending it an appropriately Victorian vestment to match the context of Buckley and the general: "such a vetriol of venom, that queen's head affranchisant, a quiet stinkingplaster zeal could cover, prepostered or postpaid!" (*FW* 101.23–25).

3. John Nash's account of hypocrisy in and around the *Wake* also discusses Shaun's passages in the context of such aspects of the transition of the Irish postal service from British to Irish management as the repainting of the postboxes and the issuing of overprinted and entirely new national postage stamps (153–56).

4. Cf. Hayman, 36; Joyce, "Continuation . . . [12]," 21; Van Mierlo, 349, 351.

5. "Linguistic landscape," a concept that has recently become very influential in sociolinguistics, was defined by Rodrigue Landry and Richard Y. Bourhis in 1997 as involving the "language of public road signs, advertising billboards, street names, place names, commercial shop signs, and public signs on government buildings" and having as one of its main functions that it "serves as a distinctive marker of the geographical territory inhabited by a given language community" (25).

6. Untitled news item, *Irish Times*, 10 March 1917, 3.

7. For example, "Concrete Problems," in the *Irish Times* of 17 July 1922.

8. For an account of universal languages in the context of linguistic rights, including a brief summary of the case of Esperanto, see Phillipson.

9. See also "League of Nations: Agenda for the Third Session."

10. For example, "The New Language" (1905), "What Is Esperanto?" (1906), "Esperanto" (1922), and "Irish and Esperanto" (1934). A search of the *Irish Times* using the terms "esperanto language neutral" revealed fourteen relevant items between 1900 and 1939.

11. Rosiers and Van Mierlo assert that Joyce read this book in the winter of 1937–38 and took notes (in notebook VI.B.46) on Volapük, Esperanto, and other auxiliary languages (58, 65–68).

12. See, for instance, "The International Esperanto Congress" (1905) and "The Esperanto Congress" (1907).

13. *Letters* 1:234–35; Hayman 255. For a Freudian interpretation of the same passage, see Ferrer.

14. Joyce, "Extract" 111 (my italics); cf. *FW* 173.35–36.

15. "Continuation . . . [12]" 23; cf. Hayman, 224; *FW* 423.35–36.

16. "Continuation . . . [12]" 23; cf. Hayman, 224; *FW* 424.2.

17. "Continuation . . . [12]" 22; cf. Hayman, 224; *FW* 423.9.

18. It is not impossible that Jolas is projecting some of his own views on Joyce here; see Jolas 272–73.

19. For a wide-ranging and insightful discussion of the parallel aims and overlapping networks of early twentieth-century European avant-garde and the Esperanto movement, see Benedikt Hjartarson's "Anationalism and the Search for a Universal Language."

Works Cited

"Administration of Justice (Language) Act (Ireland) 1737." legislation.gov.uk.
"Austrian Constitution of 1867." In *Modern Constitutions*, edited by Walter Farleigh Dodd. Chicago: University of Chicago Press, 1909. ecommons.cornell.edu/handle/1813/1443.
"Celtic Association and Dublin Street Plates." *Irish Times* (Dublin), 13 May 1905, 19.
"Concrete Problems." *Irish Times*, 17 July 1922, 5.
Conley, Tim. "Language and Languages." In *James Joyce in Context*, edited by John McCourt, 309–19. Cambridge: Cambridge University Press, 2009.
The Constitution of the Czechoslovak Republic. Prague: Société l'Éffort de la Tchécoslovaquie, 1920. Internet Archive.

"Constitution of the Irish Free State (Saorstát Eireann) Act, 1922." irishstatutebook.ie.
Crispi, Luca, and Sam Slote, eds. *How Joyce Wrote "Finnegans Wake": A Chapter-by-Chapter Genetic Guide*. Madison: University of Wisconsin Press, 2007.
Crispi, Luca, Sam Slote, and Dirk van Hulle. Introduction to Crispi and Slote, *How Joyce Wrote "Finnegans Wake,"* 3–48.
Crowley, Tony. *Wars of Words: The Politics of Language in Ireland, 1537–2004*. Oxford: Oxford University Press, 2005.
Cuhaj, George S., ed. *2013 Standard Catalogue of World Coins, 1901–2000*. Iola, WI: Krause, 2012.
———. *Standard Catalogue of World Paper Money: General Issues, 1368–1960*. 12th ed. Iola, WI: Krause, 2008.
"Czech-German Talks: Concessions to the Slovaks." *Irish Times*, 23 June 1938, 8.
"Deaf Mutes' Sports: International Contests." *Irish Times*, 18 August 1924, 5.
Deane, Vincent. Introduction to *The "Finnegans Wake" Notebooks at Buffalo: VI.B.10*, by James Joyce, edited by Vincent Deane, Daniel Ferrer, and Geert Lernout, 4–13. Turnhout: Brepols, 2001.
———. Introduction to *The "Finnegans Wake" Notebooks at Buffalo: VI.B.16*, by James Joyce, edited by Vincent Deane, Daniel Ferrer, and Geert Lernout, 4–13. Turnhout: Brepols, 2003.
"Dublin Corporation." *Irish Times*, 8 January 1901, 8.
"Dublin Street Names: Drastic Changes Suggested." *Irish Times*, 1 December 1921, 7.
"Esperanto." *Irish Times*, 27 July 1922, 6.
"The Esperanto Congress." *Times* (London), 13 August 1907, 7.
"A Feast of Stamps." *Irish Times*, 31 December 1919, 4.
Ferrer, Daniel. "Wondrous Devices in the Dark: Chapter III.4." In Crispi and Slote, *How Joyce Wrote "Finnegans Wake,"* 410–35.
"Free State Stamp: A Very Creditable Issue." *Irish Times*, 6 December 1922, 4.
"Gaelic Compulsory in P.O. Appointments." *Irish Times*, 2 April 1923, 5.
"Gaelic in the Post Office." *Irish Times*, 3 February 1922, 6.
"Germanising Knocke." *Irish Times*, 8 April 1915, 5.
"Germanising Serbia." *Irish Times*, 9 April 1916, 6.
Gibson, Andrew. *Joyce's Revenge: History, Politics, and Aesthetics in "Ulysses."* Oxford: Oxford University Press, 2002.
Hayman, David, ed. *A First-Draft Version of "Finnegans Wake."* Austin: University of Texas Press, 1963.
Hjartarson, Benedikt. "Anationalism and the Search for a Universal Language: Esperantism and the European Avant-Garde." In *Decentering the Avant-Garde*, edited by Per Bäckström and Benedikt Hjartarson, 267–97. Amsterdam: Rodopi, 2014.
"The International Esperanto Congress." *Irish Times*, 17 August 1905, 6.
"Irish and Esperanto." *Irish Times*, 8 January 1934, 8.
"The Irish Free State Stamps." *Irish Times*, 25 February 1922, 3.
"Irish Free State Stamps: The New Overprints." *Irish Times*, 13 December 1922, 7.
"Irish Language and the Municipal Elections." *Irish Times*, 2 January 1901, 6.

Jespersen, Otto. *An International Language.* London: George Allen and Unwin, 1928.
Jolas, Eugene. *Man from Babel.* Edited by Andreas Kramer and Rainer Rumold. New Haven, CT: Yale University Press, 1998.
Joyce, James. "Continuation of a Work in Progress [7]." *transition* 7 (October 1927): 34–56.
———. "Continuation of a Work in Progress [12]." *transition* 12 (March 1928): 7–27.
———. "Extract from Work in Progress." *This Quarter* (Milan) 1.2 (Autumn–Winter 1925–26): 108–23.
———. "The Home Rule Comet." In *Occasional, Critical, and Political Writing,* 155–59.
———. "Ireland at the Bar." In *Occasional, Critical, and Political Writing,* 145–47.
———. "L'Irlanda alla sbarra." In *Occasional, Critical, and Political Writing,* 217–19.
———. *Letters of James Joyce.* Vol. 1. Edited by Stuart Gilbert. New York: Viking, 1957; issued with corrections, 1965.
———. *Letters of James Joyce.* Vols. 2–3. Edited by Richard Ellmann. New York: Viking, 1966.
———. *Occasional, Critical, and Political Writing.* Edited by Kevin Barry. Translations from the Italian by Conor Deane. Oxford: Oxford University Press, 2000.
Judson, Pieter M. *Guardians of the Nation: Activists on the Language Frontiers of Imperial Austria.* Cambridge, MA: Harvard University Press, 2006.
Kamusella, Tomasz. *The Politics of Language and Nationalism in Modern Central Europe.* Basingstoke, Hants.: Palgrave Macmillan, 2008.
Landry, Rodrigue, and Richard Y. Bourhis. "Linguistic Landscape and Ethnolinguistic Vitality: An Empirical Study." *Journal of Language and Social Psychology* 16 (1997): 23–49.
Landuyt, Ingeborg. "Shaun and His Post: *La poste et les moyens de communication* in VI.B.16." *Papers on Joyce* 3 (1997): 21–47.
"League and Esperanto: Possibilities to Be Explored." *Irish Times,* 14 September 1921, 4.
"League of Nations: Agenda for the Third Session." *Irish Times,* 4 September 1922, 6.
"A League of Nations Flag." *Times* (London), 13 December 1920, 11.
"The League of Nations Union." *Times* (London), 8 June 1926, 13.
MacCabe, Colin. *James Joyce and the Revolution of the Word.* London: Macmillan, 1978.
McAlmon, Robert. "Mr Joyce Directs an Irish Word Ballet." In *Our Exagmination Round His Factification for Incamination of Work in Progress,* by Samuel Beckett et al., 105–16. 1929. London: Faber, 1961.
McCourt, John. *The Years of Bloom: James Joyce in Trieste, 1904–1920.* Dublin: Lilliput, 2000.
McMillan, Dougald. *Transition 1927–38: The History of a Literary Era.* Amsterdam: Meulenhoff; London: Calder and Boyars, 1975.
Mecsnóber, Tekla. "James Joyce and 'Eastern Europe': An Introduction." In *Joycean Unions: Post-Millennial Essays from East to West,* edited by R. Brandon Kershner and Tekla Mecsnóber, 13–45. European Joyce Studies 22. Amsterdam: Rodopi, 2013.
Melchiori, Giorgio. "The Languages of Joyce." In *The Languages of Joyce: Selected Papers from the 11th International James Joyce Symposium,* edited by Christine van Bohee-

men, Carla Marengo, and Rosa Maria Bollettieri Bosinelli, 1–18. Philadelphia: John Benjamins, 1992.

Milesi, Laurent. "The Dream of a Universal Language: A Topology of Foreign Languages in the *Wake*." Master's thesis, University of Dijon, 1983.

———. "Language(s) with a Difference." Introduction to *James Joyce and the Difference of Language*, edited by Laurent Milesi, 1–27. Cambridge: Cambridge University Press, 2003.

"Minorities Treaty between the Principal Allied and Associated Powers (the British Empire, France, Italy, Japan and the United States) and Poland, Signed at Versailles (28 June 1919)." Ungarisches Institut München. forost.ungarisches-institut.de/sammlung.php?q=002.

"Murty's Letter: 'The Wearin' of the Green.'" *Irish Times*, 8 April 1922, 5.

Nash, John. *James Joyce and the Act of Reception: Reading, Ireland, Modernism*. Cambridge: Cambridge University Press, 2006.

"News in Brief." *Times* (London), 10 June 1919, 10.

"The New Language." *Irish Times*, 10 August 1905, 5.

Phillipson, Robert. "International Languages and International Human Rights." In *Language, a Right and a Resource: Approaching Linguistic Human Rights*, edited by Miklós Kontra et al., 25–46. Budapest: Central European University Press, 1999.

Rosiers, Erika, and Wim Van Mierlo. "Neutral Auxiliaries and Universal Idioms: Otto Jespersen in Work in Progress." In *James Joyce: The Study of Languages*, edited by Dirk Van Hulle, 55–70. Brussels: Peter Lang, 2002.

Sailer, Susan Shaw. "Universalizing Languages: *Finnegans Wake* Meets Basic English." *James Joyce Quarterly* 36.4 (Summer 1999): 853–68.

"Sign Language." *Times* (London), 4 March 1936, 12.

"Silent Service in St. Paul's." *Times* (London), 19 August 1935, 13.

"Towards Settlement." *Irish Times*, 7 September 1938, 6.

Van Mierlo, Wim. "Shaun the Post." In Crispi and Slote, *How Joyce Wrote "Finnegans Wake,"* 337–83.

Wales, Katie. *The Language of James Joyce*. Basingstoke, Hants.: Macmillan, 1992.

Weber, Eugen. *Peasants into Frenchmen: The Modernization of Rural France, 1870–1914*. Stanford, CA: Stanford University Press, 1976.

"What Is Esperanto?" *Weekly Irish Times*, 14 April 1906, 21.

Yildiz, Yasemin. *Beyond the Mother Tongue: The Postmonolingual Condition*. New York: Fordham University Press, 2012.

5

Rights and Losses

The Ends of Minority Recognition in Joyce and International Law

RICH COLE

The Struggle to Define Rights

Did the citizens of Dublin want political recognition and rights as Irish or as persons? Research into the legal question of recognition has overwhelmingly sought to emphasize the Irish side of Joyce's writing. Over the past two decades, in particular, critical examination of the historical paradoxes of an oppressive British regime in radicalizing the Irish Citizen Army has converged on the composition of the "Cyclops" episode, now consistently read for its reconstruction of the era's republican jingoisms and anti-imperialistic propaganda. This method of analysis has enabled critics to say much about the various forms of Irish resentment directed back at colonial law and order. Notably, Joyce's deliberately stereotypical depiction of the drunken character called only "the citizen," who delivers his occasionally humorous, though more often alarmingly racist or xenophobic, zingers—"To hell with the bloody brutal Sassenachs and their *patois*" (12.1190–1191)—has been pressed into service as analogy for the few ineffective ways in which the dispossessed and marginalized population could express their dissatisfaction with the stiflingly Whiggish legalese of the British Empire, a regime that tended to solidify its gains by normalizing the injustices it perpetrated against the colonized population through legal institutions and practices.

Yet determining the exact brand of Irish nationalism Joyce sought to underscore has provoked intense debate and disagreement. Three competing models have emerged. First, there are the critics who share Emer Nolan's view that "Joyce imitates the polite newspaper-column chit-chat typical of what he saw as the genteel coteries of Celtic Revivalism" (105); these formal experimentations allowed Joyce to embed in his text seemingly innocuous and well-mannered forms of populist history. But Nolan's claim that Joyce's fragmentary compositional method restages the uses and abuses of history by the popular press remains quite distinct from Neil Levi's alternative suggestion that once "the very language of the concrete, local, organic, and heroic is shown to be abstract, mobile, and subjectless," the "romanticized myth of origins is not that different from, and is even a by-product of, the increasingly abstract and standardized modernity from which the nationalist wishes to distinguish himself and his country" (385). In either formulation, Joyce's references to the popular vernacular demonstrate the important role Irish print culture played in translating the twilight of past traditions for the mass public. Both also assert that Irish subjects repeatedly self-identify—that is, their identities as modern subjects are produced—by forming passionate attachments to standardizing mass cultural practices. However, only Levi finds this process of subject formation to be an inevitable outcome, and one by all indications Joyce evidently experienced, because his parodic writing style so often communicates the anxieties about representation and abstraction caused by modernity's ungrounding of history and subsequent proliferation of myths about origins. For better or for worse, any process of resistance would, in turn, invariably end up further shattering into montage the very conditions of historical fragmentation it intended to escape. Conversely, in Nolan's view, Irish subjects were in fact frequently able to define a clear sense of agency for themselves and concretize their revolutionary actions precisely in opposition to the normative constructions of Irishness disseminated by the abstract, depoliticizing, and "levelling modern discourse of the newspapers" (106). To underscore Ireland's troubling entrance into a modern cultural regime, which tended to occlude British imperialism's history of violence, character dialogue in *Ulysses* is "continuously used to mock and combat the endless leveling discourse of the modern which appears unable to render the reality of the conflict" (107). This process of ideological formation hardened the resolve of irredentists and ultimately advanced Ireland's tragic if necessary turn to republican violence. More to Nolan's point, Joyce's attention to these competing versions of history redraws a forgotten line from the discursive practices of 1904 Dublin to the "symbolism and theatricality of the 1916 Rebellion" (122). To put forward a third critical approach, Neil Davison more brazenly asserts that the Irish patriot in *Ulysses* "doesn't have time for Celtic twilights; his sentiments are more of the 'bloodyminded' Jacobin type. . . . The nation to him must be forged through violence; Joyce underscores this call to arms with the citizen's paramilitary phrases: 'stand and deliver'; or 'on point duty'" (214). But what, we might also ask, in order to make each case, do such critical disputes tend to exclude?

Strangely unremarked in *Ulysses* criticism, all three reading models repeatedly bracket Joyce's references to nationalism as occurring in isolation from the juridical revolution being undertaken in international law after World War I. This critical blind spot has endured despite the historical evidence indicating that a significant number of the proceedings and treaties brought forth with the formation of the League of Nations regularly made the headlines of daily newspapers in Ireland, Europe, and across the Atlantic. The minority issue came to the fore after the armistice with editorials in the world press demanding that minority protections be included in the peace treaties. In mid-June 1919, the same month James Joyce famously scrapped an earlier draft of "Cyclops" and began to write a second *Ulysses* wherein Bloom's double minority status as an Irish Jew would serve as the site of intense scrutiny, the unrecognized Irish Republic sent a group of representatives to the Paris Conference in the hopes that the sovereign independent state declared at the 1916 Easter Rising would be recognized.

To begin to unpack this archival concurrence, it is worth briefly returning to Michael Groden's careful assessment of Joyce's notebooks. Groden concludes that "'Cyclops' constitutes the first total break with the original techniques," because Joyce "decided to drop the interior monologue" (124–25) and informed Frank Budgen that "Stephen no longer interests me to the same extent [as Bloom]. He has a shape that can't be changed" (135). A subsequent redraft "sometime after draft V.A.6." eliminated Stephen; Joyce began to restructure the episode "to focus more coherently on Bloom" (142). These first few months into the redevelopment of "Cyclops" mark a key transitional period, largely because Leopold Bloom, the stigmatized, Europeanized Jew, comes to show all the signs that he might to try to emancipate himself. In the final text, Bloom's argumentativeness reaches a spirited pitch in the pub debates. His inability to keep silent on matters of injustice ranging from "race" (12.1467) to "Force, hatred, history, all that" (12.1481) demonstrates his desire to establish a political position. But his delivery also suffers from imprecision. As he interjects into the pub conversations, Bloom's injunction to recognize "injustice" (12.1474) frequently makes visible his own subjugated status, and often with results counterproductive to the desired effects. Bloom's attempt to draw attention to "Persecution"—which, by his rather abstract definition, occurs in "all the history of the world . . . Perpetuating national hatred among nations" (12.1417–1418)—appeals to a universal level of shared humanity, and thus transcends any single form of national sovereignty. Yet the problem with Bloom's universalism is not simply that the abstract language he relies on is insufficiently pluralistic and therefore cannot accommodate the Jewish or Irish cultures to which he belongs. Instead, the issue is that inasmuch as he expresses a commitment to the irrevocability of a shared language of human suffering, his obsession with recognizing the universal history of injustice is also what comes to stigmatize his own limited citizenship status.

Leopold Bloom may not be regarded as a stateless person, at least not in the conventional sense of the term. He does not entirely identify himself as an exile without a homeland; nor does he seek refuge on foreign soil where he was not born. The crux of the problem, instead, involves a multiplicity of belongings that emerge into public view when he simultaneously identifies as an Irish citizen as well as a Jewish person who does not quite fit within the increasingly restricted cultural value system of Irish nationalism. Bloom's universal rhetoric of inclusion highlights the trouble with a modern system of national recognition that makes it increasingly difficult to hold more than one identity category at the same time. As the fight for a unified vision of Irish independence gained in public support, fervent nationalism coalesced into a powerful struggle against imperialism, and in accordance the possibility to claim other forms of belonging were increasingly viewed as an impediment to the effort to produce a coherent and effective form of national solidarity in the fight for self-determination. Although Bloom clearly holds an Irish birthright, he must repeatedly voice this inalienable right to citizenship when challenged by the Irish patriot in the pub to declare his *true* nationality. Further, the moral vigor required for him to prove his right to belong on Irish soil demonstrates that he holds a simultaneous affiliation with a political viewpoint that requires looking beyond national lines, to a universal language of inalienable rights, in the effort to shore up his own public standing to rightfully reside in Dublin. And this appeal to a larger set of values is precisely what sets him apart from those patriots in the pub who more plainly identify with the immediate goal of Irish political independence. Bloom's universal appeals thus serve as a troubling reminder that not all cultural identifications are equally recognized in different geographical precincts, especially not in Ireland, where nationalist patriotism has come to serve as the moral flashpoint for the righteous fight against colonial subjugation. Nationalism itself, one might also argue, is largely defined by demarcating the limits of pluralistic, cosmopolitan identifications. At the national level, persecuted minorities often remain unable to speak out as equals on matters of human suffering, nor does it seem possible to find ways to liberate themselves from the dominant forces that grant recognition, without a concurrent stigmatization of their own lower standing in the community. Out of this loss of public standing a distinction emerges: the rights language used to locate and recognize universal human suffering reveals itself to be remarkably abstract and ineffective for Bloom to justify his heterogeneous public attachments. It provokes skepticism toward him rather than granting irrevocable dignity and respect as one might expect. An obvious reason for this distrust of the language of rights involves how it was instrumentalized by the British legal regime as a formidable tactic in the oppressive effort to extend the juridical boundaries of colonial rule onto Irish soil.

But this is not the full story. As Joyce draws attention to the complications inherent in the aspirational politics of recognition, he also demonstrates the conflicted ascendance of modern rights claims within the very fight for Irish freedom. His text registers a tension between the rise of modern nationalism, as it functions to draw clear boundaries where a specific set of national rights can be exercised, and the emerging global language of rights recognition that the Irish irredentist movement would increasingly come to deploy in the hope of gaining an advantage over colonialism in the new age of global rights. The international deployment of rights language relies on establishing an often-vexed politics of victimization in order for a minority group to assert a justifiable claim to universal rights necessary for the international powers of global justice to intervene.

The "Cyclops" episode itself is structured by a succession of calls for recognition, and the identificatory power of these scenes derives partly from the embittered, parochial speech of the Irish reactionaries in the barroom, but especially from a series of moral separations—from Bloom's Jewishness, his appeals to cosmopolitan ideals, his argumentativeness, and his desire for inclusion, all of which have the unintended effect of creating a noticeable enough difference between him and the other Dubliners in Barney Kiernan's pub to continually set one category of minority identifications apart from the other. Jewishness and Irishness constitute two distinct identity categories that do not seem to easily mix in Bloom's politics of recognition. What is it exactly about the uneven structure of dependency in the desire for recognition from a higher authority that fails Bloom just as it failed Ireland in her bid for inclusion in the League of Nations? The question is entwined with the struggle to (re)define rights.

In this pursuit of a new definition of rights, the politics of recognition must be reconceived as an ongoing process, the value of which lies in the fact that it enables citizens to repeatedly engage in shared political activity, quite apart from the political end-states reinforced by a language of exclusion and otherness. The very notion of colonial subordination, an exploitive relationship that involves closing off some people's practical possibilities and blocking the equal realization of freedoms in public life, may in fact be dispelled by recognition claims that open up new forms of political belonging consistent with simply being treated as a co-participant in an ongoing political process. Such claims, if effective, ensure that a colonized population may gain access to the rights and legal authority necessary for participatory self-government. The citizens in Joyce's Dublin repeatedly make this connection each time they place their hopes for freedom in gaining entry into a newly forming international legal system of minority protections; yet just as often they fail to grasp the strengths and weaknesses that this desire for juridical recognition installs in the Irish national consciousness.

To read *Ulysses* against the historical backdrop of the League of Nations requires an assessment of the human consequences of legal demands. For this tension lies at the heart of the Irish irredentist movement. Minority rights claims from Michael Collins as well as Joyce's 1907 discussion of treaties provide crucial contexts for discerning the local impact of international law on Dubliners. The effectiveness of each rights claim, moreover, must be tested against the secondary problem of *how* the politics of recognition has so often come to serve the interests of colonial power in the way that it has. It is to this problem of persistent loss of identity, a resoundingly familiar trope in Irish history, that Joyce provides a strikingly perceptive response: he repeatedly stages scenes of minority recognition in "Cyclops" to demonstrate the difference between international calls for rights that break down borders between persons and ones that turn differences into oppositions, and identities into property.

A New Global Morality?

After the war, an optimistic mood for change arose. Irish republicans seized the moment to press for international support of their separation from the British Empire. "Delegates were appointed and in its 1919 'Message to the Free Nations of the World' the Dáil called upon 'every free nation to support the Irish Republic by recognizing Ireland's national status and her right to its vindication at the Peace Conference'" (Keatinge 134). The high point of this pressure came in June, when the League's council voted 60–1 for Ireland's case to be heard. Over the next few weeks, however, Ireland's efforts to enter the League would quickly unravel at each stage of the diplomatic proceedings. By the time the delegation's case was eventually reviewed at the conference, the small nation's bid for membership fell on deaf ears. "Woodrow Wilson was unmoved," Patrick Keatinge notes, by appeals for self-determination by the Irish delegation, as well as from many Irish sympathizers in America, who had repeatedly voiced the conviction that it was up to their president, as leader of a free nation, to take action by backing the cause globally (135). Although flanked by this searing criticism, the only public concession that Wilson made came when he "subsequently argued that Ireland's case could at some time in the future be considered by the League of Nations" (135). But delay was of little interest to Irish Republicans; worse yet, it was salt in the wound. Speculative talk of the good life on the horizon, of a new international order yet to take shape, only confirmed it was still out of reach for Ireland. To publically recognize Ireland's cause for freedom while also limiting the political options available by delaying and by extending the course of colonial domination served to exacerbate the Irish predicament. What the Irish delegation also learned too late was that the leaders of the major powers had decided early on, behind closed doors, to focus their negotiating efforts on diplomatic compromises in order to swiftly construct a peaceful solution. As urgency for signing a deal between the major powers increased by the day, controversial questions related to morality and global justice were reprioritized and deferred for future consideration.

Not only did the League fail to promptly grant Ireland's entry as a sovereign state, but once its legally binding covenant was signed, it immediately systematized Ireland's subordinate status by not including the Irish on the official list of protected minorities. This secondary deferral of international legal recognition was no accident. Although the Treaty of Versailles was painstakingly drafted to set up minority protections, Britain's influence over the negotiations would repeatedly undermine Ireland's ongoing efforts by pushing for minority protections to cover only religious, ethnic, and linguistic groups under threat in Eastern Europe. All other claims for national or cultural autonomy, ones that might implicate colonialism and its territories in the process, were consequently rejected in the treaty text. Ireland's failed hopes were further confirmed when her closest ally, the United States, dropped out of the League in the spring of 1920. Recognition might come, the Irish delegation was repeatedly told, but not now. Moreover, as Carole Fink clarifies, it soon became apparent that the peacemakers of the League of Nations who signed on for protections proceeded to systematically seal off and "contain considerable numbers of minorities who would, paradoxically, be victims of the 'self-determination' of their new masters" (277). Thus the Treaty of Versailles repeatedly functions as a hall of mirrors for the colonized minority, perpetuating Ireland's subordinate status by excluding it from the group of largely Mitteleuropean protectorates.

The losses stemming from these failed transnational legal proceedings had two negative consequences upon Irish society back home. First, diplomatic collusion between the major powers resulted in failure to grant Ireland the international right to self-government as necessary to engage in its own negotiations at the League of Nations or elsewhere under England's purview. The legal covenant signed by forty-four states caused additional injury, because Ireland's subordinate status as a British colony meant that no grievances would be heard by the League's juridical council set up to monitor international minority disputes. These lapses left the Irish vulnerable to further colonial manipulation within their own borders. Perhaps the only beneficial outcome of these troubling diplomatic losses was that back in Ireland the failed bid for recognition had irreversibly stepped up awareness about the local and global dimensions of rights action. But finding effective ways to use these juridical processes—that is, to sharpen rights as weapons against colonialism—would after this moment also require contending with the public cynicism toward international law that had grown out of the losses.

The xenophobic citizen in "Cyclops" plays an integral part in the novel's reconstruction of this tension in legal history between national and international pressures. His very presence belabors the question of what constitutes a pure, uncontaminated Irishness that must be defended. The core issue in early twentieth-century discussions about the protection of minorities was whether or not any group of persons could ever secure rights as an isolated group in a productive way that did not collapse differences, foster false unities, and ultimately contribute to further forms of human cruelty. Even the most ardent advocates of the advancement of international law—including Michael Collins, who spoke for Ireland's entry into transnational treaties as a means to undo the legacy of colonial power—had to confront the difficulty of achieving minorities' emancipation without fully opening the can of worms that contained past damages and would inevitably lead to questions of historical reparations. Indeed, taking on too much responsibility for righting wrongs might cause the process of regaining freedom to stall in disputes. For a new way forward to appear on the political horizon, a fine balance would need to be found between accommodating questions of historical damage, without shirking responsibility, while also recognizing that too much dwelling on past wrongs could jeopardize peaceful negotiations and lead to further injury. When talk about freedom stalls, the path to violence appears clearer.

In the "Cyclops" episode, the citizen and J. J. begin "arguing about law and history with Bloom sticking in an odd word. /—Some people, says Bloom, can see the mote in others' eyes but they can't see the beam in their own" (12.1235–1238). Bloom's allusion to Matthew 7:3 is suggestive, because in discussing the oppressive blindness of colonial rule, he tacitly exposes the citizen's incendiary rhetoric as it commits the sin of spitefully externalizing the site of blame on his neighbor. Foreigners invaded Irish soil, "Swindling the peasants, says the citizen, and the poor of Ireland. We want no more strangers in our house" (12.1150–1151). The citizen also appears to enjoy his own outrage. More curiously, perhaps, the unsettling historical injury the citizen evokes again by recounting it, however justified or sinful, runs the risk of counterproductively producing a mob mentality among Irish nationalists one that seeks to avenge hurt as much as it also reaffirms it, and thereby discursively recodifies trauma as revenge—that is, his call for vengeance threatens to simply invert the structure of colonial violence once directed at Ireland, and such a reproduction of violence cannot be understood as a complete revolutionary break from the historical logic of oppression. To break the circuit of colonial rule requires an entirely new way forward. Perhaps as a way to redirect this blame, and to fracture the psychic structure of Irish recognition that forms the monocular view in "Cyclops" (to "see the mote in others' eyes"), Joyce includes a more self-effacing reminder: "The strangers, says the citizen. Our own fault. We let them come in. We brought them. . . . brought the Saxon robbers here" (12.1156–1158). The citizen's nativist talk about internationalism and its discontents illuminates how a disadvantageous global network of political and economic power "stole from us" the very right to exert control over the rich resources on Irish soil, as well as the financial profits produced by the Irish labor force (12.1200). His xenophobic dialogue exemplifies the rise of antiglobalist sentiments at a time when Irish national sovereignty had been jeopardized by an exploitive British colonial system that was internationalist in scope and reach. The political effort to correct such national failures, to shore up Irish borders, gave rise to Irish demands for political recognition as a sovereign state with the right to self-determination.

To date, the critical account that comes closest to dealing with such issues has been advanced by Rebecca Walkowitz. In *Cosmopolitan Style: Modernism Beyond the Nation*, Walkowitz focuses on the confusion of political identities that emerged alongside the rise of liberal cosmopolitanism. Despite nationalism's best efforts to delineate "common origins, common traditions, and common desires," Walkowitz argues, such movements are simply not enough to coherently explain the individual differences between Irish persons, because doing so would "need to bypass the disparate, quotidian experiences of living in the same place in order to produce collective, affirmative narratives of identification" (56). She includes a brief discussion of the impromptu debate between the pub-goers in "Cyclops" as a contest between two very different rhetorical structures of collective belonging. Bloom's rather inarticulate call for a universal cosmopolitanism is contrasted with the citizen's anti-Semitic nationalism. To safeguard his essentialist conception of Irish identity, his biting criticism "makes fun of Bloom's rhetoric (he calls Bloom 'a new apostle of the gentiles')" (76); yet Walkowitz argues that Bloom, as the novel's defender of cosmopolitan decency, also lands a few rhetorical punches on behalf of the rights of man. At the very least, Bloom's moralizing, global talk exposes a nascent curiosity in public conversations during the period about how framing pain and persecution in universal terms, as international legal talk, might somewhat paradoxically allow the Irish to gain their own set of national protections and rights by sharing their recognition in common with other humans outside Ireland's territorial borders.

Empire's Law

A significant legal qualification is necessary. The struggle for decolonization in Ireland was accompanied by a shifting conception of identity whereby individuals-as-citizens slowly recognized themselves existing outside the implicit roles assigned by British common law as a rights-and-duty bearer. Of course, legal recognition takes various forms, and not all of Joyce's characters demonstrate a willingness to self-identify with the British circumscription of the legal personality. In pursuing these kinds of legal questions it is important to keep in mind that the Dublin law courts referenced by Joyce were built as the first extension of common law outside England. Under this system, human beings acquire legal personhood when they are born, and as such their identities are incorporated in accordance with the traditions of English law. Denis Breen, who appears sporadically throughout the day as he walks around Dublin looking for legal counsel, epitomizes the desire for increased incorporation and protection of his legal personality under British common law. Yet the form of legal recognition he seeks fundamentally sets him apart: his willingness to embrace British protocols of legal personhood as the means to regain public face in Dublin is precisely what alienates him from the other Irish characters.

In the "Cyclops" episode, a stark contrast exists between Breen with his determination to sue for libel and the other male patrons in Barney Kiernan's pub who voice their suspicions about British processes of litigation. They spy Breen walking with legal books under his arm, and begin to speculate about the extent to which this constitutes a mutinous act against Irish patriotism:

> I didn't know what was up and Alf kept making signs out of the door. And begob what was it only that bloody old pantaloon Denis Breen in his bathslippers with two bloody big books tucked under his oxter and the wife hotfoot after him, unfortunate wretched woman, trotting like a poodle. I thought Alf would spit.
> —Look at him, says he. Breen. He's traipsing all round Dublin with a postcard someone sent him with U. p: up on it to take a li . . .
> And he doubled up.
> —Take a what? says I.
> —Libel action, says he, for ten thousand pounds.
> —O hell! says I. (12.252–262)

Breen is willing to go to court over a cryptic postcard he received containing a possibly disparaging comment about his sexuality. But the postcard is not what tarnishes his reputation. His exclusion from Irish masculinity's circle of trust happens only when he chooses to defend himself by assimilating his public image into colonial legal customs set down on Irish soil. Breen's private legal advocacy is thus not only a treasonous public act, placing a British system of individual rights above the willingness to fight for a shared Irish identity, it also epitomizes a gendered dilemma at this moment in "Cyclops." The insurmountable distance between British colonial law and the Irish Brotherhood becomes observable when Breen chooses to fight his battles not through fisticuffs but instead through the oblique, feminized systems of Lady Justice. Breen's predilection for law is paralleled in the novel with Bloom's similar inability to ascertain the Irish masculine codes outlining which battles to fight and how to fight them. In the eyes of the hypermasculine citizen, both men are cowards with "noble gait" who hide behind "sacred scrolls of law" (12.246–247) instead of raising a clenched fist to "Stand up to it then" and defend themselves and their dignity "with force like men" (12.1475). Moreover, the citizen's anti-legal sentiments underscore the irony that in the unlikely event Breen does find a lawyer, and wins the defamation suit, the juridical ruling to clear his name would immediately be undercut, viewed disparagingly as a *sissy win* by the Irishmen in the pub. To the extent that a lawful victory would demonstrate Breen's legal personhood as protected by the court system, then, it would also signal his incorporation as property of the furtive, feminizing colonial code of law, which the other men fear, loathe, and define their own Irish masculinities against.

Yet although both Breen and Bloom are social outcasts, clearly they do not stand together. Breen is a pragmatist, not a reformist, and therefore not really much of an outsider figure at all. He does not aim to challenge or overthrow English law and instead attempts to use the existing juridical establishment to lash out at every injustice he recognizes around him. Bloom is different; he remains resolute in the pub debate with the citizen to work out the murky philosophical details of exactly what his own legal recognition might consist of. His utopian platitudes are motivated by his dissatisfaction that his double identification as an Irish Jew cannot be accounted for by any one configuration of national belonging. He therefore struggles to communicate a clear notion of what defines a free nation in the broadest terms, first by suggesting: "A nation is the same people living in the same place"; after being cruelly mocked by the citizen, however, he attempts to qualify his claim, but ends up contradicting it: "Or also living in different places" (12.1422–1427). Bloom's failure to define the territorial boundaries of national citizenship in a way that does not exclude part of his identity also means that his only recourse left is to the international legal terminology of human "persecution" and universal "injustice" (12.1417, 1474). But clearly his poorly articulated statements do not carry the rhetorical force to unite the men in the pub in a way that does not also exclude himself as a member the Irish community in the process.

"Ireland, says Bloom. I was born here. Ireland" (12.1431). But upon further consideration he feels compelled to elaborate: "And I belong to a race too, says Bloom, that is hated and persecuted. Also now. This very moment. This very instant" (12.1467–1468). His inclusion of "also" sets up a parallel between the fight against racial persecution of Jewish people and Irish anti-imperialist struggles. But the failure to fully correlate these two fights, as both function to illuminate a more widespread pattern of universal suffering to stand up against, gives rise to a curious paradox, or even hypocrisy, in Irish Republican efforts to form a decidedly unified national front in the fight against colonial oppression. The colonial logic of English rule had cast all Irish people as one homogeneous unit: as one Irish identity to be conquered and converted with a civilizing logic of British imperialism. Rather than outright refusing the singularity of any one identification, the fight for Irish cultural belonging reproduced this imperialist logic of political recognition in such a way as to narrow or even exclude questions of diversity, cultural difference, and local variations across the island of Ireland. The pressure to adhere to the restrictions associated with national conformity, to become one unified nation, was further exacerbated by a new network of global relations, a modern system of geographical borders that increasingly defined nationhood through the regulation and control of human population flows. Yet despite these twin pressures which problematize the republican pursuit of self-determination, talk in the pub of colonial injustice never goes so far as to critique the myriad of hypothetical pitfalls that might accompany the rise of Ireland as a modern nation-state. Until such time as the national cause for freedom has been won, larger diplomatic solutions related to struggles for diversity would need to be delayed far into the future. In turn, talk of humanity in general, or minorities in particular, remained incongruent with the anti-imperialist task at hand. Regardless of such differences, and internal squabbles, all were born in Ireland and continued to live under British colonial restrictions.

The act of self-identification unfolds, therefore, on multiple fronts and frontiers as the colonized subject comes to explore the competing ways in which they have internalized an external divide limiting the ability to form revolutionary collectives and direct hostilities outward to fight for future liberty and justice. Consequently, the slippery excesses of identity in Joyce's scenes of recognition function as highly politicized encounters with difference—some instrumentalized for colonial projects and some not—but each encounter complicates a totalizing understanding of Irish identity for subjects who repeatedly attempt to grasp how their subjugated status fits them into the world picture. It is precisely this struggle against legal hegemony that so often locates the pathological structure of oppression.

Moreover, the trouble with the desire for recognition is that even when it is returned the gratification remains partial. Frantz Fanon has suggested that the colonized subject must learn to read the psychological limits of his or her own desire for recognition in order to avoid being passively acted upon by the Hegelian form of reciprocal recognition conferred between the slave and the colonial master: "The only way to break this vicious circle that refers me back to myself is to restore to the other his human reality, different from his natural reality, by way of mediation and recognition" (192). Clearly Fanon's suggestion that the politically oppressed must seek alternative forms of recognition that subvert the colonial gaze in order for their shared political identity as humans to become visible is much different than to suggest, as Walkowitz does, that "political recognition" is somehow always tied to national forms of belonging, "bypassing disparate experiences" and ultimately producing "literature that repeats familiar generalizations" (56). So what happens in cases when the desire for political recognition goes unfulfilled—not returned by the ultranationalist "collective personality"—and thus falls outside the "social façade" that "repeats familiar generalizations"? (56). Perhaps as a way to fill in this gap, Walkowitz recommends engaging in cosmopolitan reading practices beyond the nation, because it enables readers to imagine the possibility of all citizens as equal under the sign of universal values. Certainly this task is aspirational. But to cast aside discussion of the more thorny dynamics of political recognition in the process seems like a dangerous game to play when dealing with a subjugated minority living under a colonial system that, by definition, repeatedly fails to grant equality and self-determination. It is precisely because Walkowitz succumbs to this temptation—according cosmopolitan forms of universal sameness a higher value than minority rights recognition—that her moral rhetoric installs a liberal universalist hierarchy and thus begins to assume an uncanny likeness to the discourse of colonialism for which it was to serve as antidote.

Decolonizing Recognition

In "Ireland as the Pivot of the League of Nations," published in the *Guardian* on December 7, 1921, one day after the Anglo-Irish Treaty ratified a controversial truce and put Ireland on the edge of civil war, Michael Collins attempted to make global politics the central issue around which the Irish people could unite. He reiterated in the press that for too long democratic nation-states around the world had stood silent while Ireland was repeatedly denied its right to self-determination. In a stunning rejoinder he added, "For centuries England strove to reduce Ireland to the position of an English province," but its colonial oppression should not, must never, serve as what defined its people. Accordingly, "Ireland has never been a British colony. She has been a separate nation kept subject by a more powerful neighbour for that neighbour's own advantage, but she has never ceased to fight for her freedom." Precisely because of Ireland's conflicted status in world politics, Collins specified the pressing importance for the League of Nations to swiftly recognize her right to join and become its "pivot." Yet entry was delayed for several more years; additionally, the treaty did not unite Ireland toward freedom as Collins hoped. Nonetheless, the international plea, along with its potential ramifications to forge the solidarity of the nation-state, demonstrates a remarkable attempt to walk a fine line between being recognized as injured, subordinated by colonial history, and being marked or identified by it. His trepidations in this respect anticipate Wendy Brown's warning to minority groups that the injuries they suffer also risk becoming what defines their identity. A wounded attachment, Brown says, is a negative identification, undesirable because "In its emergence as a protest against marginalization or subordination, politicized identity thus becomes attached to its own exclusion" (73). What Collins attempted to grasp, then, was how, if Ireland was to truly emerge onto the world stage, there also seemed to be a pressing need to recognize a kind of split, a fracture of consciousness between a productive side and a destructive side of minority identifications.

The people at the heart of Joyce's republic demonstrate a need to reach a final stage of self-examination that might allow them to synthesize these two poles, but too often the possibilities for liberation are foreclosed when his characters come to internalize, to identify themselves too completely with, the weaknesses and injuries caused by the colonial legal apparatus. The forfeiture of agency implied by this configuration of the political subject is repeatedly framed as the product of Ireland's inability to broker effective international treaties. Personal vulnerability is thus an index of dealings with a colonial power negotiating in bad faith. In "Eumaeus" we learn that the international financial arrangement was Ireland's Achilles' heel, whereby it had "all the riches drained out of it by England levying taxes on the poor people that paid through the nose" (16.991–992). Joyce frequently directs his readers to the Empire's legal discourse of injury using terms such as liability, damage, penalty, debt and repayment, functioning to accentuate the pain so often inscribed in political belonging. The Irish Catholic, in Bloom's estimation, aspires toward "that muchinjured but on the whole eventempered person" (16.1081–1082). This hypersensitivity to injury, not surprisingly, is what often causes the character called the citizen to take "umbrage at something or other," a response that seems to precondition the terms for further harm. In his religion, in particular, the Irish subject finds a kind of spiritual site that enables him/herself to redirect and project blame rather than attempting to find a clear way out of the nation's own self-reinforcing politics of victimization. Joyce makes this point repeatedly: "The Irish catholic peasant. He's the Backbone of our Empire" (16.1021–1022).

As far back as 1907, in "Ireland, Island of Saints and Sages," Joyce lectured on what he termed the "moral effects" from bad dealings with Empire (173). "The English," Joyce wrote, "now disparage the Irish because they are Catholic, poor, and ignorant; however, it will not be so easy to justify such disparagement to some people. Ireland is poor because English laws have ruined the country's industries" (*CW* 167). Delivered at Università Popolare, the lecture underscores Joyce's increasing fascination with Trieste's growing irredentist spirit. Living in the city, he frequently observed mass public demonstrations against the Austro-Hungarian government. His friendship with several Triestine organizers in the struggle for independence gave him insights into Ireland's own clash with empire. Further, Leopold Bloom's identification as part of a long-suffering minority is the product of what Joyce heard living among a Hungarian Jewish population. Throughout "Cyclops," Bloom's multiethnic identification as a cultural Everyman is scorned, though in one scene his questionable Hungarian Jewish heritage is singled out as a disguised threat:

> —A wolf in sheep's clothing, says the citizen. That's what he is. Virag from Hungary! Ahasuerus I call him. Cursed by God.
>
> . . . .
>
> —Saint Patrick would want to land again at Ballykinlar and convert us, says the citizen, after allowing things like that to contaminate our shores. (12.1666–1672)

Off the island, too, Joyce's geographical distance in exile from Dublin provided a clearer indication of how the Irish struggle was being reported on in newspapers across the Continent. "In most of the wired reports in the local papers," John McCourt clarifies, "Joyce would have read of Ireland as a place of poverty, famine and insurrection, a country, as he put it in 'Ireland, Island of Saints and Sages,' destined to be 'the everlasting caricature of the serious world'" (108).

The Irish foolishly, naively, and repeatedly signed bad international treaties. Such failures, Joyce wrote in this essay, limited their capability to garner international respect as a nation capable of guiding its own self-determination:

> The economic and intellectual conditions that prevail in his own country do not permit the development of individuality. The soul of the country is weakened by centuries of useless struggle and broken treaties, and individual initiative is paralysed by the influence and admonitions of the church, while its body is manacled by the police, the tax office, and the garrison. No one who has any self-respect stays in Ireland, but flees afar as though from a country that has undergone the visitation of an angered Jove. (171)

Rights coming out of the treaties were a matter of the collective and collectivities, and they calibrated the ratios of legal power in a way that held the demands of the Empire above the colonies.

As Joyce underlines the human consequences of legal demands, he repeatedly draws attention to the looming promise of new configurations and realignments of global treaties. These adjustments to international agreements promise to produce new forms of Irish recognition and increase Ireland's legal function and rank on the world stage. The anticipation reaches a fever pitch amid the "medley of cries" signaling the long-awaited arrival of one of the last delegates to a world leaders' convention:

> The arrival of the worldrenowned headsman was greeted by a roar of acclamation from the huge concourse, the viceregal ladies waving their handkerchiefs in their excitement while the even more excitable foreign delegates cheered vociferously in a medley of cries, *hoch, banzai, eljen, zivio, chinchin, polla kronia, hiphip, vive, Allah,* amid which the ringing *evviva* of the delegate of the land of song (a high double F recalling those piercingly lovely notes with which the eunuch Catalani beglamoured our greatgreatgrandmothers) was easily distinguishable. (12.596–604)

A chorus of worldwide universal harmony momentarily takes shape. But Joyce's zany catalogue of national exclamations (*hoch* from the German for "three cheers," and so on) also casts doubt on the verity of a global community of equals universalized in song. The tone varies between the sweet consonance of cheers and a sardonically phrased "medley of cries" — a bitter reminder of failed treaties for historic Ireland, which gave rise to wounded attachments entrenched within the very notion of Irish identity. The passage forms part of Joyce's extended parody of a newspaper's feature story on the global conference as both large-scale social event and well-orchestrated publicity stunt. In a key moment of erudition, evoking the failure of the modern powers to forestall and defuse the bloody outbreak of World War I, as well as anticipating the moralizing "never again" rhetoric in calls for a global diplomatic solution, such as the League of Nations, to end all wars, Joyce plays with German compound words: "Kriegfried Ueberallgemein" (12.569)—*Kriegfried* literally translating as "warpeace" and *Ueberallgemein* as "overalluniversal." His text not only stages a satire of the inflated sentimentality of world events and the collusion of the media with the spectacle of power as both embellish the rhetorical mode of documentation to assert their importance. More strikingly, the globalized legalese serves to index the ongoing negotiations between nation-states at the 1919 Paris Conference. Joyce carefully omits the Irish "sláinte" from the list, a calculated move emphasizing the hypocrisy of universal calls for global minorities to be protected. Wasn't Ireland's exemption from the League's global covenant exactly the type of "nameless barbarity" against which "All the delegates without exception expressed themselves in the strongest possible heterogeneous terms" (12.569–571)? The elision recalls Michael Collins after the Easter Rising pleading with foreign democratic states to recognize the instantiation of the Irish free republic. And it evokes Ireland's unofficial delegation sent to the League of Nations, its failures to gain recognition. Joyce's text also echoes much further back. His allusions to international legal rights movements serve as painful reminders of Connolly's realization in 1914 when he first "heard the news that the Second International had failed" (MacCabe 168). Following an unprecedented global turn of events, not even efforts for the mobilization of international unions would be able to unite the world's suffering humanity. The outbreak of the Great War dashed Ireland's hopes for a global labor movement to end colonial exploitation.

These failed opportunities register the false promise of freedom in cosmopolitan aspirations as much as they demonstrate the pain installed at the core of the desire for political recognition. In pointing out these consequences, "Cyclops" demarcates a frequent turn from optimism to resentment. But what if the text is also constructed in a way that reopens a desire for futurity to cut through the resentment that would only seem to close down the possibilities for freedom? Such a shift in minority discourse would involve anchoring the project of sovereign agency in a bid for acknowledgment that avoids the eternal repetition of pain. Joyce underscores the ways in which media representations, for better or worse, play a role in defining minority identities for the wider global audience. Another parody of the world press records: "The fashionable international world attended *en masse*" (12.1266), this time for a wedding event mixing celebrities and socialites with political leaders. When news of the event reaches the men in the pub, it is met with a litany of complaints. They resent the lost opportunity for political efficacy. Any potentially transformative outcome of the gathering has been restricted, largely by the mass public's appetite for frivolous coverage of world affairs. Only once the folded sections are flipped through in a fevered effort to find more titillating and sensational global headlines does the newspaper, as a cultural object, attract more serious attention. The men in the pub start "Hanging over the bloody paper with Alf looking for spicy bits instead of attending to the general public." The pages eventually stop at a disconcerting "Picture of a butting match, trying to crack their bloody skulls, one chap going for the other with his head down like a bull at a gate. And another one: *Black Beast Burned in Omaha, Ga*. . . . a sambo strung up in a tree with his tongue out and a bonfire under him" (12.1321–1326). As they fixate on the persecution of the subjugated African American, the media's skewed representation of the subaltern "Black Beast" creates an empathic distance from the scene of suffering. The image is coded with otherness. This inscription of difference does not allow the Irish patriots to fully engage in decolonized forms of mutual recognition with another subjugated minority group that would render visible their shared, often vexed desires for rights recognition. It is no accident, moreover, that in the struggle for international sympathy it is these kinds of images—tragic depictions of minority "persecution," to use Bloom's hackneyed term—that can turn colonial struggles into an odd competition for acknowledgement, one that appears to attract serious if less substantial attention than the international institutions put in place to defend rights.

None of this is to say that the bid for decolonizing recognition is fixed, but it does require retooling the terms of engagement. Thus, even those exchanges of recognition that express a spirit of inclusion—such as the Irish emancipation or contemporary liberal multiculturalism—deal, at best, with the symptoms of oppression, while simultaneously working to challenge the problematic of sovereign agency in which those effects are rooted. At times, this means that depictions of suffering will in many ways only repeat existing relations of injustice. Joyce's scenes of recognition register the seeming impossibility of improving the conditions of life for subordinated groups to the extent that they are so often conditioned on other, external social stratifications like the law, which so frequently distribute vulnerability and dependence. The question about decolonizing recognition he leaves us with, which to a large extent still resonates for minority groups today, involves contending with these representations, and transcending the compassion fatigue in world politics that prevents moving minority status beyond simple legal recognition to the level of a collective responsibility.

Works Cited

Brown, Wendy. *States of Injury: Power and Freedom in Late Modernity*. Princeton: Princeton University Press, 1995.

Collins, Michael. "Ireland as the Pivot of the League of Nations." *Guardian*, 7 December 1921.

Davison, Neil R. *James Joyce, "Ulysses," and the Construction of Jewish Identity: Culture, Biography, and "the Jew" in Modernist Europe*. Cambridge: Cambridge University Press, 1998.

Fanon, Frantz. *Black Skin, White Masks*. Translated by Richard Philcox. New York: Grove Press, 2008.

Fink, Carole. "The Paris Peace Conference and the Question of Minority Rights." *Peace & Change* 21.3 (July 1996): 273–88.

Groden, Michael. *"Ulysses" in Progress*. Princeton: Princeton University Press, 1977.

Keatinge, Patrick. "Ireland and the League of Nations." *Studies: An Irish Quarterly Review* 59.234 (Summer 1970): 133–47.

Levi, Neil. "'See That Straw? That's a Straw': Anti-Semitism and Narrative Form in *Ulysses*." *Modernism/modernity* 9.3 (September 2002): 375–88.

MacCabe, Colin. *James Joyce and the Revolution of the Word*. London: Macmillan, 1978.

McCourt, John. *The Years of Bloom: James Joyce in Trieste, 1904–1920*. Dublin: Lilliput, 2000.

Nolan, Emer. *James Joyce and Nationalism*. New York: Routledge, 1995.

Walkowitz, Rebecca L. *Cosmopolitan Style: Modernism beyond the Nation*. New York: Columbia University Press, 2006.

6

Dublin Inc.

Municipal Corporation Reform in "Ivy Day in the Committee Room"

CELIA MARSHIK

It is the stuff of casual conversation. Over plates of mutton hash, Simon Dedalus tells his wife about a meeting with Father Dolan that settles the educational futures of Stephen and Maurice. Simon interrupts his own story of Stephen's behavior at Clongowes with "And, by the way, who do you think he told me will get that job in the corporation? But I'll tell you that after" (*P* 72). The character never does "tell you that after," and the corporation is not mentioned elsewhere in Joyce's first novel. Although *Portrait* intimates that the Catholic clergy have their fingers on the pulse of local employment, such concerns scarcely register for Joyce's young protagonist.

First-time readers are likely to assume that "the corporation" is a business enterprise, but the corporation referenced here and throughout Joyce's fiction is the Dublin Corporation. Joyce had, of course, experience with business (as opposed to municipal) corporations, including his 1909 involvement in the Cinematograph Volta and his short-lived attempt to sell stock in *Ulysses*. But given the lack of Irish economic development during Joyce's lifetime, and given the intense regionalism of Joyce's fiction, the Dublin Corporation emerges as *the* corporate form of significance in *Dubliners*, *Portrait*, and *Ulysses*. Moreover, Joyce's metropolitan sensibilities—and the city-centered worldview of his characters—suggest that the Dublin Corporation is not only the corporate game in town but the most tangible form of governance his characters experience. Although a focus on matters of state means that his characters almost can't *see* the Corporation, Joyce's authorial presence imagines that things might be otherwise.

In this essay I argue that Joyce deploys references to the Dublin Corporation to highlight the legal anomaly of local self-governance in the context of the colony as well as the anomalous location of the Corporation as between the individual and the state. While the limitations of Dublin Inc. are in part an artifact of Joyce's historical moment, they also point to the more general problem of weak cities—of municipalities whose rights and powers pale in contrast to those of states and nations. Joyce's representations of the Dublin Corporation are often critical, but his criticism of the institution and what the city's inhabitants made of it contains glimpses of possibility—of the hope that Ireland's capital city, and cities elsewhere, might be governed in a manner that is representative, free of corruption, and for the greater good. This aspect of Dublin Inc. has passed unnoted, in part because we as readers remain unfamiliar with details of the Dublin Corporation's history, details with which Joyce and his contemporaries would have been familiar. While Ireland's status as a colony has necessarily complicated the focus on Dublin's municipal governance, looking at the rights that residents of the city enjoyed through corporation recovers the important role of local governance even in a system of centralized state power.

My essay begins with a history of the Dublin Corporation as well as of municipal corporations more generally. While the complexities of this history (and of legal theories of municipal corporations) require more time and attention than can be given here, I will detail the rights retracted and granted through different iterations of Irish corporations, which were the focus of significant parliamentary reforms during Joyce's youth. I will then turn my attention to "Ivy Day in the Committee Room," a story that has been read as a lens on Irish *national*, but not *municipal*, politics. As I argue, our attention to "Ivy Day" should not detract from the story's equally important interest in "the Committee Room," a site of local governance acutely upended by recent changes to corporation law. If most of Joyce's characters seem unable to envision a strong municipal corporation, recovering the legal context for their conversation illuminates changes that could have opened to door to a different type of home rule.[1] Joyce's story, I demonstrate, reveals an interest in reformism and structures of municipality; more important, "Ivy Day in the Committee Room" suggests that strong municipalities make for strong nations and that nationalist efforts cannot ignore the city-as-home in a focus on the state.²

. . .

The Dublin Corporation of Joyce's day was both the product of a particular national history *and* of a piece with other municipal corporations. Its problems, as well as its promise, point to the position of municipal corporations in the context of the colony and municipal corporations generally. As Gerald Frug argues in "The City as Legal Concept," incorporated cities have long been plagued by a disabling interstitiality: a city is "an intermediate entity which is neither the state nor the individual, neither political nor economic, neither public nor private, yet which has autonomy protected against the power of the central state" (1081). In its early incarnation, the corporate municipality was "in some aspects a protector of, while in other ways a threat to, both individual rights and state power" (1099). From 1439, the year of the first corporate charter (1087), kings and occasionally British landowners granted charters to localities to establish government services (and revenue collection) that a centralized government could not offer, but the trend in modern municipal corporations is toward what Frug calls "weak cities": corporations that exercise little power because their sphere of influence (the "local") is parsed very narrowly (1063). Frug, like other legal theorists before him, argues that this need not be the case—that state governance might be decentralized so that cities could exercise more control over banking, utilities, and other economic and infrastructural matters. Indeed, in the United States there was a late nineteenth-century legal movement for municipal home rule that proposed constitutional amendments to protect city autonomy (1115–16).³ While this movement did not apparently spread to Great Britain, the role of municipal corporations in Ireland comes into sharper focus when one considers that the bid for "home rule" might have been launched in the name of cities instead of the state. And, while the Dublin Corporation was dogged by problems peculiar to a political situation far removed from those that confront us in the twenty-first century, the issue of decentralized power continues to plague many cities because of legal choices that were naturalized in the nineteenth and twentieth centuries.⁴

A brief history of the Dublin Corporation underscores the tension between local governance and the prerogatives of the larger state as well as a particular irony: ancient forms of the Corporation were more powerful than those that emerged during Joyce's lifetime. Corporate municipal bodies in Ireland came into being under the Tudors. In this period, and indeed up until the nineteenth century, "there was no distinction . . . between public and private corporations, between businesses and cities" (Frug 1082). As Peter Gale writes in his 1834 *Inquiry into the Ancient Corporate System of Ireland*, early Irish corporations offered universal (male) suffrage for residents and worked as economic engines for the same. Indeed, Gale argues that Irish corporations ranked "among the wisest, freest, and most salutary of our legal and social institutions" and hopes that "recollections of what corporate bodies were, may give some notice of what they might still become" (4, 5). While this view of early corporations seems utopian, Frug's much more dispassionate study reveals that early modern towns operated like fraternal associations instead of "mere locations for individual effort" (1089). In other words, early modern municipal corporations functioned much more like the body memorialized in the word "corporation"—"A body corporate legally authorized to act as a single individual" in the words of the *OED*—than their contemporary counterparts.

The first great downfall of Irish (and, indeed, British) corporations occurred during the reign of James I, when corporation officers began to be required to take the Oath of Supremacy, effectively eliminating Roman Catholics' ability to hold office (Cassell 7:264; Gale 43–62). The iniquities of Irish municipalities afterwards would take too long to rehearse here; while all British corporations were in need of reform by the early nineteenth century,[5] an 1833 Parliamentary commission on municipal corporations identified the "grossest abuses" in Ireland (Cassell 7:265). Joyce was clearly aware of this dark period in Dublin Inc. As John Anderson notes, *Finnegans Wake* refers to Daniel O'Connell's duel with John D'Esterre: "the gauntlet upon the hand which in an hour not for him solely evil had struck down the might he mighthavebeen d'Esterre of whom his nation seemed almost ready to be about to have need" (*FW* 52). The incident resulted from an 1815 speech in which O'Connell referred to "The Corpo" as a "beggarly corporation," an insult that D'Esterre took up on behalf of Corporation members (Anderson 2:88). When Anderson asserts that "The Dublin Corporation had always been reactionary and bigoted against Catholics"

(2:88), however, he (like many others) ignores early incarnations of the Corporation, which had not "always" been at odds with Catholics. As Gale's history of the corporation suggests, the much-needed "revision" of corporate rights could be thought of as a "restoration and extension" of previous civil liberties (157).

The hope for revision came to tentative fruition with the August 10, 1840, passage of the Municipal Corporation Reform (Ireland) Act, which was based on an 1835 law that reformed English and Welsh corporations. The act put significant changes in place, including a provision that enfranchised all male householders inhabiting a structure worth an annual rent of £10. While the £10 qualification limited voting rights to a relatively small portion of city dwellers—Matthew Potter notes that "the purpose of reform was not to introduce the masses into the political process but to make local government more broadly representative of the respectable middle classes"—the result of the act was "the overthrow of the Protestant ascendancy in most Irish cities and towns outside Ulster" (*Municipal Revolution* 77, 124).[6] Irish corporations thereafter became properly representative bodies in terms of religion if not class, but such reforms did not satisfy Irish nationalists, who "regarded local government as a stepping stone to the attainment of self-rule, not as having much value in itself" (126). Doubtless this attitude was partly due to provisions in the act like one that detailed a reorganization of the Royal Irish Constabulary, thus embedding a police force that answered to the Lord Lieutenant (not corporation officers) in the very statute that restored long-lost voting rights to many Irish Catholics. In other words, the 1840 law at once asserted and limited the rights of municipal government in Ireland, rendering Dublin and other Irish corporations strong in some matters and quite limited in others.[7]

When Joyce was born on February 2, 1882, then, Dublin Inc. was firmly controlled by nationalist interests, but it was not yet a properly democratic body (O'Brien 73). As a young boy, he may have heard about changes on the horizon: as early as 1892, English politicians like Arthur Balfour were attempting to put through a bill on Irish local government in the hope of appeasing nationalists (and perhaps even defusing calls for home rule). Such efforts were mocked in an 1892 cartoon in *Punch* titled "GIFT FROM THE GREEKS" and captioned RIGHT HON. ARTHUR. "IF I CAN ONLY GET THIS THROUGH, IT OUGHT TO SETTLE 'EM!" (see figure 1).

Figure 1. "Gift from the Greeks." Cartoon by Sir John Tenniel, engraving by Joseph Swain. *Punch*, 27 February 1892, 103.

Part of what makes this image intriguing is that the cartoonist does not identify where Balfour intends to deposit the Trojan horse. Is the building in the background Dublin Castle, the Houses of Parliament, or some other structure? The cartoon seems to promise that yet another corporation reform could backfire on either the English or the Irish, ambivalence that points to the potentially high stakes of new legislation. Strong local government might pave the way to home rule; alternatively, genuine control over local matters might defuse—might "settle"—calls for the same.[8] When we remember that, across the Atlantic, reformers were calling for home rule in the name of municipalities, not states, the stakes of corporation reform emerge as quite high. Stronger Irish cities could preserve the union while providing greater freedoms, or they could serve as stepping stones to its dissolution.

Six years would elapse before the final passage of the Local Government (Ireland) Act on August 12, 1898. The sixteen-year-old Joyce could not have failed to notice this momentous change, one of such importance that writers of all stripes have since referred to it as a "revolution."[9] This act, as Potter writes, "democratised municipal and Poor Law administration by extending their previously restricted franchises to all householders and occupants of a portion of a house, including women, for the first time. In addition, the property qualifications for municipal councilors were abolished, thus facilitating the emergence of working-class councillors" ("Rise and Fall" 42). In brief, the 1898 law established universal suffrage in local elections, removing barriers of class, sex, and creed imposed for centuries.

While the impact of this reform was significant, Dubliners (like most Irish citizens) were largely unenthusiastic about the bill and subsequent law, which Richard Haslam characterizes as "a virtually unwanted gift." As he writes,

> There was no agitation in its favour. The Irish Parliamentary Party's feelings about county government were soured by the belief, widely held, that the English Local Government Act, 1888, which was the model used for the Irish Act, was a reward to Chamberlain and the other liberal unionists for their help in defeating Gladstone's (and Parnell's) first Home Rule Bill in 1886. Therefore the new Act was met with suspicion and grudging acceptance. (27)

Here, as earlier, one sees the ways in which the laws that governed Irish municipal corporations were always imbricated with national political aspirations. The assumption that strengthening municipalities and extending the franchise was a reward for voting against home rule neatly demonstrates the tension between local and national governments. Because the state, and not the city, then as now enjoyed the most political and economic power, even "revolutionary" changes to municipal voting rights seemed of little value. And yet, the 1898 law was to have far reaching consequences.

The Local Government (Ireland) Act helped to consolidate nationalist control of the Dublin Corporation, both through the Nationalist Party proper and new parties in sympathy with the Nationalists' larger aims. And if nationalists had not particularly wanted the power that came with running a municipal corporation, they quickly began to use the body as a bully pulpit, however ineffectual. O'Brien writes that

> At the very first meeting of the Corporation after the election in 1899, the first order of business was not a much-needed declaration of war against the slums but a pledge of devotion to the cause of self-government and a promise to use every legitimate means to secure its triumph. But this was a task that could only be tackled successfully at Westminster or on the battlefield, in neither of which areas the Corporation operated. (84)

Not everyone agreed with the "intrusion" of national politics into the work of the Corporation (79), and political control of Dublin Inc. had consequences few could anticipate. As O'Brien notes, "Nationalist councilors, as the majority, became the butt of most of the criticism directed against the corporation both inside and outside the council chamber" (95). Home rule of the municipal variety was thus not entirely satisfying. Despite the many complaints lodged against the Corporation post-1898, Dublin's *Municipal Yearbook and Public Services Directory* regularly opined that "The Corporation, in the face of difficulties little dreamed of in English municipalities, has done, and is doing, a splendid work" (Donald 434).

As this brief tour through the history of the Dublin Corporation has suggested, by the time Joyce was a young adult, the "body" of the city had become much more inclusive and representative of Irish political aspirations than it had been for centuries. After 1898 all city residents, both male and female, were able to vote in local elections.[10] While this right was not always valued by Dubliners, city and county government in Ireland was properly democratic at the time *Dubliners*, most of *Portrait*, and *Ulysses* are set. And although it may be tempting to disparage the right to local self-determination, as many nationalists did, such an attitude overshadows additional reforms that might have been pursued in the name of the city instead of the state. In "Ivy Day in the Committee Room," the stakes of corporation governance emerge as incredibly high even as the romance of Ivy Day clouds the matter.

. . .

Joyce's short story is set on October 6, 1902, and thus it takes place shortly after the 1898 Act had eliminated the £10 qualification and extended the franchise to women. October 6 was, of course, "Ivy Day," an annual occasion to remember Parnell by wearing an ivy leaf. The setting for the story brings the characters together in "the Committee Room," the Nationalist Party's ward headquarters. Space and date thus intermingle here, and the time of the story's setting—its reference to a Parnellian counterpoint to the present—tends to dominate analysis. I want to suggest that Joyce's work pivots on the tension between his story's physical and temporal settings: "Ivy Day in the Committee Room" offers a picture of the Corporation's possibilities as well as its limits, and it registers what is at stake in both the Corporation and the 1898 Act.

As readers will doubtless remember, "Ivy Day in the Committee Room" opens as canvassers for municipal elections gather. Mr. O'Connor, who has retreated from inclement weather, uses a canvassing card intended to promote Richard J. Tierney to light his cigarette. The flame from the card briefly illuminates the ivy leaf in his lapel, and at the level of image, the story suggests the inadequacy of Corporation governance when compared to (state) home rule. As the tale develops, it becomes apparent that Tierney figuratively lights a fire under no one: that this candidate emerges in ironic contrast with the idealized politician encapsulated in the memory of Parnell. Joyce's story represents several characters who, like Tierney, embody "the dark opposite of Parnell" (Beards 293), and it seems possible that no officer of the Dublin Corporation could live up to that memory.

That is not to suggest that the Corporation election fails to rouse any passion. Joe Hynes, who stops by, supports Colgan. Although readers of Joyce's story hear very little about this candidate, what details we do learn emerge after Old Jack speaks scornfully of him. Hynes responds, "Is it because Colgan's a working-man you say that? What's the difference between a good honest bricklayer and a publican—eh? Hasn't the working man as good a right to be in the Corporation as anyone else—ay, and a better right than those shoneens that are always hat in hand before any fellow with a handle to his name?" (*D* 121). Here Joyce draws attention to a political landscape made possible by the 1898 Local Government Act, which extended the franchise and the right to hold office to bricklayers and other working-class men. Before 1899, someone like Colgan could not have run for corporation office, and Colgan himself might not have been able to vote.[11] After 1899, the Labour Electoral Association contested ten of the sixty council seats (O'Brien 78). Colgan is presumably a candidate for this party, which held between five and eight positions on the municipal council between 1899 and 1914 (93).[12]

The import of Colgan's candidacy—and the electors who might vote for him—has been obscured by misunderstandings of Irish municipal electoral law, and specifically by ignorance of the 1898 Act. Don Gifford's monumental *Joyce Annotated*, for example, footnotes the phrase "Municipal Elections" with the assertion that "franchise in Dublin was confined to male citizens over 21 who were £10 householders, i.e., those whose houses were listed on the tax rolls as being worth £10 in 'annual rent.' In 1901, there were 34,906 eligible voters out of a population of 290,638 in Dublin" (89). The conditions Gifford here describes would have been accurate for elections held between 1840 and 1898 under the Municipal Corporation Reform (Ireland) Act. They do not, however, pertain to the landscape of "Ivy Day," which is set in 1902. After the 1898 reforms, all adult inhabitants of the city who met residency requirements could vote, regardless of their income and property value.

This recent development in the history of Dublin Inc. registers through Hynes's continued advocacy of Colgan. The character asserts, "One man is a plain honest man with no hunker-sliding about him. He goes in to represent the labour classes. This fellow you're working for only wants to get some job or other" (*D* 121). Here Colgan emerges as an alternative to Tierney, as characters hash out who should serve Dublin Inc. in a political climate altered by an extended franchise. It is tempting to imagine how clearly Joyce's story might have made this point by representing a female character engaged in this debate; *Dubliners* cannot go quite that far, but Hynes's arguments highlight the impact of legal reforms on Dublin's municipal corporation.

As Hynes continues, his paean to Colgan increasingly makes clear the differences between Labour and Nationalist candidates—differences that could emerge only after the formation of the Labour Electoral Association in 1899.[13] Hynes asserts that "it's labour produces everything. The working-man is not looking for fat jobs for his sons and nephews and cousins. The working-man is not going to drag the honour of Dublin in the mud to please a German monarch" (*D* 121). Such rhetoric doubtless sounds hackneyed to our ears, but Hynes's arguments would have been less familiar to his interlocutors. The character suggests a fundamental difference between Colgan and Tierney, who O'Connor concedes may vote to present an address of welcome to King Edward VII. I will return to the stakes of this address in a moment, but it is here important to remember the new political landscape created by the Local Government (Ireland) Act. If the Labourites could not hope to gain a majority of seats in the governing body of the Corporation, they could and did use the expansion of the franchise to put pressure on the Nationalist ranks. Colgan may or may not be elected in the fictional life that continues after the end of "Ivy Day in the Committee Room," but candidates like him worked to pressure Nationalists to adopt aspects of the Labour platform, such as improvements in working conditions. Pre-1898, organized labor needed to settle for labor spokesmen within Nationalist ranks; post-1898, the L.E.A. could field its own candidates and put genuine political pressure on the Nationalists, who had not particularly supported the extension of the franchise to men like Colgan.[14]

The class, and thus political, differences between Tierney and Colgan are underlined later when Mr. Henchy shares his canvassing strategy, which downplays Tierney's Nationalist party affiliation. Henchy blusters: "'He's a big rate payer,' I said. 'He has extensive house property in the city and three places of business and isn't it to his own advantage to keep down the rates?'" (*D* 131). Henchy not only reveals the ethical bankruptcy at the heart of Tierney's campaign, which elides the candidate's Nationalist affiliation, but also a fundamental reason that the Dublin Corporation was weak. Like candidates then and now, Tierney appeals to voters' pocketbooks, and as a "big rate payer," he has every incentive to keep taxes low. And yet, lack of revenue is largely what kept the Dublin Corporation poor and economically vulnerable. Scholars agree that "the activities of the Dublin Corporation were constrained by its poverty, and [Mary E.] Daly has pointed out that 'no British city, nor indeed Belfast, operated within such tight financial limits as did Dublin'" (Potter, *Municipal Revolution* 145). While Dublin lacked a robust tax base in part because wealthy Protestants had relocated to nearby townships (see D'Arcy), Tierney's example indicates that citizens who could well afford to contribute to the municipality's revenue protected their wealth. The irony of Henchy's pitch could not be bitterer: Tierney's campaign is pitched in terms that ensure an impoverished municipality, one that has less power to undertake public improvements, to care for the poor, or to support the limited number of cultural institutions Dublin then enjoyed.[15]

Of course, Joyce's characters do not see this for themselves, largely because they are so intent on cadging drinks and thinking about Dublin's colonial, as opposed to municipal, position. The conversation about the Corporation's potential address of welcome to King Edward later continues, and the canvassers for Tierney debate whether Nationalist councilors should follow their "ideals" and vote against the address or extend Dublin Inc.'s welcome to the king. Here we see "Ivy Day" and "the Committee Room" in tension, as this debate emphasizes the position of Dublin as a colonial city, one in which citizens have a great deal of (realized and unrealized) control over local matters but little control over the state. The latter situation obscures the former; in their focus on state politics, characters doubly beggar the city. In keeping the rates down—refusing to exercise a power Dublin's municipal leaders did hold—the Nationalists economically weaken their city and thus their ideological position. Henchy forcefully argues that Tierney and others should vote for the address of welcome because "what we want in this country . . . is capital. The King's coming here will mean an influx of money into this country" (*D* 131). *Dubliners* here makes the point that weak cities cramp the aspiration to wider forms of self-determination; in other words, a lack of municipal home rule qualifies the drive to national home rule. In the relationship between cities and states, one often sees the impulse to centralized power—and certainly this was the case with Irish cities.[16] "Ivy Day in the Committee Room" thinks more creatively about possibilities for power sharing between city and state, as the story suggests that without *de*-centralized power (strong municipal corporations), an Irish state will never come into being.

In 1903 the Corporation voted down an address of welcome, a historical fact that underlines the stakes of the election depicted in Joyce's story. The proposed address was defeated by only three votes, with Nationalists arrayed on both sides of the measure; all Labour votes were cast against the proposal (O'Brien 88). Someone like Tierney might have voted to approve the address, while someone like Colgan would not. "Ivy Day" leaves open the question of who should represent inhabitants of the ward, but the story lays bare why the 1898 Act and subsequent elections mattered. Labour, however minoritarian, provided a new model of Dublin futurity that differed from the Nationalists'. Even though he never enters the committee room, Colgan seems much more in line than Tierney with the sympathies of Joyce and *Dubliners*.[17]

"Ivy Day in the Committee Room" concludes after Hynes recites "The Death of Parnell," a bathetic memorial to Ireland's "Uncrowned King." The response to said poem is both emotional and underwhelming, and the story's anticlimax has led to a widely shared assessment aptly expressed by Hugh Kenner: "Political activity in the vacuum left by his [Parnell's] departure consists of a few futile gestures, sporadic interviews with voters, and much meditative drinking of stout by an October fire" (61). It is certainly true that Irish nationalist politics are stymied in the story, and that alcohol—here as elsewhere in *Dubliners*—serves to dull the pain.[18] This type of assessment is correct as far as "Ivy Day" goes, but as I hope this discussion has suggested, we (like Joyce's characters) seem to have trouble seeing "the Committee Room" behind the figure of Parnell. Joyce's story positions (state) home rule as an unreachable goal, but at the same time, his tale provides glimpses of (municipal) home rule recently shaken up by legislation that extended voting rights as well as expanded the number of people eligible to serve as mayors, sheriffs and councilors.

Although the Dubliners do not appreciate the fact that they have lived through a (municipal) revolution, readers can see the way the Corporation has been transformed—or, rather, the ways the laws governing who can vote and hold office in the Corporation have been transformed. They also see how the elections might matter, both in terms of internal Corporation matters (the rates) and external state politics (the address). Historian Pauric Travers has argued that the years 1890 to 1910 have "been seen as a barren landscape" but "that view has now been replaced by a new orthodoxy which sees these years as a lost opportunity" (13). "Ivy Day in the Committee Room" presents this lost opportunity through a depiction of Corporation elections in a time of revolutionary changes at the municipal level. We simply have to remove the sprig of ivy in our eye to see it.

In his explanation of "why city powerlessness matters," Gerald Frug notes that we so accept our current political landscape, one in which nations, not municipalities, dominate the political conversation, that it is difficult to imagine the outlines of strong municipal corporations (1067). This was as true for Joyce's characters as it is in our own day: no wonder we too focus on Charles Parnell, Ivy Day, and (state) Home Rule when teaching Joyce to our students. And yet, Frug (citing Hannah Arendt's *On Revolution*) argues that cities offer a unique form of "public freedom": municipal corporations provide a venue "to participate actively in the basic social decisions that affect one's life" (1068). In the case of Dublin, active participation was possible only after 1898, when men and women of all classes could finally vote in corporation elections *and* run for corporation offices. If Joyce's texts cast a skeptical eye on the men who involved themselves in Dublin Inc.—if their version of "public freedom" often seems the freedom to profit from the public purse[19]—"Ivy Day in the Committee Room" gestures toward alternatives. For every Tierney, there is a Colgan: a new player in local democracy hoping to make the Corporation representative, fiscally sound, and independent.

Notes

A version of this essay appeared in *James Joyce Quarterly* 50.4. This revision is reprinted with permission.

1. Few critics have thought about Joyce's relationship to the Dublin Corporation, but there are happy exceptions. Chapter 2 of Michael Rubenstein's *Public Works: Infrastructure, Irish Modernism, and the Postcolonial* examines Joyce's representation of public utilities managed by the Corporation, which literalizes Dubliners' "material connection[s] and interdependence" (63). And in "'Vartryville': Dublin's Water Supply and Joyce's Sublation of Local Government," Anne Marie D'Arcy takes up the rancorous relationship between the Corporation and the surrounding townships, which came to a head over the Vartry Water Supply Scheme.

2. By "nationalist" I mean those individuals committed to a range of positions including Irish Home Rule and/or separatism. My essay seeks less to complicate our understanding of Irish nationalism than to explore the perceived (and, I believe, faulty) opposition between nationalism and local governance.

3. For an example, see Goodnow, *Municipal Home Rule*.

4. For a detailed account of the Dublin Corporation's particular limitations, see Haslam, "Origins of Irish Local Government," 17. See Frug for a history of British and American municipal corporations as well as an argument for the importance of increasing city powers.

5. See Finlayson, "Municipal Corporation Commission and Report, 1833-35," 37-38.

6. According to Cassell, the £10 qualification for Irish voters was insisted on by mem-

bers of the House of Lords. See Cassell 264–67 for a detailed account of the debate over the bill.

7. As Potter observes, "boroughs were given very limited powers, mainly to make bye-laws for the good government of the borough and to prevent and suppress nuisances (dangerous or unsanitary buildings, or places)" (*Municipal Revolution* 87).

8. John Redmond, future leader of the Irish Parliamentary Party, said of a later version of this legislation, "If this Bill is worked successfully, I believe it will constitute an unanswerable argument for Home Rule" (Travers 16).

9. The Fabian Society published a tract with a section titled "The Irish Revolution of 1898" and enthused, "Up until that date the mass of the Irish people had no more power over the local government of their own country than over the government of Russia" (2). Potter calls it "The Irish Municipal Revolution," and Pauric Travers asserts, "The Local Government Act can fairly be described as revolutionary, since it effected a sudden and total transformation in political control" (13).

10. The fact that women could vote in Irish local elections was first recognized by Carol Shloss in "Molly's Resistance to the Union: Marriage and Colonialism in Dublin, 1904," 536–37.

11. D'Arcy makes a similar point, observing that after 1898 "a bricklayer like Colgan in 'Ivy Day' could at least contest an election" (262). As her rhetoric suggests, D'Arcy views this fact as less momentous than I do.

12. Don Gifford tentatively identifies Colgan as a member of "the United Irish League" (90), but given that Hynes advocates for Colgan strictly through references to the candidate's class, it is far more likely that he was running as a Labour candidate than under the banner of a party devoted to land reform.

13. The L.E.A. was initially a rather informal party; readers may be more familiar with its later incarnation, which was organized under the auspices of James Larkin and James Connolly in 1911. For a detailed account of Larkin's and Connolly's work, see Mitchell, *Labour in Irish Politics, 1890–1930*, chapter 1, "Irish Labour Creates a Political Party" (25–46).

14. As O'Brien writes, the Nationalist attitude toward working-class voters was ambivalent: "the voting workman was an unknown quantity who might come to realize that the domination of municipal government, in Dublin as elsewhere, by Nationalist councilors . . . had done little to improve his physical surroundings" (78).

15. I am here in sympathy with Rubenstein's argument that we might see in taxation or "civic finance generally, the seeds of a project of liberation" (90). His argument that *Ulysses* indirectly celebrates the shared indebtedness and interdependence of municipal citizens is, this essay argues, prefigured in the comparatively direct treatment of taxation (or rather, the avoidance thereof) in "Ivy Day in the Committee Room."

16. On the centralization of power in Ireland before and after independence, see Haslam and Travers.

17. I am in agreement with Frank Callanan, who argues that in "'Ivy Day' Joyce . . . mitigated the naturalistic bleakness of *Dubliners* through his treatment of the abandonment of Parnell by introducing an idea, however heavily qualified, of political agency" (92).

18. Variations on this reading note the economic aspirations of the canvassers. Deane, for example, writes: "It is the linkage between a political conviction that does not or cannot in these circumstances endure and the consequent and subsequent addictive consumerism which these marginalized canvassers crave to indulge . . . that Joyce dwells on here" (32).

19. Joyce's fiction may have exaggerated this aspect of the Dublin Corporation. As O'Brien argues, "it seems fair to suppose that the jobbery and nepotism endemic to municipal administration were no worse and, given the moderate resources of the [Dublin] Corporation, probably less common than in other large municipal governments in the United Kingdom" (97).

Works Cited

Anderson, John P. *Joyce's "Finnegans Wake": The Curse of Kabbalah*. 10 vols. Boca Raton, FL: Universal, 2009–14.

Beards, Richard D. "'Ivy Day in the Committee Room': The Identity of Tierney." *Studies in Short Fiction* 14 (1977): 290–93.

Callanan, Frank. "The Parnellism of James Joyce: 'Ivy Day in the Committee Room.'" *Joyce Studies Annual* 2015.1 (2015): 73–97.

Cassell, John. *Illustrated History of England*. Rev. ed. 9 vols. London: Cassell, Petter and Galpin, 1865–74.

D'Arcy, Anne Marie. "'Vartryville': Dublin's Water Supply and Joyce's Sublation of Local Government." *Joyce Studies Annual* 2013.1 (2013): 252–93.

Deane, Seamus. "Dead Ends: Joyce's Finest Moments." In *Semicolonial Joyce*, edited by Derek Attridge and Marjorie Howes, 21–36. Cambridge: Cambridge University Press, 2000.

Donald, Robert, ed. *The Municipal Yearbook and Public Services Directory*. London: Edward Lloyd, 1908.

Fabian Society. *Local Government in Ireland*. Tract 99. London: Fabian Society, 1900.

Finlayson, G.B.A.M. "The Municipal Corporation Commission and Report, 1833–35." *Bulletin of the Institute of Historical Research* 36.93 (1963): 36–52.

Frug, Gerald. "The City as Legal Concept." *Harvard Law Review* 93.6 (April 1980): 1057–1154.

Gale, Peter. *An Inquiry into the Ancient Corporate System of Ireland and Suggestions for Its Immediate Restoration and General Extension*. London: Richard Bentley; Dublin: Yates, 1834.

Gifford, Don. *Joyce Annotated: Notes for "Dubliners" and "A Portrait of the Artist as a Young Man."* Rev. ed. Berkeley: University of California Press, 1982.

Goodnow, Frank J. *Municipal Home Rule: A Study in Administration*. New York: Macmillan, 1895.

Haslam, Richard. "The Origins of Irish Local Government." In *Local Government in Ireland: Inside Out*, edited by Mark Callanan and Justin F. Keogan, 14–40. Dublin: Institute of Public Education, 2003.

Kenner, Hugh. *Dublin's Joyce*. London: Chatto and Windus, 1955.
Mitchell, Arthur. *Labour in Irish Politics, 1890–1930*. Dublin: Irish University Press, 1974.
O'Brien, Joseph V. *"Dear, Dirty Dublin": A City in Distress, 1899–1916*. Berkeley: University of California Press, 1982.
Potter, Matthew. *The Municipal Revolution in Ireland: A Handbook of Urban Government in Ireland since 1800*. Dublin: Irish Academic Press, 2011.
———. "The Rise and Fall of Local Democracy." *History Ireland* 19.2 (March/April 2011): 40–43.
Rubenstein, Michael. *Public Works: Infrastructure, Irish Modernism, and the Postcolonial*. Notre Dame, IN: University of Notre Dame Press, 2010.
Shloss, Carol. "Molly's Resistance to the Union: Marriage and Colonialism in Dublin, 1904." *Modern Fiction Studies* 35.3 (1989): 529–41.
Travers, Pauric. "A Bloodless Revolution: The Democratisation of Irish Local Government, 1898–9." In *County and Town: One Hundred Years of Local Government in Ireland*, edited by Mary E. Daly, 12–23. Dublin: Institute of Public Administration, 2001.

7

"Nobody Owns"

Ulysses, Tenancy, and Property Law

ANDREW GIBSON

"Rattle his bones. Over the stones. Only a pauper. Nobody owns" (*U* 6.332–333). Bloom thinks of these words in "Hades" as he watches a carriage bearing a small child's coffin. They come from Thomas Noel's then well-known poem "The Pauper's Drive." (Noel, we should note, was sometimes thought of as a Chartist poet, and was anthologized in literature of social protest.) For Joyce, the last two words surely have different tones, with different implications: the pauper child belongs to no one, no one owns *to* it (Noel's song emphasizes this, and it is the only meaning we can be certain is in Bloom's thoughts); the pauper child owns nothing, but then no one in Joyce's Dublin possesses very much at all, which is what Joyce meant when, speaking of Marxist criticisms of his work, he told Eugène Jolas, "I don't know why they attack me. Nobody in any of my books is worth more than a thousand pounds" (14); and no one really owns anything anyway, proprietorship is in the end a fiction. All these tones and meanings will be at issue in what follows.

In starting to think about Joyce and property law in a British-Irish historical context, at least four crucial factors are worth keeping in mind. First, the historical priority of Brehon Law: from the Norman invasion to the Tudor plantations, Brehon Law was a principal basis of dispute with the colonizer. In Foster's words, it "imposed a powerful obstacle to the spread of English law" (26). This had a specific bearing on questions of land and property. It was only in the early seventeenth century that judges in Ireland refused any longer to recognize the key ancient Brehon concepts of tanistry and gavelkind. Tanistry was the system of legal inheritance whereby the Irish septs or family divisions each had a particular figure, the tanist, to whom alone it assigned an inalienable portion of land. Tanistry ensured that land to be inherited passed "to the eldest and worthiest male of the blood and name of the deceased" (Wylie 2). Clearly a great deal depended on how one defined "worth." Gavelkind was the Brehon system of partible inheritance whereby, on the death of the head of a sept, his successor "assembled all the males . . . and divided the lands at his discretion between them" (Finlason 85–86n). Thanks to the immense labors of Eugene O'Curry and John O'Donovan, between 1863 and 1901, a detailed knowledge of Brehon Law became possible again.[1] It was particularly important to Home Rulers and nationalists. But if, in the late nineteenth century, the politics of the land issue "ensured a considerable interest in the forms of landholding which had existed in autonomous Gaelic society" (Nicholls 3), few nationalists advocated any return to them. At the same time, however, the rediscovery of Brehon Law, however garbled in the transmission,[2] confirmed the sense of the historical conditionality of post-Kinsale (post-1601) Irish property law, its lack, so to speak, of deeply rooted, traditional purchase.

The second point, however, may initially startle anyone avid for a postcolonial (or anticolonial) reading of Joyce and property law. Property law in Ireland was a nightmare from which many august nineteenth-century eminences were trying to awake it. But though the aridly pompous tones of English legal authority, as Joyce parodies it,[3] are amply evident in, say, J. C. Wylie's monumental *Casebook on Irish Land Law*—see for example *Attorney-General v Cummins* (131–37)—the cause of the nightmare was not the imposition of the colonizer's alien legal system. Had English property law been comprehensively and scrupulously applied in Ireland, the political benefits would have been substantial if not decisive. Writing in 1866, nationalist MP Isaac Butt eloquently contrasted the legal status of the prosperous English farmer in Kent with the Irish peasant who scraped together a living at very best (11). At the same time, to pick up on Foster's terms again, by the nineteenth century the major obstacle to such a development was certainly not Brehon Law. It was landlord interest, however much or little the issue on occasion was by now more legal-historical than real and present.[4] In this respect, the dreadful snarls and thickets of Irish property law remained an index not of the effects of a colonial importation but of another failure of that "disappointed bridge" (*U* 2.39) the Union, because almost a century of work failed to create any decisive union of British and Irish property law.

The case for English property law in Ireland was repeatedly, more or less explicitly, made on both sides of the Irish Sea during the nineteenth century. In a public letter of 1843, Daniel O'Connell pleaded: "All that would be necessary to resolve the land question [in Ireland] would be to repeal a few Acts of Parliament and to restore [sic] the common law of England with respect to the relation of landlord and tenant" (quoted in Lavelle 10). In *Principles of Political Economy* (1849), John Stuart Mill argued that Irish cottier tenure—the practice of letting land in small portions directly to the peasantry—was determined, not by custom, as in England, "but by competition." From that fact flowed all manner of what others took to be endemically Irish vices, from lethargy, apathy, and disaffection to agrarian violence. Butt lamented that "in England the landlord lets his farms in tenantable or . . . inhabitable order. . . . In Ireland, he lets . . . only the raw material of the soil" (19).

But we can derive the case in question with particular clarity from two texts published in 1870, one by an English legal scholar and expert and the other by a notorious radical Irish nationalist cleric, not just because they appeared only a few years before the formation of the Land League and Joyce's birth, but also because, in their different ways, both express the profound frustration and weariness many felt at the seeming intractability of the issue of Irish land law after seventy years of Union, and the gross political failure it represented. In *The Irish Landlord Since the Revolution*, the Reverend Patrick Lavelle asserted that Ireland had entirely failed to benefit from the comparatively enlightened land law prevailing in England, because the legal system worked to ensure that the landlords had "a monopoly of political power" (12). The effects of the Penal Laws on land ownership had been that only Protestants could take leases in reversion giving the present occupant the first title to a future renewal. This reduced the Irish to cottier status, left them vulnerable to exorbitant demands for rent, and deprived them of commonage, by enclosures. The repeal of the Penal Laws, the Union, and Catholic Emancipation had done little or nothing to turn this situation round. Landlord rights remained supreme. Tenants consequently suffered the evils of rack-renting, short-term tenure, swift and easy eviction, and the turnover of the land they had briefly occupied to consolidation and grazing.

In *The History of Law of Tenures of Land in England and Ireland*, W. F. Finlason put historical and legal flesh on this argument. Justice in land law depended on common law. Formally, common law applied in both England and Ireland. But "by reason of different circumstances in the two countries," its application was "practically different" (iii–iv). English common law recognized tenant right, inheritable tenancy, and the legal claims of tenants who had made improvements to their property. Indeed, it had inherited these safeguards from Roman law and the Institutes of Justinian. Thus long leases and systems of compensation were the norm in England. The magisterial figures of the English tradition of jurisprudence like Thomas de Littleton, Edward Coke, and William Blackstone had all seen "tenancy at will" (year by year and subject to landlord whim) as merely feudal and more or less pernicious. But tenancy at will was the norm in Ireland. Common law depended on agreement by custom, was local and voluntary, and needed the consent of both landlord and tenant classes. But the right to land in Ireland had been determined by the so-called "right of conquest"[5] and by dispossession, which together made any such consent impossible. Out of this sprang rampant landlord self-interest, aggression, wilfulness, disregard for tenants' improvements, and continuing tenant belligerence. Here custom could not begin to take hold.

Thus the question of land law did not mitigate the colonial trauma. Rather the reverse: if the problem had to do in the first instance with the planters or colons and not the colonial power in itself, land law was where the trauma remained perhaps most vividly, scaringly evident.[6] It was the site par excellence of the intractable colonial face-off. Hence—the third factor—throughout the nineteenth and into the early twentieth century, land law and politics are inextricable from one another. Of course, great, indignant minds, not necessarily Catholic, nationalist, or even Irish ones, had long associated them with one another: Jonathan Swift, Edmund Burke, Mill. Less impressively, the Westminster parliament had been trying more or less ineffectually to deal with Irish land law since the Union: this led to the extensive legislation of the early and mid-nineteenth century. By 1878, however, political stagnation and agricultural depression had significantly enhanced arguments for the transfer of land ownership to the occupying cultivators, and had led to the assertion of what J. J. Lee calls "new historic" (as opposed to landlord) rights (96). It is thus between 1878 and 1904, a period running more or less from Joyce's birth to his departure from Ireland, that the question of land assumes a new dimension and takes on an altogether new intensity. This is a period in which land law takes center stage in Ireland, witnessing the formation of the Land League (1879), with Charles Stewart Parnell, Michael Davitt, and John Devoy at its head, the Land War (1879–82), the Plan of Campaign (1885), and, at Westminster, the Land Act (1881, granting, at least nominally, the famous "3 Fs," fair rent, free sale, and fixity of tenure), the Arrears Act (1882), and the Land Purchase Act (1885). For reasons beyond the scope of this essay, however, the new legislation failed to break landlord power. If, by 1914, three-quarters of tenants were buying out their landlords (Vaughan 36), that was due to the Land Acts that came, significantly, at the end of the period in which Joyce's work up to and including *Ulysses* is set, 1903 and 1904.

The period of Joyce's early life, then, is one of huge turbulence around the question of land law, but also of unresolved tensions which do not start to relax until 1904. This is repeatedly evident in his early work. But why should it be, why focus on agrarian issues when Joyce's concerns are so patently urban, on mediaeval residues when, as we have amply recognized since Hugh Kenner's *Dublin's Joyce*, Joyce's world is modern-metropolitan?[7] The answer—my fourth factor—is that, as far as land and property law is concerned, such oppositions are delusive. Firstly, Irish towns were not protected or sealed off from agrarian issues and disturbances. The leadership of the Land League was in large part composed of townsmen, shopkeepers, journalists, and publicans (often because the peasantry owed them money).[8] Furthermore, nationalists perceived questions of property and tenancy in Dublin through the lens of the agrarian situation. Secondly, as far as property was concerned, Joyce's Dublin was very unmodern indeed. People did own their houses, of course. But these were in the affluent, comfortable, Protestant-dominated, chiefly southern suburbs, to which those with the money to do so had increasingly fled during the nineteenth century. With specific exceptions—the Conroys in "The Dead" live in Monkstown, for instance—Joyce has little or no interest in the suburbs. In that respect we should distinguish quite clearly between Joyce's Dublin and Dublin per se. Joyce's Dublin is inner Dublin.

In Joyce's Dublin, "nobody owns" their homes. Joyce's people rent, and do so in particular circumstances that, again, close any imagined gap between city and country, precisely because Irish property law was as it was;

indeed, city rents were often based "on agricultural usage" (Daly 195). The *Freeman's Journal* noted in 1898 that "the Kingstown man of today is as much at the mercy of a ground landlord as was the peasant tenant at will" (2). No less a figure than the Lorcan Sherlock referred to in *Ulysses* (*U* 10.1011, 15.1380) asserted that, when it came to property, urban and rural interests were the same (Daly 311). At all events, tenement living was "the norm" in Dublin as a whole (Daly 279). This was notably the case in north Dublin, whose aristocratic and professional residents increasingly quit in the nineteenth century, surrendering their property to landlordism.

The conditions of renting in Dublin were in large part determined by the very property law that prevailed in the country: the legal problems inside and outside the city were "similar" (Daly 282). Finlason remarked, for example, on the involvement of a third (and often fourth and fifth) party in Irish property, notably in the practice of "mischievous sub-letting" in the countryside (100). Landlords frequently granted long leases to tenants who sublet to others who sublet to others again. At the bottom of the ladder came the actual occupant, who was almost always a tenant at will. So, too, in Dublin, some tenements were said "to have five levels of ownership; the average was apparently three" (Daly 283). This not only racked up rents. It also meant that, like most peasant tenants, most urban ones were on yearly leases, and could very promptly be evicted, and that no one bothered to improve properties, or even carry out necessary repairs; certainly neither the urban nor the rural tenant, whose legal status meant that any improvements would only benefit the landlord. James Connolly even suggested that, like many rural landlords, Dublin tenement owners threatened tenants with a rent rise if they did not vote for the right party (46).

Inordinate rents also meant that tenants grossly overcrowded properties. Shocked observers recognized that this had significant consequences for sanitation and public health. Not surprisingly, city-dwelling tenants, like their peasant counterparts, regularly "flitted," and did their best to diddle or outwit landlords if they saw opportunity for it. True, most of the city landlords were small businessmen, and indeed Catholic (to whose interests, very often, the city corporation and Dublin MPs were all too closely allied).[9] But this is less important than the legal structure that determined the occupation of property, which was itself determined by a colonial history and was in the first instance about land. As in rural Ireland again, the often well-meaning legislation of the later nineteenth century did not amount to substantial reform. Major legislation seemed impossible, because it would lead to properties being closed down and large numbers of Dubliners reduced to living on the streets.

The Joyce of *Ulysses* responds to this situation in complex ways. I shall consider three of them here. The first we may call nationalist. It is at its simplest in Stephen's association of Fenianism with Brehon legal terms, when he identifies Kevin Egan's colonel Richard Burke as "tanist of his sept" (*U* 3.247). The tone of the passage conflates Fenian violence with a romantic aura of the Brehon past. But such identifications are not confined to Stephen. In "Eumaeus" we learn that, when young, Bloom "was in thorough sympathy with peasant possession as voicing the trend of modern opinion" (*U* 16.1589–1590)—which effectively meant taking a position on Irish land law. Similarly, in his role as comically utopian prophet of "the new Bloomusalem," as part of the "new era . . . about to dawn," Bloom promises "Three acres and a cow for all children of nature," which, again, is in effect a promise of legislation (*U* 15.1542, 1687). Here Joyce extends broadly nationalist sympathies to include the Jewish outsider, as nationalism too often did not. So, too, in the satire in "Oxen of the Sun" on the narrative voice which places Bloom as a "tenant at will" of "the empire," and thereby fuses imperialism, anti-Semitism, and legal feudalism (*U* 14.911).

What I have called nationalist responses, however, are sometimes less so than they are registrations or perceptions of a state of affairs which are nationalist-oriented. Take for example a grim little sentence from Stephen's meditation on Richie Goulding: "Houses of decay, mine, his and all" (*U* 3.105). At its bottom there is a murky sediment of historical and legal fact. Catholic Ireland often did live in decaying housing for reasons that were inseparable from the legal situation. The law did not require landlords to be responsible for decent upkeep of property. But, as we have seen, there was no point in tenants carrying out works on the properties they inhabited, since landlords could abruptly evict them without paying compensation for any improvements they had made. Stephen is partly noting the melancholy consequences of the political and legal formations at issue here, the material conditions to which they led. So, too, his tendency explicitly and somewhat resentfully to connect Ulstermen with landed interest—Deasy through his family connection with Sir John Blackwood (*U* 2.278–288), George Russell through a sardonic echo of his words "exploitable ground" (*U* 9.106, 272)—partly has its origins, if somewhat distantly, in land law. Why Ulstermen in particular? There were still plenty of southern Anglo-Irish landlords to resent. But the legal situation very much favored Ulster, for in Ulster English common law was operative in matters of land, as in the rest of Ireland it was not. In Ulster the whole system had been modified along English lines, because tenants were often not Irish but "new English," and landlord and tenant would frequently have been fellow soldiers. By the nineteenth century, English-style tenant rights prevailed in Ulster. The landlord class could not only "exploit" the "ground," but do so relatively untroubled. This provided the Ulster landowning class, as it did their tenants, with a kind of assurance that southern landlords and tenants lacked. As Joyce presents them, in their different ways, Deasy and Russell both possess it.

But it is in the matter of Father Cowley's tenancy that the question of property law as seen from the point of view of a disadvantaged Catholic community is most striking. What is in question here is the familiar triangular structure underwritten or at least encouraged by Irish land law: (Protestant) landlord, here the Reverend Hugh C. Love, (Catholic) tenant, and third party, in this instance Reuben J. Dodd, Jewish moneylender. Third parties in property matters were actually of various kinds: landlords' agents, subletters, gombeen men. In one way or another, they were likely to deflect, conceal, and complicate the fundamental legal relation of landlord and tenant and to take its strain. Since the Famine at least, the gombeen man had bridged the economic gap in which injustice had left the tenantry by stepping in to offer it credit, or goods on credit, at inflated rates. Dodd appears to have performed precisely this function for Cowley, and indeed Cowley refers to him as a gombeen man (*U* 10.200).

In "Wandering Rocks" Cowley and his companions are nastily anti-Semitic about Dodd (*U* 10.892, 950). Joyce means them to sound unpleasant. But he is also acutely aware how far this particular expression of anti-Semitism is a function of a colonial structure of which property law is a part. The irony of the situation is that Ben Dollard suggests that Cowley take refuge in the fact that Love has "distrained for rent" (*U* 10.943). This will mean that Dodd's writ against Cowley "is not worth the paper it's printed on," because the landlord "has the prior claim" (*U* 10.945–946). Legally the landlord did indeed have priority over any third party. Nonetheless, ironically, Dollard is inviting Cowley to fall back on the construction of the landlord-tenant relation under Irish law, to exploit the inequity of a colonially determined relation legally fixed in place. With his "refined accent," his genteel antiquarianism, and his interest both in the families of the original Cambro-Norman occupiers of Irish land (the FitzGeralds) and in precise location (*U* 10.415–416), Love is the person who gets off scot-free in all this. But the novel exacts its revenge. There he cannot preserve his immunity. In "Wandering Rocks" he is presented satirically; in "Sirens" Dollard revises his focus, brooding caustically on Love, not Dodd ("Love or money," *U* 10.533–534); and in "Circe" Joyce appropriately identifies Love with Haines (as another "*sentimentalist . . . who would enjoy without incurring the immense debtorship for a thing done,*" *U* 9.550–551), and sticks a carrot up his ass for good measure (*U* 15.4700, 4706). By contrast, "Circe" gives Dodd great Dublin street slang to speak (*U* 15.1922–1923).

If Cowley and the others turn on the wrong person, the third party, the Jew, then Joyce himself rectifies the balance. Here, as in many respects, *Ulysses* is a work of justice, a justice beyond Irish land law as Joyce knew it. The justice it administers, however, is considered, which means that Joyce delimits it. If there is a will to justice in *Ulysses*, there is also a will to freedom, and the second must set limits to the first, because the will to justice always threatens to drag a historical situation back into the unfreedom and the nightmare of continuing historical antagonism. Alongside the nationalist responses to the consequences of Irish land law in *Ulysses*, there is thus also a critique of them, a skepticism as to their integrity, a desire to get them in (comic and ironic) proportion. This is predictably most evident in the citizen, who, for all his nationalism, has apparently seen the legal situation as an opportunity "for grabbing the holding of an evicted tenant," which means he now has "the Molly Maguires looking for him to let daylight through him"—extralegally, of course (*U* 12.1314–1315). So, too, those victims of Irish property law the evicted tenants themselves do not get off lightly in *Ulysses*. In "Circe" the "Irish Evicted Tenants" demand that Bloom undergo an extralegal colonial punishment, if a South African one ("Sjambok him!," *U* 15.1883–84), and in "Eumaeus" the narrator gripes about Parnell's "beloved evicted tenants" having turned on him (*U* 16.1396; cf. 1731). Joyce's point seems clear enough: opposition to Irish land law did not necessarily breed righteous anger and programs of reform. It also went hand in hand with chicanery, vindictiveness, scapegoating, and extralegal violence.

But the point at which Joyce most clearly draws a line under the nationalist engagement with land law comes with Bloom's "ultimate ambition" as described in "Ithaca," the purchase of his "country residence" (*U* 17.1497, 1657). We have been prepared for this by "Eumaeus," where it is already clear that the mature Bloom has modified his youthful nationalist views on Irish property and ownership ("a partiality . . . which, realising his mistake, he was subsequently partially cured of," 16.1590–1591). The passage involves a fantasy of a comfortable, affluent suburban life quite beyond the scope of Joyce's (inner) Dublin. It is a modern life, and its legal basis Bloom and the narrator imagine as being modern, too. Bloom would come into possession of his home precisely *not* by "primogeniture, gavelkind or borough English" (*U* 17.1499), borough English being a custom that transferred the right to inherit to the youngest son, and so was analogous to primogeniture and gavelkind. Nor would he possess his "desmesne" in "perpetuity" (*U* 17.1500). He would rather "purchase [it] by private treaty in fee simple" (*U* 17.1504). Under English law, "fee simple" meant freehold ownership. "Private treaty" meant that vendor and buyer agreed on the price. These are the terms of modern property law in countries with established common law, Both went a long way back in English common law, while remaining comparatively foreign in Ireland. The implication is clearly that it is as well to be indifferent to ancient and deeply rooted colonial antipathies, if what is at stake is modernity or modernization. Bloom would also take out a mortgage. Again, the point is how far modern legal agreements over property outdistance the feudalism that has so crippled Ireland, since Bloom's will include "a saving clause envisaging forced sale, foreclosure and mutual compensation in the event of protracted failure to pay the terms assigned, otherwise the messuage to become the absolute property of the tenant occupier upon expiry of the period of years stipulated" (*U* 17.1667–1671).

Of course, that Bloom's fantasy is so obviously unrealizable (and thus comic) may reduce the weight we might be inclined to give it, and remind us of political and historical circumstances again. But its modernity nonetheless indicates the limits of Joyce's sympathy with any position on Irish land law that takes its bearings from the Irish historical legacy and the passions it has generated alone. In any case, Joyce's last word on the subject is not necessarily the one that seems evident in the "Ithaca" passage. There was a strain in late nineteenth-century nationalist thought about

Irish land that, though allied to the Parnellite and Fenian traditions, was distinct from them. It was socialist, and its sources were British as much as Irish. It went beyond radical nationalists like Lavelle, whose goals ended with fair rents, and who did not challenge tenure. It argued for common Irish ownership of Irish land. As Michael Davitt put matters, the "soil of Ireland" should be "returned to the people of Ireland" (quoted in Cashman 91). Davitt became the most eminent Irish supporter of the cause of land nationalization and legislation promoting State ownership of land.[10] In Ireland, the idea had been current among radical and socialist groups "from at least the 1870s" (King, 40). In England and Scotland, to whose radical groups the Irish ones were often close, it went as far back as the Chartists and beyond.

We should thus underline the fact that, according to "Eumaeus," the young Bloom not only specifically sympathized with "peasant possession," but even went "farther than Michael Davitt" on the issue (*U* 16.1589, 1592). But a certain wistfulness for this radically egalitarian view of property and property law, a position that, probably even by late 1903, Joyce knew he could not strictly maintain, also haunts *Ulysses* as a whole, threads its way fitfully through it, notably perhaps in "Hades," where death is the great leveler and where humanly produced, colossal inequities may seem unreal. "Nobody owns" (*U* 6.333). "The masters of the Mediterranean are fellahin today" (*U* 7.911). In "Lestrygonians," Bloom broods:

> Houses, lines of houses, streets, miles of pavements, piledup bricks, stones. Changing hands. This owner, that. Landlord never dies they say. Other steps into his shoes when he gets his notice to quit. They buy the place up with gold and still they have all the gold. Swindle in it somewhere. Piled up in cities, worn away age after age. Pyramids in sand. . . .
> No-one is anything. (*U* 8.485–493)

The emphasis here is familiar from late nineteenth-century radical and socialist literature. The great American influence on Irish agrarian nationalism Henry George, for example, wrote of the folly of the concept of a "right to possess and to pass on the ownership of things that in their nature decay and soon cease to be" (31). But Joyce puts the point far more compellingly than anyone else. No one is anything, nothing is proper to anyone, no one has anything to own. There is, in the end, no property. Since Joyce himself never owned any, he lived out this truth. Somewhere quite deep beneath the surface of *Ulysses*, in fact, there is an obscure, melancholic dream of the end of property law.

Notes

A version of this essay appeared in *James Joyce Quarterly* 50.4. This revision is reprinted with permission.

1. See O'Curry and O'Donovan's six-volume *Ancient Laws of Ireland*.
2. MacNeill points to some examples of this in *Early Irish Laws and Institutions*.
3. For an example of Joycean parody that aims at both English legalese and Brehon Law, see *U* 12.1115–1140.
4. For arguments to this effect, see Vaughan, *Landlords and Tenants in Mid-Victorian Ireland*.
5. On which see Finlason, 98 and passim.
6. Revisionist historiography questioning this account emerged only in the 1970s and after. For an example of it, see Vaughan, 67–102. Joyce could not have been aware of it.
7. See for example Kenner, *Dublin's Joyce*; Moretti, *The Modern Epic: The World System from Goethe to García Márquez*; and Begnal, *Joyce and the City*.
8. See Clark, 149–79.
9. See for example Daly, 288–92, 315–19. According to Daly, the Corporation repeatedly gave preference to landlord over tenant and public interest. She cites as an example the mayor-to-be who owned a house that collapsed in 1902. It had been previously ruled unsafe by the Sanitation Department, but remained standing (288). Daly concludes that, where housing matters were concerned, the Corporation was "a seriously negligent, perhaps even corrupt institution" (315).
10. See King, 39.

Works Cited

Begnal, Michael, ed. *Joyce and the City: The Significance of Place*. Syracuse, NY: Syracuse University Press, 2002.
Butt, Isaac. *Land Tenure in Ireland: A Plea for the Celtic Race*. Dublin: John Falconer, 1866.
Cashman, D. B. *The Life of Michael Davitt: Founder of the National Land League*. Glasgow: Cameron & Ferguson, 1882.
Clark, Samuel. "The Social Composition of the Land League." *Irish Historical Review* 7.27 (March 1951): 149–79.
Connolly, James. *Workers' Republic*. Edited by Desmond Ryan. Dublin: Three Candles, 1951.
Daly, Mary E. *Dublin, the Deposed Capital: A Social and Economic History, 1860–1914*. Cork: Cork University Press, 1984.
Finlason, W. F. *The History of Law of Tenures of Land in England and Ireland, With Par-*

ticular Reference to Inheritable Tenancy; Leasehold Tenure; Tenancy at Will; and Tenant Right. London: Stevens & Haynes, 1870.

Foster, R. F. *Modern Ireland, 1600–1972*. London: Penguin, 1989.

George, Henry. *The Irish Land Question: What It Involves and How Alone It Can Be Settled: An Appeal to the Land League*. New York: Appleton, 1881.

Jolas, Eugène. "My Friend James Joyce." In *James Joyce: Two Decades of Criticism*, edited by Seon Givens, 3–18. New York: Vanguard, 1948.

Kenner, Hugh. *Dublin's Joyce*. Bloomington: Indiana University Press, 1956.

King, Carla. *Michael Davitt*. Dundalk: Dundalgan Press, for the Historical Association of Ireland, 1999.

Lavelle, Patrick. *The Irish Landlord Since the Revolution*. Dublin: W. B. Kelly, 1870.

Lee, Joseph. *The Modernisation of Irish Society, 1848–1918*. Dublin: Gill & Macmillan, 1973.

MacNeill, Eoin. *Early Irish Laws and Institutions*. Dublin: Burns, Oates & Washbourne, 1935.

Mill, John Stuart. *Principles of Political Economy, with Some of Their Applications to Social Philosophy*. London: John W. Parker, 1848.

Moretti, Franco. *The Modern Epic: The World System from Goethe to García Márquez*. Translated by Quintin Hoare. London: Verso, 1996.

Nicholls, K. W. *Land, Law and Society in Sixteenth-Century Ireland*. Cork: National University of Ireland, 1976.

O'Curry, Eugene, and John O'Donovan, eds. and trans. *Ancient Laws of Ireland*. 6 vols. Dublin: Alexander Thom, 1863–1901.

Vaughan, W. E. *Landlords and Tenants in Mid-Victorian Ireland*. Oxford: Clarendon, 1994.

Wylie, J.C.W. *A Casebook on Irish Land Law*. Abingdon, Oxon.: Professional Books, 1984.

8

Pro Bono Publico

Urban Space in "Cyclops"

ROBERT BRAZEAU

This essay examines the production of public space and codes that circulated around alcohol consumption in turn-of-the-century Ireland. I contend that in "Cyclops" Joyce demonstrates an intimate awareness of the emerging and established judicial and discursive reality that surrounded consumption, and that this knowledge is implicated in subtle and obvious ways in the chapter. Building on this argument, I then offer a reading of how Joyce explicitly figures urban space as an abstraction of relations of power and economic exchange in order to argue that, for Joyce, the city is simultaneously real and abstracted. This argument borrows from the work of Edward Soja and more heavily still from Henri Lefebvre's *The Production of Space*. As Dianne Chisholm and I contend elsewhere, historical changes are only truly historical when they render a change in the design, construction, or administration of space,[1] and Joyce shows, in "Cyclops," a keen interest in how public space is made and remade as new forms of knowledge and authority replace older ones. This, in fact, serves as the abiding thesis of the present essay: space, while it frequently seems a given, is produced by political and cultural codes and by the power/knowledge complex that attempts to write itself into human reality through, among other methods, the spatialization of politics and culture.

In this respect, the approach that I am taking to the text is conversant with an increasingly fertile strand in modernist studies. Whether gathered under the rubric of "alternative modernities" (Goankar) or "geomodernisms" (Doyle and Winkiel) this approach prioritizes the role of geography and the representation of specific, discrete locales in its explication of modern social and political life. Susan Stanford Friedman, one of the most consistent champions of this approach, holds that emphasizing the spatial in our explication of modernity allows critics and historians the opportunity to understand the ways in which modernity unfolds differently in different zones. Borrowing from the geographer Edward Soja, who advocates "a triple dialectic of space, time, and social being" in his "retheorization of the relations between history, geography, and modernity (*PG* 12), Friedman argues for a methodology that would always "spatialize" its inquiries into how modernity emerges as a local phenomena even while it tends to be seen as a global force. A similar interest animates Arif Dirlik's excellent essay "Rethinking Colonialism: Globalization, Postcolonialism, and the Nation." Dirlik avers that "the understanding of colonialism as system has retreated before a situational approach that valorizes contingency and difference over systemic totality" (433). Dirlik is quick to point out the value inherent in thinking about capitalism, imperialism, and modernity as global systems, but also helpfully draws theoretical attention to the merits of thinking through these larger systems in terms of their effects in discrete, local—that is, geographically specific—zones.

More specifically, however, this essay argues that Joyce shows, in "Cyclops," an interest in recent legislation in Ireland (1898 and 1902) that sought to curb the number of pubs that populated the island but, because it was poorly thought through, achieved an effect antonymic to its purpose. The irony is that this legislation by late-colonial authorities attempts to curb behaviors that, "Cyclops" seems to contend, are the result of colonial rule in the first instance. In order to support my claims here I rely on contemporary work by David Lloyd and on the monumental project articulated in Henri Lefebvre's *The Production of Space*. At the center of "Cyclops" are the pub and its role as a cultural and political institution and the codes that go into producing and regulating behaviors in this environment.

As in the short story "Counterparts," Joyce is going to suggest in "Cyclops" a connection between Irish habits around drink consumption and English colonialism. In the earlier story Joyce explicitly connects Farrington's consumption of alcohol to his emasculation in the workplace and, later, in social space. There we see clearly that as a colonized man, Farrington turns to drink to obviate his sense of inefficacy. And there we also see that his alcoholism aggravates rather than alleviates the crisis in masculinity that he experiences. His only outlet for his aggression is in the home, and while Joyce is careful not to paint a sympathetic picture of Farrington—indeed, one of the most compelling aspects of the story is how it remains critical of Farrington and the causes of his behavior at the same time—its interest in the sociological causes of Irish intemperance is of central significance to it.

David Lloyd addresses the damaging overconsumption of alcohol depicted in the story in his essay "Counterparts: *Dubliners*, Masculinity, and Temperance Nationalism." Arguing that forms of alienated labor and subjectivity coalesce in the depiction of Farrington as animated by feelings of humiliation, frustration, rage and violence (193), Lloyd positions the spaces of labor against the presumed soothing rhythms of the pub and the forms of masculinity visible in that environment. Lloyd's argument is persuasive, and I find little with which to argue in it, but here I want to inquire somewhat more specifically into how that space was itself being regulated and administered at the time. Two pieces of legislation passed on either side of the turn of the century are implicated in both "Counterparts" and "Cyclops" and their representation of public space in early twentieth-century Dublin: the Inebriates Act of 1898 and the Licensing Act of 1902.

The first of these pieces of legislation, the Inebriates Act of 1898, offers, with the benefit of historical hindsight, a clear translation of a relatively new way to address an old problem: the emerging discourse of forensic toxicology would quickly isolate alcoholism as a mental ailment, and this new sensibility would find its way into social and legal codes. The Inebriates Act calls for the founding of "inebriate reformatories" throughout England, Scotland, and Ireland, and gives to local authorities the right to incarcerate, for up to three years, anyone who commits a crime in a state of inebriation. While its main thrust is the punishment of criminal wrongdoers, it also provides for the remediation of inebriates through the measure of hospitalization even where their behavior is not implicated in any criminality. In short, the Inebriates Act, prodded by forensic toxicology, evinces an understanding that excessive alcohol consumption is a social problem in need of legal remedy, and it aims to provide exactly this remedy.

While following in clear ways from the ideology underlying the Inebriates Act of 1898, the Licensing Act of 1902 approaches the perceived problems of excessive consumption from another angle. Rather than focusing primarily on the ill effects of consumption and the behavior of the individual consumer, the Licensing Act takes a "city planning" approach to the problem and is suffused by the assumption that spirit consumption in Ireland is exacerbated by the number of pubs in the city. Viewed from the vantage point of basic economics, it would be easy to see that this line of thinking confuses cause for effect: the pubs remain open because people drink, rather than, as the statute would have it, the other way around. Not a logical document by any stretch of the imagination, this act quite clearly shows the difficulty that the colonial administration in Ireland was having in its first serious legal approaches to this fraught social and juridical issue.

The Licensing Act consists of four parts, with the last two being primarily administrative rather than directly legislative. The first part outlines a number of highly specific issues related to drunkenness—being drunk in public while caring for a child, for example, might mean a month in prison—and also declares it illegal for the owner of licensed premises to permit anyone to become intoxicated while on those premises (whether the owner or the premises are licensed is actually a gray area; it appears that the licence was attached to the premises and the owner together). This part also provides for some legal protection from a habitually inebriated spouse. In short, the first section covers a variety of situations where the excessive consumption of alcohol might cause or aggravate some legal problem, and it outlines possible penalties associated with these behaviors. In this, the first section of the 1902 act simply extends the scope of the 1898 act that it is essentially replacing.

As the final section of part I makes clear, the focus of the Licensing Act is on the remaking of public space. The definition—"the expression 'public space' shall include any place to which the public have access, whether on payment or otherwise" (4)—is a broad one, and would appear to cover, with some exceptions, almost any space that is not a private dwelling. Importantly, however, gentleman's clubs were immune from its legislative reach, inscribing a class bias into this piece of legislation, since it does not betray any felt need to change the consumption of alcohol among the wealthier segment of the populace. Military and naval clubs were also beyond the legal purview of the act.

But even as the Licensing Act was clearly directed at curtailing the number of licensed pubs in Ireland, it had what was, in retrospect, a fatal flaw. Part II section 11(4) offers the following limitation on the purview of the act in its clause pertaining to grandfathered licenses:

> On any application for the renewal of a licence for the sale by retail of intoxicating liquors to be consumed on the premises, the licensing justices may require a plan of the premises to be produced before them, and to be deposited with their clerk, and on renewing any such licence they may, by order, direct that, within a time fixed by the order, such alterations as they think reasonably necessary to secure the proper conduct of the business shall be made.

What is being stipulated here, and later in section II.16(1–4), is the condition under which a retired licence can be sold and reactivated even where the new premises would fall within one statute mile of an existing pub. This legislative proviso would have been absolutely necessary, of course, because when any property is sold, it is sold with certain zoning restrictions and affordances, and those become an important part of the value of the property. In an obvious example, if someone were to buy a house simply to live in it, the zoning attached to the property would likely be of little import. However, if someone wanted to buy a property in order to live in it and run a beauty salon or law office out of it, then they would do well to look for a property that is already zoned for those uses. In the case of liquor licenses in Ireland at this time, even where a license had been effectively dormant, it remained as a value attached to the property and could, therefore, be sold or reactivated by the existing owner or any new owner. The Circuit Court, to which such applications would have been made in 1902, reserved the right to insist on changes to the existing property, but the act seems to curtail the authority of even that court, since nowhere does it suggest that a licence would not be granted to the new or existing owner of a dormant licence.

In practice the act caused a number of people to sell or reactivate dormant licenses and thereby significantly increased the number of pubs in City Centre in the years immediately following its inception. In fact, the current pubscape of Dublin owes its profile largely to the 1902 act and the proliferation of pubs that it caused. It is worth pointing out that the Licensing Act was in place for almost six decades, and its replacement, the Intoxicating Liquor Act of 1960, only modestly reworks it, so a significant component of how public space was configured in late-colonial Dublin issues directly from the 1902 act.

As Lloyd argues in the case of "Counterparts" and Joyce is intimating in "Cyclops," Irish habits around drink are in part produced by colonial domination, so the attempt to confront the condition with more domination (and the 1902 act is representative of just this) is more likely to exacerbate than alleviate the problem. Furthermore, that the government's action actually leads to more pubs opening is the final and, for Joyce, farcical irony of this obviously failed piece of legislation. It would be one thing if this poorly thought-through law missed the mark and simply left things as they were, but the fact that it directly causes an increase in the number of pubs in Dublin points to the fundamental disconnect between the beliefs of the ruling class and the behavior of the populace at large.

The history of the 1902 act is relevant to our reading of "Cyclops" because in this chapter Joyce is keenly attentive to the forces going into the production of public space and culture in late-colonial Ireland. Moreover, the chapter exhibits a keen interest in the specific mechanisms by which space is brought into being and rendered discrete from other spaces or zones in the city. The sense that space is both constructed and policed in "Cyclops," or rather that it is only constructed by the persistent policing of codes and practices, is suggested throughout the chapter but is emphasized in our earliest introduction to the Citizen.[2] As Joe Hynes and the narrator enter the pub, the Citizen greets them:

—Stand and deliver, says he.
—That's all right, citizen, says Joe. Friends here.
—Pass, friends, says he. (12.129–131)

Space and identity are seen to be mutually constitutive and are formed in the act of crossing the border that separates the inside of the pub from the the city proper. The Citizen's oath to the men is parodic in that he does not literally have the power to disallow entry to the pub, but the point of the exchange is to suggest that some form of perceived connection, here attached to a sense of a shared cultural bond, is a requirement for entry into this specific space.

We see something similar in the later passage where the Citizen notices Bloom pacing back and forth in front of Barney Kiernan's, agitatedly waiting for Martin Cunningham to arrive. Bloom, it appears, is hesitant to enter the pub, and there is little doubt that his past has conditioned him to understand that he will be treated as an outsider in this space. Rather than subject himself to such treatment, he would rather wait for the group outside. This behavior, of course, catches the Citizen's attention:

> —There he is again, says the citizen, staring out.
> —Who? says I.
> —Bloom, says he. He's on point duty up and down there for the last ten minutes.
> And begob, I saw his physog do a peep in and then slidder off again. (12.377–381)

The description is a compelling one. Not only is Bloom's presence couched, as was the oath, in militaristic terms—he is on "point duty"—but, I would argue, there is a sense that a somewhat firmer boundary is in play for both Bloom and the Citizen than the actual or material constraints would suggest. All I mean by this is that Bloom is literally free to enter the pub and the Citizen has no practical authority to prevent this. However, Bloom clearly understands that some other, less tangible prohibition is affecting how freely he feels he can move through the different spaces of the city. In this, Joyce demonstrates an interest in how both space and ideology are constructed via a process of inclusion and exclusion. Bloom is an outsider, and as such his outsider status has to be rendered against an inside. Similarly, ideologies construct themselves simultaneously at the core and periphery of their worldviews, by articulating a sense of belonging that is also a sense of the non-belonging of the other. The Citizen notices Bloom on the sidewalk in part because he is aware that both the pub itself and his worldview are constituted by what they exclude, by what they hold or at least attempt to hold at their boundaries, and this militaristic terminology helps us to understand the affective depth of what is being negotiated here between the Citizen and Bloom even before their confrontation.

As Edward Soja remarks, the presence of a regime of regulation is integral not only to how space is formed in the first instance but also to how space is organized politically. Soja enumerates three important aspects of what he calls "the political organization of space":

1. Control over the distribution, allocation, and ownership of scarce resources (including land, money, and power—the ability to make authoritative decisions). This is largely a coordinative or administrative function aimed at satisfying the needs of society as a whole.
2. The maintenance of order and the enforcement of authority. This function revolves around the resolution of conflict both within and between societies.
3. The legitimation of authority through societal integration. Here the emphasis is on the creation and maintenance of institutions and behavior patterns which promote group unity and cohesion. (*PO* 7)

And Soja adds the following summary to this very helpful list:

> The political organization of space therefore functions within societies primarily as a means of structuring interaction between its component units (individuals and groups). Its major purpose is to create and maintain solidarity within the society by shaping the processes of competition, conflict, and cooperation as they operate spatially. (*PO* 7)

Lastly, but importantly for our purposes, Soja clarifies that this sense of "solidarity" is achieved largely through the operations of kinship and culture: "Kinship relations thus create bonds not only through blood ties but also as a primary vehicle of culture, which in turn helps cement the society through language and tradition" (*PO* 8).[3]

This brief précis of Soja's informative essay goes a long way toward helping us unpack the earliest moments of encounter between Bloom and the Citizen. As the chapter develops, however, the difference and distance between the two is not only transacted on the level of the physical and spatial but, of course, on the level of the cultural. As Soja makes clear, the terrain of culture is one of the important ways in which the spatial comes into being in the first instance, and where a physical, spatial boundary can no longer be maintained, the power to police inclusion and exclusion devolves to an apparatus of culture. "Cyclops" quite meticulously registers the shift from one to the other as Bloom transgresses the affective boundary between the street and the pub. That is, when the distance in space between the Citizen and Bloom collapses, the cultural distance between them, at least as it is understood by the Citizen, carries the weight of policing identity. "Cyclops" contains numerous references to how the differences between

Bloom and the Citizen are articulated, and as they are not central to my present inquiry into the production of space, I will offer only a brief gloss on the most significant of these. Most of the characters in the chapter mark Bloom's presumed Jewishness with some form of anti-Semitic utterance, but the narrator and the Citizen are most egregious in this regard. While many critics have offered extended arguments on this topic, Neil Levi's reading of the complexity that Bloom brings to the social relations that are established (or are establishing themselves) in the chapter is perhaps the most compelling. For Levi,

> "the Jew" as imagined by modern anti-Semitism solves the problem of finding a concrete embodiment, or, more precisely, a *personification*, for powerful social and economic forces that otherwise lack a material manifestation. The Jew serves to personify processes within finance capital that have no concrete manifestation, that are quite literally *unrepresentable*. (376)

I will return to Levi's essay in just a moment, but suffice it to say here that Bloom's Jewishness marks him as culturally different from the other men in the chapter. This discourse reaches its most disturbing apex in the imputation of contagion that the Citizen levels at Bloom: "Saint Patrick would want to land again at Ballykinlar and convert us, says the citizen, after allowing things like that to contaminate our shores" (12.1671–1672).[4]

However, this is not the only way in which Bloom is marked as the other in "Cyclops." His abstemiousness marks him as different from the Citizen (and other men in the pub), as do his liberal humanism and relatively modern social and philosophical views. However, Joyce is careful to show the broader operation of a culture of masculinity forming around the rituals of alcohol consumption (and Bloom's lack of belonging to it) rather than the more straightforward difference between Bloom and the Citizen. So it is not the Citizen but Joe Hynes who is featured in the following important exchange with Bloom:

> ... And says Joe:
> —Could you make a hole in another pint?
> —Could a swim duck? says I.
> —Same again, Terry, says Joe. Are you sure you won't have anything in the way of liquid refreshment? says he.
> —Thank you, no, says Bloom. (12.755–760)

Interestingly, Hynes places the order for drinks before asking Bloom if he will have one, which possibly suggests that he knows the answer before extending the offer. It may also be the case that Hynes feels the need to go further than the others might in his attempts to include Bloom because he is mindful that he owes Bloom money and that Bloom sees him standing drinks.[5]

I want to return here, briefly, to one of the aspects of Soja's definition that was not addressed in my previous look into the formation of culture as implicated in the production of space in the chapter and which is, in my view, central to a thorough-going reading of Joyce's representation of how space signifies in "Cyclops." Soja remarks that "the major purpose" of the political organization of space is to shape "processes of competition, conflict, and cooperation" (7). Where divergent interests operate within the same spatial context, the organization of that space will take place around the imperative to mediate these moments of competition or conflict. In "Cyclops," what we come to see is that the hostility directed at Bloom, primarily by the Citizen, functions to cover schisms, some of which are deep, some of which are relatively minor, between the other men, all of whom are engaged in forms of competition, cooperation, and, later in the chapter, conflict. In the parlance of "Cyclops" itself, we could call the overt conflict between Bloom and the Citizen a "blind" to deflect (or partially deflect) our attention from the other forms of conflict in the chapter. The narrator, for example, lets slip that the Citizen might be grabbing land in rural Ireland, which would mean that he is capitalizing on the misfortune of his countrymen; this would render his overt nationalism yet another "blind" to cover his exploitative behavior:[6]

> And he took the last swig out of the pint. Moya. All wind and piss like a tanyard cat. Cows in Connacht have long horns. As much as his bloody life is worth to go down and address his tall talk to the assembled multitude in Shanagolden where he daren't show his nose with the Molly Maguires looking for him to let daylight through him for grabbing the holding of an evicted tenant. (12.1311–1316)

Land-grabbing here constitutes yet another way in which forms of economic competition are played out in the register of the spatial. In fact, it represents a way in which space and spatial consciousness are constructed as an object of economic and political contest. The narrator in "Cyclops" appears to side with the Citizen in overt ways, but we are aware that a deeper sense of conflict and competition resides at the core of their relationship. What is compelling in "Cyclops" is that the proximity in space of the two in Barney Kiernan's requires that this potential for antagonism between them be either sublated or redirected at another. In this case, that other is Bloom. And this complex of competition and sublation is one of the important networks of affiliation and contest that organize the spatial in this chapter. Etienne Balibar has argued that a characteristic component of nationalism is exactly the drive to either understate or obliterate personal difference within the culture so that "it is the symbolic difference between 'ourselves' and 'foreigners' which wins out and which is irreducible" (94). In "Cyclops," Joyce never quite lets the differences between the men in the pub collapse, and therefore the attempt to mark Bloom as wholly other never quite succeeds.

What makes unpacking this network of association, conflict, and competition of greater moment in "Cyclops" is that, as we move toward the hostile confrontation between Bloom and the Citizen, we are going to see not only that the attribution of subterfuge and secrecy that ultimately lands on Bloom is misplaced (he has not bet on the race, so has not won anything) but that such behavior is, as I have been arguing, more characteristic of the other men in the pub, all of whom are engaging in forms of secret competition and conflict under the guise of overt conviviality:

—Don't tell anyone, says the citizen.
—Beg your pardon, says he.
—Come on boys, says Martin, seeing it was looking blue. Come along now.
—Don't tell anyone, says the citizen, letting a bawl out of him. It's a secret.
And the bloody dog woke up and let a growl. (12.1762–1766)

Secrets and blinds abound here. The men in the pub, pretending to share similar views and values, secretly compete and connive, while Bloom, who is keeping nothing of significance from anyone, is disparaged as a hypocrite and dissembler. It is central to the chapter that the confines of the pub render necessary these forms of affiliation and contest. But even that is not correct: in the context of "Cyclops" the place called "the pub" is not demarcated by the walls and objects found in 8, 9, and 10 Little Britain

Street; rather, "the pub" is the name that is given to the networks, relationships, inscriptions of subjectivity, and forms of belonging or rejection that dominate within that environment and organize the flow of goods and information.

The view that space is primarily organized by flows of goods, people, and information, and the concomitant assertion that it is simultaneously real and abstract, is at the center of Henri Lefebvre's monumental work *The Production of Space*. Public space, as Lefebvre argues, is not public space because that is where the preexisting body called the public can meet but, rather, is such because a sense of what constitutes public being writes itself into the codes and institutions that dominate in that environment. Public space is produced by cultural codes that cohere around gender and sexuality, class, race, and around more subtle social indicators as well (manliness and sexuality are related but also very different, of course). Space is produced, according to Lefebvre, via a series of social relationships that are conditioned by the spaces in which they occur but then also work, reciprocally, to define and redefine any space. This lengthy passage from Lefebvre offers a very good sense of his definition of urban space:

> The form of social space is encounter, assembly, simultaneity. But what assembles, or what is assembled? The answer is: everything that there is *in space*, everything that is produced either by nature or by society, either through their co-operation or through their conflicts. Everything: living beings, things, objects, works, signs and symbols. Natural space juxtaposes—and thus disperses: it puts places and that which occupies them side by side. It particularizes. By contrast, social space implies actual or potential assembly at a single point, or around that point. It implies, therefore, the possibility of accumulation (a possibility that is realized under specific conditions).... Urban space gathers crowds, products in the markets, acts and symbols. It concentrates all these, and accumulates them. To say "urban space" is to say centre and centrality. (101)

The pub is, of course, one such space of accumulation, where a network of meanings forms and reforms in elastic ways that are nevertheless guided by a set of codes that are more or less agreed upon by the regular denizens of the pub. That Bloom fails to master these codes is obvious, but that they can be mastered is equally so, since both Martin Cunningham and others seem to navigate the demands put to Irish masculinity in this habitus with fluency and ease. Cunningham is aware, for example, that merely entering the pub requires him to have a "half one" (12.1668–1670) and it is also Cunningham, later, who senses that the Citizen is on the verge of violence against Bloom (12.1764). In both cases we see Cunningham adroitly read and decode the cues in this highly dense semiotic space.

Lefebvre's explication of space, especially urban space, emphasizes the role of the established and spontaneous networks that form within the city. He alludes to this aspect of space relatively early in the same chapter where he remarks that "social space contains a great diversity of objects, both natural and social, including the networks and pathways which facilitate the exchange of material things and information. Such 'objects' are thus not only things but also relations" (77). Indeed, as the analysis continues, Lefebvre becomes increasingly attentive to the consequences that ensue from the assumption that space is defined by the production and flow of information in casually forming networks. It is helpful to quote Lefebvre at length:

> So-called social reality is dual, multiple, plural. To what extent, then, does it furnish a reality at all? If reality is taken in the sense of materiality, social reality no longer has reality, nor is it reality. On the other hand, it contains and implies some terribly concrete abstractions (including, as cannot be too often emphasized, money, commodities, and the exchange of material goods), as well as "pure" forms: exchange, language, signs, equivalences, reciprocities, contracts, and so on.
>
> According to Marx (and no one who has considered the matter at all has managed to demolish this basic analytical premise), merely to note the existence of things, whether specific objects or "the object" in general, is to ignore what things at once embody and dissimulate, namely social relations and the forms of those relations. (81)

Arguably we are, with this passage, very close to understanding a central premise of Joyce's articulation of public space in "Cyclops." The chapter works steadily to keep our attention on the mode of relation that forms between the denizens of the pub and how those relations are nurtured or spoiled as they are realized as a product of the flow of information and commodities. To put this somewhat differently, what Joyce has us focus on in the context of "Cyclops" is the abstractions and exchanges that form reality as well as the reality they bring into being. The ontologically "real" materiality of the pub never fully recedes in the face of the depiction of the abstractions, but the chapter is complicated by this dual drive to explore both the space that is produced and the forces going into its production.

These relations, especially as they explicitly serve to facilitate the flow of information, are central to the depiction of pub culture in the chapter. And, importantly, as we saw in the first half of this essay, the city itself is formed via the negotiation of similarly intangible relationships between the imperial government and the Irish citizenry. All space becomes formed within a network of social relations, and the challenge of assessing the role and operation of these networks resides in keeping attention on the abstractions around which the ontologically real becomes formed rather than falling into a descriptive or unproblematic stance that takes space as a given or that prioritizes its material (rather than abstract) manifestation.

I want to conclude this essay by discussing two important scenes from near the end of the chapter which, I think, draw out compelling aspects of the arguments about space made by Lefebvre and which also point us to the fact that Joyce is attentive to the abstract quality of social space. The first immediately precedes the often-quoted passage where Bloom is asked to define what constitutes a nation. In a way that is revelatory in the context of this discussion, part of the difficulty he experiences in that task derives from his inability to locate an abstraction (the nation) within the confines of an ontologically given terrain. The nation is, above all, a set of codes and relations, networks and ideas about itself, rather than an easily construed material or ontological given. But the section I want to draw attention to comes immediately before this, and contains the only usage of the word "space" in all of "Cyclops":

> —Well, says J. J. We have Edward the peacemaker now.
> —Tell that to a fool, says the citizen. There's a bloody sight more pox than pax about that boyo. Edward Guelph-Wettin!
> —And what do you think, says Joe, of the holy boys, the priests and bishops of Ireland doing up his room in Maynooth in His Satanic Majesty's racing colours and sticking up pictures of all the horses his jockeys rode. The earl of Dublin, no less.
> —They ought to have stuck up all the women he rode himself, says little Alf.

And says J. J.:
—Considerations of space influenced their lordships' decision. (12.1399–1408)⁷

Typographically, the final punch line is set apart from the text, perhaps to punctuate its elocutionary flair somewhat more effectively. However, it also calls attention to itself sitting under the initials "J. J." which here refer directly to J. J. O'Molloy but also throughout "Cyclops" refer, perhaps, to Joyce himself. Is this yet another Cyclopean blind, or does it signal Joyce's attempt to insert something closer to his own presence within the epistemological space of "Cyclops"?⁸ What is especially compelling about the use of the initials "J. J." here rather than the full "J. J. O'Molloy" is that the punch line draws specific attention to the organization and administration of space, the "consideration of space" that dominates the chapter itself.

However, it is in a later passage that the fullness of the abstraction that social space represents is brought more acutely into focus—specifically by the reference late in the chapter to the destruction of the city caused by the paramilitary fighting during the Easter Rising and the War of Independence.⁹ Guerrilla combat on city streets and shelling from British ships on the Liffey represent another, more brutal, method by which space is made and remade in the city of Dublin, and Joyce refuses to shy away from the images of colonial domination and its effect on the space of the city in "Cyclops." As Bloom is chased out of the pub by the Citizen and Garryowen, with the Citizen throwing a biscuit tin at him, we read:

> The catastrophe was terrific and instantaneous in its effect. The observatory of Dunsink registered in all eleven shocks, all of the fifth grade of Mercalli's scale, and there is no record extant of a similar seismic disturbance in our island since the earthquake of 1534, the year of the rebellion of Silken Thomas. The epicentre appears to have been that part of the metropolis which constitutes the Inn's Quay ward and parish of Saint Michan covering a surface of forty-one acres, two roods and one square pole or perch. All the lordly residences in the vicinity of the palace of justice were demolished and that noble edifice itself, in which at the time of the catastrophe important legal debates were in progress, is literally a mass of ruins beneath which it is to be feared all the occupants have been buried alive. (12.1858–1869)

According to the British Geographical Survey, there was indeed an earthquake felt in Ireland in 1534. While its epicenter was near Denbighshire in northern Wales, the quake achieved a maximum power of 4.5 on the Richter scale and was felt in Dublin.[10] The reference to Silken Thomas forges a connection between the spatial and the geopolitical that unites much of what we read in "Cyclops" regarding the ideology of political nationalism and the production of space in Dublin. The allusion to Thomas's rebellion functions in many ways here, since it is largely credited by historians with effectively forcing Henry VIII to pay greater attention to Irish affairs, especially after 1533 and the first fissures in his relationship with the Catholic Church, which led to the attenuation of his support among Catholics in Ireland. As R. Dudley Edwards asserts, "not until this period had any of the Anglo-Irish ever taken arms, in conjunction with the Irish, against the king" (687). As well, the short-lived and unsuccessful rebellion was a significant historical prompt behind the passage of yet another statute that figures largely in Irish history: the Kingdom of Ireland Act (1542). Joyce, it appears, is nothing if not thorough in his recondite allusive universe, connecting the violence of the Anglo-Irish War with the earlier uprising, and seeing both the historical and what, in 1904, would have been the future (1920) as joined along a continuum.

In this, space comes to clearly show its abstract underpinnings, and material or ontological reality recedes in the face of trajectories of continuity between past and future. The city is not the collection of objects, people, and places that we encounter in a day, but is rather formed in a set of abstract economic, political, and social relations that are always in a state of becoming or derealization that defies the presumed solidity or materiality of urban space. The city, then, is an abstraction formed in the commingling of relations of power, allegiance, competition, and conflict. While space does not permit a thorough reading of the relationship between the interchapters and the diegetic text of "Cyclops," it could be argued effectively that the interchapters serve to attenuate the view of the city as ontological space and, again, draw out the abstract properties of the urban: the interchapter revolving around "the land of holy Michan" (12.68–99), for example, grafts history and codes constituent of Catholic belief onto the urban geography in, I contend, an effort to loosen the hold of the material or ontological in our cognition of the spatial and urban. Indeed, the language in the passage referring to Thomas's rebellion would be just as appropriate for one of the interchapters, and at the end of "Cyclops" Joyce can be seen to collapse the distinction between the two. As well, it is worth pointing out that Joyce the geographer is, in both the interchapter regarding St. Michan's and the later passage regarding the rebellion of Silken Thomas, insisting on a reading of the past and the future that explicitly spatializes its historical enquiry, and in this respect shows a keen interest in the city as a fluid, shifting space where power forms and reforms the urban surrounding. For Joyce, it seems, and I do not mean this to sound glib, a continuum connects wrongheaded and unsuccessful statutes like the Licensing Act of 1902 and the destruction that occurred during the Rising, and in both cases the text on which this program of oppression is written is the material city itself and the physical spaces that compose it.

Walter D. Mignolo has argued persuasively that modernity could not come into being in the way we understand it without coloniality. The latter, Mignolo claims, is something like the outer husk of the former—that part of modernity that it would like to disavow but which was, in every way, its enabling historical circumstance: "Coloniality . . . is the hidden face of modernity and its very condition of possibility" (722). According to Mignolo, Western modernity consolidates an image of itself that "exhibits chronological movement" (722) as it advances from premodernity into a rational and always improving future, but in order to succeed in this, it must repress its own dubious origins in the colonial enterprise. By focusing his and our attention on space, Joyce brackets the fiction of temporal and cultural progress that is constituent within English colonial modernity in Ireland in order to reveal its deeper stratifications and self-defeating delusions. For Joyce, the distant past and the near future, as they converge in Dublin's City Centre, and as they fold themselves into urban spatial formations, reveal the failures of a coloniality that is often repressed within modernity's gleeful self-understanding. Of equal importance to our reading of "Cyclops," Joyce evinces a keen awareness of the demands that political nationalism makes on subjects to repress difference in support of a group identity that is shown to be fractious and flawed. Viewed in this way, "Cyclops" becomes an oddly affirmative celebration of the failure of these discourses that would seek to dominate from above by the forces that insist from below.

Notes

A version of this essay appeared in *James Joyce Quarterly* 50.4. This revision is reprinted with permission.

1. See Chisholm and Brazeau, introduction to *Journal of Urban History* special issue "The Other City."

2. I capitalize the word "Citizen" when referring to this character despite the fact that Joyce does not do so in *Ulysses*. Where I quote from the text and the character's name is included in the passage cited, I retain Joyce's spelling.

3. It should be noted that Soja himself does not seriously credit the notion of literal "blood ties" as the primary conduit of a sense of social cohesion. Rather, he argues that even where this sense of direct kinship is only imagined, it nevertheless remains powerfully operative.

4. Note as well that the Citizen's view is phrased in terms of a lost, ideal community. Jean-Luc Nancy explores this aspect of the discourse of nationalism in his essay "The Inoperative Community": "We should become suspicious of the retrospective consciousness of the lost community and its identity (whether this consciousness conceives of itself as effectively retrospective or whether, disregarding the realities of the past, it constructs images of this past for the sake of an ideal or a prospective vision)" (10).

5. It is unlikely that there is any genuine fondness between Hynes and Bloom, since it is Hynes who uses the derogatory term "Shylock" to refer to the mortgager of Dignam's life insurance policy at 12.766. The use of the term, or the fact that it comes from Hynes (or both), seems to throw Bloom somewhat, as evidenced by his mistaken use of "admirers" for "advisers" at 12.767–769.

6. It would also complicate his later condemnation of Bloom as "swindling the peasants . . . and the poor of Ireland" (12.1150).

7. It is worth noting, here, the elision between the "sticking up" of pictures of the horses and the violence suggested in sticking up the actual women, as Alf Bergan suggests. A reading of the gender dynamic that works its way through the chapter is beyond the scope of the present essay but will be offered in a subsequent analysis of "Cyclops."

8. There is a compelling example of this earlier in the chapter as well, when we read the following, offered as it is in an almost offhand way: "And J. J. and the citizen arguing about law and history with Bloom sticking in an odd word" (12.1235–1236).

9. An earlier reference to the Croke Park Massacre of 1920 is also found in "Cyclops," at 12.869–871, and this is another allusion that ties together the policing of behavior and space, of course.

10. See the UK Historical Earthquake Database at www.earthquakes.bgs.ac.uk/historical/.

Works Cited

Balibar, Etienne. "The Nation Form: History and Ideology." In *Race, Nation, Class*, edited by Etienne Balibar and Immanuel Wallerstein, translated by Chris Turner, 86–106. London: Verso, 1999.

Chisholm, Dianne, and Robert Brazeau. Introduction to "The Other City: (De)Mystifying Urban Culture," special issue, *Journal of Urban History* 29.1 (2002): 1–4.
Dirlik, Arif. "Rethinking Colonialism: Globalization, Postcolonialism, and the Nation." *Interventions* 4.3 (2002): 428–48.
Doyle, Laura, and Laura Winkiel, eds. *Geomodernisms: Race, Modernism, Modernity*. Bloomington: Indiana University Press, 2005.
Edwards, R. Dudley. "Venerable John Travers and the Rebellion of Silken Thomas." *Studies: An Irish Quarterly Review* 23.92 (1934): 687–99.
Friedman, Susan Stanford. "Planetarity: Musing Modernist Studies." *Modernism/modernity* 17.3 (2010): 471–99.
Gaonkar, Dilip Parameshwar. *Alternative Modernities*. Durham, NC: Duke University Press, 2001.
Joyce, James. *Ulysses*. Edited by Hans Walter Gabler. New York: Random House, 1986.
Lefebvre, Henri. *The Production of Space*. Translated by Donald Nicholson-Smith. Cambridge: Blackwell, 1991.
Levi, Neil. "'See That Straw? That's a Straw': Anti-Semitism and Narrative Form in *Hello,*" *Modernism/modernity* 9.3 (2002): 375–88.
Lloyd, David. "Counterparts: *Dubliners*, Masculinity, and Temperance Nationalism." In *Future Crossings: Literature between Philosophy and Cultural Studies*, edited by Krzysztof Ziarek and Seamus Deane, 193–220. Evanston, IL: Northwestern University Press, 2000.
Mignolo, Walter D. "The Many Faces of Cosmo-polis: Border Thinking and Critical Cosmopolitanism." *Public Culture* 12.3 (2000): 721–48.
Nancy, Jean-Luc. "The Inoperative Community." In *The Inoperative Community*, edited by Peter Connor, 1–42. Minneapolis: University of Minnesota Press, 1991.
Soja, Edward W. *The Political Organization of Space*. Washington: Association of American Geographers, Commission on College Geography, 1971.
———. *Postmodern Geographies: The Reassertion of Space in Critical Social Theory*. London: Verso, 1989.

PART III

Joyce's Legal Languages
and Sources

9

"Eating orangepeels in the park"

Largesse, Libel, and Public Action in *Ulysses*

ANNE MARIE D'ARCY

> I gave bax of biscums to the jacobeaters and pottage bakes to the esausted
>
> FW 542.29–30

That the public response to Queen Victoria's final visit to Dublin (4–26 April 1900) made an indelible impression on Joyce is borne out by his frequent recollection of the event in his writings: from his 1907 lecture, delivered at the Università Popolare in Trieste and generally entitled "Ireland: Island of Saints and Sages" in English, to some oblique references in *Ulysses* and *Finnegans Wake* which have hitherto been overlooked. The visit, although apparently hastily convened, had a thoroughgoing imperialist agenda which sought to celebrate, in the face of "the possibility of Irish political autonomy or devolution" (*U* 17.759–760), the centenary of the passing of the Acts of Union (Union with Ireland Act 1800 (39&40 Geo.3 c.67) of the Parliament of Great Britain, and the Act of Union (Ireland) 1800 (40 Geo.3 c.38) of the Parliament of Ireland), while also acknowledging the Irish contribution to the (Second) Anglo-Boer War of 1899–1902, most notably through the formation of the Irish Guards regiment on 1 April 1900. In this context, it is no accident that the motto adopted by the Irish Guards, *Quis separabit*, is that of the "true blue" (*U* 2.275) Volunteers of the eighteenth century, which became in turn the motto of the Order of Saint Patrick, or as Joyce puts it in *Finnegans Wake*, "the quis separabits"

(*FW* 255.35).¹ Moreover, the close association between the establishment of the Irish Guards and the Irish contribution to the British war effort was embodied in the appointment of Field-Marshal Frederick Sleigh Roberts, first Earl Roberts of Kandahar, Pretoria, and Waterford, as first colonel of the regiment. Roberts had taken "Bloemfontein" (*U* 15.796) on 13 March 1900, then Johannesburg and the rest of the Transvaal, before returning to Britain in December, whereupon he was created earl. The intense pride felt by Dublin's Protestant middle classes in the Irish provenance of "Bobs" and his newly formed regiment, as recognized in Queen Victoria's visit, is recalled with bitter irony by Joyce in the name of Mina Purefoy's son, "darling little Bobsy (called after our famous hero of the South African war, lord Bobs of Waterford and Candahar)" (*U* 14.1331–1332). Bobsy's happy infancy provides a notable contrast to the thousands of Boer infants who died in the first concentration camps of the modern age.² This telling detail reminds us that these camps were engendered by "the genius of two commanders, Lord Roberts and Lord Kitchener," whom Joyce ironically claims as "Irish" (*OCPW* 117) in his Trieste lecture.³ Indeed, it is equally ironic that even though she has lost a child in infancy, Molly Bloom is blind to the possibility that the creator of any "concentration camp" is "a deathsman of the soul" (*U* 9.130-135). However, she is aware that "singing the absent-minded beggar and wearing a brooch for Lord Roberts" (*U* 18.377–378) have cost her dearly in terms of the middle class, albeit predominantly Catholic, nationalist circles she moves in, at least since her marriage.

Perhaps the most striking feature of Joyce's initial recollection of Queen Victoria's visit is how curiously divergent it is from the "endless streets full of enthusiastic people" described in her diary and in such contemporary newspapers as the *Times* and the *Irish Times*, if not the *Freeman's Journal* (Victoria's diary quoted in Murphy 286). Joyce points out that the British war effort "needed recruits and volunteers from Ireland to demonstrate the now-famous valour in the field in whose recognition the English government allowed the Irish regiments to carry the three-leafed emblem of Irish patriotism on St Patrick's Day. In fact, the queen came to win the easy sympathy of the country and to increase the lists of recruiting sergeants" (*OPCW* 117). Commenting on her entry to Dublin, which is later parodied in the "Circe" episode of *Ulysses*, Joyce notes the "Officials and their wives, unionist clerks and their wives, tourists and their wives," who "stood on decorated balconies, and when the procession appeared, they began to shout greetings and wave handkerchiefs." By contrast, "the crowd watched the sumptuous procession and its sad central figure with eyes of curiosity, almost pity,

> When the carriage passed by, they followed its wake with ambiguous glances. This time there were no bombs or cabbages, but the queen of England entered the capital of Ireland in the midst of a silent people. (*OCPW* 118)

Yet Joyce was aware of the metaphorical bomb that exploded on 7 April 1900 in the *United Irishman* in the form of an article by "Maud Gonne, beautiful woman" (*U* 3.233) denouncing the royal visit. The imminent appearance of this article during the queen's visit precipitated a search of Bernard Doyle's printing works at 9 Upper Ormond Quay by Inspector John Lowe and Sergeant Robert Montgomery of "the G division" (*U* 16.133) and the subsequent seizure of this edition on the eve of publication on the grounds it was "calculated to produce dissent, disaffection, and disloyalty."[4] As in the case of the first suppression of the *United Irishman* on 7 February 1900, copies of this edition were also seized in the post by order of "the Lord Lieutenant," as Gonne surmised, and as evinced by the newspaper wrappers transferred from the Chief Secretary's Library, Dublin Castle, to the National Library of Ireland in 1921 (Gonne and Yeats 128:83, 482:83n1). Gonne's article had originally appeared on 1 April 1900 as "La reine de la disette" in "a special Queen's no of *l'Irlande libre*" (Gonne and Yeats 122:73). This was a monthly journal she had established in Paris in 1897 to commemorate the centenary of the 1798 rebellion under the umbrella of the Boulangist paper, *la Patrie*, published by her lover "M. Millevoye" (*U* 3.233).[5] Translated into English as "The Famine Queen," the article not only elicited the second suppression of the *United Irishman* but also served as catalyst to the criminal libel case taken by Gonne against Ramsay Colles: the proprietor, publisher, and editor of a "very loyal" society journal, the *Irish Figaro* (formerly the *Dublin Figaro*) (Wade 339).

In addition to his professed occupation of journalist, Richard William Colles (1862–1919), better known by his pen name, "Ramsay Colles, M.A., LL.D., J.P., M.R.I.A, F.R. Hist. S., F.R.S.L., F.R.S.A.I, etc.," was a self-styled "leader of thought" and "one of the brightest intellects in the kingdom," as his long-running advertisement for Phosferine, "the greatest of all tonics," proclaimed. In addition to being the Irish representative of the Maha Bodhi Society, he was a committed Freemason, being an erstwhile member of the Duke of York Lodge, No. 25, which included Lord Roberts and Lord Kitchener, as he is keen to point out in his "frankly egotistical" memoir, published in 1911 (Colles 265). Here, he echoes the Purefoys' admiration for Roberts in *Ulysses*, and Colles was, in fact, related to the Irish branch of the Purefoy family, who were seated in Leicestershire from at least the thirteenth century, settling in Ireland as good "Williamites" (*U* 12.1380).[6] Like the Purefoys in *Ulysses*, Colles was "well connected" to "Dublin Castle" (*U* 8.361–362) and entirely familiar with the workings of "the Treasury Remembrancer's office" (*U* 14.1335), which was a byword for the imperialist attitude toward the finances of Ireland.[7] Indeed, it was rumored that Colles acted as an informant, "drawing secret service pay from the castle" (*U* 8.444), and that the *Irish Figaro* "was subsidised by Dublin Castle" (Gonne 201). In 1896 he became a justice of the peace, that is, a borough magistrate appointed under the 1808 Dublin Police Magistrates Act (48 Geo.3. c.140). However, he remained no stranger to litigation in his capacity as publisher and journalist, most notably the libel case taken against the *Irish Figaro* by Dr. Joseph Edward Kenny, nationalist member of Parliament for Dublin, College Green, and coroner for the City of Dublin, in May 1895. Rather curiously, Colles persisted in claiming friendship with Kenny in his memoir, after the coroner's untimely death on 9 April 1900. Here, he summarily dismisses Kenny as someone who "was at one time mixed up with the Home Rule Party."[8] To counteract the publication of "The Famine Queen," Colles not only penned scathing retorts over the next fortnight in his own journal, but also printed a poster advertising what proved to be his final attack: "Absolutely without a rival. 'Irish Figaro,' Saturday, 21st April, 1900. Miss Maud Gonne's Pension from the Government."[9] As Padraic Colum later recalled, the number of these "posters plastered everywhere" was out of proportion to the modest distribution of this "undercover organ of the Castle." By contrast,

> The article so publicized had nothing more to disclose than that the pension due to Colonel Gonne as an army officer was paid into the estate from which Maud Gonne and her sisters drew an income. But that a striking figure in the nationalist movement was in the pay of the other side was the impression given people who looked at the poster and did not read the article. (Colum 58–59)

Thus it was the advance distribution of this poster, as opposed to the publication of the article itself, which ensured Gonne's triumph in her "sensational libel action" against Colles (Gonne 201). However, "Arthur Griffith did not wait for that," as Colum put it. On the morning of 9 April, in the wake of the first article attacking Gonne in the *Figaro*, Griffith "went round and horsewhipped the editor in his office," located at 7 Grafton Street, deploying a "sjambok he had brought back from South Africa. For this he was given his first term in prison."[10] Griffith was sentenced to a fortnight in jail that same afternoon by John Alexander Byrne, KC, one of the divisional police justices of Dublin, because he declined the option of paying a fine of "one pound or fourteen days and ordered to find two sureties of five pounds each to keep the peace." Thus he "was sentenced to another fourteen days, exclaiming as he left the dock, 'I'll not enter into any bail to keep the peace towards Mr Colles.'"[11] According to Gonne's own account, Griffith reacted with such ire because Colles (whom she consistently refers to as Collis in her letters) likened her to Herodotus as *mendaciorum pater* (father of lies).[12] As she tells Yeats in a letter dated Good Friday, 13 April:

> Collis in the *Figaro* had called me a *liar* & expressed doubts as to the possibility of a liar being a lady & all this in defence of the loyal Dublin Fusiliers & their bravery. The editor of the U.I. seems to have exceptionally decided views on the responsibilities of an Editor, he said that no lady on the staff of the U.I. should be insulted so he called on Collis in his office. . . . Collis didn't defend himself but sprang to the window & yelled for help & finally got a policeman. . . . Every body I have seen even some unionists say Griffith was quite right & Collis only got what he deserved. I called on Griffith in Mountjoy & found him in very good spirits not with standing wearing prison dress of an extraordinarily ugly description. (Gonne and Yeats 122–23:74)

In an *Irish Figaro* article of 14 April, Colles dismissed Griffith's action "as the offences of a manikin, for that is all Mr Arthur Griffith is, I may say this Griffith is only a specimen of a crowd of reptiles known as the Transvaal Committee," which included Gonne herself. Indeed, the Irish Transvaal Committee was formed on 10 October 1899 in the Celtic Literary Society rooms, 32 Lower Abbey Street, with Gonne in the chair. In his memoir, Colles attempts to consign the irruption of Griffith into his office to the realms of *opera buffa*, but even with the benefit of hindsight, he reaffirms his assertion that Gonne is a "liar," once more begging the question, "Can a Liar be called a Lady?" (Colles, 47). Joyce burlesques this incident in the "Circe" episode of *Ulysses* when the Irish Evicted Tenants call for Bloom to be flogged: "Sjambok him!" (*U* 15.1882–1883).[13] In deploying the sjambok, with its strong connotations of colonial abuse of power, Joyce not only alludes to "the grim ironies to Irish pro-Boerism," exemplified by the Irish Transvaal Committee, but also reminds us of the inherent irony of turning the anti-Semitic Griffith's weapon of choice on Bloom, his putative ally (Gibson 199).[14]

While Griffith was "detained in custody in Mountjoy prison" (*U* 15.1169–1170), Gonne, in addition to preparing for court, forged ahead with the organization of the Patriotic Children's Treat and the unveiling of a plaque at 65 High Street, commemorating the birthplace of the United Irishman "Napper Tandy" (*U* 3.260). With a summons for malicious libel secured against Colles on 21 April, the case was fixed for hearing on 26 April in "the solemn court of Green street" (*U* 12.1121). The next day was Easter Sunday, and fifteen women gathered after twelve-o'clock Mass in the Celtic Literary Society rooms, with the intention of presenting to Griffith a blackthorn stick with a silver collar to replace his sjambok. Yet gradually the focus of this meeting shifted to organizing a public event as a sovereign counteractive to Children's Day as the mass congress and exhibition of the "beloved subjects" (*U* 15.1542) of tomorrow, in that most contested of colonial spaces, the Phoenix Park, devised as the propagandistic zenith of the royal visit.[15] On 6 April, at least according to unionist sources, "a vast concourse of children, to the number of 50,000, from the city and the country, assembled in the Phoenix Park to see the Queen and to be seen by her Majesty" (McCarthy 482). Indeed, 52,000 was the figure generally reported in official channels, but the number of children who attended was closer to 18,000–20,000 from the country, and 13,000 from the city, as reported in the *Freeman's Journal*.[16] However, the *United Irishman* put the number of city children considerably lower, "Out of the 35,000 children which made up the school attendance in Dublin only 5,000 allowed themselves to be used for a Unionist demonstration, and these 5,000 were chiefly from the Masonic, Industrial and Workhouse Schools."[17] Even the arch-unionist Michael John Fitzgerald McCarthy was forced to concede that "despite all explanation, the vast majority, indeed almost all the Catholic children, both at the male and female National Schools, and at the Industrial Schools, were successfully bamboozled into holding aloof, and losing the sadly-needed day of enlightenment and pleasure." Yet notwithstanding the exact number of children extended in lines for over half a mile, from John Henry Foley's equestrian statue of "general Gough in the park" (*U* 15.795) to the main entrance to the Viceregal Lodge, they "were hospitably entertained at the expense of a citizens' committee" (483–86). This Citizens' Reception Committee was headed by the Lady Mayoress, Maud Pile, and Caroline, Lady Arnott, in the company of many others with titles and surnames familiar to readers of *Ulysses*, most notably the Countess of Fingall, Mrs Dockrell, the Misses Fitzgibbon, Mrs Mooney, Mrs Conolly Norman, Mrs Kenny, Mrs Rowe, and Miss Towers. In addition to "the erudite and worshipful chairman of quarter sessions sir Frederick Falkiner, recorder of Dublin" (*U* 12.1874–1875), several aldermen and burgesses of the city of Dublin were involved in the organization of the event, having already been excoriated as "The Queen's Own" in the *United Irishman* of 10 March 1900:

> Councillor Joseph Downes, Baker, Inns'-quay ward
> Alderman Meade, Builder, Trinity ward
> Councillor Pile, Lord Mayor, Fishmonger, Fitzwilliam ward
> Councillor Bernard Gorevan, Draper, Usher's quay ward
> Councillor Reuben Dodd, Solicitors' Clerk, Wood-quay ward

Ramsay Colles attended as part of the committee of eight men responsible for "arranging and controlling the children," which was "assisted by some hundreds of stewards."[18] In this context, he is castigated by the *United Irishman* as that "Miserable creature, Colles."[19]

Certainly, the highly symbolic image of the Famine Queen feeding the loyalist Five Thousand, due to the low turnout from Dublin schools on Children's Day, was interpreted in terms of the triumph of "the Roman catholic church" and "the Irish nation" (*U* 17.15–16) over a particularly invidious attempt at Souperism. In turning the corner of Duke Street into Dawson Street, which Joyce elides to create an emblematic juxtaposition of "Gray's confectioner's window of unbought tarts" (13 Duke Street) and "the reverend Thomas Connellan's bookstore" (51b Dawson Street), Bloom muses on the origin of Souperism:

> *Why I left the church of Rome?* Birds' nest women run him. They say they used to give pauper children soup to change to protestants in the time of the potato blight. Society over the way papa went to for the conversion of poor jews. Same bait. *Why we left the church of Rome*. (*U* 8.1069–1074)[20]

Here, Bloom's contention that these women run Connellan gives us an acute sense of the debt that the apostate, "fair-haired priest of Athlone" owed to the Irish Church Missions: Anglican proselytizing organizations dedicated to the mass conversion of Catholic Ireland to the Church of Ireland, which also helped staff Smyly's Homes and Free Day Schools for Necessitous Children. These homes and schools were founded by Ellen Smyly (1815–1901), who established the Birds' Nest, for girls and infants, at Mounttown, County Dublin in 1859. The home, dedicated to the memory of Mrs Elizabeth Whately and Mrs Blanch Wale, the wife and daughter of the former Protestant archbishop of Dublin, was relocated to 19–20 York Road, Kingstown, and declared open on 9 April 1862.[21] By 1904 the Smyly *magisterium* included the Ragged Boys' Home in Grand Canal Street (1852), the Coombe Ragged Day Schools and Boys' Home in Skinner's Alley (1853), the Girls' Home and Infants' Day School in Luke Street (1854), the Elliot Home for Waifs and Strays in Townsend Street (1872), the Home for Big Lads in Townsend Street (1883), the Helping Hand Home in Hawkins Street (1888), and a branch of the Birds' Nest called Nead le Farrige at Spiddal, County Galway (1882). The uncompromisingly anti-Romanist ethos of these homes for "ragged boys and girls" (*U* 15.1602) became a sectarian flashpoint, casting a long shadow over the Save the Dublin Kiddies campaign during the 1913 lockout, while the "rescue" of foundlings by doughty clergymen was reported throughout the Irish Catholic diaspora:

> A short time ago it transpired that in Glencree Reformatory out of 150 criminals, 120 had graduated in Mrs Smyly's Schools. Last month a curate of St Kevin's rescued a boy from one of the bird's nests. The boy told the priest that at the Birds' Nest in Kingstown there was placed a statue of the Blessed Virgin; again and again he was asked—but he refused—to spit on the statue of the immaculate Mother of God.[22]

Notwithstanding this luridly hagiographic account, it would be difficult to overestimate the degree to which the Birds' Nest was a place of terror in

Dublin Catholic consciousness for several generations.[23] This terror feeds into the report published in the *United Irishman* on 31 March 1900 regarding the impending Children's Day:

> The "Souper" gang is always with us. A committee of which some of the most prominent members were friends and supporters of Mrs Smyly has been formed in Dublin to "give the poor children" a free breakfast on the occasion of the visit of the Queen of England. Not alone is the "free breakfast" intended as an act of political proselytism, but is, we are confident, from the personnel of the committee, intended to be used for purposes of religious proselytism.[24]

In *Finnegans Wake*, Joyce recalls the Children's Tea in Kingstown Town Hall, 5 April 1900, organized by the "rampant royal commissioners" (*FW* 448.19–20) of the township to celebrate the presence of the royal yacht, the *Victoria and Albert II*, in the harbor, "from the slime of their slums and artesaned wellings, rickets and riots, like the Smyly boys at their vicereine's levee" (*FW* 209.32–34). Here, the event is compared parodically to the Levée at the Castle: the afternoon party exclusively for men which marked the opening of the summer season. By contrast, the Children's Tea was boycotted by the pupils of "the Christian Brothers Schools" and "Convent Schools, Kingstown," who were "singing 'God Save Ireland' at the time the feasters were winding up their entertainment with 'God Save the Queen.'"[25] Indeed, the sense that Children's Day amounted to nothing more than "allsods of esoupcans that's in the queen's pottage" (*FW* 289.4–5) was preceded by nationalist outrage concerning the "instructive treat" (*U* 12.551) offered to the children of the North Dublin Union Workhouse in honor of Queen Victoria's Diamond Jubilee on 22 June 1897, which was declined by the governors.[26] Bloom recalls this nexus of associations, "north Dublin union, lord mayor in his gingerbread coach, old queen in a bathchair. . . . Children fighting for the scrapings of the pot. Want a souppot as big as the Phoenix park" (*U* 8.709–715). We are reminded of Stephen's and Bloom's shared sense of the blighted, bloody, Edomitic inheritance of Ireland, which toasts its ruler in the language of the dispossessed, "I am tired of my voice, the voice of Esau. My kingdom for a drink" (*U* 9.981).

However, from a unionist perspective, Children's Day was an opportunity to showcase "the generosity of Irishmen" (McCarthy 484), embodied in the donation of a ton of biscuits by such favored sons of Providence as "Messrs Jacob *agus* Jacob," and a ton of jam and 10,000 bags of sweets from "Williams and Woods" (*U* 12.1825; 18.942). In addition to 300 gallons of milk from "the Lucan dairy" (*U* 18.271), Messrs Downes (*D* 102) donated 1,800 buns to the Phoenix Park, while Messrs Johnston, Mooney and O'Brien (*P* 250) donated 3,000 buns. By contrast, "James Rourke's city bakery" (*U* 16.55–56) and Kennedy's (cf. *FW* 7.10–11) emerged as bakers and confectioners to the patriotic children. In terms of the principal bakers and confectioners of Dublin, it would appear that only "Boland's breadvan" (*U* 4.82) had no part to play in this ideological bunfight. Messrs M'Cluskey donated 750 oranges to the Phoenix Park, while Hamilton Drummond, seed merchant and nurseryman, poet and historical novelist, magistrate and prominent member of the Council of the Unionist Registration Association, donated 2,500. For Bloom, these particular donations take on a political complexion; they suggest to him that all that remains of an Irish child's birthright under British rule is a soupy mess of pottage, imbued with Orangism: "The Patriot's banquet. Eating orangepeels in the park" (*U* 8.516–517). Here, Bloom's imagery recalls that of Mr Daedalus in *Stephen Hero*, who warns his son against ending up "a loafer eating orangepeels and sleeping in the Park" (*SH* 222), but in this context Joyce's oblique reference to the staunchly unionist, albeit not axiomatically orange, hue of Children's Day ironically recalls the Patriotic Children's Treat.[27] Indeed, Joyce once again recalls the political cynicism which motivated the royal visit, symbolized by the Esauic orts of Children's Day, in Biddy the Hen's "orangeflavoured mudmound" (*FW* 111.34), but we may also note the references in *Finnegans Wake* to "the knock out in the park where oranges have been laid to rust upon the green" (*FW* 3.21–22), and "a few spontaneous fragments of orangepeel, the last remains of an outdoor meal" (*FW* 110.29–30).

In stark contrast to the pervasively unionist motivation in establishing the Citizens' Reception Committee, with all of its attendant associations of Souperism which Bloom acknowledges in ironic resignation, the establishment of the Ladies' Committee of the Patriotic Children's Treat stemmed directly from Gonne's publication of "The Famine Queen," and the subsequent events touching on Griffith's defense of her honor and on her libel case against Colles. The Patriotic Children's Treat, which took place on 1 July 1900 in Clonturk Park, has been described as "an incredible spectacle of the strength and fervour of Irish nationalism in Dublin—the largest political rally in the city up to that time" (Trotter 84). It enrolled "30,000 schoolchildren who refused to be bribed into parading before the Queen of England," according to the *United Irishman*, though the actual number of attendees may have been considerably lower.[28] Gonne put this number at 20,000, recalling in her memoir that "all our time, for two days and nights before it, was spent in cutting up hams and making sandwiches in a big store we had secured in Talbot Street":

> Headed by beflagged lorries piled with casks of ginger beer and twenty-thousand paper bags containing sandwiches, buns and sweets, that wonderful procession of children carrying green branches moved off from Beresford Place, marshalled by the young men of the Celtic Literary Society and the Gaelic Athletic Association on the march to Clonturk Park. . . . The Patriotic Children's treat became legendary in Dublin and, even now, middle-aged men and women come up to me in the streets and say: "I was one of the Patriotic Children at your party, when Queen Victoria was over." Queen Victoria's children's Treat had been eclipsed. (270)[29]

While it would appear from contemporary reports of donations received that the food was simpler than that on offer on Children's Day, the Patriotic Children were accompanied by at least six marching bands, which Bloom seems to recall, "Halffed enthusiasts. Penny roll and a walk with the band . . . The not far distant day. Homerule sun rising up in the northwest" (*U* 8.470–474). Although the idea may not have been her brainchild originally but that of William Rooney, the event was undoubtedly spearheaded by Maud Gonne, fresh from her legal triumph over Colles, and fulfilling Millevoye's vision of her as "the Joan of Arc of Ireland," as Joyce puts it in a letter to Stanislaus on 15 March 1905.[30] Certainly, the total capitulation of Colles in the courtroom and, by extension, of the Castle regime, did a great deal to burnish Gonne's moral armor and secure her position as the self-fashioned, female saviour of Ireland.

After an adjournment from 26 April, Colles appeared on 4 May before Ernest Godwin Swifte to answer the summons previously taken out against him by Gonne. Under the instruction of "Friery the solicitor" (*U* 18.1070), who was also county coroner for North Dublin, Gonne was represented by that redoubtable Liberal, William Huston Dodd, then Third Sergeant-at-Law in Ireland, and "John F Taylor," who would appear to have lived up to MacHugh's estimation of his deliberative rhetoric on "the revival of the Irish tongue" as "the finest display of oratory I ever heard" (*U* 7.792–796).[31] Indeed, Taylor was described on his death on 7 November 1902 as "one of the most brilliant men of his generation, and was eminent alike as a lawyer, journalist, historian, public speaker, and politician" (*Law Times* 68). Under the instruction of Messrs Horan and Shortt, Colles was represented by James Henry Mussen Campbell, then Unionist member of Parliament for St Stephen's Green (1898–1900) and later first Baron Glenavy (1921), yet also Cathaoirleach of the First Seanad of the Free State (1922–28). In stating the case for the prosecution, Sergeant Dodd focused on section 8 of the Law of Libel Amendment Act 1888 (51 & 52 Vict. c. 64). Under this section an "order of a judge at Chambers" must be "first had and obtained" in order to take issue against a "person responsible for the publication of a newspaper" for criminal libel. This follows on, *ejusdem generis*, from the preceding reference to "any proprietor, publisher, editor"; thus the act is intended to cover those responsible for the production of the newspaper.[32] Dodd pointed out that although the *Irish Figaro* was "apparently conducted by a company," which meant that the proprietor, publisher, or editor would be covered by the act, in this case "the company was not possessed of any assets and not worth proceeding against." Moreover, an application for permission to instigate proceedings for criminal libel is not required when the intended prosecution is issued against the author of an article in a newspaper as defined by the Newspaper Libel and Registration Act 1881 (44 & 45 Vict. c. 60), nor would any poster advertising the article penned by Colles, even though he was also proprietor, publisher, and editor of this newspaper, be covered by this section.

Arthur Griffith was duly called as a witness for the complainant, stating that in his opinion the poster intimated that Gonne was "a government agent." However, in his cross-examination of Griffith, Campbell sought to discredit Griffith's assessment by pointing to his role as proprietor, publisher and editor of Gonne's "infamous and scurrilous" article, "The Famine Queen." In his subsequent cross-examination of Gonne, Campbell quoted at length from "The Famine Queen," also suggesting she might well be the author of several anonymous articles in the *United Irishman*. He then proceeded to question her credentials as a bona fide Irishwoman, suggesting that her military background made her pro-Boer statements all the more "scurrilous and scandalous." In addressing the bench, Campbell returned to the application of section 8 of the 1888 act, stating that the summons was originally taken out in relation to the statements appearing in the newspaper itself, but upon realizing that "no prosecution would lie for these statements without the leave of a judge of the High Court," the "miserable and cowardly course had been adopted of changing the object of attack and going for the poster." Swifte dismissed this on the grounds that Colles was "proven to be the manager and the editor," which made him responsible for the content of the poster, if not the article itself, in these capacities. In giving his decision, Swifte "held in the first place that the placard complained of was not a newspaper." While he was of the mind that some of Gonne's statements were "perfectly shocking," such opinions "did not prevent her from putting the criminal law into action." Finally, he stated that the poster printed and distributed by Colles was calculated to hold Gonne "up to hatred and contempt," and the statements complained of were defamatory; thus, a prima facie case had been established for proceeding to trial. According to the *Freeman's Journal*, applause broke out in the gallery, and Gonne exited the court to loud cheers from "people in the courtyard," escorted by John O'Leary, who remained *l'ultimo Feniano* (*OPCW* 237-239) in Joyce's estimation.[33]

On Saturday, 12 May 1900, Colles unreservedly withdrew his accusation before Recorder Falkiner in Green Street Courthouse and tendered an apology, via Campbell, "for the mistake and any misconception as to Miss Gonne's position, due either to the statement in the paper or the placards announcing it." Taylor accepted the apology on Gonne's behalf, stating she had "no desire whatever to act in any severe manner" toward Colles, having taken "this proceeding merely for the purpose of making it quite clear that her character in public was consistent with everything with regard to her action and her life in private."[34] Again, the *Freeman's Journal* records that Gonne "was cheered on appearing in the street," a sentiment apparently shared by the prosecuting counsel: "Meeting me later in London, Mr Campbell apologized to me . . . 'Believe me, Miss Gonne, I never liked a case less and I was glad you won.' He owned that Dublin Castle had paid for Ramsey Collis' [sic] defence" (Gonne 201). Indeed, there were several theories as to Colles's incentive in circulating the libel, but one of the most common is summed up by "Máire," a member of the organization which sprang from the Ladies' Committee of the Patriotic Children's Treat, Inghínidhe na hÉireann, or "Daughters of Erin" (*U* 15.1936):

There was in Dublin in 1900 an editor who ran a weekly paper—
they passed into oblivion long ago. The paper was then dying; the
editor hit upon the expedient of slandering a woman. This, being an
unusual hit in a paper published in Ireland, succeeded for a week.
(quoted in Ward 17)[35]

It was also suggested that Colles was paid by Dublin Castle to target Gonne, being in constant need of funds to fuel his life in high society: a rumor Joyce alludes to in "the fallowing for the Durban Gazette . . . From a collispendent" (*FW* 602.20).[36] Gonne firmly believed Colles was a Castle agent, and his assertion in his memoir that the false information had been supplied to him in the form of "a strong hint to a blind horse from John Mallon of Lower Castle Yard" (*U* 16.1192) would appear to point in this direction.[37] As her Good Friday letter to Yeats evinces, Gonne was under surveillance by "Mr Mallon's brigade" in the wake of the publication of "The Famine Queen" and in anticipation of the Napper Tandy commemoration, "One stands opposite my Hotel all day & I think night too, another follows me around even into the shops, I have never seen such open & impudent shadowing before" (123:74).

Although Joyce does not comment directly on either the trial of Griffith, or the libel action of Gonne, he returns on a number of occasions to two of their principal outcomes: the realization of the Patriotic Children's Treat as a mass demonstration, and the subsequent establishment of Inghínidhe na hÉireann. The Patriotic Children's Treat was established at the suggestion of one of Griffith's closest allies, and one of Joyce's bêtes noires, William Rooney, whose eminently patriotic verse Joyce would excoriate posthumously in his initial review for the *Daily Express*.[38] In addition to cofounding with Griffith the Celtic Literary Society (1893) and Cumann na nGaedhael (1900), Rooney also helped establish and edit the *United Irishman* (1899), and was regarded as "the Davis of the latest national movement" (*OCPW* 61). According to Máire Killeen, who was engaged to him until his death on 6 May 1901, Rooney was present in the Celtic Literary Society rooms on Easter Sunday, albeit in the outer room when Gonne "proposed that we give effect to his suggestion in the *United Irishman* that a treat be given to the patriotic children who had refused to attend at the treat given when Queen Victoria had visited Ireland seeking recruits for the South African War."[39] However, Killeen notes it was Gonne who "suggested that we form a society," which initially gave rise to the Ladies' Committee of the Patriotic Children's Treat. Gonne assumed the position of president, while other executive positions were held by Alice Furlong (vice president), May O'Leary-Curtis (honorary treasurer), Judith Rooney (honorary treasurer), Annie Egan (honorary secretary), and Sarah White (honorary secretary).[40] By the autumn, the Ladies' Committee of the Patriotic Children's Treat was reconstituted as Inghínidhe na hÉireann, holding its inaugural once again in the Celtic Literary Society rooms, with Jenni Wyse-Power, that is, "John Wyse Nolan's wife" (*U* 8.950-951), taking a prominent role, eventually becoming vice president.

The objects of Inghínidhe na hÉireann were listed in the *United Irishman* on 13 October 1900:

I.   The re-establishment of the complete independence of Ireland
II. To encourage the study of Gaelic, of Irish literature, history, music and art, especially amongst the young, by the organising and teaching of classes for the above objects
III. To support and popularise Irish manufactures
IV. To discourage the reading and circulation of low English literature, the singing of English songs, the attending of vulgar English entertainments at theatres and music halls, and to combat in every way English influence, which is doing so much injury to the artistic taste and refinement of the Irish people
V.   To form a fund called the National Purposes Fund, for the furtherance of the above objects.

In the pursuit of these objects, the Ninnies, as they were affectionately termed by contemporary Dubliners, organized "classes for children over nine years old" for "the teaching of Gaelic, Irish history, Irish songs," and regular céilís for adults and children alike. They also performed tableaux vivants and participated in plays, most notably the three performances by W. G. Fay's Irish National Dramatic Company on 2-4 April 1902 at "St Teresas hall Clarendon St" (*U* 18.375) of Æ's *Deirdre*, and *Cathleen ni Houlihan* by Yeats and Lady Gregory, featuring Gonne as Cathleen.[41] In the "Circe" episode of *Ulysses*, Joyce parodies Æ's performance as Cathvah the Druid in his one and only play, allied to his lifelong identification with "Mananaan" (*U* 9.190) or "Mananaun MacLir" (*U* 15.2261-2276).[42] Moreover, the "Maid Maud ninnies" (*FW* 586.6-7), dressed in the widow's weeds affected by Gonne in memory of the martyrs of 1916, mockingly laud Bloom as he is immolated by his own "phoenix flames" (*U* 15.1935–1936), in a tableau vivant which recalls the *relaxado en persona* of an *Auto da Fé*. In "Scylla and Charybdis" Joyce also recalls his drunken visit on 20 June 1904 to the rehearsal rooms of the Irish National Theatre Society at 34 Camden Street, "the night in the Camden hall when the daughters of Erin had to lift their skirts to step over you as you lay in your mulberrycoloured, multicoloured, multitudinous vomit!" (*U* 9.1192–1194).[43] In addition to these references to the theatrical exploits of Inghínidhe na hÉireann, Joyce in "The Dead" incorporates a telling detail into his portrayal of Miss Ivors, who wears a "large brooch which was fixed in the front of her collar" bearing "an Irish device" (*D* 187).[44] Here, Joyce's reference recalls the symbol of Inghínidhe na hÉireann: a specially commissioned, trilobed, pseudopenannular brooch, based on the design of the late eighth-century, silver-gilt Cavan Brooch.[45] The Cavan Brooch was also referred to as the Queen's Brooch because the monarch was presented with a copy when she visited the library of Trinity College on 7 August 1849; thus the appropriation of this particular Insular artefact is yet another example of Gonne's acutely personalized, competitive defiance as "Servant of the Queen."[46]

Finally, Joyce draws attention to yet another aspect of the legal and civil events leading up to the foundation of Inghínidhe na hÉireann, which reminds us of the principal, practical purpose of the royal visit of 1900: a recruitment drive for the Anglo-Boer War, because "Irish soldiers had as often fought for England as against her, more so, in fact" (*U* 16.1041–1042). If Gonne's testimony during her libel case was to be believed, her father was one such man, in the manner of "the best admirals and generals" like Lord Roberts and Lord Kitchener, yet she had come to the opinion that, like the licencee of the cabman's shelter at Butt Bridge, "rumoured to be or have been Fitzharris," she "cared nothing for any empire" and "considered no Irishman worthy of his salt that served it" (*U* 16.1017–1018, 1044, 1024–1025). Her opinion was well known, and the dichotomy between her virulent anti-imperialism and her military upbringing in Dublin, in a manner rather grander than that of Molly Bloom in Gibraltar, formed the basis of the libel circulated by Colles, seemingly at the behest of John Mallon, erstwhile scourge of the almost invincible Fitzharris. Yet it would appear that Bloom shares the sentiments of Gonne, and by extension Inghínidhe na hÉireann, who waged an unremitting campaign against the policy adopted during the Anglo-Boer War of not confining soldiers to barracks in the evening, most notably the "royal Dublins, boys, the salt of the earth" (*U* 15.785), in order to encourage enlistment:⁴⁷

> royal Dublin fusiliers. Redcoats. Too showy. That must be why the women go after them. Uniform. Easier to enlist and drill. Maud Gonne's letter about taking them off O'Connell street at night: disgrace to our Irish capital. Griffith's paper is on the same tack now: an army rotten with venereal disease: overseas or halfseasover empire. (*U* 5.68–72)

Yet Joyce remains acutely aware that whether a young man went out to die with "the Dublins that won Tugela" (*U* 18.402–403), under orders issued from Command Headquarters in the Phoenix Park "in the service of our sovereign" (*U* 15.788–789), or as a "hero boy who went to his death with a song on his lips as if he were but going to a hurling match in Clonturk park" (*U* 12.644–646), they each answered their respective callings with "the voice of Esau" (*U* 15.1220).

Acknowledgments

In addition to the readers and editors, I am particularly grateful to the late Adrian Hardiman, Michael Laffan, and Niall Ó Brolcháin for help with specific queries, and Jonathan Mills for his incisive comments regarding various drafts of this essay. I acknowledge the support of the University of Leicester in granting me Academic Study Leave, and would like to thank in particular the School of English, Trinity College Dublin, for granting me a Visiting Research Fellowship which facilitated the essay's completion.

Notes

1. See D'Arcy, "*Dindsenchas*, Mr Deasy and the Nightmare of Partition in *Ulysses*," 20, 27.

2. The official figures inscribed on the Nasionale Vrouemonument (National Women's Memorial) at Bloemfontein state that 4,177 Boer women and 22,074 Boer children perished in British concentration camps. However, this total of 26,251, allied to the 1,676 Boer men in the overall count of 27,927, may be an overestimation, with the actual figure based on camp records being closer to 25,000 Boers, with at least 14,000 black victims. See van Heyningen, *Concentration Camps of the Anglo-Boer War*.

3. However, Joyce is mistaken in stating that Roberts was "born in Ireland" (*OCPW*

117); rather, he was born in Kanpur (Cawnpore) on 30 September 1832 to General Abraham Roberts of Waterford and his second wife, Isabella Bunbury of Kilfeacle, Co. Tipperary.

4. "Dublin Paper Suppressed," *New York Times*, 7 April 1900.

5. Cf. Pomeranz, "Maud Gonne and M. Millevoye," 169. The phrase "Famine Queen" originates in "Over the Frontier" in the *United Irishman* of 20 January 1900.

6. See *Visitation of... Leicester in the Year 1619*, 32–37; *Visitation of... Warwick in the Year 1619* 254–55; *Visitation of... Warwick 1682–1683*, 109–10.

7. In addition to the Official Report, House of Commons (4th ser.), "Irish Treasury Remembrancer" (HC Deb 13 May 1908, vol 188, cc1159-60), see O'Brien, *Dublin Castle and the Irish People*, 321–22: "In 1872, the new officer was appointed under the title 'Treasury Remembrancer and Deputy Paymaster.' The Treasury Remembrancer then is the agent of the English Treasury in Ireland. He advises the Treasury on matters relating to 'Imperial' expenditure in the country. He is also the Deputy Paymaster General; and all officials are paid by him."

8. Colles, *In Castle and Court House*, 140. In addition to being the defendant in several libel cases, Colles was the initial receiver in a landmark case on the receiver's duty of care; cf. *Robinson Printing Co. Ltd v. Chic Ltd* (1905) 2 Ch 123.

9. "Miss Maud Gonne," *Freeman's Journal*, 5 May 1900.

10. Colum, *Arthur Griffith*, 60. See Lyons, *Some Recollections of Griffith and His Times*, 10.

11. Colles, 52. The extension of the sentence by two weeks would explain the proverbial "month in Mountjoy" that Colum and others seemed to recollect. In addition to Colum, 60, see "Irish Editor to Go to Prison," *New York Times*, 10 April 1900.

12. The title *mendaciorum pater* was coined by the Spanish humanist scholar Juan Luis Vivès, who in *De disciplinis libri xx*, 2:5, wrote: "Herodotus, quem verius mendaciorum patrem dixeris, quam quomodo ilium vacant nonnulli, parentem historiae."

13. See Nohrnberg, "'Building Up a Nation Once Again,'" 116, though it is not the case as stated here that Griffith "publicly assaulted" Colles because he had accused "Maud Gonne of being a spy." Griffith's assault had nothing to do with the accusation on which the libel case was based.

14. On the dissipation of Griffith's youthful anti-Semitism, see D'Arcy, "Joyce and the Twoheaded Octopus," 874–75.

15. See Condon, "The Patriotic Children's Treat," 169–73.

16. "The Queen's Visit: The Children's Demonstration in the Park," *Freeman's Journal*, 9 April 1900.

17. "Patriotic Children's Treat," *United Irishman*, 5 May 1900.

18. "Children's Demonstration," *Freeman's Journal*, 9 April 1900.

19. "For the Children," *United Irishman*, 28 April 1900.

20. It has been argued that Joyce is overly reliant in retrospect on Thom's Directory, because Katherine Gray's shop was not actually on the corner of Duke Street (see Slote, "Thomistic Representation," while "Connellan's bookstore was one shop up Dawson past the corner" (Kenner, "Joyce and Modernism," 99).

21. "York Road" is more usual than "York Street"; cf. Gifford, *"Ulysses" Annotated*, 186.
22. "Dublin Notes," *New Zealand Tablet*, 11 January 1895.
23. Cf. Andrews, *Dublin Made Me*, 9–10, in which the author describes the Birds' Nest as one of the menacing "horrors" of his childhood "where children might be brought and turned into Protestants."
24. Cf. McCarthy, *Five Years in Ireland*, 485.
25. "Children's Treat at Kingstown," *Freeman's Journal*, 9 April 1900.
26. Cf. McCarthy, 596. True to form, the Guardians of the North Dublin Union sent a letter to Wilhelmina of the Netherlands, thanking her for the evacuation of "old Oom Paul" (*U* 18.394) and expressing regret "that the Boer people should ever come under the ruthless heel of a nation remarkable for its cruelty, covetousness, and rapacity" ("Irish Sympathy for Boers," *Times* (London), 18 October 1900).
27. Pace Gifford, 172–73.
28. "Patriotic Children's Treat," *United Irishman*, 7 July 1900.
29. In addition to Condon, 174–78, see Bobotis, "Rival Maternities," 78–79.
30. *Letters*, 2:85. Cf. Gonne: "Why don't you free Ireland as Joan of Arc freed France?" (64).
31. See "The 'Irish Revival': The Law Students' Debating Society," *Freeman's Journal*, 25 October 1901. See also Bender, "Language of the Outlaw." Maud Gonne was present at this debate, as were Joyce and his erstwhile Irish teacher, Pádraig Pearse. Gonne described Taylor as "the most brilliant orator I ever heard" (90).
32. In addition to www.legislation.gov.uk/ukpga/Vict/51–52/64/section/8/enacted, see Halsbury et al., *The Laws of England*, 18: 644, 656, 697–98, 704, 711–12, 725–30, 740–46.
33. "Miss Maud Gonne," *Freeman's Journal*, 5 May 1900.
34. "Miss Maud Gonne's Case," *Freeman's Journal*, 15 May 1900.
35. Cf. "Máire," *Bean na hÉireann* (*"The Women of Ireland"*). May 1910.
36. See *Oxford English Dictionary*, 2nd ed., s.v. "fallow," *v.* 1a. Joyce associates the word not only with such urban gazettes as the *Irish Figaro* but also with the *Dublin Gazette*, the official newspaper, published 1705–1922, "by authority" of the Irish Executive, based in Dublin Castle.
37. Cf. Colles, 53–54.
38. See "An Irish Poet," *Daily Express*, 12 December 1902 (*OCPW* 61–63).
39. Bureau of Military History WS 321: Witness: Máire Ó Brolcháin, Vice President Inghíni na hÉireann, 1900; Member Sinn Fein, 1905–1921, 9. Killeen was certainly elected vice president in 1903 (cf. *United Irishman*, 31 October 1903, 5), before marrying Rooney's close friend, Patrick Bradley (Pádraig Ó Brolcháin) on 30 June 1904. Arthur Griffith acted as best man. That Rooney conceived of the Patriotic Children's Treat, cf. also Papers of Sighle Humphreys (1899–1994), UCD Archives, IE UCDA P106/1226 (10–12).
40. See "Patriotic Children's Treat," *Freeman's Journal*, 30 April 1900. The actor Máire Quinn was elected honorary secretary, while her sister Margaret became treasurer; see also "Patriotic Children's Treat," *Freeman's Journal*, 7 July 1900. Cf. "Inghínidhe na hÉireann ('Daughters of Erin')," *United Irishman*, 27 and 31 October 1900.

41. In addition to http://catalogue.nli.ie/Record/vtls000648851, see Quinn, "Cathleen ni Houlihan Writes Back."

42. In addition to http://catalogue.nli.ie/Record/vtls000516067, see Paterakis, "Mananaan MacLir in *Ulysses*"; MacQuarrie, *Biography of the Irish God of the Sea*, 337–83.

43. This incident gave rise to "Satire on the Brothers Fay"; cf. Ellmann, *James Joyce*, 61–62, 167, 771, 773.

44. Joyce's original, eminently Chaucerian detail of the brooch's motto is as emblematic in its own historical context as the rather more ambiguous *Amor vincit omnia* emblazoned on the Prioress's brooch in the *Canterbury Tales*, as for "many of the activists, the existence of the brooch among their possessions is the only indication of their membership of the organization" (McCoole, *No Ordinary Women*, 154). There were also enamelled metal badges featuring a harp, the words "Daughters of Ireland," and a Celtic cross produced for Inghínidhe na hÉireann by P. Quinn & Co., Belfast, who also produced badges for the Irish Volunteers and other Nationalist organizations.

45. Cf. Foster, *Fictions of the Irish Literary Revival*, 151.

46. The brooch commissioned by the Provost and Senior Fellows of Trinity College for presentation to Queen Victoria was made by Edmond Johnson for West and Son, of Wicklow gold; it featured a pearl from Lough Eske, County Donegal. It was donated after her death to the National Museum of Ireland by her son the Duke of Connaught.

47. Here Bloom recalls the handbills produced by Inghínidhe na hÉireann "on the shame of Irish girls consorting with the soldiers of the enemy of their country," which were distributed to such "couples in the streets, with the result that almost every night there were fights in O'Connell Street" (Gonne 267). In addition to http://catalogue.nli.ie/Record/vtls000261392, see Pearl, *Dublin in Bloomtime*, 15; Cheng, *Joyce, Race, and Empire*, 226–28.

Works Cited

Andrews, C. S. *Dublin Made Me: An Autobiography*. Dublin: Mercier, 1979.

Bender, Abby. "The Language of the Outlaw: A Clarification." *James Joyce Quarterly* 44.4 (2007): 807–12.

Bobotis, Andrea. "Rival Maternities: Maud Gonne, Queen Victoria, and the Reign of the Political Mother." *Victorian Studies* 49.1 (2006): 63–83.

Cheng, Vincent. *Joyce, Race, and Empire*. Cambridge: Cambridge University Press, 1995.

Colles, Ramsay. *In Castle and Court House: Being Reminiscences of 30 Years in Ireland*. London: T. Werner Laurie, 1911.

Colum, Padraic. *Arthur Griffith*. Dublin: Browne and Nolan, 1959.

Condon, Janette. "The Patriotic Children's Treat: Irish Nationalism and Children's Culture at the Twilight of Empire." *Irish Studies Review* 8.2 (2000): 167–78.

Cork Examiner. "Children's Day in the Phoenix Park." 9 May 1900.

D'Arcy, Anne Marie. "*Dindsenchas*, Mr Deasy and the Nightmare of Partition in *Ulysses*." *Proceedings of the Royal Irish Academy* 114C (2014): 295–325.

———. "Joyce and the Twoheaded Octopus of *judéo-maçonnerie.*" *Review of English Studies* 64.4 (2013): 857–77.
Ellmann, Richard. *James Joyce.* Rev. ed. New York: Oxford University Press, 1982.
Foster, John Wilson. *Fictions of the Irish Literary Revival: A Changeling Art.* Syracuse, NY: Syracuse University Press, 1987.
Freeman's Journal. "Children's Demonstration." 9 April 1900.
———. "Children's Treat at Kingstown." *Freeman's Journal,* 9 April 1900.
———. "The 'Irish Revival': The Law Students' Debating Society." 25 October 1901.
———. "Miss Maud Gonne." 5 May 1900.
———. "Miss Maud Gonne's Case." 15 May 1900.
———. "Patriotic Children's Treat." 30 April 1900.
———. "Patriotic Children's Treat." 7 July 1900.
———. "The Queen's Visit: The Children's Demonstration in the Park." 9 April 1900.
Gibson, Andrew. "'Strangers in My House, Bad Manners to Them': England in 'Circe.'" In *Reading Joyce's "Circe,"* edited by Andrew Gibson, 179–221. European Joyce Studies 3. Amsterdam: Rodopi, 1994.
Gifford, Don. *"Ulysses" Annotated: Notes for James Joyce's "Ulysses."* With Robert J. Seidman. 2nd ed. Berkeley: University of California Press, 1988.
Gonne, Maud. *The Autobiography of Maud Gonne: A Servant of the Queen.* Edited by A. Norman Jeffares and Anna MacBride White. Chicago: University of Chicago Press, 1994.
Gonne, Maud, and William Butler Yeats. *The Gonne-Yeats Letters, 1893–1938.* Edited by Anna MacBride White and A. Norman Jeffares. London: Hutchinson, 1992.
Halsbury, Earl of, et al., eds. *The Laws of England: Being a Complete Statement of the Whole Law of England.* 31 vols. London: Butterworth, 1907–17.
Humphreys, Sighle. Papers, 1899–1994. University College Dublin archives.
"Irish Treasury Remembrancer." HC Deb 13 May 1908, vol 188, cc1159–60.
Kenner, Hugh. "Joyce and Modernism." In *James Joyce,* edited by Harold Bloom, 91–102. Philadelphia: Chelsea House, 2003.
Law Times and Journal of Property. "John F. Taylor." Vol. 114 (1903): 68.
Lyons, George A. *Some Recollections of Griffith and His Times.* Dublin: Talbot, 1923.
MacQuarrie, Charles W. *The Biography of the Irish God of the Sea from the Voyage of Bran (700 A.D.) to Finnegans Wake (1939): The Waves of Manannán.* Lewiston, N.Y.: Mellen, 2004.
"Máire." *Bean na hÉireann ("The Women of Ireland").* May 1910.
McCarthy, Michael J. F. *Five Years in Ireland: 1895–1900.* Dublin: Hodges, Figgis, 1901.
McCoole, Sinéad. *No Ordinary Women: Irish Female Activists in the Revolutionary Years, 1900–1923.* Dublin: O'Brien, 2003.
Murphy, James H. *Abject Loyalty: Nationalism and Monarchy in Ireland During the Reign of Queen Victoria.* Cork: Cork University Press, 2001.
New York Times. "Dublin Paper Suppressed: Article Signed by Maud Gonne on 'The Famine Queen' the Cause." 7 April 1900.
———. "Irish Editor to Go to Prison." 10 April 1900.

New Zealand Tablet. "Dublin Notes." 11 January 1895.
Nohrnberg, Peter C. L. "'Building Up a Nation Once Again': Irish Masculinity, Violence, and the Cultural Politics of Sports in *A Portrait of the Artist as a Young Man* and *Ulysses*." *Joyce Studies Annual*, 2010, 99–152.
O'Brien, R. Barry. *Dublin Castle and the Irish People*. London: Kegan Paul, Trench, Truebner, 1909.
Paterakis, Deborah Tannen. "Mananaan MacLir in *Ulysses*." *Eire-Ireland* 7.3 (1972): 29–35.
Pearl, Cyril. *Dublin in Bloomtime: The City James Joyce Knew*. London: Angus and Robertson, 1969.
Pomeranz, Victory. "Maud Gonne and M. Millevoye." *James Joyce Quarterly* 11.2 (1974): 169.
Quinn, Antoinette. "Cathleen ni Houlihan Writes Back: Maud Gonne and Irish National Theater." In *Gender and Sexuality in Modern Ireland*, edited by Anthony Bradley and Maryann Gialanella Valiulis, 39–59. Amherst: University of Massachusetts Press, 1997.
Slote, Sam. "The Thomistic Representation of Dublin in *Ulysses*." In *Making Space in the Works of James Joyce*, edited by Valérie Bénéjam and John Bishop, 191–202. London: Routledge, 2011.
Times (London). "Irish Sympathy for Boers." 18 October 1900.
Trotter, Mary. *Ireland's National Theaters: Political Performance and the Origins of the Irish Dramatic Movement*. Syracuse: Syracuse University Press, 2001.
United Irishman. "For the Children." 28 April 1900.
———. "Inghínidhe na hÉireann ('Daughters of Erin')." 27 October 1900.
———. "Inghínidhe na hÉireann ('Daughters of Erin')." 31 October 1900.
———. "Over the Frontier." 20 January 1900.
———. "Patriotic Children's Treat." 5 May 1900.
———. "Patriotic Children's Treat." 7 July 1900.
———. "The Queen's Own." 10 March 1900.
Van Heyningen, Elizabeth. *The Concentration Camps of the Anglo-Boer War: A Social History*. Johannesburg: Jacana, 2013.
The Visitation of the County of Leicester in the Year 1619. Edited by John Fetherston. Harleian Visitation Series 2. London: The Harleian Society, 1870.
The Visitation of the County of Warwick 1682–1683. Edited by W. Harry Rylands. Harleian Visitation Series 62. London: The Harleian Society, 1911.
The Visitation of the County of Warwick in the Year 1619. Edited by John Fetherston, Harleian Visitation Series 12. London: The Harleian Society, 1877.
Vivès, Juan Luis. *De disciplinis libri xx*. 3 vols. Cologne: Johannes Gymnicus, 1536.
Wade, Alan, ed. *The Letters of W. B. Yeats*. London: Hart-Davis, 1954.
Ward, Margaret, ed. *In Their Own Voice: Women and Irish Nationalism*. Dublin: Attic, 1995.

10

The Law in/of *Finnegans Wake*

A Starchamber Quiry

TERENCE KILLEEN

> Stay us wherefore in our search for righteousness, O Sustainer...
>
> *Finnegans Wake*, Rose-O'Hanlon edition

I

Joyce's early note-taking for the work that was to become *Finnegans Wake* was remarkably random. With no very clear idea of where the work was going, or exactly what he was doing, he took notes from a variety of sources, apparently on the principle that they might prove useful eventually. Despite the haphazard nature of this exercise, there were certain favored sources—sources that suggest already a particular orientation of Joyce's interests, a particular horizon, perhaps, for the work to come.

One of the principal providers at this early stage was newspapers. In fact, newspapers continued to be a fruitful source of material throughout the writing of *Finnegans Wake*, though their importance waned somewhat as the work went on. The very first notebook that Joyce compiled contains notes from the *Irish Times*, the *Daily Mail*, the *Daily Sketch*, and several other English papers, as well as many from the Irish periodical the *Leader*.

From the beginning, court reports were particular objects of Joyce's attention. By and large, his interest in the material he was reading was lexical: he was culling unusual words and phrases that for many different reasons appealed to him. For instance, from an *Irish Times* report of 2 December 1922 concerning an ambush in Collinstown, County Dublin, Joyce retained the phrase "Peter the Painter" (a German Mauser automatic pistol named after the leader of the anarchist Siege of Sydney Street).[1] Joyce's interest is not at all in the circumstances of the ambush or the political reasons behind it (it was a minor episode of the Civil War); his interest is entirely in the lexical unit "Peter the Painter," which is sufficiently unusual and distinctive to feature possibly in the projected work. And in fact "Peter the Painter" does get into the finished work: "when the hyougono heckler with the Peter the Painter wanted to hole him" (*FW* 85.5–6).

Similarly, notes he derived from court reports record instances of unusual locutions, particularly in the testimony of witnesses, the kind of locutions that are frequently followed in court reports by the words "laughter in court." A report from the *Connacht Tribune* of 16 February 1924 noted in notebook VI.B 1 (which incidentally is not the first notebook) provided the phrase "was 25 yrs coming to / Tuam," meaning the witness had been a regular visitor to Tuam for the past twenty-five years. Obviously Joyce was both entertained and intrigued by this way of expressing such a simple idea. So, as very often, it is the verbal dimension of the court report that appealed to Joyce.

However, at least some of the court reports—and one in particular—were also clearly of interest to Joyce because of their content.

As Vincent Deane, one of the *Notebooks* series editors, writes in his introduction to VI.B 10 (actually the very first notebook): "Apart from the sensational nature of the deeds which give rise to them, accounts of crimes and law cases owe their peculiar interest to their unique revelations of character and daily life."[2] In VI.B 10 the court case that left the largest trace in *Finnegans Wake* is recorded, obliquely. This was the trial in London of Frederick Bywaters and Edith Thompson for the murder of Thompson's husband, Percy, on 3 October 1922. Following a lengthy trial the pair were convicted, and, despite an appeal and a good deal of public disquiet, they were hanged on 9 January 1923.

Joyce took a very keen interest in this case, as is evidenced by Arthur Power's account of their conversations at the time of the trial.[3] Joyce believed that Edith Thompson, at least, should not have been convicted and that her execution was due in large part to her status as an adultress. Ironically, most of the public comment on the case at the time was highly supportive of Bywaters, who had actually carried out the killing, and regarded Mrs. Thompson as the real instigator of the act, and therefore the more culpable of the two. The public comment is highly relevant, for this is the aspect of the case that Joyce seized on. His most extended note is a virtual condensed transcript of a vox pop set of interviews that appeared in the *Daily Sketch* of 14 December 1922. In keeping with the general tenor of public opinion, this survey took place in the context of a petition for the reprieve of Bywaters only—Thompson is not mentioned. The article, summarized by Joyce on pages 71–72 of notebook VI.B 10, elicits opinions from people in many walks of life, among them a waitress, a bus driver, a sailor, and an actress. Joyce transcribed the opinions with unusual fidelity. They formed the basis for *FW* 58–61, which retains the structure of the vox pop with various would-be representative individuals ("a dustman nocknamed Sevenchurches" (*FW* 59.16–17), based on the *Daily Sketch*'s "a dustman named Churches").

The extent of Joyce's interest in this case is confirmed by the much later notebook VI.B 33, which dates from 1931. This volume features extensive notes from a book that is largely a transcript of the evidence in the Bywaters-Thompson trial, edited by the English criminologist Filson Young.[4] The book also includes long excerpts from Edith Thompson's remarkable letters to Bywaters prior to the murder. Joyce's notes from this work, which cover some twenty-nine pages of the notebook, are taken fairly impartially from Filson Young's introduction, from the transcript of the trial, and from Edith Thompson's letters, though in fact it is from the letters that Joyce mainly incorporated material into *Finnegans Wake* itself.

At the time he took these notes, Joyce was writing part II, chapter 1, and this is the section in which most of the notes found a home. The chapter features strongly the voice of Issy, the daughter, and Mrs. Thompson's simpering, somewhat infantile style of writing suits Issy's voice very well. For instance, every word in the sentence "I know it is difficult but when your goche I go dead" (*FW* 251.25–26) comes from Thompson's letters, including the word "goche," which may be a mistranscription of *fâché*.[5]

Why such interest in this court case? No other attracted Joyce's attention to this degree. One answer is that the case features a triangle that has a particular relevance for *Finnegans Wake*: that of an older man, a younger wife, and a younger man. This is the structure of the Tristan and Isolde legend, which was definitely a very early element in the writing of

Finnegans Wake.⁶ The analogy is striking, and if Joyce was seeking for ways to generalize, to universalize the triangle structure of the Tristan legend, here was a ready-made true situation that provided a perfect parallel.

That said, it is also true that the Bywaters-Thompson case appears in *Finnegans Wake* only vestigially. Its presence in the text can be perceived only with the help of the notebooks: no one could have guessed it, had the notebooks not survived. In this it is very unlike the Tristan-Isolde motif, which features extensively and by name throughout the work. The problems raised by the presence of a "shadow text" beneath the actual text of *Finnegans Wake*, a shadow text that can be traced only via external sources, are beyond the scope of this essay; however, the importance of this case to Joyce's overall conception of the book is clear both from the extensive nature of the notes he took (and their quite extensive use) and above all from the fact that Joyce's discovery of this trial and its consequences took place so early in the book's genesis. It is that that gives the Bywaters-Thompson case its deserved prominence in *Finnegans Wake* studies, for it means that it is a crucial jumping-off point in the work's initial framing.

This case is clearly exceptional in Joyce's writing of *Finnegans Wake*, but the texture of many other legal cases is also deeply interwoven into the work. A casual phrase, "wipe the street up with the clonmellian" (*FW* 443.10), derives from a report of a court case in the *Daily Mail* of 8 December 1922 dealing with a blackmail allegation: a witness told the court that a defendant said he would "wipe the streets" with the plaintiff.⁷ Of course, as with the Bywaters-Thompson issue, these shards and fragments of long-ago court reports would be irretrievable without the labors of diligent scholars among the notebooks; but they do leave the particular scent of their legal origins on the text, and it is possible for a skilled reader to, as it were, sniff them out, to register a faint resonance of a particular discourse that traverses the individual sentence and somehow leaves its trace behind. Very often, that trace has its origins in long-forgotten court testimony, preserved in this most unlikely of ways.

II

In addition to the inspiration gained from court reports, Joyce also took a more focused interest in legal matters at various times in the writing of *Finnegans Wake*. He consulted diverse legal tomes—not, in general, the more serious law books,[8] but works for the general reader which could be highly informative about the law in many of its aspects. Among these works a particularly interesting instance is Maud I. Crofts's *Women under English Law*. Notes derived from it take up the first few pages of notebook VI.B 33. For instance, the legalistic-sounding phrase "compellably empanelled at quarter sessions" (*FW* 529.6–7) derives directly from Crofts's book. Similarly, the sentences "True bill. By a jury of matrons" (*FW* 242.21–22) also derive from Crofts, who defines a "true bill" and also explains "a jury of matrons."[9] Other legal terms from Crofts's book, sometimes distorted, such as "jackticktating," "feme sole," and "durant coverture," feature prominently in *FW* 243, part of Glugg's (Shem's) declarations about his parents during the Children's Games chapter, II.1.

Joyce's use of Crofts's book, when taken with his many citations of court cases (far more could be given), is further evidence of the importance of the law in his conception of *Finnegans Wake*. We can now see how this legal interest works out in the book itself.

Part I chapter 4 features a lengthy trial followed by court deliberations and a verdict of sorts (*FW* 85–96), all done in due form. A remarkable feature of this trial is that it is partly based on the "Maamtrasna murders" in Connemara in 1882. This was a case in which a number of men were tried and hanged for the murder of a family named Joyce. At least one of those tried, an elderly man called Myles Joyce, was widely believed to be innocent. He spoke only Irish, and his evidence was barely comprehended by the court through a very inadequate interpreter. James Joyce had written about the case before, for the Trieste newspaper *Il Piccolo della Sera* in 1907.[10] Here, of course, *Finnegans Wake* being a comic work, the treatment is very different. Yet it remains true that the Maamtrasna murder trial underpins this very baroque passage just as it underpins Joyce's original essay, where the trial becomes an exemplar of Ireland's position at the bar of world opinion. Two factors make the relevance of the Maamtrasna case indubitable. One is the reference at the start of this passage to the defendant, Festy King, as "a child of Maam" (*FW* 85.22–23), clearly alluding to Maamtrasna. The other factor is that when Festy finally gives evidence (*FW* 91.4–33), he does so through the medium of an Irish language that is in fact, with a different phonetic rendering, English: "mhuith peisth mhuise as fearra bheura muirre hriosmas" (*FW* 91.4–5), when said out loud, reveals itself to be "with best wishes for a very merry Christmas").[11]

This echoes the situation of Myles Joyce in the original Maamtrasna trial, who could testify only in Irish, which was not understood by the court.

The trial itself follows a fairly "normal" court report pattern, with a recognizable sequence of examination and probably cross-examination. We are told of the charges against Festy (one of throwing stones and the other of indecent exposure). There follows an account of the "evidence" from a couple of witnesses, succeeded by Festy King's own hilarious expostulation, protesting his innocence, naturally, which throws the court into chaos. After this, the four judges feel unable to do other than pronounce "their standing verdict of Nolans Brumans" (*FW* 93.1), a term that, as Roland McHugh notes, sounds very close to "nolens volens," as well as alluding to Bruno of Nola.[12] In any case, Festy King leaves the court, bequeathing a "vinesmelling" (*FW* 93.8) fart as a memorial of his presence. He is roundly rebuked by the members of the female bar, who are happy to see him go. That would seem to conclude matters, but there is an epilogue in which the four judges (who are the book's Four Old Men, perhaps best known under their combined name, derived from the Four Evangelists, Mamalujo) gather in their chambers, where, over quite a few drinks, they discuss the case, arguing about it, and then move on to exchange their usual confused versions of Irish history.

To make any sense of this dense passage—and there are many details that are still, and may always remain, deeply puzzling—it is necessary to put it in the context of the part of *Finnegans Wake* in which it appears. It is embedded in part I chapter 4, a chapter that, along with chapter 3, is devoted to a quest for HCE, who has undergone several metamorphoses since he first appeared in chapter 2. The trial in chapter 4 is part of that quest. Is Festy King another manifestation of HCE? Probably, though as the case progresses he begins to take on distinct shades of HCE's son Shem, the feckless writer character. (And in fact there is a letter from Joyce to Sylvia Beach in which he clearly refers to the defendant by the Shem siglum.)[13]

In any case, the most relevant comment on this trial is "Well, even should not the framing up of such figments in the evidential order bring the true truth to light . . ." (*FW* 96.26-27). As *Finnegans Wake* statements go, this is pretty clear; it states that even recourse to the idiom and setting of the law—noted of course as a means of bring the "true truth" to light—has not succeeded in establishing the facts in this instance.

Finnegans Wake stages this bind, the bind between the need to establish what happened during the encounter in the park set out in part I chapter 2 and the impossibility of finding any language or linguistic form capable of giving it expression. But while this appears to be the book's formal dilemma, its recourse to the language of the law—a special linguistic universe—is in many ways self-delighting. All special discourses are grist for this book's mill. Law, with its refined circumlocutions, its frequently tendentious distinctions, its apparent linguistic abstraction from the actual matters it is dealing with, provides a special instance of a discourse that is ripe for exploitation in *Finnegans Wake*'s unique terms. And Joyce's painstaking assembly of citations from legal documents in the notebooks proves how important this discourse was for him in bringing together the "active elements" (as he called them himself) that would eventually "fuse" to create *Finnegans Wake* (*Letters* 1: 204).

The passage goes on to say that despite this failure, "by such playing possum our hagious curious encestor bestly saved his brush with his posterity" (*FW* 96.34–35)—in other words (in other words!) that by playing dead and thus eluding the attentions of the law and other agencies, HCE managed to preserve himself for posterity. And indeed shortly thereafter he turns into a fox (hence the "brush" in the quoted passage) who is hotly pursued but who manages to elude his pursuers, thus reinforcing the point about his untraceability. This is one of the prime functions of the law in this text—as an exemplar of the way in which even the most searching inquiry is sometimes doomed to fall short of its object.

III

One way in which in the law proves useful to the author of *Finnegans Wake* is as a source of parodic discourse. The law's tendency to use its own semi-private language, to employ terms that are exclusive to it—often a cause of irritation among the public—is a boon to an author who can very precisely utilize such locutions for purposes sometimes very far from those for which they are normally employed. An extended example is provided by *FW* 572–76. It begins as a case cited from Roman law—and of course Roman law remains one of the primary underpinnings of the law today, as evidenced by the amount of Latin still used in it.

The case concerns one Honuphrius, about whom we are informed in the first place that he is engaging, or preparing to engage, in sexual activities with "Felicia, a virgin" (*FW* 572.23) and with Eugenius and Jeremias, "two or three philadelphians" (*FW.* 572.24). All four, we are told, are "consanguineous to the lowest degree" (*FW* 572.25)—so, in other words, incest is very much involved. Honuphrius's wife, Anita, has been informed by her maidservant, Fortissa, that Honuphrius wants her to commit adultery with Magravius, "a commercial, emulous of Honuphrius" (*FW* 572.30). If readers are not yet confused, they soon will be, as multiple characters are introduced, all engaging in some act of unnatural copulation with a close relative, or else urging their wives or friends to some such act, in a debauched scenario made all the more explicit by the chaste legal Latinate prose in which it is described. In the slightly moralistic language of the completed book's very first expounders, Campbell and Robinson, "One is struck with horror that such matters can be discussed in the boring terminology of everyday legal experience."[14] The scenario is presented as a sort of "case stated" ("cases stated" arise where a lower court feels that in the course of a trial an important point of law has arisen that only a higher court can resolve), a conundrum (it is called a "proposer" in *FW* 572.19–20) for the higher court to resolve. And a knotty conundrum it is. The ultimate question posed is "Has he [Honuphrius] hegemony and shall she [Anita] submit?" (*FW* 573.32). Hegemony, which is not a particularly legal term, seems here to refer to Honuphrius's power to compel Anita to have sexual congress either with him or with some other male. So the question comes down to the power of a husband over a wife—an issue at other points in the book, notably the end of part III, chapter 3. Almost all the characters mentioned in this convoluted saga are recognizable as derived from the principal figures in the book. Honuphrius and Anita, for instance, are clearly HCE and ALP, the main male and female elements. So things are not quite as murky as they at first seem.

It is worth noting that this passage appears at a very late stage in the book, in the penultimate chapter. By this point, many permutations of these basic figures—HCE, his wife, their children, the Four Old Men, the twelve customers at HCE's pub, the boots at the inn, the maidservant Kate—have been run through. They should have grown familiar to us. So by the time page 572 is arrived at, it is possible to play around with these figures, to put them into highly unlikely, not to say grotesque, positions. Joyce in a way "riffs" on them, putting them through the hoops one more time. Something similar happens in the Ithaca episode of *Ulysses*, where the treatment of Bloom and Stephen becomes very detached, their travails apparently of far less concern to the narrator than the formal question-and-answer mode in which the episode is couched. We don't have to feel as moralistic about the whole scenario as Campbell and Robinson did, and indeed more recent commentary is far more relaxed about it. A general point about earlier treatments of *Finnegans Wake* is indeed how moralistic they tend to be; even William York Tindall, in his 1969 *Reader's Guide to "Finnegans Wake,"* still seemed rather shocked at the content of this passage. For all kinds of reasons, we are now less easily shocked, and perhaps more open to the comic.

This passage leads on to an even more legalistic scene. That *Finnegans Wake* can switch perspective with dizzying rapidity from the personal to the social and the historical is well known, and this is what happens here. There has been a hint already in the Honuphrius passage, where it is mentioned that the aforesaid Honuphrius "pretends publicly to possess his conjunct in thirtynine several manners" (*FW* 573.19–20), a clear reference to the thirty-nine articles of faith of the Church of England. In this subsequent passage, *FW* 573–76, the reference to the churches, to church history, and to history in general becomes much more explicit. This is a trial—a civil action for damages—over an unpaid and possibly dud cheque. The case is heard before a judge and jury all of whom are named Doyle, and a key witness is called Ann Doyle. As the name would suggest, the Doyles, and especially Ann Doyle, represent the Irish Catholic population.[15] Ann is a junior partner in a firm called Tangos, "a foreign firm" (*FW* 574.5), apparently the Irish Catholic Church, which is being challenged over the validity of the cheque by a rival firm called Pango, apparently the Anglican Church, and possibly also the English crown. Eventually Judge Jeremy Doyle rules that Ann has been a slave since the time of the Norman Conquest and therefore not entitled to sign any cheque, that Pepigi, the permanent trustee of the Tangos firm, is a corpse, and that therefore the value of the cheque cannot be recovered.

This passage features many legal terms, mostly used in their correct sense. Thus "the lodgment of the species" (*FW* 574.17) refers to the act of depositing money—though the use of the term "species" rather than the correct "specie" suggests that rather more is going on. To "particularise" (*FW* 574.18) is to allege a special issue in the defense. Many other such terms are scattered throughout. There is a great deal of citing of faux-legal authorities, as beloved by learned judges: "D'Oyly Owens holds (though Finn Magnusson of himself holds also)" (*FW* 574.1–2). There is some marvellous wordplay, particularly the memorable "went outside his jurisfiction altogether" (*FW* 574.34). Hard though it is to credit, this court case is an allegorical account of Irish ecclesiastical and general history since the Norman conquest—the reference to "Hal Kilbride" (*FW* 576.6), or Henry VIII, is an important clue—presented in the guise of an action at civil law. It is therefore quite a serious subject, but presented, as always, in an absurdist comic mode. To such unlikely uses, in a work like this, can the law be applied.

The most sustained use of a legal framework—a "jurisfiction"—to underpin the structure of *Finnegans Wake* occurs in part III chapter 3 (*FW* 474–554). This, the longest chapter of the book, takes the form of an inquiry, a "sworn starchamber quiry" (*FW* 475.18–19) conducted by the Four Old Men upon the prostrate form of Yawn, as the Shaun figure is now known in the third of his four "watches" in part III. It is in part a séance, since through Yawn's body come the voices of most of the characters of the book. Moreover, as the inquiry goes on, the identities of the interrogators seem to change: the Four Old Men having proved pretty ineffectual, they are supplanted by a younger, sharper team, a sort of "braintrust" (*FW* 529.5). However, the term "sworn starchamber quiry" clearly indicates that this is a kind of tribunal, an inquisitorial exercise designed to elicit the truth about some issue. As such, it resembles more the style of investigation practiced in continental Europe than the adversarial court system common in the Anglo-American tradition and also in use in Ireland. Such investigations in the Anglo-Saxon tradition are held via tribunals of inquiry, which have considerable legal powers but are not courts. (The original star chamber in medieval England was a kind of superior court with greater powers than ordinary courts. It became, as time went on, a byword for abuse of the legal process. However, it is certainly true that "inquiry" was one of its functions.)

The inquiry in this instance is not adversarial; in fact, the only disputes occur among the inquirers themselves, not between the subject of the inquiry and the inquirers. Quite a bit of the text is taken up with rows between the Four Old Men, which greatly hamper the progress, such as it is, of the inquiry. Nonetheless, progress is made: we delve deeper into the experience, first of Shaun, then gradually of many of the other major figures in the book, ending with the primal persona of HCE himself, the work's progenitor, who delivers himself of a long speech going back to the very foundation of Dublin itself and bringing the chapter to an extremely powerful and moving conclusion.[16] One could well feel, comparing the book's portrayal of the trial system and the inquiry system as methods of eliciting the truth, that the latter is far more effective.

And this relative success, as compared with the tangles and contradictions that the various trial scenes appear to involve, may betoken a superior valuation of the inquiry mode in the course of the work as a whole. This goes back, perhaps, to the purpose of the inquiry, as compared to that of the trial: the difference is that one involves *judging*, the application of a moral and social standard to the action committed, while the other is engaged merely in finding out what actually happened, without passing judgment upon it. The limitations of the trial format are perhaps best articulated in this passage: "Thus the unfacts, did we possess them, are too imprecisely few to warrant our certitude, the evidencegivers by legpoll too untrustworthily irreperible where his adjugers are semmingly freak threes but his judicandees plainly minus twos" (*FW* 57.16–19). It is also evident from elsewhere in the work that the twelve jurors at HCE's trial are deeply hostile to him: "by reverendum they found him guilty of their and those imputations of fornicolopulation with two of his albowcrural correlations" (*FW* 557.15–17). It is as if the book has started on a course that it has found is not going to work, but it has to plow ahead anyway until, toward the end in part III chapter 3, it hits upon a way that, despite many obscurities, does lead to rather more enlightenment than anything that has gone before.

This exploration of the function of the law in Joyce's last work confirms one's sense that the *Wake*'s general principle is heuristic rather than teleological: that it is not an apocalypse, a last judgment, a prophetic book, or a secret scripture. Rather, in accordance with its circular structure, it is a series of probes, an ongoing, endless inquiry which finally escapes the structure of judging in which law itself seems inevitably caught up.

The law, then, is ultimately one of several forms of discourse that are tried out in this work in its ongoing project, never achieved, "to sneeze out a likelihood that will solve and salve life's robulous rebus" (*FW* 12.33–34). This is the project gestured at in my epigraph (rendered much more pointed in the new Rose-O'Hanlon edition)—the doomed "quest for righteousness," for the truth about the fall of Finnegan and the consequences thereof. In this quest the law is a privileged form of discourse for two reasons. One is the law's unique claim to authority: only religion can claim to be more authoritative, more grounded, than the law, and yet this particular case proves too painful and problematic to resolve. The other reason is that the law is to a remarkable extent its own linguistic universe, providing its own highly specialized terminology and idioms, as well as the unique linguistic structure of the trial mode: statement of claim, defense, testimony, cross-examination, summing-up, judgment.[17] Such a highly elaborate linguistic and social structure could not but feature strongly in this work, and even if, as has been shown, the "quest" ultimately and inevitably fails, law's huge contribution to this essentially linguistic universe—the material it provides for all the fun that is had along the way—matters far more.

Notes

Epigraph: The epigraph quotes the Danis Rose and John O'Hanlon edition. The standard edition of *Finnegans Wake* up to this point, the 1939 Viking edition, reads "search for tighteousness" (5). In an ongoing scholarly scandal, Rose and O'Hanlon have not released the apparatus for their editorial decisions in their edition. However, consultation of the *James Joyce Archive* (*Finnegans Wake*, book I, *Galley Proofs*, 1: 293) confirms that Joyce's original manuscript inscription was "righteousness"; this was subsequently misread by a typist as "tighteousness" (ibid., 292), and the error was incorporated into all subsequent editions.

1. Deane, Ferrer, and Lernout, *Notebooks*, VI.B 10: 65.
2. Ibid., 8.
3. Power, *Conversations with James Joyce*, 72–76.
4. Young, *Trial of Frederick Bywaters and Edith Thompson*.
5. The letter of Mrs. Thompson to Bywaters, as it appeared in the trial record, reads: "Je suis goche darlint and disappointed" (Young, *Trial*, 227). René Weis in *Criminal Justice*, 92, speculates that "goche," in the context, is a mistranscription of "fâché," which Thompson may have actually written.
6. For a recent account of the importance of the Tristan legend in Joyce's early work on *Finnegans Wake*, see Ferrer, *Brouillons d'un baiser*. See also Hayman, *The "Wake" in Transit*.
7. Deane, Ferrer, and Lernout, *Notebooks*, VI.B 10: 84.
8. Nonetheless, in a letter to his brother Stanislaus on 18 July 1931 he does quote "Hargreave's Laws of England,"—rightly corrected by Richard Ellmann in *Letters* 2: 637 to "Halsbury's"—perhaps the fundamental work on English law. As Vincent Deane writes in his introduction to notebook VI.B 33, Joyce's interest in works on marriage law was certainly stimulated by the complicated question of his own marriage to Nora in 1931. He

became something of an expert on the topic. See Deane, Ferrer, and Lernout, *Notebooks*, VI.B 33: 5, and Bowker, *James Joyce*, 410–29, the best treatment of the subject.

9. Crofts, *Women under English Law*, 12, 14. A "jury of matrons" was a jury of women who, at a time when women were debarred from juries, were empaneled to decide on a claim by a woman prisoner who had been condemned to death that she was pregnant. If the jury found the claim was correct, sentence was deferred until after the birth, though Crofts states (14) that in practice in latter years the sentence was always commuted to penal servitude for life. It is also worth mentioning that the phrase "true bill" is used by Mr. Kernan in the story "Grace" in *Dubliners*, suggesting it was a fairly standard term for something, usually unpleasant, that is accepted as a fact (*D* 159).

10. Joyce, *Occasional, Critical, and Political Writing*, 145–48.

11. A device also used by Myles na Gopaleen (Flann O'Brien) in his *Irish Times* column.

12. McHugh, *Annotations to "Finnegans Wake,"* 93.

13. Banta and Silverman, *Letters to Sylvia Beach*, 125.

14. Campbell and Robinson, *Skeleton Key to "Finnegans Wake,"* 269.

15. Notebook VI.B 10 links the name Ann Doyle to An Dáil, the newly founded Irish parliament; see Deane, Ferrer, and Lernout, *Notebooks*, VI.B 10: 32.

16. One of the voices that come through in the course of this inquiry, that of Anna Livia, has recently been the subject of an extremely searching and revelatory exposition: Devlin and Zhang, "ALP's Polyvocal Testimony in III.3."

17. It is this comparative neglect of the linguistic dimension of the work that is the main shortcoming of Edmund L. Epstein's recent and very helpful *Guide through "Finnegans Wake,"* probably the most useful text on Joyce's last work to appear for some time. Epstein does a superb job, born of a lifetime's acquaintance with the work, in elucidating the overarching narrative of *Finnegans Wake*—but sometimes at the expense of the work's intricate verbal arabesques.

Works Cited

Banta, Melissa, and Oscar A. Silverman, eds. *James Joyce's Letters to Sylvia Beach, 1921–1940*. Bloomington: Indiana University Press, 1987.

Bowker, Gordon. *James Joyce: A Biography*. London: Weidenfeld and Nicolson, 2011.

Campbell, Joseph, and Henry Morton Robinson. *A Skeleton Key to "Finnegans Wake."* London: Faber, 1947.

Crofts, Maud I. *Women under English Law*. London: National Council of Women of Great Britain, 1925.

Deane, Vincent, Daniel Ferrer, and Geert Lernout, eds. *The "Finnegans Wake" Notebooks at Buffalo*. 9 vols. Turnhout: Brepols, 2001–4.

Devlin, Kimberly J., and Mingming Zhang. "ALP's Polyvocal Testimony in III.3: A Collaborative Interpretation." *James Joyce Quarterly* 49.1 (Fall 2011): 91–107.

Epstein, Edmund L. *A Guide through "Finnegans Wake."* Gainesville: University Press of Florida, 2009.

Ferrer, Daniel, ed. *Brouillons d'un baiser: Premiers pas vers "Finnegans Wake."* English text with facing translation by Marie Darrieussecq. Paris: Gallimard, 2014.

Hayman, David. *The "Wake" in Transit.* Ithaca, NY: Cornell University Press, 1990.

Joyce, James. *Finnegans Wake.* New York: Viking, 1939.

———. *Finnegans Wake.* Edited by Danis Rose and John O'Hanlon. London: Penguin, 2012.

———. *James Joyce Archive: A Facsimile of the Buffalo Notebooks.* Edited by Michael Groden. 63 vols. New York: Garland, 1978.

———. *Occasional, Critical, and Political Writing.* Edited by Kevin Barry. Translations from the Italian by Conor Deane. Oxford: Oxford University Press, 2000.

McHugh, Roland. *Annotations to "Finnegans Wake."* 3rd ed. Baltimore: Johns Hopkins University Press, 2006.

Power, Arthur. *Conversations with James Joyce.* 1974. Dublin: Lilliput, 1999.

Tindall, William York. *A Reader's Guide to "Finnegans Wake."* London: Thames and Hudson, 1969.

Weis, René J. A. *Criminal Justice: The True Story of Edith Thompson.* London: Hamish Hamilton, 1988.

Young, Filson, ed. *The Trial of Frederick Bywaters and Edith Thompson.* Edinburgh: W. Hodge, 1923.

11

The Logos of Trademark

Joyce, Bass Ale, and Brand Insignias

JONATHAN GOLDMAN

The legacy of James Joyce incorporates seemingly contradictory ideas. Joyce's work earned a reputation for time-consuming difficulty while offering up an easily graspable writerly persona—that of the elusive avant-garde genius par excellence. The apparent incongruity between the incomprehensible and the instantly comprehensible can be reconciled by reading Joyce alongside trademark law. Joyce generates a codified, caricatured version of authorial identity that echoes trademark's basic conception as "a sort of shorthand symbol used to indicate the trade origin of goods" (Great Britain Patent Office 4), while promoting a particular form of literary consumption that signals the singular quality of his work. The coexistence of complexity and simplicity that inflects Joyce's renown, furthermore, mirrors the underlying complexities of trademark law, which relies on contrary principles of distinction and reproducibility and reconceives the relationship between consumers and objects.

Branding, Modernism, and Criticism

This essay examines Joyce through the aperture of trademark discourse—as seen in legal and visual texts from Joyce's time—to show how trademark law in the late 1800s and early 1900s provided modernist culture with new ways to imagine the author/artist's relation to the marketplace. At the center of the essay is Leopold Bloom's fixation on the Bass Ale logo, which was, as many Joyce readers know, the first case under Britain's Trade Marks

Registration Act of 1875, and which makes numerous cameos in modernist art. In *Ulysses*, I will argue, the Bass triangle is used to equate consumption of the object with recognition of the code that signals and distinguishes it, an idea that resonates with Joyce's particular self-construction as author. I will suggest that, because trademark is a phenomenon of Joyce's historical moment and a preoccupation of his culture, its processes inflect both his self-branding and his narratives. Indeed, the overlap between these aspects of Joyce's work—his authorial imprimatur and his textual techniques—is clarified by reading trademark laws in tandem with *Ulysses*.[1]

Spurred by the example of the Bass logo (technically a *logomark*, a nonrepresentational printed graphic), whose author is lost to history, this essay focuses on registered icons rather than brand names. There have been forms of branding and brand marks for centuries, but my specific concern here is with corporate emblems. Registration and government protection of trademarks emerged as a central concern in the late nineteenth century for English-speaking cultures and retained relevance through the first half of the twentieth. In 1862, Great Britain's Merchandise Marks Act prohibited merchants from fraudulently using company brand names and insignias (Poland 3). This was superseded by the more emphatic 1875 law, which was the first to place the government in charge of validating ownership of such marks, inaugurating formal registration of trademarks through the United Kingdom Patent Office and offering legal recourse in the event of infringement, starting on 1 January 1876 (Great Britain Patent Office 20). Revisions of Britain's trademark registration laws passed in 1883, 1888, 1905, 1919, and 1938 but not again until 1994 (ibid. 8), showing that, while its heritage is Victorian, British trademark becomes a modernist concern, undergoing continual modification during Joyce's 1882–1941 lifetime.

Scholars have paid incomplete attention to trademark's presence in Joyce, even though its principles have lurked within the Joyce narrative, including his biography. In his legal imbroglio with literary bootlegger Samuel Roth, Joyce invoked the idea of legal ownership of the brand name, which falls under trademark law. His representatives in the United States "sought and won an injunction barring Roth and his publishing company from 'using the name of the plaintiff [Joyce] for advertising purposes or for the purposes of trade,'" according to Robert Spoo, quoting from legal briefs (108). The gambit deployed a central tenet of trademark: that a brand name, in order to perform its function, must refer to a sole purveyor who controls its use.² This principle happens also to animate the authorial brand name as it arises in recent modernist criticism, sometimes in reference to Joyce but rarely incorporating analysis of the legal regime that subsumes brand names.³ For recent scholars, the brand name usually serves as a metaphor for the forging of modernist reputations, a figure for modernist writers' engagement with the marketplace and the attendant discourses of advertising, self-promotion, and celebrity. In this view, Ezra Pound's command that writers "make it new" smuggles in the stipulation that writers be distinct, stamp their work as the product of a sole creator designated by author name. The figure of trademark thus can be heard in high modernist rhetoric and underlying recent scholarship. Its rhetorical roles, along with the Roth influence in *Ulysses*'s print history, spotlight the relevance of trademark to Joyce and the gap in criticism that this essay begins to fill.

I doubt I would have pursued this topic without the example of critics such as Spoo and Paul K. Saint-Amour, who engage Joyce alongside copyright issues—the system of intellectual property that overtly addresses literary production and the legal regime that governs the circulation and accessibility of texts.⁴ Unlike copyright criticism, though, I am looking at the legal regime not for the way Joyce and his publishers and agents made litigious use of it but for the way its principles guide his work. While copyright implies originality, and the putative ownership of material by one discrete entity, trademark is based on subtly different concepts. These include distinctiveness (the difference of one object from others, and the value that difference generates) and recognizability (the instant identifiability of one object amid the marketplace of objects).

Distinctiveness and recognition are written into the text of the 1875 law, which invites individual merchants and companies to register the "name of an individual or firm printed in some particular and distinctive manner; or a written signature or copy of a written signature of an individual or firm; or a distinctive device, mark, heading label or ticket" (Wood 87–88). The statute characterizes a "distinctive" trademark as an instantly recognizable code for authenticating a product's manufacturing history and quality. It is on the surface an attempt to deter the duplicitous from defrauding consumers. The 1875 act exemplifies how the language of early trademark law assumes and promotes the market's inherent "good will" toward consumers (Heymann 80). At the same time, the trademark broadcasts the commodity's distinctiveness vis-à-vis others. The notion of trademark assumes that the marketing benefits that accrue to a brand are desirable enough for this authentication. Trademark discourse is thus unclear regarding whose rights it is protecting.

That ambiguity is not the only vexation inherent to the legal regime. For instance, trademark communicates the notion of distinctiveness through printed logos, images that are infinitely reproducible. It thus relies on an interdependence of singularity and multiplicity. Furthermore, trademark is predicated on a relationship between the signifying mark and the commodity that does not exist until authenticated by the legal regime, meaning the government that approves and enforces that relationship. One cannot trademark a word that names or describes the product, such as "beer" or "bitter." Neither can one trademark a picture of the commodity. Even in early incarnations of the law, the registered trademark had to be an otherwise unrelated referent, such as, say, "Plumtree" for a canned meat product, a name noted in *Ulysses* as a "registered trade mark" (*U* 17.604).

Undergirded by these principles, trademark creates a system of identification that detaches the insignia from both the manufacturing source of the object and the experience of the commodity. Instead, it promises a repetition of earlier moments of consumption. In trademark, meaning derives from consumption of the brand logo, a re-experience of the brand's recognizability and state-protected status.

The Case of Bass

It might seem counterintuitive to treat Joyce alongside a nonlinguistic device; the un-obviousness of the enterprise is reflected in the relative lack of writing on the topic. One critical trailblazer, John Rocco, addresses the Bass logo in a 1996 *James Joyce Quarterly* article, arguing that the emblem's appearance in *Ulysses* resonates with Joyce's technique (399–409), a view with which I agree, though I reach my conclusion quite differently. The significance of the Bass Ale triangle and its deployment in *Ulysses* stem from both Bass's status as the first case of the 1875 act, entered into the rolls on 1 January 1876 (Bamforth 57), and the emblem's ensuing appearances in modernist art. Its appearances in visual culture come to signal trademark's processes and contradictions writ large. These make the Bass logo into, one might say, the insignia of trademark law, the trademark that refers to trademark.

The Bass Ale Corporation, located at Burton-on-Trent and dating to the 1700s, scored the first legally protected British trademark not by merit but by industry and foresight. The Bass brewers, as indicated by their promotional text, registered their trademark to prevent customers from getting tricked into consuming an inferior product. The company's 2011 bottle proclaims:

> As Bass Ale's popularity grew, unscrupulous imitators tried to pass off inferior products as Bass by copying the unique Red Triangle logo. In 1875, concerned for the reputation of their beloved brew, Bass Brewers applied for and were granted Britain's first registered trademark.[5]

By registering the trademark, the company makes the icon signify the brand and the brand signify marketplace prestige and exceptionalism. The brewery and the state cosign a guarantee that buying a bottle marked with the red triangle means purchasing a product brewed to the standards of the Bass Corporation, whether the transaction occurs in London, Dublin, or Paris.[6]

That Bass's trademark, during the late nineteenth century, necessitated legal protection, that the brand was known as far away as the Continent, can be seen by its appearance in Edouard Manet's 1882 painting *Un Bar aux Folies-Bergère*. This, Manet's ultimate work, launched the Bass logo's journey in modern art. Exhibited in Joyce's birth year, the painting helped to establish the Bass triangle as representing the complexities of trademark discourse, setting in motion a pattern of using the emblem to contemplate the branding of the artist/author.

Manet's nightclub scene includes two bottles marked with the red triangle sitting sentry on either end of the marble bar, behind which stands a uniformed woman employee. The painting's appropriation of a registered trademark, the precursor to twentieth-century product placements by Jasper Johns, Andy Warhol, and Mr. Brainwash, foregrounds numerous theoretical concerns that will persist through trademark discourse at the turn of the century and through Joyce's inclusion of the Bass bottle in *Ulysses*.

Setting two Bass beers among a crowd of bottles whose labels are unreadable connotes the characteristic of being uncharacteristic, of standing out in a crowd. The interplay of distinction, reproducibility, and commodification is written into the picture, signaled by visual connections between the Bass logo, the bartender's red floral triangle at her bodice, and Manet's own name in signature, adjacent to a Bass bottle at the bottom left. Manet pairs the Bass logo with his painted signature, prompting Carol Armstrong to see the name as "a trademark, the logo for a product" (285). Armstrong, in keeping with contemporary critical tendency,[7] uses the term "trademark" metaphorically—Manet's name is not and cannot be a registered device—to imply that the signature functions as a mark of distinction. This parallel of logo and signature proposes a contrast between the mechanical reproducibility of the trademark and the supposed corporeal connection of the signature. Resolving the contrast is the fact that the artist's signature, like the brand, is bound into a relation determined by the marketplace. The art market is itself girded by ideas of distinction and prestige. That is to say, the name Manet invokes legal and commercial regimes in order to signal "the artist," a gesture revisited by later texts of modernism.

Repetition and Recognition

Manet's 1882 use of the red triangle and its implications in *Un Bar* prefaces a series of Bass appropriations that place trademark at the center of modernist concerns over distinction and reproducibility. Some twenty Pablo Picasso pieces from the 1910s harp on Bass, occasionally omitting the logo in favor of the brand name, according to Rocco (402).[8] Picasso's disciple Juan Gris, Georges Braque, and the less known but equally representative modernist painter Henry Hayden all produced important Cubist works depicting the logo while living in Paris during the years just prior to Joyce's arrival or once Joyce was there,[9] completing *Ulysses*, commencing *Finnegans Wake*, and fighting his legal battles. The repetitions of the Bass brand and label emphasize the exemplary status of the trademark and, even in omission, highlight recognizability as its central characteristic. They also, by virtue of announcing an intertextual connection between different painters and works, signal the relation of trademark to the artistic imprimatur. The Bass trademark's journey from Manet to the years during and after World War I—the moment of high modernism—confirms its role as an abstract for brand logos, a sign that, even when appropriated and recontextualized, refers to the processes and contradictions of trademark and how they relate to authorial identity.[10]

While trademark proclaims the singularity of the commodity and the object's distinction from other marketplace objects, it also relies on repetition and sameness. It addresses the relationship between consumer and corporation but also incorporates the idea that a brand logo signifies itself rather than the product or its origin. Such counterintuitive ideas become increasingly visible in the trademark discourse of the *Ulysses* years. In the paintings of the 1910s and 1920s, for example, the Bass trademark's recognizability is reinforced by its repetition, and it matters more that the triangle refers to a brand than that it refers to a beer. These complexities surface in legal writings of the time, as well. In a 1927 *Harvard Law Review* article considered a legal landmark, F. W. Schechter writes that trademark

> indicates, not that the article in question comes from a definite or particular source, the characteristics of which or the personalities connected with which are specifically known to the consumer, but merely that the goods in connection with which it is used emanate from the same—possibly anonymous—source or have reached the consumer through the same channels as certain other goods that have already given the consumer satisfaction, and that bore the same trademark. (819)

Here, the mechanical reproducibility of the insignia is essential to that commercial goodwill that buttresses trademark: the replication is responsible for corroborating present and past experiences of consumption. Schechter describes the way a trademark, instead of guaranteeing the commodity's manufacture history and origin, instead promises a repetition of those experiences in the customer's past; the consumer will primarily reexperience the trademark and secondarily the product and brand. Extending this logic, one can see that trademark announces and thus asserts that the current moment of consumption replicates prior instances, making it irrelevant whether the present matches the past on an aesthetic or sensory level. That is to say, trademark determines the replication of that experience by making customers consume the sign, which determines the subject's empirical experiences and thus creates its own narrative of the material past.

The ideas latent in Schechter and the modern-art appearances of the Bass logo, all closely contemporary to *Ulysses*, cast trademark as a system of objects that signify, primarily, their previous iterations. This premise aligns with our current moment; Rosemary Coombe says that the brand trademark has evolved into culture's "quintessential self-referential sign" that "replaces the products themselves as the site of fetishism" (55–56). Trademark's force in our contemporary marketplace, she argues, is largely independent of the commodity. Even in the case of first encounter between customer and commodity, the trademark is the object of consumption. My own reading agrees that trademarks are by nature tautological signs, referring primarily to recognition of themselves, their present iterations rewriting the past to underwrite the present and make promises about future consumption. It is a kind of fiction, one that emerges in Joyce's own writing.

The Fictions of Trademark

Regardless of whether Joyce was aware of the Bass logo's appearances in the art world, his use of trademark suggests its significance to *Ulysses* and to Joyce's authorial identity, meanwhile demonstrating that he participates in the zeitgeist of trademark. In Joyce, the trademark indeed emerges as an emblem of itself, conveying primarily the recognition of signs. His authorial self-fashioning echoes this logic. Joyce's literary technique, notably his polyvalent use of style, contributes to an identity based not on one characteristic but on the idea of characteristics, recognizable codes: Joyce's figurative trademark is his self-positioning as a metaphorically trademarked entity. He makes distinction the sign of his writing. To echo Daniel J. Boorstin's famous dismissal of celebrity, he is distinctive for being distinctive. Thus his work emphasizes consumption of the sign, creating an easily accessible code for the authorial brand.

Joyce channels his meditation on trademark through Bloom, the ad canvasser, who stares intently at a Bass bottle for a while. It is, therefore, intuitive to understand Bloom's fixation as an example of his attention to publicity depicted throughout *Ulysses*. Mark Osteen reads the scene as proof that Bloom "is subjected to the power of goods to arrest and magnetize attention" (221). Garry Leonard goes further, arguing that Bloom is derided for his interest and saying that "the consumer mesmerized before the product" represents "a degraded version" of religious worship (38). Indeed, Bloom continually ruminates over, and internalizes, products and publicity: transferring his marital frustration into an obsession with the slogan for Plumtree's Potted Meat, identifying Pear's Soap as the solution for Bantam Lyons's hygienic difficulties, reading the *Agendath Netaim* tree-planting campaign propaganda, admiring Catholicism's strategic mystifications, crossing paths with sandwich-board men, attempting to renew a logomark newspaper advertisement, and plotting ways to attract consumer attention for a variety of enterprises. No other logo enraptures Bloom like the Bass logo, though; the extremity of his ardor invites a reading of *Ulysses* with regard to the triangle's status and legal history and its repeated appearances in modernist painting: contexts that reflect Joyce's own trademarking.

The Bass logo's immediate context, the "Oxen of the Sun" episode, signals the idea of trademark in two ways. One is the literal branding evoked by the chapter title and its corresponding episode in *The Odyssey* in which the sailors steal livestock belonging to the sun god's herds. "Oxen," that is, reminds us of the historical origin of branding, a mark of possession burned onto bodies, animal or otherwise. In Homer, Odysseus's crew land in trouble when they disregard Helios the sun god's claim over his cattle and sheep—herds and flocks that, like those of the famous Maverick family in Texas, are not branded. Thus the episode title evokes the insignia of ownership and its relation to consumption. Secondly, "Oxen of the Sun" excavates the notion of writing, and particularly style, as literary property and examines literary property as authorial identity.[11] In this chapter, Joyce flaunts his masterful stylistic mimicry, narrating the episode in forty formally distinct passages, each corresponding to an historical moment in English letters, most aping a particular writer.[12] The episode deploys these distinct styles to offer an author who can speak in any voice, whose ability to imitate is inimitable. The ventriloquistic variability suggests that the episode is *Ulysses* in miniature, a distillation of the novel's overall technical play.[13] Joyce asserts his distinct stylistic identity through reproducing other voices, and the "Oxen" episode is a central site of this process.

Ulysses mentions the Bass bottle in three moments occurring over several pages. The bottle and its brand are obscure at first, but each depiction incrementally illuminates the brand identity, until the third one announces that this is indeed a Bass beer bottle that Bloom beholds. Conversely, only the first instance clearly delineates the trademark image. That is, the overt description of the Bass logo is set in an inverse relationship to the overt announcement of the brand. These moments combine to devalue the relationship between the logo and the beer it represents.

The triangle first materializes, made strange, in a passage meant to echo the opium-inflected writings of Thomas De Quincey. Bloom, lost in thought, envisions "a ruby and triangled sign" situated among the heavens (*U* 14.1108–1109). The sign is appointed as the "forehead" of the constellation Taurus, the bull. As part of a constellation, the triangle is figuratively affixed to an outline traced only in theory, to a culture's imaginary design existing in two dimensions. It resides on the surface of an intangible object, as if to indicate the irrelevance of what lies beyond the sign itself. The reference to the bull, and thus to Great Britain, offers a vague hint of the triangle's commercial and legal function (while also implicating the icon within the episode's discussion of English-Irish history). Here, despite its color and shape, the logo is hardly recognizable. Neither the bottle, the beer, nor the brand is mentioned.

The dark picture brightens in the subsequent reference. As Don Gifford notes, Joyce depicts Lenehan complaining of his failed wager on a racehorse that he mistakenly believes is owned by the Bass chief executive (434). "If I had poor luck with Bass's mare perhaps this draught of his may serve me," he says, reaching for a bottle with a "scarlet label" (*U* 14.1161–1164). Lenehan is stayed from disturbing the bottle when Buck Mulligan alerts him to Bloom's continued transfixed stare. The text thus hints that this bottle has been the focus of Bloom's reverie for some duration. Lenehan's lament offers a coded clue to the identity of the label and, thus, an explanation of the ruby triangle from several passages earlier. It also replays motifs of the episode, since it satirizes animal ownership through Lenehan's brand misattribution. Again the novel shows a tenuous relationship between logo, logos, and commodity.

The third appearance unambiguously names the brand and its geographical source, though it depicts the triangle itself only indirectly.

> During the past four minutes or thereabouts he had been staring hard at a certain amount of number one Bass bottled by Messrs Bass and Co at Burton-on-Trent which happened to be situated amongst a lot of others right opposite to where he was and which was certainly calculated to attract anyone's remark on account of its scarlet appearance. (*U* 14.1181–1185)

The description alludes to the triangle through its "scarlet appearance" designed to attract attention to the bottle and by the brand name and the location of the brewery. *Ulysses*, like Manet's *Un Bar*, emphasizes that this one label is instantly identified, since it does not name other brands among the bottles arrayed on the table—though there is some syntactical confusion about whether it is the Bass bottle or Burton-on-Trent that is situated amongst the anonymous, brandless objects. The words "number one" designate the specific variety of the Bass product (there existed at the time a Bass Number Two, whose logo became the second registered trademark) while slyly alluding to that logo's primacy in British trademark law.

This instance implies that trademark conflates recognition of an icon with consumption of the product. The passage does not refer to the logo's triangular shape but, in suggesting a backwards glance at the previous references to the bottle, it offers a clarification. The "ruby and triangled sign" acts as the last word. That is, the retrospective view portrays the logo as an object for consumption rather than as a brand signifier. Indeed, throughout these passages, there is no mention of actually drinking the bottle's contents; on the contrary, poor Lenehan's attempt is stymied, and Bloom surreptitiously dumps the beer out so as to mask his socially unacceptable abstinence (*U* 14.1194–1197).

The logo, not the beverage, remains the relevant object of consumption throughout the narrative transformations among styles that are based on the works of De Quincey, Landor, and Thomas Babington Macaulay. While the "Oxen" episode changes authorial identities through its evolving literary voices, shifts that reveal an author who can appropriate any style, the Bass logo's primary reference—to itself—is immutable. My understanding of Joyce's treatment of Bass here differs from that of Rocco, for whom the multiple portrayals of the icon suggest indeterminacy. Rocco writes, "Joyce undermines the stability of the trademark by giving it to us in three different voices." He adds that the logo serves as "an object of the everyday world that has the power to be transformed" (404). While noting that the logo undergoes linguistic metamorphosis, Rocco misses the retrospective assertion of its meaning as trademark and object of consumption. The second and third inclusions of the Bass bottle invoke the brand's trademark history and cast the triangle as a sign of the experience of trademark, even one detached from the commodity.

Ulysses's mercuriality announces style, the abstracted notion of style, appropriated from its sources, as Joyce's dominant literary feature; stylistic instability is the primary characteristic of the text. In this regard, however, no single style represents Joyce. As Franco Moretti writes, "it is no accident that Joyce does not found a school, and that those who use him as a model and imitate one of *Ulysses*'s many styles betray the fundamental intention of his novel: the systematic refusal to accept *one* style as the privileged vehicle of expression" (206). Since Joyce's chief technical characteristic is his variability, his writing undermines the idea of a trademark style. While his mutability depends on appropriating and reframing voices, *Ulysses* depicts prior literary styles as less polyvalent, displaying the difference between Joyce's technique and that of previous literary generations. That is, in "Oxen," when he links the voices to specific historical authors and genres, he creates those references partly by revealing and disseminating his strategies and sources among his literary accomplices. "Oxen" imagines a prior reading of each style and insists that the two past and present moments of consumption match. (If they do not, surely that is a failure on the part of the reader rather than the writer.) This revision of the experience of style echoes the effect of trademark. It also operates on literary history: consider that without their inclusion in *Ulysses* some of these writers would surely be less known and read than they are today. Establishing his literary sources serves to emphasize the technique and de-emphasize narrative, portraying literary history as a progression of traceable styles. Meanwhile, what is traceable to Joyce remains stylistic variety and imitation, the ethos of style.

Iconotypography

The Bass logo looms in Joyce's work not only because it is a token that conveys the idea of instant recognition and the system of trademark but also because it is nonmimetic and visual, characteristics that ultimately play to Joyce's recognizability and codification. In Joyce, visuality, the displayability of writing, attends moments of stylistic change. For example, *Ulysses*'s formal variations, perhaps most eruptive in the episodes "Aeolus," "Scylla and Charibdis," "Sirens," "Circe," and "Eumaeus," accompany shifts in the viewable surface of the text. Simply put, the episodes where Joyce's style becomes most opaque and least penetrable look different from others and from texts that draw less attention to technique and therefore do not foreground their author-brand as emphatically. The *Wake* later revisits and exaggerates this. The atypical typography creates a textual iconography that Joyce overtly aligns with his distinction as an author. In a 1923 letter, written after the publication of *Ulysses* and during his early efforts on the *Wake*, Joyce counsels his friend Arthur Power to look at the illuminated *Book of Kells*: "I have taken it about with me, and have pored over its workmanship for hours. You can compare much of my work to the intricate illuminations. I would like it to be possible to pick up any page of my book and know at once what book it is" (*Letters* 2: 545). Delighting in the elaborate markings of the medieval text, Joyce hopes that the printed surface of his own work, in its uniqueness and recognizability, will mark his writing.

Joyce's focus on the visible surface of the book inflects his earliest narratives; from *Dubliners* onward, for example, he resists the use of unsightly quotation marks (*Letters* 2: 353). In *Ulysses* he imagines the visual recognizability of his authorial brand. As Bloom journeys from the newspaper's printing press to its editorial offices in "Aeolus," the tactility and visuality of the printed medium are set in contrast to the airy insubstantiality of speech and oral culture. The episode's most notable features are its boldface inter-titles, which constitute the novel's earliest radical typography. All novelists depend on visuality in that their words must be visible to be read, and they must be read in order to be understood and thus to create meaning. But Joyce's distinction (also apparent in a few of his contemporaries, including Gertrude Stein and E. E. Cummings), which is traceable to predecessors (Jonathan Swift, Laurence Sterne), is that his words create meaning by being seen but not necessarily understood. His relation to and incorporation of trademark discourse formulate a striking implication: that reading the texts is not the sole, not even the primary, experience of his work. To consume Joyce, his writing suggests, is to scan the page and recognize the insignia of the author at a glance. Indeed, in Joyce's ruminations about the *Book of Kells,* he describes handling it and gazing upon it but says nothing about reading the words or deciphering their meaning. Reading is an afterthought in this system—again bringing Joyce close to trademark. A nonrepresentational trademark is not read; the Bass logo is not read; a red triangle is seen and apprehended. It has two dimensions only and cannot be penetrated. Although Joyce's writing is notorious for being difficult to access and necessary to excavate, his negotiation of the visual suggests the opposite: that his text's meaning depends on instant and easy recognition.

An explication of this effect comes from a perhaps unlikely—because famously unsympathetic to Joyce—source: Stein. An avant-garde stylist and astute collector of modernist artwork, Stein maintained her own interest in trademark, having arranged for a circular imprint of her famous quotation "Rose is a rose is a rose is a rose" from "Sacred Emily" (187) literally to be branded on editions of her books. In what might be considered an irony, Stein perceives and summarizes Joyce's system of generating texts that codify his authorial brand even without being read. She calls Joyce and the Cubist Georges Braque "the incomprehensibles whom anybody can understand" (*Autobiography* 212). The remark casts Joyce's venerated difficulty and depth as a secondary aspect of his text. His writing, Stein hints, first and foremost promotes itself as recognizable at a glance, comprehensible in a moment, identifiable instantly, not meant to be penetrated at all, merely viewed for its surface, and she indicates that Joyce's stylistic variability, his multiplicity of meaning, and his implicit and explicit demands that readers study his work slowly and carefully are secondary to this textual identity. Stein identifies Joyce as instantly recognizable and announces that identification, not penetration, is the appropriate treatment of his work. The chief characteristic of Joyce, in other words, is his self-branding; his trademark is his trademarking. Like a logo that turns the act of consumption into an experience of the brand but not the product or the company, Joyce's trademark turns the act of reading Joyce into recognition of his recognizability. The redacted version of textual identity may seem to contradict Joyce's repute and other modernist narratives of difficulty; as I have shown, however, this version of the writerly subject is dependent on difficulty, using the opacity of the writing to offer an easily consumable insignia of the author.

Joyce and the Culture of Trademark

Joyce's culture uses the late-1800s emergence of modern trademark to reconceive the relationship between an artist/producer and the marketplace, a discourse that, in return, helps recast how trademark operates. Joyce shares in this exploration, constructing an authorial identity that parallels the processes of trademark. In so doing, he places distinction—in the form of visual identifiability—at the forefront of his authorship. Seeing him this way contradicts or at least recolors numerous entrenched narratives of

Joyce and of modernism, specifically the idea that the textual value and authorial distinction are linked through depth rather than surface. As the Bass Ale logo takes on the role of suggesting the processes of trademark, Joyce exemplifies the fiction of trademark—the authorial self-fashioning, particular to modernism, predicated on instant recognition and consumption rather than engaged explication and comprehension.

The presence of trademark in Joyce implies that the world of avant-garde aesthetics and high culture helped foment early twentieth-century trademark culture. It implicates Joyce and modernism with our own society's proliferation of trademark icons and our everyday, sometimes unconscious, negotiation with them. In particular, Joyce and the artists appropriating and recirculating the Bass logo contribute to our current conditions by making recognizability a central value for everything and everyone circulating in the marketplace of signs. We are awash in logos and brands, insignias and possessions of corporate regimes whose sway extends from electoral politics to our daily diet options and whose legal status sometimes seems to outweigh that of the individual. Social movements are predicated on opposition to corporate influence and culture; corporate emblems are recognized around the globe; protesters carry United States flags that substitute company logos for stars against the blue field. Our trademarks stir desire and "mobilize emotional connotations," according to Jean Baudrillard (209). He points to a line of thinking implied throughout this essay but not pursued: that the consumption of Joyce's trademark contributes to consumer identity and accrues capital in the marketplaces of culture, much as corporate trademarks today, in the words of Naomi Klein, "provide the essentials of lifestyle and monopolize ever-expanding stretches of cultural space" (16). By participating in trademark's revising of the act of consumption, Joyce can be seen as helping mark the path for a culture that recognizes experience through signs that happen to be corporate emblems, iconic properties registered and protected by the state.

Notes

An earlier version of this essay appeared in *James Joyce Quarterly* 51.1. This revision is published with permission.

1. I use the notion of imprimatur outlined throughout Jaffe's *Modernism and the Culture of Celebrity*.

2. Landes and Posner state, "To perform its naming function a trademark or brand name (these are rough synonyms) must not be duplicated" (167).

3. See, for example, Dettmar and Watt, *Marketing Modernisms*; Rainey, *Institutions of Modernism*; Turner, *Marketing Modernism between the Two World Wars*; Wicke, *Advertising Fictions*. For a rare consideration of brand appearances in modernism, see McDonald, "Product Placement: Literary Modernism and Crisco."

4. See Saint-Amour, *The Copywrights*, and his edited collection *Modernism and Copyright*. See also Glass, *Authors, Inc.*, 57–93, for his treatment of Mark Twain's fight for copyright.

5. This legend is on a Bass Ale bottle purchased on 6 April 2011.

6. The licensing of brand names to other sources of manufacture did not yet exist in 1876.

7. The tendency is prevalent among critics who have called attention to the confluence of modernism and celebrity culture. Examples include Jaffe, writing of Pierre Bourdieu's "trademark concept, cultural capital" (13), and Hammill, who writes of "[Mae] West's trademark wit" (81).

8. Sources differ slightly on the total Picasso works that include images of Bass Ale.

9. Among them are Braque's *Still Life with Bottle of Bass* (1914), Hayden's *Still-Life With a Guitar, Bottle of Bass and Fruit* (1918), and Gris's *La Bouteille de Bass* (1925).

10. The beer lends its name to the title of "Bass Ale Blues," a 1925 jazz recording by the Original Memphis Five. A band that illustrates a propensity for speciousness in branding, the Original Memphis Five were neither original nor originally from Memphis; they appropriated both the song's melody and their group's name from the jazz pioneer W. C. Handy, and all of them hailed from New York. The tune bears a marked musical resemblance to Handy's canonical "Beale Street Blues," while the two song titles are similar as well, suggesting the Original Memphis Five were making frivolous use of the word "original." In this way and others, the band highlights contradictions within the system of trademark; indeed, they regularly produced music under various pseudonyms. At least there were five band members. See Kirchner, 157, 767. Concerning the band name, see Yanow, 166, 184.

11. Saint-Amour, *The Copywrights*, 68–98.

12. Gifford, 432–36.

13. I write about style and Joyce's authorial self-production in *Modernism Is the Literature of Celebrity*, 57–64, and mention the Bass bottle in this context on pages 63–64. Several moments of this essay are reconsiderations of ideas and material I treat there.

Bibliography

Armstrong, Carol. *Manet Manette*. New Haven, CT: Yale University Press, 2002.
Bamforth, Charles. *Beer*. Oxford: Oxford University Press, 2003.
Baudrillard, Jean. *The System of Objects*. Translated by James Benedict. New York: Verso, 1996.
Coombe, Rosemary J. *The Cultural Life of Intellectual Properties: Authorship, Appropriation, and the Law*. Durham, NC: Duke University Press, 1999.

Dettmar, Kevin J. H., and Stephen Watt, eds. *Marketing Modernisms: Self-Promotion, Canonization, Rereading*. Ann Arbor: University of Michigan Press, 1995.
Gifford, Don. *"Ulysses" Annotated: Notes for James Joyce's "Ulysses."* With Robert J. Seidman. Berkeley: University of California Press, 1988.
Glass, Loren. *Authors Inc.: Literary Celebrity in the Modern United States, 1880–1980*. New York: New York University Press, 2004.
Goldman, Jonathan E. *Modernism Is the Literature of Celebrity*. Austin: University of Texas Press, 2011.
Great Britain Patent Office. *A Century of Trade Marks: A Commentary on the Work and History of the Trade Marks Registry, Which Celebrates Its Centenary in 1976*. London: Her Majesty's Stationery Office, 1976.
Hammill, Faye. *Women, Celebrity, and Literary Culture Between the Wars*. Austin: University of Texas Press, 2007.
Heymann, Laura A. "The Birth of the Authornym: Authorship, Pseudonymity, and Trademark Law." *Notre Dame Law Review* 80.4 (2004): 1377–1450.
Jaffe, Aaron. *Modernism and the Culture of Celebrity*. Cambridge: Cambridge University Press, 2005.
Joyce, James. *Finnegans Wake*. New York: Viking, 1939.
———. *Letters*. Vol. 1. Edited by Stuart Gilbert. New York: Viking, 1957. Corrected ed., New York: Viking, 1966.
———. *Letters*. Vols. 2–3. Edited by Richard Ellmann. New York: Viking, 1966.
———. *Ulysses*. 1922. Edited by Hans Walter Gabler with Wolfhard Steppe and Herbert Cahoon. New York: Garland, 1984.
Kirchner, Bill, ed. *The Oxford Companion to Jazz*. New York: Oxford University Press, 2000.
Klein, Naomi. *No Logo: Taking Aim at the Brand Bullies*. New York: Picador, 2002.
Landes, William M., and Richard A. Posner. *The Economic Structure of Intellectual Property Law*. Cambridge, MA: Harvard University Press, 2003.
Leonard, Garry. *Advertising and Commodity Culture in Joyce*. Gainesville: University Press of Florida, 1998.
McDonald, Gail. "Product Placement: Literary Modernism and Crisco." *Modernist Cultures* 2 (May 2006): 21–30.
Moretti, Franco. *Signs Taken for Wonders: Essays in the Sociology of Literary Forms*. Translated by Susan Fischer, David Forgacs, and David Miller. London: Verso, 1983.
Osteen, Mark. *The Economy of "Ulysses": Making Both Ends Meet*. Syracuse, NY: Syracuse University Press, 1995.
Poland, Harry Bodkin. *Trade Marks: The Merchandise Trade Marks Act, 1862*. London: J. Crockford, 1862.
Pound, Ezra. *Make It New: Essays*. New Haven, CT: Yale University Press, 1936.
Rainey, Lawrence. *Institutions of Modernism: Literary Elites and Public Culture*. New Haven, CT: Yale University Press, 1998.
Rocco, John. "Drinking *Ulysses*: Joyce, Bass Ale, and the Typography of Cubism." *James Joyce Quarterly* 33 (1996): 399–409.

Saint-Amour, Paul K. *The Copywrights: Intellectual Property and the Literary Imagination.* Ithaca, NY: Cornell University Press, 2013.
Schechter, F. W. "The Rational Basis of Trademark Law." *Harvard Law Review* 40 (April 1927): 819.
Spoo, Robert. *Without Copyrights: Piracy, Publishing, and the Public Domain.* New York: Oxford University Press, 2013.
Stein, Gertrude. *The Autobiography of Alice B. Toklas.* 1933. New York: Vintage, 1990.
———. "Sacred Emily." In *Geography and Plays.* Boston: Four Seas Press, 1922.
Turner, Catherine. *Marketing Modernism between the Two World Wars.* Amherst: University of Massachusetts Press, 2003.
Wicke, Jennifer. *Advertising Fictions.* New York: Columbia University Press, 1988.
Wood, J. Bigland. *The Law of Trade Marks Including the Merchandise Marks Act, 1862 and the Trade Mark Registration Act, 1975.* London: Stevens and Sons, 1876.
Yanow, Scott. *Classic Jazz.* New York: Hal Leonard, 2001.

PART IV

Circulation and Its Legalities

12

Literature Meets Law in Court

The Trials of *Ulysses*

JOSEPH M. HASSETT

The potential of an obscenity trial to illuminate the relationship between law and literature is captured in Arthur Miller's great metaphor of the trial as a crucible for testing competing ideas. Literature and law meet each other head on when a book is alleged to be obscene. Literature asserts a primal claim to be heard. The law of obscenity seeks to silence certain books on the ground that their very presence is so harmful to society that they should be banished and their publishers imprisoned.

This clash was described in apocalyptic terms by Jane Heap as she faced criminal charges in 1920 for publishing an episode of *Ulysses* in the *Little Review*, which she coedited with her lover, Margaret Anderson. Heap wrote that "Art is and always has been the supreme Order" and thus is the only human activity "that has an eternal quality." Standing on this premise, she commented on her impending trial in what can only be described as a harumph: "What legal genius to bring Law against Order!" (5). Anderson saw the issue the same way. She believed that a work of art could not be obscene. The only pertinent question to be asked about *Ulysses*, she wrote, was whether it was a work of art ("Obvious" 9).

The views of Anderson and Heap would be substantially vindicated thirteen years later by a judicial decision that cleared *Ulysses* of obscenity charges, a watershed event that accorded literary criticism a prominent role in obscenity cases. Indeed, the role of literary criticism in obscenity trials became so central that the 1960 English trial exonerating *Lady Chat-*

terley's Lover was described as "probably the most thorough and expensive seminar on Lawrence's work ever given" (Sparrow 35).

Anderson and Heap, however, were convicted of a crime in 1921 for publishing an episode of a work that was later declared the greatest English-language novel of the twentieth century. The struggle between law and literature never ends. It is as old as Plato who, distrusting poets' seductive appeal to the emotions, banned them from his republic.[1] It is as recent as the next politician who promises more vigorous enforcement of obscenity laws. Given the never-ending nature of the struggle between law and literature, it is worth examining how obscenity cases are won or lost, and the two trials of *Ulysses* are good case studies, because different approaches brought very different results.

The case against Anderson and Heap began when John Sumner, secretary of the New York Society for the Suppression of Vice, issued a warrant complaining of the distribution of the July–August 1920 number of the *Little Review*, which contained the last section of the "Nausicaa" episode of *Ulysses*. As Pound put it in an October 1920 letter to Joyce, Nausicaa had "been pinched by the po-lice."[2] The episode under attack unfolds on Dublin's Sandymount Strand, where Gerty MacDowell sits on a rock while a Benediction ceremony takes place in the adjacent Star of the Sea church. The first part seems to be Gerty's interior monologue, but the texture of the voice is so unremittingly the trite language of consumer-oriented magazines that it overwhelms the notion of a real Gerty separate from the language. Gerty's monologue becomes startlingly alive when she notices that Leopold Bloom, sitting on a nearby rock, is staring at her. As the reader hears Gerty's perception of the Benediction, she swings her foot in time with the *Tantum ergo* hymn and then, with fireworks from a nearby bazaar commencing overhead, leans back to allow the increasingly excited Bloom to see her "nainsook knickers, four and eleven, on account of being white," while a streaking rocket "sprang and bang shot blind blank and O! then the Roman candle burst and it was like a sigh of O! and everyone cried O! O! and it gushed out of it a stream of rain gold hair threads and they shed and ah! they were all greeny dewy stars falling with golden, O so lovely! O so soft, sweet, soft!"[3]

As Vladimir Nabokov observed, the newness of this passage emphasizes the difference between cliché—words that were once original and vivid but have become hackneyed—and live lyrical language: "what Joyce does here," Nabokov wrote, "is to cause some of that dead and rotten stuff to reveal here and there its live source, its primary freshness." Nabokov instanced the "real beauty" and "luminous pathetic charm" of the "church service as it passes transparently through Gerty's consciousness." The description of the fireworks, he added, "is really tender and beautiful: it is the freshness of poetry still with us before it becomes a cliché" (345–46).

The fact that Bloom ejaculates as the rocket bursts into beautiful display becomes apparent from several musings in the Bloomian interior monologue that now takes control of the narrative. The *Little Review*'s attorney John Quinn, in a letter of 16 October 1920 to Pound,[4] identified the musings that triggered the prosecution:

> Near her monthlies, I expect, makes them feel ticklish. . . . But then why don't all women menstruate at the same time with the same moon?
> Wonder if it is bad to go with them then.
> Mr. Bloom with careful hand recomposed his shirt.
> Did she know what I? Course.
> Lord, I am wet.
> For this relief much thanks.
> Short snooze now if I had. And she can do the other.[5]

As Bloom lingers on the Strand, the reader has immediate access to his typically wide-ranging reverie as he ponders the vagaries of sexual attraction ("Pretty girls and ugly men marrying"); philosophizes that a woman's "First thoughts" about men "are best," instancing an occasion about which Molly will later elaborate ("Molly, lieutenant Mulvey that kissed her under the Moorish wall beside the gardens" when she was fifteen); sees his encounter with Gerty in a humanizing context ("Still it was a kind of language between us"); meditates on the central role of women in birth and death ("Nature. Washing child, washing corpse. Dignam"); and postulates an erotic current connecting people and their environment ("Like to be that rock she sat on. Also the library today: those girls graduates. Happy chairs under them").[6]

As the reverie continues, Bloom frames his encounter with Gerty in terms of his initial sexual experience with Molly on Howth, and her betrayal with Blazes Boylan, which coincides with what Nabokov calls Bloom's "love at a distance" with Gerty (348). Having noted that his watch stopped at half past four, with the speculation "Very strange about my watch. Wonder is there any magnetic influence between the person because that was about the time he," Bloom pulls all the strands together while gazing toward Howth: "All quiet on Howth now. The distant hills seem. Where we. The rhododendrons. I am a fool perhaps. He gets the plums and I the leavings." These musings lead Bloom to reflect on the circular pattern of life: "Curious [Molly] an only child, I an only child. So it returns. Think you're escaping and run into yourself. Longest way round is the shortest way home. And just when he and she. Circus horse walking in a ring."[7]

John Sumner's response to Joyce's stylistic innovation was to charge Anderson and Heap with violating a New York statute that criminalized the distribution of "any obscene, lewd, lascivious, filthy, indecent, or disgusting" material. Then-prevailing judicial decisions, following a half-century-old Queen's Bench decision, *Regina v. Hicklin,* L.R. 3 Q.B. 360 (1868), defined a work as obscene if it tended to excite sexual desire.

There were a variety of possible approaches to defending Joyce's prose:

First, there is the seemingly obvious argument that exciting sexual desire—an enterprise necessary to preserving the species—ought not be declared out of bounds for literature. Anderson and Heap put this position more broadly. For them, literature, by definition, could not be obscene.

A second approach, at the level of the minor premise, is the argument that, in fact, the book does not excite sexual desire. This appeals to the advocate as the path of least resistance because it operates within the contours of existing legal precedent.

Midway between these approaches is the tenebrous field where the arguments of lawyers can attempt to reshape the law. Two subsidiary rules stated in *Hicklin* presented obstacles. The first was that the obscenity of a work is to be measured not by its effect on the law's typical reagent, "the reasonable man," but on the most susceptible potential readers, "those whose minds are open to such immoral influences." The second was that *any* obscenity in a book violated the statute, no matter how beautifully written the book might be as a whole. As one New York court put it:

> Charm of language, subtlety of thought, faultless style, even distinction of authorship, may all have their lure for the literary critic, yet these qualities may all be present and the book be unfit for dissemination to the reading public.[8]

This view has ancient roots. It was the very beauty of Homer and Sophocles that convinced Plato of their danger. Under this approach, the better the writing, the more dangerous the obscenity.

The task of the advocate for Anderson and Heap was to find the ideas, verbal formulae, and persuasive force to change the judge-made *Hicklin* rules so that Joyce's literary achievement would weigh more heavily than the shock effect of Bloom's wet shirt or Gerty's monthlies. New York lawyer John Quinn, who had given the funds that enabled Ezra Pound to bring *Ulysses* to the *Little Review*, was an almost automatic choice to defend Anderson and Heap. But he was unsuited to the task for a number of reasons. The first was his belief that unwitting recipients of magazines through the postal system should be protected from *Ulysses*. His 16 October letter to Pound reflects his view that "There are things in 'Ulysses' published in number after number of 'The Little Review' that never should have appeared in a magazine asking privileges of the mails. In a book, yes. In a magazine, emphatically no."

Second, Quinn was representing Joyce in trying to negotiate a contract for publication of the novel as a whole, and he believed that serialization would lead to a criminal conviction that would scare publishers away from the book.

Third, because his law practice depended on the favor of a group of Catholic Irish-American businessmen, politicians, and judges, he was reluctant to be publicly perceived as a "free smut, free sex advocate"—a phrase he had previously used to warn Ezra Pound.[9]

Finally, Quinn suffered from misogyny compounded by prejudice against Anderson and Heap's lesbianism. His 16 October letter to Pound rants against the "female urinal" from which the *Little Review* was published and accuses his clients of having the "perverted courage of the bugger and the Lesbian." A troubling part of his mind associated the periodic publication of the magazine with the menstrual cycle. His letter fulminates about his clients' "menstrual defecations," "the monthly mensurations," as he put it, by which Anderson and Heap have "urinally and menstrually violate[d] the law." A follow-up letter of 21 October 1920 continues the same fixation on periodicity.[10] Borrowing a word from one of the Bloomian musings being attacked by Sumner, Quinn refers to issues of the *Little Review* as "monthlies."

Quinn's limitations had grave consequences because, despite the generally forbidding terrain created by the *Hicklin* precedent, there was room for maneuver. Judge Learned Hand, in a 1913 opinion in a case in which Quinn represented the defendant, had characterized *Hicklin* as reflective of "mid-Victorian morals" and questioned "whether in the end men will regard that as obscene which is honestly relevant to the adequate expression of innocent ideas, and whether they will not believe that truth and beauty are too precious to society at large to be mutilated in the interests of those most likely to pervert them to base uses."[11]

Judge Hand's opinion was an open invitation to the advocate for an author like Joyce to establish that the law ought not bar portrayal of the serious and beautiful way in which reality reveals itself in the sexually tinged imagination. Moreover, that very case was articulated for Quinn in a long letter written by a brilliant student of literature who had trained as a barrister in Dublin, eighty-one-year-old John Butler Yeats (hereafter "JBY"), father of the poet William Butler Yeats. JBY realized that "it is really a great issue . . . whether the books of Joyce and such as he are to go free or not." He recognized in Joyce "an intense feeling for what is actual and true" and saw that "[t]he whole movement against Joyce and his terrible veracity, naked and unashamed, has its origin in the desire of people to live comfortably, and, that they may live comfortably, to live superficially" (70, 73).

JBY's keen eye focused on the statutory term "filthy," the etymological root of obscene. "That such a man" as Joyce "should write filthiness," he insisted, "is incredible" (70). Citing two fellow graduates of Trinity College Dublin, he argued that Joyce's "intense feeling for what is actual and true" stands midway between worship of "the beautiful," as exemplified by Wilde, and fixation on "the ugly," as exemplified by Swift. "Beauty was the God of [Wilde's] heaven," he wrote, "and ugliness its devil." In contrast to him stood Swift, who "died in mental misery; broken down by what?—his passion for the ugly, by that constant contemplation of the hideous." Dante, JBY argued, "never shrank from the hideous and the obscene" and taught Joyce "that terrible hardness, that hardness of which Wilde had so little and Swift too much" (71–73).

JBY's powerful ideas fared worse than the seed that fell upon rock. Quinn perverted them terribly in his argument at a preliminary hearing on the charges against Anderson and Heap before City Magistrate J. E. Corrigan, a member of the Irish-Catholic coterie on which Quinn depended. Converting JBY's aesthetic argument into a moral one, Quinn urged that it is beauty that corrupts, but filth that deters, and contrasted "the strong hard filth of a man like Joyce with the devotion to art of a soft flabby man like Wilde."[12] This is bad criticism and worse advocacy. The idea of confessing filth but pleading hardness in avoidance was not an inspired one.

Quinn's other argument was another perversion of JBY, who had noted that "Joyce brings with him what will protect him from the silly, . . . for Joyce is very difficult reading." Quinn reduced this subtle observation to what he called the "syllogism" that the reader would either understand the "Nausicaa" episode or not. "If he understood what it meant," Quinn argued, "then it couldn't corrupt him, for it would either amuse or bore him. If he didn't understand what it meant, then it could [also not] corrupt him." Magistrate Corrigan had no trouble resisting Quinn's syllogism. The passage "where the man went off in his pants," Corrigan ruled, was unmistakable in meaning and "smutty, filthy within the meaning of the statute." So much for the syllogism.

Quinn's account of the ensuing trial before three city court judges, contained in letters to Joyce and Shane Leslie,[13] shows how far he departed from Heap's absolutism and Anderson's desire for a defense based upon her belief that *Ulysses* was the "the prose masterpiece of my generation" ("Ulysses" 24). Branding the judges as "stupid," Quinn told Joyce that he had made "what many people in court called a brilliant argument," which he described as "the only tack that could be taken with the three stupid judges." This bit of brilliance—what he characterized to Shane Leslie as a "frank appeal to the three judges' ignorance"—was the assertion "that no one could understand what the thing was about" and thus it could not corrupt anyone.

Before Joyce had time to digest this revelation, Quinn was regaling him with the "good point" he made that the anger manifested in the prosecutor's argument was "my best exhibit" because it showed that "what 'Ulysses' does" is to make people angry, but "it doesn't tend to drive them to the arms of some siren."

Confusing the effect of being the prosecutor in an obscenity trial with the effect of reading the book, Quinn deprived the occasion of the seriousness it demanded. "The judges were rocking with laughter," he wrote to Joyce, "and again I thought I had them." The joke was on his clients.

Anderson and Heap were fined fifty dollars each, and it was stipulated that no further installments of *Ulysses* would be published. Quinn had decided in advance of trial that there would be no appeal from the assumed conviction, and he informed Anderson a few days before the trial that he would not make a record of "witnesses, experts and critics, and passages of comparative literature" for an appeal as he would have done had he "thought there was a fighting chance in the matter."[14]

Although he sufficiently altered his view at the last minute to concede that expert testimony might be admissible to mitigate punishment,[15] the thrust of the expert testimony he offered, as Anderson noted in "'Ulysses' in Court," was directed only to the point that *Ulysses* would not corrupt readers, but did not demonstrate its quality as literature (24). No appeal was taken. Within about a year of the time an appeal would have been decided, New York's highest court ruled in another case that the book in an obscenity proceeding must be considered as a whole, and that expert opinion can be considered as to an author's reputation and a book's merit.[16] Joyce's work had been found obscene without Quinn's having sought an appellate ruling on these important issues.

Quinn lacked the personal conviction to force the courts to confront the right of *Ulysses* to be heard. Moreover, his bias against Anderson and Heap and his antipathy to their enterprise made him unsuitable for the fundamentally important task of protecting their right to publish. Joyce's biographers Ellmann (503–4) and Bowker (286), JBY's biographer William Murphy (521), and Quinn's own biographer B. L. Reid (454–56) have not challenged Quinn's judgment that the case against Anderson and Heap was unwinnable. In fact, a recent book by Kevin Birmingham advances the extraordinary notion that Quinn's defense constituted "sophisticated legal creativity" (168), but this view is based on the erroneous suggestion that Quinn introduced a completely out-of-context-discussion of Learned Hand's *Kennerley* opinion in the midst of an argument avowedly addressed to the "ignorance" of judges Quinn perceived as "stupid." Birmingham has since clarified that his reference to a Quinn memorandum that cited *Kennerley* was to papers previously filed in a different court in support of an unsuccessful motion to have the case transferred there.[17] Birmingham's approach is an extreme form of deference to Quinn's view that the case was unwinnable, but Quinn thought the same thing about the case against James Branch Cabell's *Jurgen* in 1920,[18] and he was proved wrong when his successor won the case (Holt 73–74). Without hindsight or speculation, it is clear that the arguments Quinn advanced were poor ones, and unworthy of *Ulysses*.

Better arguments were advanced in 1932, when Random House founder Bennett Cerf and attorney Morris Ernst set out to bring *Ulysses* to the public. Although they had the benefit of publication of the complete novel in Paris, they had to deal with the concluding Molly Bloom monologue, which Joyce characterized in a letter to Frank Budgen as "probably more obscene than any preceding episode."[19] Importantly, they brought a willingness to insist upon the veracity and value of Joyce's work. Ernst argued that Joyce had "cast light into some of the murky chambers of the human mind. It is only by such exposure that we can hope to banish darkness and taint. Joyce's penetration and courage deserve praise, not condemnation" (Moscato and LeBlanc 267).

It remained necessary to come to grips with the text. Confronted with a charge that *Ulysses* is obscene, the mind of the advocate seems incapable of resisting the argument that it is too obscure to excite. Ernst put it this way: *Ulysses* "is far too tedious and labyrinthine and bewildering for the untutored and the impressionable who might conceivably be affected by it. Such people would not get beyond the first dozen pages." Referring to a decision that had relied on the difficulty of *Jurgen* in finding it not to be obscene, Ernst argued: "Beside [*Ulysses*], *Jurgen* is a child's primer" (ibid.).

One can empathize with the advocate's desire to evade the question of obscenity with the red herring of obscurity. But sooner or later, a rigorous assessment of whether *Ulysses* was barred by the statutory ban on obscene works must come to grips with the fact that the essence of *Ulysses*—its warp and woof—is Joyce's conviction that sexual desire lies at the heart of things. Ernst sought to whistle his way past this core issue, arguing, "Though the element of sex is present, it is relegated to a position of relative unimportance" (ibid. 266). To their credit, the judges faced with the task of applying the statute were not so facile. The current of erotic imagination that animates *Ulysses* could not be ignored.

The judicial wrestling with this lively question resulted in an unusual instance of resolving a legal question in terms of literary technique. Without using the term "stream of consciousness," Judge Woolsey opined that Joyce was experimenting in a new literary genre in which he attempted to show how the screen of consciousness with its ever-shifting kaleidoscopic impressions carries, as it were on a plastic palimpsest, not only what is in the focus of each man's observation of the actual things about him, but also in a penumbral zone residua of past impressions, some recent and some drawn up by association from the domain of the subconscious. He shows how each of these impressions affects the life and behavior of the character which he is describing.

The important point here is that the characters are not consciously indulging themselves in erotic imaginings. Rather, the primal energy of Eros is forcing itself on the characters. Accordingly, if there is a strong sexual undercurrent in *Ulysses*, it is not the fault of either Joyce or the reader:

> If Joyce did not attempt to be honest in developing the technique which he has adopted in Ulysses, the result would be psychologically misleading and thus unfaithful to his chosen technique. Such an attitude would be artistically inexcusable.

Woolsey's analysis brought him to the precise point JBY had made when he wrote Quinn that the reason for the outcry against Joyce was his terrible veracity. Woolsey put it this way:

> It is because Joyce has been loyal to his technique and has not funked its necessary implications, but has honestly attempted to tell fully what his characters think about, that he has been the subject of so many attacks and that his purpose has been so often misunderstood and misrepresented.[20]

Law and literature blend seamlessly here because it is Joyce's mastery as a writer that convinces Woolsey that it would be wrong for the law to silence him. Woolsey was responding to a feature of Joyce's writing pinpointed by Augustine Martin's observation that Joyce's literary achievement was the invention of "a range of technical and linguistic resources" of the necessary "power and range" to break the "sound barrier of . . . social reticence, the wall—at least the façade—between the public and private self that Victoria's reign had so consolidated, and which the Catholic Church in Ireland had so reinforced" (155). Joyce's piercing of the sound barrier between public and private showed Woolsey the way to break the hold of the Victorian *Hicklin* case on the law of obscenity.

The prosecution urged Woolsey's special attention to Molly Bloom's soliloquy. Importantly, Ernst's emphasis on the quality of *Ulysses* as literature provided Molly a platform from which she commanded serious attention. In the argument Molly crafted from her bed in Eccles Street, Woolsey could not help but find the rationale for recognizing the role of the erotic imagination. Molly's question—"what else were we given all those desires for Id like to know" (*U* 18.1397–1398)—demanded an answer from a judge being asked to ban a book that draws attention to such desire. It "didnt make me blush," argued Molly: "why should it either its only nature" (*U* 18.1386).

Woolsey's implicit acceptance of Molly's argument enabled him to swallow the admittedly "strong draught" of *Ulysses*. It remained to reconcile his conclusion with the federal law of obscenity, which still adhered to the twin views of the *Hicklin* doctrine that the measure of obscenity was the impact of isolated passages on the susceptible. *United States v. Bennett* so held. Woolsey simply plunged ahead with the *ipse dixit* that the proper test was a reading of the book in its entirety in terms of how it would affect "a person with average sex instincts—what the French would call *l'homme moyen sensuel*—who plays, in this branch of legal inquiry, the same role of hypothetical reagent as does the 'reasonable man' in the law of torts" (184).

Woolsey thus had the unenviable task of offering himself as the barometer of whether *Ulysses* excited lustful thoughts. Even the valiant Woolsey paled at this prospect. Instead, in an extraordinary departure from the notion that the advocates have a full opportunity to present their cases to the decision maker, Woolsey reported what was, in effect, the combined decision of himself and two friends. His carefully hedged report avoided the question whether and to what extent any of the three had been stimulated to lustful thoughts in the course of duty. Rather the report was that "in its entirety" the "net effect" of *Ulysses* was not "to excite sexual impulses or lustful thoughts" (184–85).

Woolsey's opinion was vulnerable to an argument that, whatever the "net effect" of *Ulysses*, it contained specific passages that were obscene, and that the book thus ran afoul of the statute under the traditional *Hicklin* rule, as adopted in *Bennett*. The government made exactly that argument in appealing Woolsey's decision to the Court of Appeals. One of the three judges agreed, but not the others: Learned Hand, who had questioned the soundness of the *Hicklin* rule twenty years previously in *Kennerley*, and his cousin Augustus Hand, two wonderfully educated judges of robust intellect and trenchant pen.

Learned Hand's private preconference memorandum to his fellow judges, now available in the Harvard Law School library, gives us an unvarnished insight into his thinking that some passages of the novel "could excite lustful feelings," but "the offending passages are clearly necessary to the epic of the soul as Joyce conceived it, and the parts which might be occasion for lubricity in the reader are to my way of thinking not sufficient to condemn a very notable contribution to literature."

Writing for the two-judge majority, Augustus Hand identified Joyce "as a pioneer" of the "'stream of consciousness' method of presenting fiction, which ... attempts to depict the thoughts and lay bare the souls of a number of people ... with a literalism that leaves nothing unsaid." Then, in one of those touches that makes judging an art, Hand, with an eye on precedents that permitted a greater range of sexual language in scientific works, framed the question before the court as "whether such a book of artistic merit and scientific insight should be regarded as 'obscene' within section 305(a) of the Tariff Act."[21] Molly would have been proud to see her insight labeled scientific.

With characteristic candor, Hand conceded: "That numerous long passages in Ulysses contain matter that is obscene under any fair definition of the word cannot be gainsaid; yet they are relevant to the purpose of depicting the thoughts of the characters and are introduced to give meaning to the whole, rather than to promote lust or portray filth for its own sake."

Again meeting the prosecution squarely, Hand observed that "it is argued that United States v. Bennett ... stands in the way of what has been said, and it certainly does." Exercising his power as an appellate judge, Hand simply interred *Bennett* as departed dogma. Citing his opinion in *United States v. Dennett* that works of physiology, medicine, science, and sex instruction are not within the statute, though to some extent and among some persons they may tend to promote lustful thoughts, Hand concluded: "We think the same immunity should apply to literature as to science, where the presentation, when viewed objectively, is sincere, and the erotic matter is not introduced to promote lust and does not furnish the dominant note of the publication."[22]

By focusing on the quality of Joyce's novel as literature, and creating a presumptive dichotomy between literature and obscenity, the *Ulysses* decision fundamentally altered the law of obscenity. At the same stroke, the decision created a significant role for literary criticism in obscenity trials by holding that, in determining whether obscenity is the dominant note of the publication, the trier of fact is to be guided by the "relevancy of the objectionable parts to the theme" and "the established reputation of the work in the estimation of approved critics...." In holding that *Ulysses* was not obscene, the court relied on the fact that "*Ulysses* is rated as a book of considerable power by persons whose opinions are entitled to weight."[23]

The government decided not to seek Supreme Court review.[24] The voyage of *Ulysses* through the courts thus came to an end. The federal decisions in the *Ulysses* case had far-reaching impact. The Supreme Court's 1957 decision in *Roth v. United States* held that a definition of obscenity like that applied by the Second Circuit in the *Ulysses* case was constitutionally required because the First Amendment to the United States Constitution protects a book that excites sexual desire so long as the book is not "utterly without redeeming social importance."

The argument that carried the day in *Ulysses* was that regard for truth itself requires that Joyce's terrible veracity be heard. That argument had its roots in the fictional reverie of Molly Bloom. Plato was right: fictions subvert orthodoxies.

Notes

This subject is developed at greater length in *The "Ulysses" Trials: Beauty and Truth Meet the Law* (Dublin: Lilliput, 2016).

1. Plato, *Republic*, 595b, 600d, 601a, 602b, 603a, 605a,b.
2. Ezra Pound to James Joyce, ca. October 1920, in Pound, *Letters*, 150.
3. "*Ulysses*, Episode XIII (Continued)," 43–44.
4. John Quinn to Pound, 16 October 1920, John Quinn Memorial Collection, New York Public Library (hereafter "Quinn Collection").
5. "*Ulysses*, Episode XIII (Continued)," 45–57.
6. Ibid., 46–52.
7. Ibid., 50–53.
8. *People v. Seltzer*, 334.
9. Quinn to Pound, 2 March 1918, Quinn Collection.
10. Quinn to Pound, 21 October 1920, Quinn Collection.
11. *United States v. Kennerley*, 120–21.
12. Quinn to Pound, 21 October 1920, Quinn Collection.
13. Quinn to Joyce, 13 April 1921; Quinn to Shane Leslie, 21 June 1922, Quinn Collection.

14. Quinn to Margaret Anderson, 5 February 1921, Special Collections Research Center, Southern Illinois University, Carbondale (hereafter "SIU").
15. Quinn to Anderson, 8 February 1921, SIU.
16. *Halsey v. New York Socy. for Suppression of Vice*.
17. E-mail, Kevin Birmingham to author, March 31, 2015. For Quinn's filing, see "Affidavit and Notice of Motion for the Transfer of Cause From Court of Special Sessions to Court of General Sessions. Jan. 12, 1921. Court of General Sessions in and for the City and County of New York," SIU.
18. Quinn to Arthur Symons, 11 April 1920, Quinn Collection.
19. Joyce to Frank Budgen, 16 August 1921, in *Selected Letters*, 285.
20. *United States v. One Book Called "Ulysses*," 5 F. Supp. 182 at 183.
21. *United States v. One Book Entitled Ulysses*, 72 F.2d 705 at 706.
22. Ibid., 707.
23. Ibid., 706, 708.
24. Harry S. Ridgley, Memorandum for Solicitor General, 10 September 1934, National Archives, Washington, D.C.

Works Cited

Anderson, Margaret. "An Obvious Statement (for the Millionth Time)." *Little Review* 7.3 (September–December 1920): 8–16.
——. "'Ulysses' in Court." *Little Review* 7.4 (January–March 1921): 22–25.
Birmingham, Kevin. *The Most Dangerous Book: The Battle for James Joyce's "Ulysses."* New York: Penguin, 2014.
Bowker, Gordon. *James Joyce: A Biography*. London: Weidenfeld & Nicolson, 2011.
Ellmann, Richard. *James Joyce*. Rev. ed. New York: Oxford University Press, 1982.
Heap, Jane. "Art and the Law." *Little Review* 7.3 (September–December 1920): 5–7.
Holt, Guy, ed. *Jurgen and the Law*. New York: McBride, 1923.
Joyce, James. *Selected Letters*. Edited by Richard Ellmann. New York: Viking, 1975.
——. "*Ulysses*, Episode XIII (Continued)." *Little Review* 7.2 (July–August 1920): 42–58.
Martin, Augustine. "Sin and Secrecy in Joyce's Fiction." In *James Joyce: An International Perspective*, edited by Suheil Badi Bushrui and Bernard Benstock, 143–55. Gerrards Cross, Bucks.: Colin Smythe, 1982.
Moscato, Michael, and Leslie LeBlanc, eds. *The United States of America v. One Book Entitled "Ulysses" by James Joyce: Documents and Commentary: A 50-Year Retrospective*. Frederick, MD: University Publications of America, 1984.
Murphy, William M. *Prodigal Father: The Life of John Butler Yeats (1839–1922)*. Ithaca, NY: Cornell University Press, 1978.
Nabokov, Vladimir. *Lectures on Literature*. New York: Harcourt Brace Jovanovich, 1980.
Plato. *The Republic*. Translated by Benjamin Jowett. New York: Modern Library, 1941.
Pound, Ezra. *The Letters of Ezra Pound*. Edited by D. D. Paige. New York: Harcourt Brace, 1950.

Quinn, John. Papers. John Quinn Memorial Collection, New York Public Library.
Reid, B. L. *The Man from New York: John Quinn and His Friends*. New York: Oxford University Press, 1968.
Sparrow, John. "*Regina v. Penguin Books Ltd.*: An Undisclosed Element of the Case." *Encounter* 18 (February 1962): 35–43.
Yeats, John Butler. "To John Quinn." October 14, 1920. Published as "A Letter: J. B. Yeats on James Joyce," edited by Donald J. Torchiana and Glenn O'Malley, *Tri-Quarterly* (Fall 1964): 70–76.

Legal Decisions

Halsey v. New York Socy. for Suppression of Vice, 234 N.Y.1 (1922).
People v. Seltzer, 122 Misc. 329, 334, 203 N.Y.S. 809, 813 (Sup. Ct. 1924).
Roth v. United States, 354 U.S. 476 (1957).
United States v. Bennett, 16 Blatch. 338, Fed. Cas. 18 No. 14, 571 (1879).
United States v. Dennett, 39 F.2d 564 (2d Cir. 1930).
United States v. Kennerley, 209 Fed. 119 (S.D.N.Y. 1913).
United States v. One Book Called "Ulysses," 5 F. Supp. 182 (S.D.N.Y. 1933).
United States v. One Book Entitled Ulysses, 72 F.2d 705 (2d Cir. 1934).

13

The Prestige of the Law

Revisiting Obscenity Law and Judge Woolsey's *Ulysses* Decision

KEVIN BIRMINGHAM

The United States of America v. One Book Called "Ulysses" is a landmark of obscenity jurisprudence, a triumph for literary expression, and one of the most widely read legal decisions in United States history,[1] and yet the man who penned it in 1933 remains largely in history's shadows. I struggled with the mystery of Judge John Munro Woolsey while conducting research for *The Most Dangerous Book*, my chronicle of the publication and censorship history of *Ulysses*, and Woolsey remained obscure until sheer luck brought me to the judge's grandson, John Woolsey III, who happens to be the brother of a friend of a friend. Woolsey shared with me multiple family documents, photographs, and home movies, and he guided me through the judge's library on a hill near the Woolseys' summer home in Petersham, Massachusetts, where his grandfather read *Ulysses* in the autumn of 1933. As if that were not enough, he also introduced me to Peggy Brooks, who is probably the last surviving person to have known the judge personally. With their help, the light of history shines just a little bit more on the judge who altered the history of modernism in the United States.

Traces of the man have always been visible. Much of what we need to know about Woolsey's philosophy regarding obscenity—and quite a bit about the judge himself—appears at the beginning of his *Ulysses* decision: "I have read 'Ulysses' once in its entirety and I have read those passages of which the Government particularly complains several times. In fact, for many weeks, my spare time has been devoted to the consideration of the decision which my duty would require me to make in this matter" (183). Woolsey's leisurely attention to *Ulysses*—which included examining the "satellite" scholarly books surrounding Joyce's novel during the judge's ample vacation—was quite possibly the most research any United States judge had ever performed in order to evaluate a novel's alleged obscenity. To some it was a form of judicial bravado. When asked his opinion of Woolsey, Judge Learned Hand, one of the nation's most distinguished jurists, complained that Woolsey was "a bit of a show off"; he thought of himself as "literary," which, Hand said, is "a very dangerous thing for a judge to be" (Gunther 289). Hand's evaluation is surprising not only because he himself was somewhat literary but also because literariness seems to have been Woolsey's great asset.

As a district judge for the Southern District of New York, Woolsey presided over several prominent federal cases in the 1930s, but the *Ulysses* controversy had a particularly rich history. Joyce's novel had been informally relegated to outlaw status since a 1921 New York trial found the editors of the *Little Review*, Margaret Anderson and Jane Heap, guilty of publishing obscenity when they serialized the second half of "Nausicaa." The guilty verdict scared U.S. publishers, and the 1922 Paris and London publications were subjected to mass burnings in the United States and the United Kingdom. For more than a decade, British and American readers had to smuggle copies of *Ulysses*, sometimes with decoy covers, past customs officials until Random House transformed Joyce's novel from contraband to classic in the eyes of the law. The publishing house imported one copy of *Ulysses* from Paris, engineered its seizure by New York customs officials under the Tariff Act of 1930, which banned the importation of obscene books, and challenged that seizure on the grounds that Joyce's novel was not obscene but, in fact, a modern classic.[2]

Woolsey's declaration that *Ulysses* could be imported into the United States paved the way for the first authorized edition of Joyce's masterpiece in an English-speaking country, and Random House printed the *Ulysses* decision as a preface to most copies of *Ulysses* it has sold since.[3] The decision was simultaneously a legal victory and a rave review. Several media outlets, including the *Saturday Review of Literature*, reprinted the decision virtually in its entirety,[4] and it was eloquent and forceful enough to inspire fan mail. Elmer Rice, a prominent anticensorship activist, wrote the judge a letter to praise him for "the wisdom, clarity and conciseness of your opinion" and to say that he was "grateful for so deep an understanding and so sensitive an analysis of the creative processes."[5] The *Ulysses* verdict was still memorable at the end of Woolsey's career. When he retired in 1943, the *New York Herald Tribune* declared the judge "no mere philological exhibitionist, but an authentic artist and scholar," and the *New Yorker* hailed *United States v. One Book Called "Ulysses"* as a "literary gem."[6] Vladimir Nabokov's fictional John Ray Jr., Ph.D., mentions Woolsey's "monumental decision" in the foreword to *Lolita* (4). The District Court case deserved such a tribute since Nabokov's novel—like so many others—escaped censorship proceedings at least partly because the *Ulysses* decision had become canonical in U.S. jurisprudence by the 1950s.

And yet its status obscures what, precisely, made the decision and the judge both artistic and dangerous. The characteristics that emerge from published and unpublished accounts of Woolsey are the judge's warmth, his gregariousness, and his self-regard. Brooks is a Woolsey family friend who worked for the judge in the summer of 1942, after she had graduated from Vassar College. She recalls the care he took with his decisions and his insistence upon writing them out in longhand and revising steadily. She believes that he cared so much about the details of his decisions because he "wanted people to admire him."[7] Woolsey was a man of letters. He read poetry to his wife and gave books as gifts—deluxe editions with slipcases and floral hard covers of Robert Frost's *A Witness Tree*, John Donne's *Love Poems*, and Elizabeth Barrett Browning's *Sonnets from the Portuguese*—though he was worldly enough to keep up with contemporary literature as well (Woolsey Jr., "Family History"). He chatted with Brooks about Mary McCarthy's recently published collection *The Company She Keeps*, particularly "The Man in the Brooks Brothers Shirt," a mildly daring story about a middle-aged salesman who seduces a young woman on a train.

Woolsey's interest in literature complemented his elite pedigree. He attended Phillips Academy Andover, Yale University (1898), and the Columbia University Law School (1901). He was the descendant of Yale presidents and a Yale founder—members of his family had been attending the university since the beginning of the eighteenth century—and he joined clubs as a way to gild his social stature. At Yale he was president of the University Club and a founder of the Kipling Club (which did not last long). He was a member of Hé Boulé, a sophomore fraternity, Alpha Delta Phi, a junior fraternity, and Scroll and Key, a senior society (they were not secret back then). During his final year of law school, he cofounded the *Columbia Law Review* and later became president of his law-school alumni association. He enjoyed membership. He was, among other things, a member of the Century Association in New York, the Graduates Club of New Haven, the Elizabethan Club at Yale, the Union Club of Boston, and the University Club of New York. He belonged to multiple country clubs, New York's Grolier Club (for bibliophiles), the American Antiquarian Society, and the Walpole Society (also for antiquarians).[8] He collected fine objects like furniture, clocks, and pewter, and he cultivated his taste for tobaccos and liqueurs.

All of this, for Woolsey—the pedigree, the books, the social clubs, the cultural trappings—went hand in hand with authority itself. A few months before his *Ulysses* decision, Woolsey gave Columbia University an eighteenth-century copy of a Jacobean mace made of Sheffield silver. He wrote to Nicholas Murray Butler, the university's president, that he wanted the mace to be "used at all commencements, at convocations, at meetings of the board of trustees and at all other university functions when its use may be appropriate as an emblem of authority for the president and trustees of Columbia."[9] Emblems of authority mattered.

United States v. One Book Called "Ulysses" was part of a trio of obscenity cases Woolsey heard in the early 1930s that, taken together, implied a trend for the federal court. Part of the reason why they have the character they do is because the defense counsel spearheading the cases was the ambitious civil-liberties lawyer Morris Ernst, who was dedicated to liberalizing the nation's sexual standards. At the time, the basis of obscenity law was an 1868 British ruling, *Regina v. Hicklin*, which advised judges to consider the potential effects of portions of a text upon anyone "into whose hands a publication of this sort may fall" (368), be they children, prurient teenagers, or impressionable young ladies—a particularly fraught category for *Ulysses*. If the material had the tendency to "deprave and corrupt" the minds of potential readers, then it was obscene and therefore subject to an array of laws empowering federal and state governments to destroy the material and imprison the people publishing it, selling it, or distributing it through the mail or through private carriers. A few federal decisions had begun challenging *Hicklin*'s dominance over obscenity jurisprudence, but in 1933 the law was still very much in flux.

In two 1931 cases, Woolsey declared that works by Dr. Marie Carmichael Stopes were not obscene: *Married Love*, a marital aid, and *Contraception*, written primarily for medical professionals. In both cases, Woolsey noted that the text in question would not "stir the sex impulses" in a normal person—a requisite feature of "obscenity" that he claimed to cull not from the extensive case history defining the term in the courts but from the *Oxford English Dictionary*.[10] It was as if the term's legal application were not appreciably different from its common usage.

Ernst immediately saw an ally in Woolsey—a judge willing to remake obscenity law nearly from scratch—and so two days after Woolsey's *Married Love* decision, he gave the judge a copy of his own book, *To the Pure... A Study of Obscenity and the Censor*, written with William Seagle. "I thought possibly it might interest you," Ernst wrote.[11] "I shall read with interest," the judge wrote back.[12] *To the Pure* attacked censorship standards as tyrannically arbitrary, a threat to democracy, and a violation of First Amendment rights, an argument that no one (including Woolsey) would abide. The meaninglessness of obscenity as legal category, according to Ernst and Seagle, forced lawyers to appeal to the whims and prejudices of judges and juries: "obscenity is only a superstition of the day—the modern counterpart of ancient witchcraft" (x). Ernst was so confident that Woolsey would be a stalwart supporter of literary freedom that he spent seven months angling for him to preside over the *Ulysses* case,[13] and their friendship grew after the *Ulysses* decision. In February 1934, Ernst had the judge over for cocktails, and Woolsey invited Ernst to the Century Association for lunch. Ernst even tried to persuade Woolsey to write his memoirs—Cass Canfield, the president of Harper & Brothers, was interested in publishing them—but the judge refused.[14] When Woolsey sent Ernst his portrait in 1935, Ernst asked if the judge might add an inscription—"some sweet phrase taken from the writings of Joyce, Woolsey, or some other author who has a flair for diction and cadence"—and the judge gladly complied.[15] The *Ulysses* decision was, one might say, nearly the cooperative enterprise of a nascent friendship.

Woolsey's Stepping-Stones

For all of the attention *United States v. One Book Called "Ulysses"* has received, Woolsey's argument is rather simple. He declares that he has read the entire novel and that Joyce's authorial intentions are legitimate. There is no "dirt for dirt's sake" (184), as he famously put it, and he repeatedly refers to the sincerity and honesty of Joyce's techniques. After approving of Joyce's intentions, he moves beyond them by noting that a lack of pornographic intent "is not sufficient" in determining a text's obscenity. Woolsey therefore considers the novel's effect—whether it would "excite sexual impulses or lustful thoughts" in "a person with average sex instincts" (184). *Ulysses* does not do this, Woolsey declares, and he makes that determination more "objective" by consulting with two friends (184).

Decades later, Ernst wrote that "it is difficult even today to find any new principle laid down" by Woolsey's decision; its importance lay, Ernst insisted, in precipitating a "psychological breakthrough" regarding censorship (Ernst and Schwartz 94). He was right. Nothing about Woolsey's argument was new, but one would not know that from the decision's reputation or even by reading the decision itself. His argument was simple because it bypassed the pressing legal issues vexing obscenity jurisprudence. Virtually every feature of his commentary—the relevance of authorial intent, the effect of a book's literary merit on its overarching effect, and even whether a judge had the "duty" to read the whole book at all—was highly contested at the time.[16] The "psychological breakthrough" of Woolsey's decision was that it treated the evolving legal standards it uses as if they were foregone conclusions. The case law underpinning *United States v. One Book Called "Ulysses"* is almost entirely missing from Woolsey's decision.[17] It stands on the shoulders of invisible giants.

Woolsey laced his decision with guidelines taken from previous cases, but he cites this case history only while making a perfunctory gesture toward the legal definition of obscenity—the *Ulysses* case, for some reason, compelled him to move beyond the *Oxford English Dictionary*. Rather than indicating how previous decisions had shaped the definition of obscenity, Woolsey merely listed seven relevant cases (two of which were his own): *Married Love* and *Contraception* (his 1931 decisions) along with *Swearingen* (1896), *Dunlop* (1897), *Dysart* (1926), *Wendling* (1932), and *Dennett* (1930).[18] Woolsey claimed to cull one formulation of the meaning of obscenity from this roundup of cases: something "obscene" tends to "stir the sex impulses." This was, of course, the same formulation he cited in previous decisions, but the definition was worth emphasizing because it excluded any books that were merely coarse or disgusting, and Woolsey wanted to close his decision by emphasizing that *Ulysses* is "somewhat emetic" but not "an aphrodisiac" (185).

And yet the case history's influence upon Woolsey went deeper than that. The most important case of his compendium was the 1930 *Dennett* decision, which involved yet another one of Ernst's clients, Mary Ware Dennett, over her educational pamphlet *The Sex Side of Life*. Judge Augustus Hand—a cousin of Learned Hand—wrote the *Dennett* decision for the Circuit Court of Appeals for the Second Circuit, and he pushed back against prevailing standards in obscenity jurisprudence. *Dennett* declared that judges in obscenity cases must consider the book as a whole ("its main effect"), its authorial intent, and the text's instructional value; a text with "truthful exposition" and "sincerity of feeling" was not likely to be obscene.[19] *United States v. One Book Called "Ulysses"* was, it seems, cast in *Dennett*'s mold, and yet Woolsey cited *Dennett* without so much as gesturing to the principles it helped establish.

Important as it was, *Dennett* was only a stepping-stone. *Ulysses* was a novel rather than a marital aid or a sex-education pamphlet, which meant that Woolsey would have to go beyond *Dennett* and his own previous obscenity decisions, leaping from a defense of instructional material to a defense of a work of fiction. And this was not a small distinction—the government pressed it when it appealed Woolsey's *Ulysses* decision to the Circuit Court. Fortunately, Woolsey also had a compelling model for the judicial practice of weighing "filth" against literary value: Judge Learned Hand's 1913 opinion in *United States v. Kennerley. Kennerley* urged jurists to protect works of "truth and beauty" even if it meant potentially corrupting a "salacious few," for truth and beauty, Learned Hand insisted, "are too precious to society at large to be mutilated in the interests of those most likely to pervert them" (120).

What was revolutionary about *Kennerley* was the way it suggested the protection of truth and beauty. Learned Hand introduced two crucial standards articulated in federal court for the first time: the goal for obscenity censorship, he argued, should not be to protect any vulnerable persons "into whose hands such material may fall" (as the *Hicklin* decision put it) but to prohibit the circulation of any books that offend or corrupt "the average conscience of the time" (121).[20] The phrase "of the time" is crucial, for Hand's second principle was that obscenity is always in flux: it is "the compromise between candor and shame at which the community may have arrived here and now" (121). Obscenity changed from place to place and from year to year. Not only was obscenity itself variable, its variability operated within the text's large meanings and values. Judges should weigh virtues against vices, candor against shame.

The *Kennerley* decision was obscure for nearly two decades. It had not been cited in any state or federal decision and remained virtually ignored by everyone but Ernst, who repeatedly referred to it in his brief for the *Ulysses* case. Ernst noted that *Kennerley* established a "living standard" for obscenity and quoted the decision liberally in his discussion of the development of obscenity law.[21] In fact, the *Kennerley* decision inspired Ernst's most ambitious defenses. Ernst and Random House sent roughly nine hundred copies of a questionnaire to librarians around the country asking for their opinion of *Ulysses*, their patrons' interest in reading it, and whether they owned (or wanted to own) a copy. Ernst then produced a United States map with a red pin marking every city or town expressing an interest in *Ulysses*. The "community" that had accepted *Ulysses* was nothing less than the entire country.[22] Ernst repeatedly pressed the *Kennerley* decision upon Woolsey, and the judge had clearly absorbed it. Woolsey was adding his own rhetorical flourish to *Kennerley's* "average conscience" standard when he began in *One Book Called "Ulysses"* to consider *Ulysses*'s "effect on a person with average sex instincts—what the French would call *l'homme moyen sensuel*" (184).

And yet Woolsey's decision officially ignored *Kennerley*. Rather than citing its community and "average conscience" standards while referencing Ernst's treasure trove of evidence from librarians across the country, Woolsey decided to collect evidence from his own social sphere, as if applying an intramural version of the community standard. He verified his determination that *Ulysses* was not "an aphrodisiac" to a person of "average sex instincts" by consulting two friends whose opinions would represent community standards in the absence of a jury. What is bizarre is not just that Woolsey did not cite *Kennerley* as the legal basis for his investigation but that his reasoning swerves away from obscenity law altogether. Woolsey's two representatives of *l'homme moyen sensuel*, he writes, play "the same role of hypothetical reagent as does the 'reasonable man' in the law of torts and 'the man learned in the art' on questions of invention in patent law" (184).[23] Why did Woolsey limit the persuasiveness of his decision by evading the case history underpinning his argument? Why cite unnamed friends instead of Learned and Augustus Hand?

Poetry and Prestige

The answer potentially lies in the judge's vanity. Anyone who was not conversant with obscenity case law might reasonably think that the principles in *United States v. One Book Called "Ulysses"* were more or less Woolsey's own inventions. Stripping away the case law also made his decision more quotable, which contributed to Learned Hand's sense that Woolsey was "a bit of a show off ... given to phrases." According to Gerald Gunther, both Judges Hand were irritated by the press coverage of Woolsey's decision, and they specifically wanted their Circuit Court decision upholding Woolsey's decree to be unquotable (288–89). And yet there were more carefully calculated reasons. Presenting debatable methods as if they were already standard practices strengthened the influence of Woolsey's decision and ensured its durable legacy. Perhaps paradoxically, scrubbing away the case history made the fluxional principles governing obscenity law seem sturdier than they actually were, as if the case history had sunk so deeply into a pattern of judicial practices that it did not need to be rehearsed.

The basis of Woolsey's *Ulysses* decision is not obscenity law. The basis is prestige. The decision's authority derives from a sleight of hand creating the illusion of a monument that builds its own foundation. Prestige is exactly this illusion. It is a conjured authority pretending to be established, self-evident, and impervious to disruption. My attention to the prestige underpinning Woolsey's decision follows a line of scholarship that begins with Pierre Bourdieu's landmark study *Distinction: A Social Critique of the Judgement of Taste*.[24] Bourdieu characterizes cultural taste not as a neutral examination of inherent value but as a set of practices and objects that validate power. Elites seize upon artifacts, artworks, texts, furnishings, and so forth as arbitrary, yet self-evident, cultural goods—inventories of cultural capital—that symbolize and justify the economic capital the elites possess. The key word in *Distinction* is not "high" culture but "legitimate" (*légitime*) culture, which is to say that cultural capital does not metaphorically buttress some preexisting hierarchy so much as it arises within a cultural regime that exists by official decree.[25] This binary of legitimate and illegitimate culture carved out by prestigious power is both the basis and the purpose of Woolsey's decision, for his decree concerning the truth, beauty, and sincerity of *Ulysses* doubles as an act of official power that literally legitimizes the novel and welcomes it into the cultural regime. In keeping with the mutual dependence of political, cultural and economic capital, Woolsey's decision bestows an aura of authority upon Joyce's novel that Random House, in turn, could wield for its own benefit and authority. Woolsey, in other words, turned *Ulysses* into a Jacobean mace.

In light of all this, there is a mischievous brilliance to Woolsey's decision, for it exposes the fact that nearly all legal judgments of literary value proceed from declarations of prestige, decrees from positions that are ostensibly beyond debate. Judges outlawed books by deciding that they would "deprave and corrupt" a hypothetical audience (while the judges themselves, of course, remained uncorrupted) because the *Hicklin* rule focused on a book's supposed *tendency* to corrupt. Liberal guidelines were also beyond debate. The literary value standard (the idea that a somewhat dirty book could be exculpated by its virtues) gained a foothold in obscenity law as a means to protect books whose value could not be disputed. While Learned Hand gestured vaguely to precious works of truth and beauty, other decisions named incontestably *légitime* authors and texts that might be censored if the books under consideration were banned. *St. Hubert Guild v. Quinn*, a 1909 New York Supreme Court Appellate Term decision, defended Voltaire by insisting upon his self-evident "genius" ("none can deny the great influence of his work"); another New York case, *In re Worthington*, exonerated François Rabelais, *The Decameron*, and Henry Fielding by invoking the hallowed names of William Shakespeare and Geoffrey Chaucer; yet another invoked the Bible.[26] By the time Augustus Hand affirmed Woolsey's decree in a decision that extolled *Hamlet*, *Romeo and Juliet*, and *Venus and Adonis*, the practice of defense by prestige was well established.

Woolsey invoked literary prestige more subtly. By focusing on *Ulysses* itself, he made judicial precedents and practices vanish, which left only careful readings conducted by himself (a Yale alum, a serious reader of serious books) and two trusted friends (also Yale alums) "whose opinion on literature and on life I value most highly." And there was, importantly, a quasi-institutional basis for Woolsey's faith in those opinions. His unnamed friends were Charles E. Merrill Jr., a small educational publisher—repeatedly misidentified as the son of the Merrill Lynch cofounder—and Henry Seidel Canby, a former Yale English professor and a founder of the *Saturday Review of Literature* (hence the *Saturday Review*'s reprint of Woolsey's decision). Merrill and Canby also happened to be two of the three members of the Century Association's Literature Committee.[27] Woolsey chose friends with credentials.

To note that Woolsey, Merrill, and Canby were not "average" members of the community, as Paul Vanderham does when he enumerates Woolsey's "well-intentioned lie[s]," is to miss what is most important about the men's role in Woolsey's decision.[28] What mattered was that they had prestige. By shifting our view of Woolsey's decision from a series of lies for the sake of literary freedom to canny sleights of hand, we can better recognize the legal stakes of his decision: Woolsey was not circumventing obscenity law—he was not grasping for some way to legalize a good book. Rather, he was performing the tricks that have always been a part of obscenity law.

The prestige of *United States v. One Book Called "Ulysses"* goes beyond consulting social-club literature committees over case law. It suffuses the language of the decision itself. Woolsey took pleasure in pointing out that Joyce's novel featured sexual content because "his locale was Celtic and his season Spring" (184). If such rhetorical flourishes were the reason why Learned Hand called him a "show off" (which was bad), they were also the reason why the *New York Sun* called him a "word fumigator" (which was good).[29] And none of Woolsey's decisions demonstrates his literary bent—the sheer pleasure of distilling a novelist's project—more than his *Ulysses* decision:

> Joyce has attempted—it seems to me, with astonishing success—to show how the screen of consciousness with its ever-shifting kaleidoscopic impressions carries, as it were on a plastic palimpsest, not only what is in the focus of each man's observation of the actual things about him, but also in a penumbral zone residua of past impressions, some recent and some drawn up by association from the domain of the subconscious. (183)

Woolsey's literary decisions were "dangerous" because they revealed that the armature of case law and the neutral voice of authority are disposable. After all, it was precisely Woolsey's literariness, his rhetorical displays (kaleidoscope, palimpsest, penumbra), and his performance of originality that made *United States v. One Book Called "Ulysses"* a foundation for decades of future state and federal decisions, a landmark in the evolving obscenity case law that Woolsey himself ignored. The institutionalization of his decision is dangerous because it underscores just how easily prestige becomes authority. The law itself is a monument that builds its own foundation.

Woolsey sought authority from prestige long before he became a judge in 1929. That is why so many of the trappings of his cultural capital mattered, from his Yale pedigree down to the colonial furniture, the pewter, and the Jacobean mace. The interdependence of the authority of the law and the prestige of culture was, in fact, the heart of his legal philosophy. In 1935, when he sent Ernst his photograph and Ernst asked for an inscription, Woolsey wrote back that the one he was sending also inspired the staging of the photographic portrait itself. The inscription, he wrote to Ernst, was "a paraphrase I made from a stanza I found on an eighteenth century sampler in a New Hampshire attic one rainy Thanksgiving afternoon."[30] A few years later, Woolsey recounted the same story of a rainy New Hampshire Thanksgiving to a journalist named Jack Alexander, who was writing a profile about the judge. Woolsey gave Alexander the impression that the stanza was, for Woolsey, emblematic of the law itself: "I fear, Sir, that you may consider these protestations unmaidenly, but by the laws of Nature we are bound to love, although the Rules of Modesty oftentimes compel us to conceal it."[31]

As a philosophy of the law, the meaning is rather simple: To be human is to be pulled between social rules and the laws of nature, and the law of the land must allow itself to be warped lest it break. And yet what seems more important than the unnamed poem's implicit philosophy—which could not have been new to Woolsey—was the fact that the judge would use an eighteenth-century poem as an emblem of the law at all. The value of the stanza is precisely that it resides in the pages of a poetry anthology rather than a legal textbook. Woolsey wanted his decisions to be upheld and admired, of course, but he also wanted them to be public. He valued English legal decisions, he said, because they were "more like conversations than essays and this informality of approach leads the man in the street when he reads a decision to be kept aware that the common law is not a thing apart, but of the web and woof of society by which and under which we all must live" (Woolf). Authority, for Woolsey, too easily became insular, whereas an effective legal decision was, like prestige, a social coin, an official token whose value ultimately derives from acceptance and circulation. Case law was a part of what made decisions insular.

Woolsey, on the other hand, rummaged through attics, leafed through dictionaries, read books and "satellite" books, and asked the opinions of his friends.

It is no wonder Woolsey was considered literary. Connecting casual conversations with heavy books, forgotten treasures with rich insights, established precedents with epiphanic moments was, after all, what Joyce was apt to do. It is what scholars do. It is what John Woolsey III did when he picked me up from the Worcester train station, drove me thirty miles to Petersham, showed me around his house, and bought me lunch. I spent Bloomsday Eve 2010 eating sandwiches with the judge's grandson—and his son—on a hillside next to the carefully preserved library where Woolsey read *Ulysses*. That is a part of the judge's enduring legacy.

Notes

A version of this essay appeared in *James Joyce Quarterly* 50.4. This revision is reprinted with permission.

1. *United States v. One Book Called "Ulysses,"* 5 F. Supp. 182 (S.D.N.Y. 1933), aff'd sub nom. *United States v. One Book Entitled Ulysses by James Joyce,* 72 F.2d 705 (2d Cir 1934).

2. The Tariff Act of 1930 allowed the secretary of the treasury to "admit the so-called classics or books of recognized and established literary or scientific merit" (19 U.S.C. § 1305). The provision marks this out as something separate from the question of obscenity, though Morris Ernst, Random House's legal counsel, would make the terms mutually exclusive: if something is a classic, it is not obscene. Ernst argued that if the treasury secretary were to grant the importation of one copy because a book is a classic, the obscenity provision of the Tariff Act should not apply to the book at all.

3. Judge John Munro Woolsey's opinion was omitted for a few years after Random House issued a new edition in 1986 prepared by Hans Walter Gabler. See Nadel, "The American *Ulysses*."

4. "Judge Woolsey on 'Ulysses,'" *Saturday Review of Literature*, 16 December 1933, 356.

5. Elmer Rice to Woolsey, 11 December 1933, Morris Ernst Papers (hereafter MEP), Harry Ransom Center, University of Texas at Austin, Box 366, Folder 4. To others, Rice praised *Ulysses* for having a "stimulating effect . . . on my erectile tissue" (qtd. in Wheeler 71).

6. "A Judge Retires," *New York Herald Tribune*, 3 December 1943; Talk of the Town, *New Yorker*, 8 January 1944. I have transcribed "A Judge Retires" from Yale University's Alumni Records and Talk of the Town from a Woolsey family clipping.

7. Interview with Peggy Brooks, New York, NY, 11 November 2009. Woolsey was indeed proud of his decision, though his pride had limits. One thousand copies of his *Ulysses* decision were printed as a pamphlet, but this was apparently the work of friends. See Henry Clapp Smith to Ernst, MEP, Box 366, Folder 4.

8. See Woolsey Jr., "Family History," and the John Munro Woolsey File, Yale University Alumni Records Office, Collection Number RU 830, Series I, Box 122. Woolsey's membership in the Walpole Society, founded in Boston in 1909, is not to be confused with another Walpole Society devoted to British art, founded in 1911. Both were named after the British writer Horace Walpole.

9. "Old English Mace Given to Columbia," *New York Times*, 14 May 1933, N3.

10. See *United States v. One Book Entitled "Contraception,"* 51 F.2d, and *United States v. One Obscene Book Entitled "Married Love,"* 48 F.2d. *Married Love*, according to Woolsey, was "informative and instructive," written "decently" and "with restraint" (823–24), and *Contraception* primarily aroused feelings of "sympathy and pity" for the women unaware of contraceptive methods (528).

11. Ernst to Woolsey, 8 April 1931, MEP, Box 393, Folder 4.

12. Woolsey to Ernst, 9 April 1931, MEP, Box 393, Folder 4.

13. Moscato and LeBlanc 172–213. Despite Bennett Cerf's pleas for a speedy trial, Ernst stalled from January through July 1933 in order to obtain Woolsey. They would have to wait another four months before Woolsey heard arguments on competing motions.

14. Woolsey to Ernst, 20 February, 5 March, and 25 March 1934, MEP, Box 36, Folder 3.

15. Ernst to Woolsey, 3 April 1935, and Woolsey to Ernst, 4 April 1935, MEP, Box 36, Folder 3.

16. Woolsey, for example, assumed in *One Book Called "Ulysses"* that authorial intent—detecting "the leer of the sensualist"—was crucial when, in fact, the intent of the author (or salesman or importer) had been explicitly negated in favor of the text's potential effects in obscenity decisions going back to *Regina v. Hicklin*. The pamphlet under consideration in *Hicklin* was *The Confessional Unmasked*, and it was no less obscene, according to Judge C. J. Cockburn's decision for the Queen's Bench, because it had been distributed as a protest against Catholicism rather than for the corruption of public morals.

17. A comparison with Augustus Hand's decision in the Circuit Court appeal underscores Woolsey's lack of citations. The Circuit Court decision discusses *United States v. Dennett*, *Halsey v. New York Society for the Suppression of Vice*, and *In re Worthington Co.* at length and examines counterarguments in *United States v. Bennett*, *Regina v. Hicklin*, *Rosen v. United States*, and *Dunlop v. United States*. It also reasserts the importance of *Dennett* and adduces *Konda v. United States*, *Clark v. United States*, and *St. Hubert Guild v. Quinn*. See *United States v. One Book Entitled Ulysses*, 72 F. 2d 705, 707–8 (1934).

18. Technically, Woolsey also cites his decision in *One Book Entitled "Contraception"* in order to establish the practice of the case: ruling upon competing motions filed for a forfeiture proceeding. See *Swearingen v. United States*, *Dunlop v. United States*, *Dysart v. United States*, and *People v. Wendling*.

19. See *United States v. Dennett*, which is the first federal decision to articulate the "whole-book" standard forcefully, though we can find an earlier federal precedent in the 1890s—see *In re Worthington Co.* Two New York State decisions, *Halsey* and *St. Hubert Guild*, also articulated a "whole-book" standard. While the practice of judging excerpts

seems harsh, it was the logical consequence of the *Hicklin* case: corruptible people, as Learned Hand pointed out in *United States v. Kennerley*, are precisely those who will read only excerpts.

20. The average-conscience and community-standards tests appeared on the state level in the 1909 New York Supreme Court Appellate Term case *St. Hubert Guild*: "the test to be applied does not require the testimony of experts, but is one falling within knowledge as the community at large of matters of literature." See Robert Spoo's essay in this volume for reasons why Judge Learned Hand's suggestions in *Kennerley* were legally nonbinding in the period.

21. "Living standard" is Ernst's phrase. See Moscato and LeBlanc 244, also 250.

22. For a discussion of the map and questionnaire, see Brockman, "American Librarians and Early Censorship of *Ulysses*: 'Aiding the Cause of Free Expression'?" Woolsey may very well have borrowed the phrase "*homme moyen sensuel*" from John Dos Passos's response to the questionnaire. See Moscato and LeBlanc 126.

23. In tort law, the conduct of a "reasonable man" is the standard against which someone would be judged to be negligent. Yet in the absence of a fixed set of rules, judging the concept involved the creation of a hypothetical "reasonable man," an idea that originated in the eighteenth century (Prosser 149–50). The "man learned in the art" is a hypothetical person whose knowledge would determine whether an invention were truly new or an improvement upon an existing patent.

24. Bourdieu's insights regarding the mutual dependence of cultural and economic capital cast a long shadow in literary studies. John Guillory, for example, applies Bourdieu's theories to university English departments in *Cultural Capital* and Loren Glass applies them specifically to Woolsey's *Ulysses* decision in "Redeeming Value: Obscenity and Anglo-American Modernism." According to Glass, Woolsey's attention to the critical apparatus surrounding *Ulysses* ratified the professionalization of literary studies and its role in the production of Bourdieu's "legitimate" culture (346–47).

25. The history of "legitimate" culture underscores its arbitrary nature. Lawrence Levine, for example, in *Highbrow/Lowbrow: The Emergence of Cultural Hierarchy in American*, chronicles how William Shakespeare was transformed from a writer of popular entertainment to a standard-bearer of legitimate culture in the late nineteenth century. Part of what makes Bourdieu's analysis so powerful is that the collapse of high and low cultures (or their constant reorganization) does nothing to diminish the political uses of cultural taste. Many recent scholars demonstrate how the new elites are the cultural omnivores. See, for example, Peterson and Kern, "Changing Highbrow Taste: From Snob to Omnivore." Joyce, as an omnivore himself, may have been a snob ahead of his time. For the idea of Joyce as a snob (though not an omnivore), see Sean Latham, "*Am I a Snob?*": *Modernism and the Novel*.

26. For a reference to the Bible, see *Halsey*.

27. See Alexander Lindey to Ernst, 7 December 1933, in Moscato and LeBlanc 317, and *The Century Association Yearbook* 99. Robert Spoo's essay in this volume also identifies the correct Merrill. Merrill was not, as Joseph Kelly speculates in *Our Joyce*, the Merrill Lynch cofounder and father of the poet James Merrill. My source for Mer-

rill's identity is Woolsey Jr., "Assorted Notes." The judge did not know the Merrill Lynch cofounder, nor was that Merrill a member of the Century Association. Several scholars before and after Kelly have similarly mistaken Woolsey's obscure friend for the flashier Merrill, including Langdon Hammer in his recent *James Merrill: Life and Art* (New York: Knopf, 2015). A review of Hammer's book by Benjamin Madden in *Modernism/modernity* insists I misidentify Merrill in *The Most Dangerous Book* despite my clear documentation and Hammer's own attempt to set the record straight in the pages of the *New York Times Sunday Book Review*. Myths persist to the degree that they are entertaining. Sometimes their origins are anxiety-of-influence misreadings. Joseph Hassett's *The Ulysses Trials* (Dublin: The Lilliput Press, 2016), for example, misrepresents both my book and an email exchange between us.

28. Vanderham borrows the phrase "well-intentioned lies" (127) from Leslie Fiedler's "To Whom Does Joyce Belong? *Ulysses* as Parody, Pop and Porn," 29. Vanderham identifies four lies, one of which is the departure from the "average conscience" test: "Woolsey's *homme moyen sensuel* is really a projection of Woolsey himself, a man distinguished from the man in the street by, among other qualities, a high degree of literary sophistication" (127).

29. "Judge John M. Woolsey," *New York Sun*, 25 May 1934, 70.

30. Woolsey to Ernst, 4 April 1935, MEP, Box 36, Folder 3. The stanza apparently inspired the placement of items on his judicial bench in his photograph.

31. Alexander 15–16. Alexander describes the paraphrase as a fragment of a letter. Copies of his article exist in the private collections of both Peggy Brooks and the Woolsey family. Editors at the *New Yorker* considered publishing Alexander's profile but ultimately decided it was too "wooden."

Works Cited

Alexander, Jack. "Federal Judge." Undated MS. Copies in the collections of Peggy Brooks, New York, and the Woolsey family, Petersham, MA.
Birmingham, Kevin. *The Most Dangerous Book: The Battle for James Joyce's "Ulysses."* New York: Penguin, 2014.
Bourdieu, Pierre. *Distinction: A Social Critique of the Judgement of Taste*. Translated by Richard Nice. Cambridge, MA: Harvard University Press, 1984.
Brockman, William S. "American Librarians and Early Censorship of *Ulysses*: 'Aiding the Cause of Free Expression'?" *Joyce Studies Annual* 5.1 (1994): 56–74.
The Century Association Yearbook. New York: Century Association, 1933.
The Confessional Unmasked: Showing the Depravity of the Romish Priesthood, the Iniquity of the Confessional, and the Questions Put to Females in Confession. London: Protestant Electoral Union, 1867.
Dennett, Mary Ware. *The Sex Side of Life: An Explanation for Young People*. Astoria, NY: M. W. Dennett, 1928.
Ernst, Morris L., and Alan U. Schwartz. "Four-Letter Words and the Unconscious." In *Censorship: The Search for the Obscene*, 93–107. New York: Macmillan, 1964.

Ernst, Morris L., and William Seagle. *To the Pure . . . : A Study of Obscenity and the Censor.* New York: Viking, 1928.
Fiedler, Leslie. "To Whom Does Joyce Belong? *Ulysses* as Parody, Pop and Porn." In *Light Rays: James Joyce and Modernism*, edited by Heyward Ehrlich, 26–30. New York: New Horizon, 1984.
Glass, Loren. "Redeeming Value: Obscenity and Anglo-American Modernism." *Critical Inquiry* 32.2 (Winter 2006): 341–61.
Guillory, John. *Cultural Capital: The Problem of Literary Canon Formation.* Chicago: University of Chicago Press, 1995.
Gunther, Gerald. *Learned Hand: The Man and the Judge.* 2nd ed. New York: Oxford University Press, 2011.
Kelly, Joseph. *Our Joyce: From Outcast to Icon.* Austin: University of Texas Press, 1998.
Latham, Sean. *"Am I a Snob?": Modernism and the Novel.* Ithaca, NY: Cornell University Press, 2003.
Levine, Lawrence W. *Highbrow/Lowbrow: The Emergence of Cultural Hierarchy in America.* Cambridge, MA: Harvard University Press, 1988.
Moscato, Michael, and Leslie LeBlanc, eds. *The United States of America v. One Book Entitled "Ulysses" by James Joyce: Documents and Commentary: A 50-Year Retrospective.* Frederick, MD: University Publications of America, 1984.
Nadel, Ira. "The American *Ulysses*: 'A Lasting Boom.'" *James Joyce Quarterly* 28 (Summer 1991): 967–81.
Nabokov, Vladimir. *Lolita.* 2 vols. Paris: Olympia, 1955.
New Yorker. Talk of the Town. 8 January 1944.
New York Herald Tribune. "A Judge Retires." 3 December 1943, 22.
New York Sun. "Judge John M. Woolsey." 25 May 1934, 70.
New York Times. "Old English Mace Given to Columbia." 14 May 1933, N3.
Peterson, Richard A., and Roger M. Kern. "Changing Highbrow Taste: From Snob to Omnivore." *American Sociological Review* 61 (October 1996): 900–907.
Prosser, William L. *Handbook of the Law of Torts.* 4th ed. St. Paul: West Publishers, 1971.
Saturday Review of Literature. "Judge Woolsey on 'Ulysses.'" 16 December 1933, 356.
Stopes, Marie Carmichael. *Contraception (Birth Control): Its Theory, History, and Practice.* London: J. Bale, 1923.
———. *Married Love; or, Love in Marriage.* New York: Critic and Guide, 1918.
Vanderham, Paul. *James Joyce and Censorship: The Trials of "Ulysses."* New York: New York University Press, 1998.
Wheeler, Leigh Ann. "Where Else but Greenwich Village?: Love, Lust and the Emergence of the American Civil Liberties Union's Sexual Rights Agenda, 1920–1931." *Journal of the History of Sexuality* 21.1 (January 2012): 60–92.
Woolf, S. J. "A Judge Who Scans the Drama of Life." *New York Times Magazine*, 11 March 1934, SM7.
Woolsey, John, Jr. "Assorted Notes." Undated papers. Woolsey family collection, Petersham, MA.

———. "Family History: The Woolseys." Undated MS. Woolsey family collection, Petersham, MA.

Legal Decisions

Clark v. United States, 211 F. 916 (8th Cir. 1914).
Dunlop v. United States, 165 U.S. 486 (1897).
Dysart v. United States, 272 U.S. 655 (1926).
Halsey v. New York Society for the Suppression of Vice, 234 N.Y. 1 (N.Y. 1922).
In re Worthington Co., 30 N.Y.S. 361 (N.Y. Sup. Ct. 1894).
Konda v. United States, 166 F. 91 (7th Cir. 1908).
People v. Wendling, 258 N.Y. 451, 180 N.E. 169 (1932).
Regina v. Hicklin, [1868] L.R. 3 Q.B. 360.
Rosen v. United States, 161 U.S. 29 (1896).
St. Hubert Guild v. Quinn, 118 N.Y.S. 582 (N.Y. App. Div. 1909).
Swearingen v. United States, 161 U.S. 446 (1896).
United States v. Bennett, 24 Fed. Cas. 1093 (C.C.S.D.N.Y. 1879).
United States v. Dennett, 39 F.2d 564 (2d Cir. 1930).
United States v. Kennerley, 209 F. 119 (1913).
United States v. One Book Called "Ulysses," 5 F. Supp. 182 (S.D.N.Y. 1933).
United States v. One Book Entitled "Contraception," 51 F.2d 525 (S.D.N.Y. 1931).
United States v. One Book Entitled Ulysses by James Joyce, 72 F.2d 705 (2d Cir. 1934).
United States v. One Obscene Book Entitled "Married Love," 48 F.2d 821 (S.D.N.Y. 1931).

14

Ulysses as Deodand

Books, Automobiles, and the Law of Forfeiture

ROBERT SPOO

If corporations can be persons under the law, books can have a soul and a conscience. The goodness or malignity of books has long been an assumption of legal thinking. In a famous passage of *Areopagitica*, John Milton, deploring prepublication censorship under Parliament's Licensing Order of 1643, denied that books were "absolutely dead things" and held that they contained "the precious life-blood of a master spirit, embalmed and treasured up on purpose to a life beyond life" (155–56). To suppress a book by legal means was to kill "the image of God, as it were, in the eye," to commit "a kind of homicide ... sometimes a martyrdom" (156). For Milton, books were subtle distillations of their human authors, with power to do good or evil, and the state's coercive force must be applied, he felt, with the kind of respect for living autonomy that the law recognized in other areas.

Milton thought it especially "lamentable" that "the work of any deceased author, though never so famous in his lifetime and even to this day," should be subjected to prepublication scrutiny by an official body of licensors who might suppress "the venturous edge" of the author's text and reduce all learning to the level of "a common steadfast dunce" (180–81). He considered such posthumous meddling to be "a treacherous fraud against the orphan remainders of worthiest men," and he announced the sweeping principle "Truth and understanding are not such wares as to be monopolized and traded in by tickets and statutes and standards" (181). These were strong words for an English author to hazard in 1644, especially one who had not sought a license for his pamphlet. Milton was asserting that the Licensing Order threatened to murder authors' defenseless children—their books—and to reduce truth to the level of a commodity controlled by an oligopoly of state examiners.

Milton was speaking out against prior restraints, but the law more commonly has sought to silence books after they were published. Such silencing has taken two legal forms: proceedings *in personam* (against authors, publishers, or booksellers) and proceedings *in rem* (against books themselves). British obscenity laws in the twentieth century, for example, targeted books no less than their publishers. Under Lord Campbell's Act, courts issued orders for forfeiture and destruction of many publications deemed obscene, including D. H. Lawrence's *The Rainbow* in 1915 and Radclyffe Hall's *The Well of Loneliness* in 1928 (Potter 18). When Random House challenged the U.S. customs ban on James Joyce's *Ulysses* in 1932, it was in the context of an *in rem* civil forfeiture action involving a single imported copy of the Paris edition.

Joyce's novel, first published as a complete book in France in 1922, had been a legal orphan in the United States ever since a portion of the work was ruled obscene by a New York court in 1921. The book's reputation for indecency had prevented Joyce from complying with the technicalities of U.S. copyright law, so the book became lawless in a double sense: a youthful offender against obscenity codes and a waif stripped of literary property rights—an outlaw without the law. The book's orphan status made it vulnerable to lawful kidnapping by the New York pirate-pornographer Samuel Roth, who began serializing extracts in his magazine *Two Worlds Monthly* in 1926. In essence, American copyright and obscenity laws had combined to separate Joyce from his intellectual offspring (Spoo, "Copyright Protectionism"). Random House's strategy was to reunite author and child by going to court to legitimize the tainted, long-suffering book, to rehabilitate the book's personhood.

But Random House and its cofounder Bennett Cerf faced a dilemma. While a favorable result in the U.S. customs case would open the harbors to *Ulysses*, it would also invite the depredations of lawful pirates who now might go to work with their greatest legal fear, prosecution for publishing obscenity, much allayed. In banning controversial modern works, obscenity law had come to function as a sort of super-copyright, vesting the government with exclusive power to control publication and making it impossible for anyone else, even authors, to disseminate works. American copyright law, in contrast, often failed to protect transatlantic works at all. Cerf worried that vigilant pirates would quickly and lawfully free-ride on his success in liberating *Ulysses* from the censor, leaving him with little more than a moral victory and a legal bill. The subtext of the customs litigation implied an anxious narrative of obscenity's red light changing to green while copyright's light still flashed an ambiguous, curious yellow.

The *Ulysses* customs case was not a criminal prosecution, but rather a civil action in which the U.S. government sought the forfeiture and destruction of a piece of physical property: one book entitled *Ulysses*, or, more precisely, one copy of a book entitled *Ulysses*. Neither Joyce nor Cerf was the target of the litigation; rather, a single copy of *Ulysses*, seized at the Port of New York, was the defendant in the case. Like other sued chattels, this book had no attorney; its defense had to be provided indirectly by Random House, which interposed its claim as lawful purchaser of the volume. It was exactly as when law enforcement today seizes an automobile alleged to have been used to transport a controlled substance. In addition to any criminal charges pending against persons involved in the prohibited activity, prosecutors may file a civil forfeiture action against the vehicle itself. The owner is usually given a chance to argue in court that her vehicle should not be declared forfeit to the state. If she succeeds, she can reclaim her automobile.[1]

This is precisely what happened in the *Ulysses* case, except that the property for which Cerf fought was not a car but a copy of a book, a book accused of having concealed in its pages not packets of narcotics but passages of obscenity in violation of the Tariff Act of 1930. If Cerf won, his victory would allow him to reclaim his copy of *Ulysses* and (here's where the analogy to sued automobiles ends) would open the New York port to all other copies of the book. That a book purchaser like Cerf could win a broader victory than a car owner stems from the fact that books are public goods, infinitely reproducible in identical form. If one copy is deemed free of obscenity by a competent court, all copies essentially share in the judgment. In contrast, when an accused automobile is restored to its owner after litigation, the next car to come rumbling down the road with a trunkful of illegal drugs cannot benefit from that victory. Cars are private goods, each with its particular identity and history. The fact that books are public goods is just what worried Cerf. He wanted to do more than simply win back the copy of *Ulysses* he had imported from Paris; he wanted to use his legal victory to print and sell thousands more copies. But since *Ulysses* was a public good that lacked a U.S. copyright, the lifting of the customs ban was a benefit that Cerf might have to share with lawful free riders.[2]

This essay is about the status of Joyce's book as a sued defendant, a legal person, in effect, whose personhood had historical roots in the ancient concept of the sacrificial deodand. Along the way, I clarify the kind of proceeding that *United States v. One Book Entitled Ulysses* was.[3] The action was not a "prosecution" (Kelly 129) or a "libel prosecution" (Nowlin 60); it did not involve "obscenity charges" or what we normally think of as a "trial" (Thomas 127-28); nor did it result in a "verdict" (Ladenson 91) or an "acquittal" (Law 219). A full appreciation of any litigation requires a grasp of what might seem at first glance to be mere technicalities of procedure (Rembar 27-28). Procedure is as important to the work of legal historians as it is to the practice of litigators. Just as procedural matters "enter into and condition all substantive law's becoming actual when there is a dispute" (Llewellyn 9), so they also give meaning to historical depictions of the work of judges and lawyers. Because procedure defines the possible within litigation, it is critical for assessing the actual performances of legal actors.

Finally, I offer a fresh appreciation of the achievement of Judge John Munro Woolsey, who gave judgment for Random House in the forfeiture action. The creativity and courage that Woolsey showed have been somewhat tarnished by recent critiques that have stressed his alleged elitism, aestheticism, and subjectivity. I argue that Woolsey's opinion should be read, not simply as a guilty signifier for privileged power masquerading as urbane progressivism, indifferent to the popular will, but rather as a flexible, imaginative response to social and legal realities that constrained judicial approaches to obscenity in the 1930s.

Books and Buicks: The Thing as Defendant

Let's return to automobile seizures. A provision of New York City's Civil Administrative Code authorizes the police to seize the motor vehicles of those accused of driving while intoxicated or of committing other offenses for which a motor vehicle can be considered an instrumentality of the crime.[4] The code permits the city to take custody of the seized vehicle and to hold it in the expectation of eventually gaining title by prevailing in a civil forfeiture proceeding initiated by the city against the vehicle. These civil actions are called *in rem* proceedings, actions brought against a thing, rather than *in personam* proceedings, actions brought against a person, such as criminal prosecutions for driving while intoxicated. The civil forfeiture action against the vehicle is independent of the criminal case against its driver and may be pursued by the city even if the criminal case is dismissed or results in acquittal. These forfeiture cases awaited the resolution of separate criminal charges and could take months or even years to run their course. Justice Sonia Sotomayor, then a judge on the U.S. Court of Appeals for the Second Circuit, authored an important opinion that required, as a matter of constitutional due process, a prompt hearing before a neutral fact finder to determine the propriety of the city's continued possession of a vehicle after its seizure by police and before the ultimate resolution of the forfeiture action in court.[5] This "*Krimstock* hearing," as it has come to be called, gives a vehicle owner an early opportunity to offer evidence, for example, that she neither knew nor had reason to know that her friend would take her car without her permission and drive it while inebriated. In this way the innocent owner might be able to recover her car without having to wait months or years for a civil court to decide that the vehicle had been operated without her knowledge and should not be forfeited as an instrumentality of crime. Justice Sotomayor's opinion introduced fairness into a practice that had often worked a deprivation of property without adequate due process.

In the *Ulysses* customs case, the seized copy of Joyce's masterpiece, like Valerie Krimstock's 1995 Toyota, stood accused as a sort of dangerous instrumentality, a *res* or thing subject to the strictures of civil forfeiture. The litigation orchestrated by Random House's lawyer Morris L. Ernst worked so well because the Tariff Act under which *Ulysses* had been seized, like New York's forfeiture law as modified by Sotomayor's opinion, had been revised to permit fairer, more efficient proceedings (Weinrib 371–72). Ernst knew the Tariff Act's new forfeiture procedure well; he had helped design it. In the late 1920s he had interested Senator Bronson Cutting of New Mexico in reforming the arbitrariness of censorship by customs officials (Ernst 161–62). Up to that time, when a book was seized by customs as obscene, the person to whom the book had been addressed could, if he or she wished, challenge the seizure in the U.S. Customs Court, but this was a weak safeguard. The addressee had the burden of proving that the book was not obscene; the collector of customs was not required to prove anything. The collector's subjective decision to pounce on the book would not be overturned unless the Customs Court was persuaded that he had substantially abused his discretion. In most cases, the seizure was upheld and the book was confiscated (Ernst and Lindey 14–16). The unpredictable squeamishness of bureaucrats was practically immune from judicial review.

The Cutting amendment changed all that. Senator Cutting sought Ernst's help in revising the Tariff Act to set up barriers against capricious seizures. The new statutory procedure, formulated by Ernst and codified in Section 305 of the Tariff Act of 1930, established a coherent mechanism for testing the validity of seizures: promptly after a seizure, customs was required to inform the U.S. Attorney of the district in which the book had been taken; the U.S. Attorney was in turn required to initiate proceedings in the federal district court (not the Customs Court) for the book's forfeiture. The government had to make a reasoned case for forfeiture, and the book's addressee was entitled to intervene as claimant and demand a jury trial. Under the Cutting amendment, the discretionary power of customs officials was subjected to meaningful judicial oversight. Automatic confiscation was a thing of the past.

The Cutting amendment also prevented the government from directing its power against the foreign sender or the domestic recipient of a seized book; those individuals were free from criminal prosecution under the revised Tariff Act (Ernst 161–62). Instead, the government was required to bring a civil forfeiture action directly against the allegedly obscene book, the legal *res*. The government was obliged to initiate this *in rem* action by filing a "libel" against the seized book—an old term used in admiralty law for the initial complaint or pleading in a lawsuit. An admiralty "libel" (from the Latin *libellus*, little book) should not be confused with the form of defamation called libel (from *libellus famosus*, a defamatory publication or pamphlet) or with older concepts of seditious or obscene libel. The *Ulysses* customs case was, technically, a proceeding in admiralty—hence the "A" in the case's docket number, A 110-59. Libel proceedings were a time-honored means of gaining legal title, for example, to ships captured as prizes at sea. During the Civil War, President Lincoln's blockade of southern ports resulted in the seizure of many belligerent and neutral vessels which were then subjected to libel proceedings by U.S. Attorneys and, following successful litigation, declared forfeit to the United States as war prizes. These vessels were defendants in *in rem* actions. Under the Tariff Act, the seized copy of *Ulysses* was, likewise, the sole defendant in an *in rem* case.

Such lawsuits, regularly filed against contaminated or contraband imports, were common during Prohibition. The National Archives Northeast Region, located in New York City, contains the records of many such forfeiture proceedings. Turning the pages of these files, one can see why indecent books and bootleg hooch occupied the same imaginative space in the 1920s and 1930s, a linkage that gave rise to the playful term "bookleggers" for underground operators like Samuel Roth. In the same box that contains the files for *United States v. One Book Entitled Ulysses*,[6] there are also records for *United States v. One Ford Truck*, a case dating from December 1932 and involving a vehicle caught transporting "intoxicating liquors" in violation of the Tariff Act and the Prohibition Reorganization Act. Other case files include *United States v. Approximately 126 Assorted Glasses, a quantity of intoxicating liquors, etc. found at Club La Lune on West 52nd Street* and *United States v. One Cash Register, Remington #A-334, 163840, a quantity of intoxicating liquors, etc. found at premises at 584 Lenox Ave., Manhattan*. Each of these cases was a forfeiture action, or libel, brought against illicit articles by George Z. Medalie, the same U.S. Attorney who in 1932 filed a libel against one book entitled *Ulysses*.

Readying *Ulysses* to Be Sued

Ernst's initial task was to make sure that customs actually seized a copy of *Ulysses*. On Cerf's instructions, Joyce's friend and assistant Paul Léon carefully pasted into a copy of the Shakespeare and Company edition a number of documents, including press extracts and critical assessments, that might serve as evidence of the book's literary importance and moral decency. In this period, American courts were often reluctant to admit evidence of critical praise for an allegedly obscene book; judges worried that the testimony of literary experts would trespass on the province of the fact finder (Gillers 237). If the seized copy actually embodied testimonials, however, those items would be harder to ignore, as a practical matter. Ernst's stratagem capitalized on a book's special status in forfeiture actions—its status as text.

After fortifying the volume with extracts, Léon dispatched it for transport aboard the S/S *Bremen*. The ship with its controversial cargo docked at the Port of New York in early May 1932. Prompted by Ernst's office, customs officials seized the volume and notified Ernst's associate Alexander Lindey that it was being held as obscene, pursuant to the Tariff Act. On 24 May, as required by the Cutting amendment, customs transmitted the volume to the U.S. Attorney for the Southern District of New York for initiating forfeiture proceedings. After a long delay, on 9 December, U.S. Attorney Medalie filed a libel that alleged grounds for the forfeiture, confiscation, and destruction of the book. A week later, Ernst interposed a claim on behalf of the addressee of the volume, Random House, as "intervenor" in the action, that is, as a third party entering the proceeding to assert its rights as owner of the challenged property.[7] Originally Ernst had hoped that retired Supreme Court justice Oliver Wendell Holmes Jr. would agree to be the book's addressee instead of Random House. Imagine if the caption of the case had read "United States v. One Book Entitled *Ulysses* by James Joyce (Oliver Wendell Holmes Jr., Claimant)." But Holmes declined, and other candidates, including Nicholas Murray Butler, president of Columbia University, and Roy Howard, codirector of the Scripps-Howard newspaper chain, also refused.[8] The primary parties were the government and the accused copy of *Ulysses*. As intervening claimant, Random House filed an answer to the government's libel, denying that *Ulysses* violated the Tariff Act. With this exchange, the issue of obscenity was formally joined.

Of Culpable Chattels: *Ulysses* as Deodand

The seized copy of *Ulysses* was now a defendant in a civil action. As noted above, the law of forfeiture makes the inanimate instrumentalities of alleged misconduct, rather than human actors, the targets of the state's power. Forfeiture has its roots in vengeance exacted on the offending thing (Holmes 10). Scholars trace forfeiture proceedings to the early English law of deodands, under which a chattel, whether an animal or an inanimate object, was adjudged a deodand (*deo dandum*, to be given to God) once a coroner's jury concluded that the chattel had caused the accidental or negligent death of a human being. Upon such a finding, the Crown was supposed to confiscate the chattel, sell it, and apply the proceeds to charitable purposes, but in practice the chattel's owner often paid a fine equal to the value of the deodand, and the sum was turned over to a charity or the victim's family, or simply added to the royal coffers (Pervukhin; Piety).

The law of deodands embodied a kind of animistic logic, a belief that if a thing caused harm to a person, the thing, rather than its human owner, was the culprit. "If an ox gore a man or a woman, that they die," the Mosaic code commanded, "then the ox shall be surely stoned, and his flesh shall not be eaten; but the owner of the ox shall be quit" (Exodus 21:28). Vestiges of this logic have survived in the modern police practice of seizing the instrumentalities of crime. Following such seizures, state and federal authorities routinely launch forfeiture proceedings against these passive conduits of alleged criminal activity. This is how *Krimstock*-type seizures became such an attractive aid in combating intoxicated driving. A forfeiture action is, in a sense, a prosecution by other means, a civil counterpart or supplement to a criminal proceeding, with the added advantage to the state of requiring a lower standard of proof than the high burden ("beyond a reasonable doubt") that prosecutors of crimes must meet.

The lineaments of the law of deodands can be glimpsed behind the libel filed against Random House's copy of *Ulysses*. No human being was the object of the law's wrath; it was the book itself, the immediate corrupter of morals, against which the U.S. Attorney sought a decree of forfeiture and destruction, by way of just punishment. One of Ernst's briefs contended, Miltonically, that the government should be required to prove its allegations beyond a reasonable doubt because the case was "something like a capital case. *Ulysses* stands before the Court as defendant. Charged with being a menace to public morals, it is fighting for its life. If condemned, it faces destruction by a means (i.e., confiscation) no less complete than that of hanging or electrocution."[9] This was no lawyerly flight of fancy. The retributive fury of the state was being concentrated upon a public enemy, *Ulysses* by James Joyce.

The highly publicized lawsuit represented a further chapter in the martyrdom of *Ulysses*. Already the victim of pirates, Joyce's novel was now a federal prisoner as well. The caption of the case—*United States of America v. One Book Entitled Ulysses*—spoke eloquently of the forces ranged against the beleaguered book, a Goliath-against-David story in which philistine might asserted its right to confiscate and destroy an instrumentality of aesthetic and moral subversiveness. *Ulysses* was coveted in its character of tangible and intangible property: pirates plying their trade on the bounding public domain wanted to reproduce it in catchpenny copies; the government sought a decree for the annihilation of its physical embodiment, a latter-day deodand offered up to appease Victorian sensibilities. Yet, just as with Roth's piracies, Joyce was able to benefit from this fresh spectacle of his victimized genius. The more *Ulysses* seemed the object of piratical desire or official condemnation, the more justified seemed its claims to literary greatness and lawful availability.

Judge Woolsey and the Average Libido

Judge Woolsey, presiding in the trial court, was no stranger to forfeiture proceedings. Prior to his judicial career, he had practiced as an admiralty lawyer and litigated numerous cases that involved libels filed against maritime vessels for unpaid debts or other legal claims.[10] Later, as a federal judge, he tried various admiralty cases, including a dispute in which a barge owner filed a libel against a steamship that he alleged had tortiously damaged his vessel.[11] It was scarcely a stretch for Woolsey when his docket came to include lawsuits against books, not boats. By the time he was assigned the *Ulysses* case, he had dismissed Tariff Act libels filed by the government against two allegedly obscene books by Marie Stopes, *Married Love* and *Contraception*, which openly discussed birth control, adult sexuality, and marriage equality.[12] Ernst and U.S. Attorney Medalie had been opponents in those forfeiture actions as well.

Reduced to its essence, Judge Woolsey's test for obscenity as set forth in his *Ulysses* opinion was as follows: a book is not obscene within the meaning of the Tariff Act of 1930 if the author's intent was not pornographic and if the book, viewed in its entirety and according to its net effect, does not tend to stir the sex impulses or lead to sexually impure and lustful thoughts in a person with average sex instincts (*U* ix–xiv). This test was bold and forthright in 1933. With its clearly delineated subjective and objective criteria, it rejected the circular jargon, prudish indirection, and scolding tone of other obscenity opinions of the day,[13] focusing instead on commonsense matters: sincere authorial purpose, the net effect of the whole work, the relevancy of the work's parts to its whole, and the libidinous impact on a normal mind. Woolsey shunned the sort of judicial voice that intoned, "Masterpieces have never been produced by men given to obscenity or lustful thoughts—men who have no Master."[14]

Without saying so, Woolsey audaciously rejected what was arguably the reigning test of obscenity in his jurisdiction, a standard derived from the

1868 English case *Regina v. Hicklin*: "whether the tendency of the matter charged as obscenity is to deprave and corrupt those whose minds are open to such immoral influences, and into whose hands a publication of this sort may fall."[15] Every part of this definition stacked the deck against a defendant. Prosecutors could point to a few words or phrases ("the matter charged") and argue that these fragments had a "tendency" to corrupt the young, the morbidly prudish, or the selectively salacious ("whose minds are open to such immoral influences") if there was any possibility of access ("into whose hands a publication of this sort may fall"). The "normal mind," which Woolsey had already invoked in deciding the *Contraception* and *Married Love* cases, was a very different test from the *Hicklin* formula. *Hicklin* protected what Ernst called the "dullest-witted and most fallible";[16] its theory was that "if one libidinous man existed in an Anglo-Saxon community, then all its members would have to submit themselves to the inhibitions of the censorship" (Ernst and Seagle 192). Paternalistic and overbroad, *Hicklin* might be called the Law of the Child; it had a devastating impact on adult Americans' access to serious reading matter.

Judge Woolsey rolled a big boulder when he pushed aside the *Hicklin* standard, but one would scarcely gather this from the critiques of recent scholars. For them, Woolsey's test slyly enthroned the educated, elite reader while only pretending to invoke the "average reader" (Kelly 60; Nowlin 60–61; Vanderham 127). His opinion "in a subtle series of shifts . . . [mapped] educated reading practices onto a construction of the normal or average reader" (Leckie 16). The average reader, under Woolsey's wand, was merely a pretext for culturally exclusive practices. But these suspicious hermeneutics, however revisionary they may seem today, misinterpret the law and the legal reality of 1933. Woolsey did not adopt the "average reader," in the critic's sense, as a test of obscenity. His chosen measure was the "person with average sex instincts," or the "normal person." Critics have thus shifted the category from average sex instincts to average reading ability, from a sexual-emotional test to a socio-educational one. In doing so, they have committed a category error. There is no reason, in principle, why Woolsey or any other educated reader could not have served as a test of average sexual maturity. That Woolsey did not try his test out on "the lower classes and the uneducated" (Kelly 120) did not destroy its legal usefulness. His sexually reasonable person was "a measure of guidance for the honest judge" (Ernst and Lindey 189), not a statistical average based on the demographics of reading. Woolsey was establishing a progressive test, within judicial conventions, for a murky, troublesome area of the law.

What was the actual legal impact of Judge Woolsey's decision? There had never been a comprehensive legal ban on *Ulysses* in the United States. Rather, the seeming blanket prohibition resulted chiefly from two cases. A serialized portion of *Ulysses* had been deemed obscene in 1921 when the New York Court of Special Sessions, applying the state's penal code, convicted the editors of the *Little Review* of publishing obscenity (Weir). Later, in 1928, the U.S. Customs Court upheld the seizure of seven copies of *Ulysses*, along with other titles, at the Port of Minneapolis, under the previous Tariff Act of 1922, a seizure upheld in *Heymoolen v. United States*.[17] Woolsey's decision did not overrule either of these cases, which had been decided by different courts under different laws. Even after the U.S. Court of Appeals for the Second Circuit affirmed Woolsey's *Ulysses* decision in 1934, the book was still vulnerable to attack from the postal authorities, state prosecutors, and vigilant vice societies; even customs officials outside of New York, Connecticut, and Vermont—the territory included within the jurisdiction of the Second Circuit—might feel free to seize the book. Just a few months after Woolsey issued his decree, an Episcopal clergyman learned that the U.S. Post Office had seized a copy of the Random House *Ulysses* that he had mailed to himself along with *Lives of the Saints* and Richard Maurice Bucke's *Cosmic Consciousness*. When the clergyman protested, the Post Office stated that it planned to hold the book without destroying it until the *Ulysses* appeal was decided; in the meantime, the good pastor could consider himself technically charged under the Comstock Act with sending obscenity through the mails.[18]

The inclusion of Judge Woolsey's opinion in the Random House *Ulysses* was intended to discourage such collateral attacks. Ernst had found that inserting judicial opinions or similar matter in newly liberated volumes—Stopes's *Enduring Passion*, Radclyffe Hall's *The Well of Loneliness*, and *The Decameron*—tended to "retard" the aggressions of law enforcement and to cause censorship groups to hesitate before commencing proceedings.[19] Cerf hoped that the opinion would "impress a number of self-appointed smut-hounds in various states sufficiently to keep them from taking any action against the book, and causing us petty annoyance for an indefinite period of time."[20] Initially, Lindey thought it would be "amusing" to print Woolsey's urbane, literate opinion alongside the *Heymoolen* judgment,[21] which had crudely fulminated against *Ulysses* and the books seized with it as "obscenity of the rottenest and vilest character," but the idea of dueling judges went no further.

For his part, Woolsey preferred to omit the technical portions of his opinion and to print only its substance in the Random House edition—he was proud of the opinion as a piece of literary criticism—but Ernst felt that inclusion of the entire document was essential. Only the complete opinion could serve as a scarecrow to ward off further official harassment of *Ulysses*. In the end, the strict precedential sweep of Woolsey's decree was modest, but the social and cultural impact of his opinion transcended its legal function and quickly became a symbol of judicial enlightenment and good sense. Ernst himself believed that the chief importance of Woolsey's decision was that it "represented a psychological breakthrough in the censorship field" rather than a foundational legal precedent (Ernst and Schwartz 94). Even so, the decision has been cited in published judicial opinions some fifty times between 1935 and 2015.[22]

In addition to Judge Woolsey's opinion, the Random House *Ulysses* contained an authenticating letter from Joyce certifying that Cerf's edition was "the only authentic one in the United States" (*U* xvii). Joyce's letter sketched a history of the publication, censorship, and piracy of *Ulysses*. Instead of writing about himself, he wrote a little biography of his book, which had had, he noted, "a life of its own," just as all books have their own destiny: "*Habent sua fata libelli!*" (*U* xv). He approached the subject as if he were composing a saint's life, or that of a misunderstood heretic, complete with journeys, persecutions, and ritual sacrifices. Copies of *Ulysses* had been "seized and burnt" by customs officials in New York and Folkestone, and Joyce's inability to "acquire the copyright in the United States" had led to the abduction and unauthorized publication of the book by "unscrupulous persons" (*U* xvi–xvii). Placed strategically just after the text of Judge Woolsey's opinion, the letter reinforced the perception of *Ulysses* as sufferer—orphan of censorship, hostage of pirates, defendant in a forfeiture action, sacrificial deodand.

John Milton argued that restraints on authorial speech struck at "the breath of reason itself" and slew "an immortality rather than a life" (156). His anthropomorphizing insistence that the law could make martyrs of books nicely captures the fate of *Ulysses* in America between 1918 and 1934. Subjected to post office seizures, a New York obscenity trial, and the lawful piracies of the wily, admiring Roth, *Ulysses* was an orphan in need of rescue when Cerf and Ernst joined forces to make it the centerpiece of a federal forfeiture action. They found the right judge, one who had presided over earlier *in rem* actions against books and who understood enough about literature and life to know that he must let Joyce's book lead him, in its full, complex personhood, and under an enlightened legal standard, to a proper judgment.

Notes

This essay is an expansion and revision of portions of my essay "Judging Woolsey Judging Obscenity: Elitism, Aestheticism, and the Reasonable Libido in the *Ulysses* Customs Case," *James Joyce Quarterly* 50.4 (2013): 1027–49, and of a few pages, 240–43, of my book *Without Copyrights: Piracy, Publishing, and the Public Domain*.

1. For judicial decisions concerning automobile forfeitures, see United States v. One 2001 Mercedes Benz ML 320, 668 F. Supp. 2d 1132 (E.D. Wis. 2009); United States v. 2001 Honda Accord EX VIN #1HGCG22561A035829, 245 F. Supp. 2d 602, 611–12 (M.D. Pa. 2003).

2. In the end, Cerf's strategies worked so well that free riders did not trespass on his informal right to publish *Ulysses*; see Spoo, *Without Copyrights*, 245–62.

3. United States v. One Book Called "Ulysses," 5 F. Supp. 182, 182–83 (S.D.N.Y. 1933), *aff'd sub nom.* United States v. One Book Entitled Ulysses by James Joyce, 72 F.2d 705 (2d Cir. 1934).

4. N.Y.C. Code § 14-140.

5. *See* Krimstock v. Kelly, 306 F.3d 40, 65–66 (2d Cir. 2002) (Sotomayor, J.).

6. Box No. 1446 (540505-06) (43220-21), U.S. District Court for the Southern District of New York, Admiralty case files nos. A110-59 to A110-80, National Archives Northeast Region, New York City.

7. Random House's Claim (Moscato and LeBlanc 167).

8. Letters, Cerf to Lindey, 28 March 1932; Horace Chapman Rose to Cerf, 1 April 1932; Cerf to Ernst, 13 April 1932, in Moscato and LeBlanc 110, 115, 118.

9. Claimant's Supplementary Memorandum (Moscato and LeBlanc 291).

10. See, for example, Piedmont & George's Creek Coal Co. v. Seaboard Fisheries Co., 254 U.S. 1 (1920); Watts, Watts & Co. v. Unione Austriaca di Navigazione, 248 U.S. 9 (1918).

11. The Jack Hammond, 41 F.2d 831 (S.D.N.Y. 1930).

12. United States v. One Book, Entitled "Contraception," by Marie C. Stopes, 51 F.2d 525 (S.D.N.Y. 1931); United States v. One Obscene Book Entitled "Married Love," 48 F.2d 821 (S.D.N.Y. 1931).

13. See, for example, People v. Berg, 272 N.Y.S. 586 (N.Y. App. Div. 1934) ("We have no purpose to excite the curiosity of the prurient by naming the book—as might be desired by those interested in its publication and sale. It is sufficient to say that it is fully

and completely of the type that the language of the [obscenity] statute condemns.... In addition, it lacks literary merit.... Filth, however it may be bedizened or its grossness concealed, must remain plain filth in all ages."), *aff'd*, 199 N.E. 513 (N.Y. 1935).

14. One Book Entitled Ulysses, 72 F.2d at 711 (Manton, J., dissenting).

15. [1868] L.R. 3 Q.B. 360, 369.

16. Claimant's Memorandum in Support of Motion to Dismiss Libel, in Moscato and LeBlanc 249–50.

17. Heymoolen v. United States, Treas. Dec. 42907 (Cust. Ct. 1928), in Moscato and LeBlanc 142.

18. Letter, Morgan Brainard to Judge Woolsey, 29 March 1934, John Munro Woolsey Papers, Yale Law School, New Haven, CT (hereafter "Woolsey Papers").

19. Letter, Ernst to B. W. Huebsch, 21 October 1931, in Moscato and LeBlanc 99.

20. Letter, Cerf to Judge Woolsey, 20 December 1933, Woolsey Papers.

21. Lindey, office memorandum, 7 December 1933, in Moscato and LeBlanc 316–17.

22. I base this count on a check of the Westlaw database on 20 September 2016. As might be expected, the Second Circuit opinion that affirmed Judge Woolsey's decree, United States v. One Book Entitled Ulysses by James Joyce, 72 F.2d 705 (2d Cir. 1934), has been cited more frequently by courts—nearly one hundred times between 1935 and 2011.

Works Cited

Ernst, Morris L. *The Best Is Yet*... New York: Harper and Brothers, 1945.

Ernst, Morris L., and Alexander Lindey. *The Censor Marches On: Recent Milestones in the Administration of the Obscenity Law in the United States*. 1939. New York: Da Capo, 1971.

Ernst, Morris L., and Alan U. Schwartz. *Censorship: The Search for the Obscene*. New York: Macmillan, 1964.

Ernst, Morris L., and William Seagle. *To the Pure...: A Study of Obscenity and the Censor*. New York: Viking, 1928.

Gillers, Stephen. "A Tendency to Deprave and Corrupt: The Transformation of American Obscenity Law from *Hicklin* to *Ulysses II*." *Washington University Law Review* 85.2 (2007): 215–96.

Holmes, O. W., Jr. *The Common Law*. Boston: Little, Brown, 1881.

Joyce, James. *Ulysses*. New York: Modern Library, Random House, 1934.

Kelly, Joseph. *Our Joyce: From Outcast to Icon*. Austin: University of Texas Press, 1998.

Ladenson, Elisabeth. *Dirt for Art's Sake: Books on Trial from "Madame Bovary" to "Lolita."* Ithaca, NY: Cornell University Press, 2007.

Law, Jules David. "'Pity They Can't See Themselves': Assessing the 'Subject' of Pornography in 'Nausicaa.'" *James Joyce Quarterly* 27.2 (1990): 219–39.

Leckie, Barbara. "'Short Cuts to Culture': Censorship and Modernism; or, Learning to Read *Ulysses*." *European Joyce Studies* 14 (2002): 9–28.

Llewellyn, K. N. *The Bramble Bush: On Our Law and Its Study*. 1930. New York: Oceana, 1996.

Milton, John. "Areopagitica: A Speech for the Liberty of Unlicensed Printing, to the Parliament of England." In *The Portable Milton*, edited by Douglas Bush, 151–205. New York: Viking, 1949.

Moscato, Michael, and Leslie LeBlanc, eds. *The United States of America v. One Book Entitled "Ulysses" by James Joyce: Documents and Commentary*. Frederick, MD: University Publications of America, 1984.

Nowlin, Christopher. *Judging Obscenity: A Critical History of Expert Evidence*. Montreal: McGill-Queen's University Press, 2003.

Pervukhin, Anna. "Deodands: A Study in the Creation of Common Law Rules." *American Journal of Legal History* 47.3 (2005): 237–56.

Piety, Tamara R. "Scorched Earth: How the Expansion of Civil Forfeiture Doctrine Has Laid Waste to Due Process." *University of Miami Law Review* 45 (1991): 911–78.

Potter, Rachel. *Obscene Modernism: Literary Censorship and Experiment, 1900–1940*. Oxford: Oxford University Press, 2013.

Rembar, Charles. *The End of Obscenity: The Trials of "Lady Chatterley," "Tropic of Cancer," and "Fanny Hill."* New York: Random House, 1968.

Spoo, Robert. "Copyright Protectionism and Its Discontents: The Case of James Joyce's *Ulysses* in America." *Yale Law Journal* 108.3 (1998): 633–67.

———. *Without Copyrights: Piracy, Publishing, and the Public Domain*. New York: Oxford University Press, 2013.

Thomas, Brook. "*Ulysses* on Trial: Some Supplementary Reading." In *The Administration of Aesthetics: Censorship, Political Criticism, and the Public Sphere*, edited by Richard Burt, 125–48. Minneapolis: University of Minnesota Press, 1994.

Vanderham, Paul. *James Joyce and Censorship: The Trials of "Ulysses."* New York: New York University Press, 1998.

Weinrib, Laura M. "The Sex Side of Civil Liberties: *United States v. Dennett* and the Changing Face of Free Speech." *Law and History Review* 30.2 (2012): 325–86.

Weir, David. "What Did He Know, and When Did He Know It: The *Little Review*, Joyce, and *Ulysses*." In "Joyce and the Law," special issue, *James Joyce Quarterly* 37.3/4 (2000): 389–412.

15

The Past and Future of Joycean Copyright

AMANDA GOLDEN

Copyright law has been a major factor in James Joyce's publication history and reception, its influence apparent in three spheres: censorship, piracy, and creative works. These categories often overlap and exist in relation to each other. Mirroring Joyce's *Ulysses*, Joycean copyright also complicates the very terms on which it operates. Joyce sought legal protection for *Ulysses* when it was not possible for the law to protect his work. As Robert Spoo and other critics have demonstrated, in form and content, *Ulysses* also complicates existing legal distinctions. This critical interest in the ramifications of copyright law has led to more informed considerations of the Joyce Estate's control over his work, particularly in blocking artistic use of Joyce's writing. The expiration of *Ulysses*'s copyright in the United Kingdom, Ireland, and the European Union in 2012 increased access to the text, and the National Library of Ireland digitally published its Joyce manuscripts.[1] Joyce's digital future will irrevocably alter reading and teaching of his work, bringing new generations closer to the creative process and redefining copyright's role in Joyce's textual history. This access can enable both freely available editions of a lesser quality and the possibility of new print and digital editions that build on previous scholarship.

Censorship prevented Joyce from publishing *Ulysses* in the United States. Following the *Little Review*'s publication of episodes from the novel in America and Sylvia Beach's publication of *Ulysses* in France in 1922, Samuel Roth brought out an error-filled pirated version in his American magazine *Two Worlds Monthly*. Joyce's legal recourse was limited, as it had not been possible to pursue an American copyright for the novel once it was held to be obscene. Nevertheless, as Spoo records in *Without Copyrights*, in 1927 Joyce sought legal action, "suing Roth and his publishing company for half a million dollars in damages for the commercial misappropriation of his name" (198). While this effort was unsuccessful, Spoo points out that

> the suit actually caused his name and fame to overflow any boundaries that could have been secured by legal process. Roth, who had positioned himself to exploit *Ulysses* just as its author was beginning to emerge into the mainstream from coterie appeal and literary scandal, and whose unauthorized disseminations greatly assisted that emergence, indelibly fixed Joyce's brand of martyred genius. (232)

As readers developed a sense of both Joyce and his novel, this idea was also in some ways independent of the public perception of *Ulysses*, which would continue to change.

Because Joyce published *Ulysses* under less than ideal conditions, generations of scholars have sought to produce editions that realize the vision of *Ulysses* that Joyce was not able to achieve. As Sam Slote recounts, each edition has brought complications:

> Because of the difficulties Joyce had in getting *Ulysses* published, the first edition was produced in France by an amateur publisher using a French printer who did not speak English. Compounding these problems was Joyce's habit of continually revising and expanding his work. One third of *Ulysses* was composed on the galley and page proofs. And so, beyond dealing with a text in a language he did not understand, Maurice Darantiere, Joyce's printer, had to contend with Joyce's barely legible handwriting. As Joyce was reviewing (and expanding) the various proofs for *Ulysses*, he knew that the text would be flawed and so the first edition begins with the statement, initialed by its publisher Sylvia Beach but actually written by Joyce: "*The publisher asks the reader's indulgence for typographical errors unavoidable in the exceptional circumstances.*" Every subsequent attempt to redress these errors in future editions wound up introducing new errors in the process. (xi)

In many ways, this is not a unique history. George Bornstein and other scholars have illustrated that historical contingencies alter texts, and that texts exist in numerous versions, apart from what the author may have intended. In *Material Modernism,* Bornstein underscores "the fluidity of modernist texts" (43). Shifting away from "a single ideal form of the text, newer theories [of editing] stress the legitimacy of various versions, the importance of social as well as authorial constructions of the text, and the historical contingency of both the linguistic and bibliographical codes" (43). The last items on Bornstein's list refer to material factors, such as the (literal) inscrutability of Joyce's manuscript, that affect the final product. Contingency also extends to the ways that Joyce's response to the law altered *Ulysses,* which has led critics to form new interpretations of the ways that its form and content continue to change.

Following the Roth case, Bennett Cerf at Random House sought to publish the American edition of *Ulysses.* Part of the reason that copyright is significant is that authors and publishers desire to be compensated for their labor. Because *Ulysses* still lacked copyright protection, a single publisher would help to ensure that Joyce received appropriate payment. But Cerf could not guarantee that others would not attempt to bring out their own editions, and Spoo explores further the convention of professional courtesy that led other publishers to respect Random House's publication of the novel. By this time Roth was serving jail time for the indecent content he had published in *Two Worlds Monthly,* in *Ulysses* and other texts. *Ulysses* was less vulnerable to piracy because the publisher would have been accountable for its obscenity, and there had been previous objections to the "Nausicaa" episode in the *Little Review* (*Without Copyrights* 219).

Despite Cerf's efforts, Roth's pirated text became the dominant American reading edition until *Ulysses* was reset in 1961. When he was rushing to file the copyright for Random House in 1934, Bennett Cerf accidentally sent the Roth typescript to the typesetters (255). While this copyright covered supplemental materials that Random House included in their edition, it was unclear whether the text of Joyce's novel was protected by copyright.[2] Cerf hoped that there was an acknowledged copyright of the episodes published in the *Little Review,* but Spoo notes in "Copyright Protectionism and Its Discontents" that although Margaret C. Anderson published the magazines

> each bearing a notice of copyright . . . it is not certain that Anderson consistently complied with the deposit and registration requirements. The Copyright Office contains a record of registration for

only the first four of twenty-three issues that serialized *Ulysses*. Although failure to deposit and register the remaining issues would not have destroyed the copyrights in those issues, it might well have impaired their enforceability. (637)[3]

In light of the legal battles that have surrounded *Ulysses*, Spoo concludes that "because *Ulysses* has never, or almost never, enjoyed genuine copyright protection in the United States—despite claims to the contrary—this epoch-making work should now be recognized for what in legal reality it is: one of the great treasures of the public domain" (635). And while the novel's copyright expired in several countries in 2012, issues involving international copyright and permission to quote from Joyce's draft materials published in facsimile after 1922 continue to plague Joyce scholarship.

Joyce's case was complicated by his working abroad. As Spoo argues, Ezra Pound and his contemporaries had to confront the practical implications of art that needed to travel: "Pound perceived clearly that literary modernism, if it was to thrive in the international context, required the freedom to cross borders. Quite simply, manuscripts and books by foreign-domiciled authors had to pass through customs and the mails before they could come to rest in the hands of American publishers, printers, and readers" (634). The subversive aspects of modernism in general "involved the transgressing of moral and ideological boundaries. . . . Yet such transgressions could scarcely occur in the absence of the first kind of border-crossing. The artistic and ideological ambitions of authors were dependent upon the sociomaterial means of producing and disseminating texts" (634). Part of Joyce's and his contemporaries' response to literary and artistic conventions has involved alluding to and adapting previous texts. As it responds to literary antecedents, *Ulysses*, Paul Saint-Amour argues in his 2003 book *The Copywrights: Intellectual Property and the Literary Imagination*, redefines the boundaries of a creative work. This has been of particular significance as Joyce's estate has restricted artists from quoting his work, which, Spoo finds, places limitations on the creation of new work.

Criticism

Because copyright reserves payment for a literary work to an author or rights holder, Saint-Amour investigates the ways that Joyce and his contemporaries responded to the changing value of their writing. The legal history he charts intersects with modernism's history, providing another dimension to a literary period that includes other forms of artistic experimentation: "since copyright law's inception, a growing number and range of texts (both 'literary' and 'nonliterary') register a self-awareness about their status as literary property. I would hardly insist that this self-awareness is historically coextensive with *modernism*, though one of this books's focal texts—Joyce's *Ulysses*—sits at the core of the current modernist canon, and partly, I will argue, as a result of its proprietary self-consciousness" (13). Moving outward from modernism, *The Copywrights* seeks to establish a broader understanding of "copyright metadiscourse—a discourse whose subject is its own literary property status" and which "is one feature of the *modern* text, and one that remains undertheorized. Unlike more ingrown kinds of formal self-consciousness or metafiction, it is directed both inward, at the text's patterns and principles of construction, and outward, at the legal, economic, and ideological operations that protect and commodify the text" (13).

As Spoo teaches us, from its title onward, *Ulysses* alludes to and adapts texts that preceded it. The fact that *Ulysses* rests on and revises so many texts complicates definitions of author and text ("Introduction" 338). One of the topics that Saint-Amour takes up in *The Copywrights* is the challenge that *Ulysses* poses to copyright law's understanding of authorship. In doing so, he builds upon the work of critics like Mark Rose, whose 1993 book *Authors and Owners: The Invention of Copyright* addresses the inadequacy of "the romantic conception of authorship" on which copyright law has drawn (Rose viii, Saint-Amour 11). Rose notes that previous scholarship, such as Benjamin Kaplan's 1967 *An Unhurried View of Copyright*, anticipates the "connection between the invention of the author as original genius and the invention of copyright" (viii). The emphasis that this formulation places on a single author does not hold for *Ulysses*; Saint-Amour observes that Joyce himself "oscillated between embracing collective authorship and wrapping himself in the mystique and privileges of the individual genius" (159). Because *Ulysses*'s innovation is inseparable from its allusions, the novel has led to what Saint-Amour calls a "tension between collective and individual modes of literary property" and reflects the ways that copyright law shaped Joyce's texts and those of his contemporaries (160).

Saint-Amour turns to the fourteenth episode of *Ulysses* to demonstrate the ways that its form and content engage the complexity of creation. "Oxen of the Sun," set in a maternity ward, addresses the ways that new life grows out of what came before. The legal concept of copyright runs counter to this reality, which, Saint-Amour argues, is integral to the episode's design: "the terminal narratives of gestation, parturition, and literary tradition that structure the episode are paired with the equally terminal narrative of copyright.... The episode, I maintain, is concerned to parody not only literary sources but copyright law itself, while simultaneously performing appropriative parody as a potent form of critical discourse and thus as an arguably fair use of sources" (17–18). Saint-Amour imagines *Ulysses*'s publication in 2002, which might begin on the copyright page with acknowledgments of permission to publish from a list of sources, but he concludes, "The Joyce of our thought experiment . . . suffers not from the stigma of obscenity but from copyright regimes that regard even the minimal appropriation and parody of private intellectual property as a far worse crime" (198). In his vision of 2002, Saint-Amour responds to the Joyce Estate's own responses to artists and critics who emulate and analyze Joyce's own strategies.

The Estate

Overseeing the Joyce Estate, Stephen Joyce has limited artists' responses to his grandfather's work. In 2000, Spoo explains, Stephen Joyce prohibited the inclusion of "eighteen words from *Finnegans Wake* in a short choral piece commissioned by Lyric FM for a Europe-wide broadcast," telling the composer, "To put it politely, mildly[,] my wife and I don't like your music" ("Introduction" 337). When Stephen Joyce denied permission for a performance based on Molly Bloom's monologue that comprises the final episode of the novel, Spoo emphasizes that it "is various *adaptations* of the episode to which he objects. . . . Mr. Joyce explained: 'This last chapter/episode was not written for the stage or to be performed, but as the concluding part of a novel'" (338). Acting in this fashion, Spoo argues, Stephen Joyce exhibits an impulse "to protect his grandfather's works from being adulterated by the kinds of transformative insights that derivative works . . . can bring to even the greatest, most comprehensive masterpieces" (338). The idea of heirs protecting their author and his work is not uncommon.[4] But in the case of the Joyce Estate, the law has intervened to assess the parameters of the control that rights holders can exercise.

Rights holders and editors are invested in the integrity of writers' work. Some of the Joyce Estate's responses to critical work have continued in the same vein as Joyce's own objections to previous publications. In order to publish more material with *Ulysses* so that Random House's copyright would cover more pages, and perhaps extend to the whole volume, Cerf wanted to include Joyce's chart of the novel's episodes. But, Spoo recounts, "Joyce refused to allow the supplement on aesthetic grounds: *Ulysses* was a work of 'pure literature' and should not contain self-exegesis" (*Without Copyrights* 253). Shifting from Joyce's interpretations to his composition strategies, scholars have published editions of *Ulysses* that draw on their research with Joyce's manuscripts and other materials. Hans Walter Gabler published his 1984 edition of *Ulysses* when the Society of Authors handled the estate's permissions (Groden 232). In contrast to "an older, more traditional notion of the text as fixed product championed by John Kidd," Bornstein submits, Gabler's mode of editing represented "a newer conception of the text as a work in progress" (4). Gabler included symbols in the text on the pages of the left-hand side of his edition, indicating different types of Joyce's alterations. Vicki Mahaffey observes, "What Gabler tried to produce was an 'ideal' record of the process of composition, an 'authoritative text free of corruption,'" that is, transmissional error (237). She points to Jerome McGann's remark that "Gabler's edition does not give us the work which Joyce wanted to present to the public; rather, he gives us a text in which we may observe Joyce at work, alone, before he turns to meet his public" (181). When Stephen Joyce was later overseeing the estate, he sought legal action in response to a new edition he feared would diminish *Ulysses*'s overall reputation.

When the Joyce Estate was charging too much for David Pierce to include an excerpt from the 1922 publication of *Ulysses* in his anthology *Irish Writing in the Twentieth Century*, he opted for part of Danis Rose's 1997 Reader's Edition of *Ulysses* instead. The Joyce Estate had previously sought legal action against Rose, and its "allegations included copyright infringement and the unfair competition tort of 'passing off'" (Spoo, "Introduction" 338–39, *Without Copyrights* 228). Rose's edition incorporates excerpts from what is called the Rosenbach Manuscript and other archival materials. The court determined that the copyright dates of the manuscripts Rose quoted were the dates on which they were published in facsimile.[5] In addition, because the form of Rose's edition does not differ substantially from previous copies of *Ulysses*,

> Justice Lloyd of the English High Court ruled that Rose's edition had infringed the copyrights in certain Joyce manuscripts, but he rejected the estate's other copyright claims. He then turned to the estate's alternative theory and carefully framed the question it raised: did Rose's edition constitute passing off—that is, was the edition so different from the "class of goods" that had come to be known to the reading public as "*Ulysses* by James Joyce" that the edition, as an instance of false labeling, substantially harmed the goodwill that the estate acquired in the "trade name" of "*Ulysses* by James Joyce"? (*Without Copyrights* 228)

While the Reader's Edition differed from the contents that Joyce published, it was still an edition of *Ulysses*; "Justice Lloyd observed that, in contrast to the estate's strained effort to turn a literary text into a commodity, a more conventional instance of passing off would be 'selling lemon juice in a plastic lemon-shaped container which customers associate with a different manufacturer'" (228). This case is indicative of the ways that an estate's interpretation and a legal interpretation can differ, an issue that Carol Shloss's lawsuit against the Joyce Estate in 2007 revisits.

While the Joyce Estate's investment in the Rose case concerned *Ulysses*'s reputation, in her essay "Privacy and the Misuse of Copyright" Shloss argues that the Joyce Estate's restriction of her access to materials and of the publication of quotations in her 2003 book *Lucia Joyce: To Dance at the Wake* grew out of a desire to protect Joyce's reputation and that of his family (244). As Shloss recounts, Stephen Joyce destroyed his letters from Lucia, an act that compromises critics' understanding of her life (246). This act and his restricting of her ability to quote prompt Shloss to ask, "What social damage would ensue if copyright claims could be used selectively to remove knowledge from the realm of collective responsibility and possible action? What other stories would remain, perforce, untold?" (258). The decision in Shloss's case has far-reaching implications, particularly for archival scholarship and women's literary history.

Spoo served as Shloss's lawyer in the case, and he argues in "Archival

Foreclosure" that the ruling questioned the legal extent of estates' ability to restrict scholarship. As he puts it,

> A cutting-edge contention of Professor Shloss's lawsuit was that the Joyce Estate was guilty of having engaged in copyright misuse—an attempt to extend its monopoly power beyond its proper economic sphere by using copyrights to shut down scholarly discussion, prevent use of public-domain materials, and interfere with Professor Shloss's access to physical documents in libraries and archives. If Professor Shloss could prove copyright misuse, the estate might be disabled from enforcing its copyrights against her, at least until the estate had purged the misconduct and its effects. (548)

Spoo stresses that the court's decision that the Joyce Estate must pay Shloss's legal fees "tells us in no uncertain terms that Carol Shloss 'prevailed' on the basis of the results she obtained. Is it precedent on questions of fair use and copyright misuse? No. Is it precedent on the attorneys' fees issue? Yes" (551). This case recognizes the significance of scholars' research using primary sources, which continues to change following the National Library of Ireland's digitization of its manuscripts in 2012, and the possibility of future digital projects.

Since 2012

The ability to publish or quote from *Ulysses* differs depending on one's country and has been inhibited in the United States by the copyright act extensions. Currently the segments that the *Little Review* published from *Ulysses* are part of the public domain in the United States.[6] Spoo has argued that the version of *Ulysses* published in Paris in 1922 can be considered part of the public domain in the United States.[7] In *Without Copyrights*, however, he also clarifies that URAA (Uruguay Round Agreements Act) gave the version of *Ulysses* published in Paris in 1922 copyright coverage in the United States in 1996 (264). After two years *Ulysses* reentered the public domain, but ten months later the copyright was extended by twenty years under the Sonny Bono Copyright Term Extension Act (264–65). *Ulysses*, like other "post-1922 works that were eligible for restoration under the URAA[,] received the double benefit of URAA revival and Sonny Bono term enhancement" (265).[8]

In the European Union, Spoo points out, *Ulysses* became part of the public domain in 2011, which has led to new editions that incorporate critical material that might have not been approved by Joyce himself (268). Slote's 2012 edition of *Ulysses* from Alma Classics follows the text of the 1939 European edition from Odyssey Press, with annotations keyed to numbers in the margins that do not disrupt the prose. The table of contents also contains the *Odyssey* title, time of day, and location of each episode. Joyce considered this "self-exegesis" and he "would allow Cerf to issue the chart separately, as publicity for the book, but not between its covers" (253). Slote's inclusion of information from Joyce's chart expands on Gabler's placement of the *Odyssey* titles in parentheses in his table of contents.

The absence of a large-scale digital edition of *Ulysses* reflects the magnitude of the task of creating one.[9] Near the close of the twentieth century, Michael Groden, who had worked on the *James Joyce Archive*, envisioned an edition of the novel called "James Joyce's *Ulysses* in Hypermedia," but it never came to fruition (240). Future scholars can learn from Gabler and other editors in order to pursue accessible digital, print, or hybrid editions of *Ulysses*. Mahaffey quotes Gabler, who in "The Synchrony and Diachrony of Texts" stressed that "the articulation of critical understanding . . . will reach its highest degree of definitiveness from a critical interpretation of the work's revisional variation," and she adds that "he identifies the variations within an evolving manuscript as 'stimuli to interpretation'" (238). Gabler's explanation resembles rationales for digitization and data visualizations, which can lead to new observations and modes of understanding texts. With regard to the efficacy of Gabler's method, Mahaffey proposes:

> Given Gabler's editorial aim to make the process of authorial composition accessible to critical interpretation, one legitimate question is whether the synoptic text actually succeeds in stimulating such interpretations. The answer at this point in time seems to be 'no,' partly because the three-volume edition, being expensive, is not widely available, and partly because the system of diacritical marks used to designate the different levels of composition have proven difficult to interpret. This prompts me to ask whether the synoptic text should not be marketed separately, without the reading text, perhaps in a more readable format. (Could colors or different typefaces be used instead of half-brackets to indicate the most important levels? . . .) (239)

The final suggestion could certainly be achieved in a digital version of *Ulysses*. The types of marks that Gabler used could be replaced with links, clearly marking portions of source materials to which the editor is referring. While the indication of the link would be within the text, shifting these materials to another screen would also retain the fluidity of the text in a different way and remove materials that recall Joyce's aversion to "self-exegesis" from the volume (though a web-based edition would not have the same limitations as pages between covers).[10]

Digital access to the National Library of Ireland's manuscripts will alter the teaching and study of Joyce, and could inform print and digital projects.[11] Because these manuscripts were not published before Joyce died in 1941 or prior to 2002, they have been part of the public domain since 2012 in the United States.[12] Following such examples as JoyceWays and Digital Dubliners,[13] future apps and resources could add new dimensions to readers' navigation of Joyce's texts alongside the past and present state of the landscapes to which he alludes.

It is also possible for readers to access versions of Joyce's texts that incorporate different forms of media and invite interaction with the texts.[14] Collaborative annotated editions of *Dubliners*, *A Portrait of the Artist as a Young Man*, and *Ulysses* already exist on the site PoetryGenius.[15] It is also within fair use for users to create free readings or performances of Joyce's texts and stream them online. Librivox has created a free audio edition of *Ulysses* made by volunteers.[16] Listeners who otherwise might not have invested in the entirety of a *Ulysses* audiobook or checked it out from a library can access episodes online or using the smartphone app.

The future for Joyce studies is promising. The copyright issues that curtailed quotation from *Ulysses* also allowed for a certain control over subsequent editions, attempting to stabilize their presence in the world. Scholarship and interpretation, however, lead to new approaches to literature and history, and, as the Shloss case demonstrates, literary executors can encounter legal limitations. With the expiration of *Ulysses*'s copyright in several countries, critics can quote more liberally and editions can speak to the changing scope of Joyce scholarship in the twenty-first century.

Notes

1. "All editions of Joyce's works published during his lifetime" are under copyright in Spain until 2021, but in Canada and Australia they are considered part of the public

domain (Saint-Amour et al.). For the National Library of Ireland manuscripts, see Ryan.

2. See Spoo's introduction to *James Joyce Quarterly*'s "Joyce and the Law" issue for further background regarding the debates over editions of *Ulysses*.

3. Spoo adds that Random House's "*Ulysses*, in its quest for protection in the United States, could expect only limited assistance from *The Little Review*'s copyrights, even if they were found to be enforceable" (640).

4. Amy Hildreth Chen argues in "The Perils of Literary Celebrity: The Archive Stories of Ted Hughes and Sylvia Plath" that the Ted Hughes Estate's decisions have emerged out of a desire to protect Hughes's image.

5. Spoo adds that the manuscript facsimiles were protected by "copyrights that were never revived because they had never lapsed, such as those in the manuscript materials published in the *James Joyce Archive* in the 1970s. In an interpretive move that recalls the text-editing theory known as 'versioning,' the court held that pre-publication versions of *Ulysses*, to the extent that they differ in some significant way from published versions, constitute independent authorial 'works' for purposes of copyright" ("Introduction" 340).

6. The publication of these texts in the United States preceded 1923; see Saint-Amour et al.

7. Ibid. The authors of this resource cite Spoo, "Copyright Protectionism and Its Discontents."

8. Under the terms of the Sonny Bono Copyright Act, the copyright of the 1961 edition of *Ulysses* will expire in 2057. For a list of dates when Joyce's publications' copyrights will expire, see Saint-Amour et al.

9. Users can read the recent publication of *The Little Review "Ulysses"* as a Kindle edition.

10. Archival materials, including the Rosenbach Manuscript and items previously published in *The James Joyce Archive*, would still require permission for inclusion, in part or in whole, in digital form.

11. Sam Slote brought to my attention Daniel Ferrer's *Brouillons d'un baiser*, which contains translations and contents from the National Library of Ireland's *Finnegans Wake* materials.

12. The digital availability of the National Library of Ireland's manuscripts (see Ryan) differs, along with copyright law, according to country. They are not part of the public domain in the United Kingdom until 31 December 2039. See Saint-Amour et al.

13. https://itunes.apple.com/us/app/joyceways/id534524278?mt=8 and http://digitaldubliners.com.

14. Existing projects include Ulysses Seen at http://ulyssesseen.com/ and Infinite Ulysses at www.infiniteulysses.com.

15. See http://genius.com/albums/James-joyce/Dubliners, http://genius.com/James-joyce-a-portrait-of-the-artist-as-a-young-man-chap-1-annotated, and http://genius.com/albums/James-joyce/Ulysses.

16. https://librivox.org/ulysses-by-james-joyce/. Performers do not need permission

from copyright holders to stream readings of a text online if they are free of charge; see https://joycefoundation.osu.edu/joyce-copyright/public-performances.

Works Cited

Birmingham, Kevin. *The Most Dangerous Book: The Battle for James Joyce's "Ulysses."* New York: Penguin, 2014.

Bornstein, George. *Material Modernism: The Politics of the Page.* New York: Cambridge University Press, 2001.

Chen, Amy Hildreth. "Archival Bodies: Twentieth Century Literary Collections." PhD diss., Emory University, 2013.

———. "The Perils of Literary Celebrity: The Archive Stories of Ted Hughes and Sylvia Plath." *Ted Hughes Society Journal* 2 (Winter 2011): 20–31.

Gabler, Hans Walter. "The Synchrony and Diachrony of Texts: Practice and Theory of the Critical Edition of James Joyce's *Ulysses.*" *Text* 1 (1981): 305–26.

Gifford, Don. *"Ulysses" Annotated.* With Robert J. Seidman. 2nd ed. Berkeley: University of California Press, 1988.

Goldman, Jonathan E. *Modernism Is the Literature of Celebrity.* Austin: University of Texas Press, 2011.

Groden, Michael. "Perplex in the Pen—and in the Pixels: Reflections on the James Joyce Archive, Hans Walter Gabler's *Ulysses,* and James Joyce's *Ulysses* in Hypermedia." *Journal of Modern Literature* 22.2 (1999): 225–44.

Joyce, James. *The Little Review "Ulysses."* Edited by Mark Gaipa, Sean Latham, and Robert Scholes. New Haven, CT: Yale University Press, 2015.

———. *Ulysses.* Edited by Hans Walter Gabler with Wolfhard Steppe and Herbert Cahoon. New York: Garland, 1984.

———. *Ulysses.* Edited by Sam Slote. Richmond (London): Alma Classics, 2012.

———. *Ulysses: A Reader's Edition.* Edited by Danis Rose. London: Picador, 1997.

Kaplan, Benjamin. *An Unhurried View of Copyright.* New York: Columbia University Press, 1967.

Latham, Sean, ed. *The Cambridge Companion to "Ulysses."* New York: Cambridge University Press, 2014.

Mahaffey, Vicki. "Intentional Error: The Paradox of Editing Joyce's *Ulysses.*" In *James Joyce's "Ulysses": A Casebook,* edited by Derek Attridge, 231–55. New York: Oxford University Press, 2004.

McGann, Jerome J. *Social Values and Poetic Acts: The Historical Judgment of Literary Work.* Cambridge, MA: Harvard University Press, 1988.

Pierce, David. *Irish Writing in the Twentieth Century: A Reader.* Cork: Cork University Press, 2000.

Rose, Mark. *Authors and Owners: The Invention of Copyright.* Cambridge: Harvard University Press, 1993.

Rossman, Charles. "The New 'Ulysses': The Hidden Controversy." *New York Review of Books*, 8 December 1988, 53–58. www.nybooks.com/articles/archives/1988/dec/08/the-new-ulysses-the-hidden-controversy/.
Ryan, Catherine. "Joyce Manuscripts Online—Beta but Beautiful!" National Library of Ireland, 15 June 2012. http://blog.nli.ie/index.php/2012/06/15/joyce-manuscripts-online-beta-but-beautiful/.
Saint-Amour, Paul K. *The Copywrights: Intellectual Property and the Literary Imagination*. Ithaca, NY: Cornell University Press, 2013.
———, ed. *Modernism and Copyright*. New York: Oxford University Press, 2011.
Saint-Amour, Paul K., Michael Groden, Carol Loeb Shloss, and Robert Spoo. "Copyright, Fair Use, and Permissions: About the Law: Joyce Works in Copyright and in the Public Domain." https://joycefoundation.osu.edu/joyce-copyright/fair-use-and-permissions/about-law/public-domain.
Shloss, Carol Loeb. *Lucia Joyce: To Dance in the Wake*. New York: Farrar, Straus and Giroux, 2003.
———. "Privacy and the Misuse of Copyright: The Case of *Shloss v. the Estate of James Joyce*." In Saint-Amour, *Modernism and Copyright*, 243–59.
Slote, Sam. Introduction to Joyce, *Ulysses*, edited by Sam Slote, v–xiv.
Spoo, Robert E. "Archival Foreclosure: A Scholar's Lawsuit Against the Estate of James Joyce." *American Archivist* 71.2 (Fall–Winter 2008): 544–51.
———. "Copyright Protectionism and Its Discontents: The Case of James Joyce's *Ulysses* in America." *Yale Law Journal* 108.3 (December 1998): 633–67.
———. "Introduction: Injuries, Remedies, Moral Rights, and the Public Domain." In "Joyce and the Law," special edition, *James Joyce Quarterly* 37.3/4 (Spring–Summer 2000): 333–62, 364–65.
———. "Litigating the Right to Be a Scholar." *Joyce Studies Annual* (2008): 12–21.
———. *Without Copyrights: Piracy, Publishing, and the Public Domain*. New York: Oxford University Press, 2013.

CONTRIBUTORS

Kevin Birmingham is the author of *The Most Dangerous Book: The Battle for James Joyce's "Ulysses."*

Robert Brazeau is associate professor of Irish studies at the University of Alberta in Alberta. He is the coeditor of *Eco-Joyce: The Environmental Imagination of James Joyce.*

Rich Cole is a doctoral candidate at University of Alberta. His recent essays appear in *Cartographies of Exile: A New Spatial Literacy; H.D. and Modernity;* and *Modernism and Affect.*

Anne Marie D'Arcy is senior lecturer in the School of Arts at the University of Leicester, director of the Medieval Research Centre at the University of Leicester, and visiting research fellow at the School of English, Trinity College Dublin. She is the author of *Wisdom and the Grail: The Image of the Vessel in the Queste del Saint Graal and Malory's Tale of the Sankgreal.*

Andrew Gibson is former research professor of modern literature and theory at Royal Holloway, University of London. His many books include *Joyce's Revenge: History, Politics, Aesthetics in "Ulysses"; Beckett and Badiou: The Pathos of Intermittency; Intermittency: The Concept of Historical Reason in Contemporary French Philosophy;* and *The Strong Spirit: History, Politics and Aesthetics in Joyce's Writings 1898–1915.*

Amanda Golden is assistant professor of English at the New York Institute of Technology. She is the editor of *This Business of Words: Reassessing Anne Sexton.*

Jonathan Goldman, professor at New York Institute of Technology, is the author of *Modernism Is the Literature of Celebrity* and coeditor of *Modernist Star Maps: Celebrity, Modernity, Culture*. He has written about twentieth-century literature and culture in publications including *The Cambridge Companion to "Ulysses," Cambridge Contexts: Bernard Shaw, Cambridge Contexts: Tom Stoppard, James Joyce Quarterly, Narrative, Novel: A Forum on Fiction, The Paris Review,* and *The Chronicle of Higher Education*.

Joseph M. Hassett is a lawyer and literary scholar residing in Washington, D.C. He is the author of *W. B. Yeats and the Muses*.

Terence Killeen is research scholar at the James Joyce Centre, Dublin. He is the author of *"Ulysses" Unbound: A Reader's Companion to James Joyce's "Ulysses."*

Celia Marshik is professor of English at Stony Brook University. She is the author of *British Modernism and Censorship* and *At the Mercy of Their Clothes: Modernism, the Middlebrow, and British Garment Culture* and the editor of *The Cambridge Companion to Modernist Culture*.

Tekla Mecsnóber teaches at the University of Groningen in the Netherlands. She has recently coedited volume 22 of the *European Joyce Studies* series, titled *Joycean Unions: Post-Millennial Essays from East to West*.

Carey Mickalites is associate professor of English at the University of Memphis. He is the author of *Modernism and Market Fantasy*.

Steven Morrison is a teaching associate at the University of Nottingham. He is coeditor of *Joyce's "Wandering Rocks."*

Robert Spoo is Chapman Distinguished Professor of Law at the University of Tulsa College of Law. His latest book is *Without Copyrights: Piracy, Publishing, and the Public Domain*.

Janine Utell is professor and chair of English at Widener University. She is the author of *James Joyce and the Revolt of Love* and *Engagements with Narrative*.

INDEX

Act of Union (1800) (Ireland), 157
Acts of Union (Union with Ireland Act of 1800), 157
Administration of Justice (Language) Act (Ireland) of 1737, 71
Adultery, 20, 26–27, 29n1, 29n4
"Aeolus" (Joyce, J.), 72, 204
African Americans, 103
"After the Race" (Joyce, J.), 31, 34–37, 45
Against authors, publishers, or booksellers. *See In personam*
Against books themselves. *See In rem*
Alcohol, 252; colonialism and consumption of, 136–37, 140; with masculinity, culture of, 143–44; in public spaces, laws governing, 6, 136–40, 151. *See also* Pubs
Alexander, Jack, 239, 243n31
Aliens, 58n1; as fiction, convenient, 56–58; question with immigration, 49–51
Aliens Act (1905): immigration and, 5, 48–53, 56–57; opposition to, 55
Anderson, John, 108
Anderson, Margaret: copyright law and, 264–65; *Ulysses* trial and, 213–14, 216, 217, 220, 229, 257
Anglo-Boer War of 1899–1902, 58n1, 157–58, 172–73, 173n2
Anglo-Irish Treaty (1921), 67, 70, 98
Anglo-Irish War, 150
Anti-Semitism, 50, 58n1, 128; economy and, 39–40, 42, 143; Ireland with immigration and, 51–56; in *Ulysses*, 51–52, 54, 86–87, 94, 99–100, 143

"Archival Foreclosure" (Spoo), 269–70
Areopagitica (Milton), 246
Armstrong, Carol, 198
Arrears Act (1882), 126
Asquith, Herbert, 50
Attorney-General v. Cummins, 123
Audiobooks, 272
Australia, 272n1
Austria, 70–73, 272n1
Austro-Hungarian Empire, 70
Authorial branding, trademark law and, 7, 195, 200–204
Authors, 247, 250–52, 268. *See also* Authorial branding, trademark law and
Authors and Owners: The Invention of Copyright (Rose, M.), 266
Authorship, copyright and, 266
Automobiles, with law of forfeiture, 248, 249–52
Autonomy, 107; in private life, 17, 28; sexual, 19–21, 29n4

Balfour, Arthur, 109–11, *110*
Balibar, Etienne, 145
Banknotes, language on, 70, 71
Un Bar aux Folies-Bergère (Manet), 197–98
Barnacle, Nora. *See* Joyce, Nora Barnacle
Bass, 208n9, 208n10; trademark law and, 193–94, 196–99, 207, 208n5, 208n8, 208n13; in *Ulysses* 194, 197, 201–3
"Bass Ale Blues" (Original Memphis Five), 208n10

Baudrillard, Jean, 207
Beach, Sylvia, 262, 263
Belgium, 74
Birds' Nest, 164–65, 174n22
Birmingham, Kevin, 220, 228, 243n27
Blackstone, William, 125
Blackwood, John, 128
"The Boarding House" (Joyce, J.), 22, 28
Boccaccio, Giovanni, 237, 257
Body, as financial being, 34–35
Book of Kells, 205
Books, 243n27; audiobooks, 272; digital, 262; with forfeiture, law of, 249–52; obscenity law and, 228, 230, 233, 241n10, 241n18, 249; suppression of, 246–48
Booksellers. *See In personam*
Boorstin, Daniel J., 200
Booth Report (1889), 50
Bornstein, George, 263–64, 268
Bourdieu, Pierre, 208n7, 236, 242n24, 242n25
Bourhis, Richard Y., 80n5
La Bouteille de Bass (Gris), 208n9
Bowker, Gordon, 220
Boyle, Robert, 54
Bradley, Patrick, 175n37
Branding: authorial, 7, 195, 200–204; licensing of names for, 208n6; "Oxen of the Sun" and, 201, 204; trademark law with modernism, criticism and, 193–96
Braque, Georges, 198, 208n9
Brehon Law, 122–23, 128
British Nationality Act (1948), 47
British Nationality and Status of Aliens Act of 1914, 53
Brooch, 172, 176n42, 176n44
Brooks, Peggy, 228, 230, 243n31
Brouillons d'un baiser (Ferrer), 273n11
Brown, Wendy, 99
Browning, Elizabeth Barrett, 230
Bucke, Richard Maurice, 257
Budgen, Frank, 221

Burke, Edmund, 125
Burke, Richard, 128
Butler, Nicholas Murray, 231, 253
Butt, Isaac, 123, 124
Byrne, John Alexander, 161
Bywaters, Frederick, 180
Bywaters-Thompson case, 7, 180–82, 190n5

Cabell, James Branch, 220, 221
Callanan, Frank, 119n17
"Calypso" (Joyce, J.), 26–27, 38–39
Campbell, James Henry Mussen, 168–69
Campbell, Joseph, 186, 187
Canada, 272n1
Canby, Henry Seidel, 237–38
Canterbury Tales (Chaucer), 176n42
Carr, Henry, 3
Casebook on Irish Land Law (Wylie), 123
Cassell, John, 118n6
Catholic Church, 124, 150, 162–63
Cavan Brooch, 172, 176n44
Celebrity, 207n1, 208n7, 208n13, 273n4
Censorship, 232, 262. *See also* Libel case, media with; Obscenity law
Cerf, Bennett: copyright law and, 264, 268; at Random House, 221, 241n13, 247–49, 257, 259, 259n2
Chartists, 132
Chaucer, Geoffrey, 176n42, 237
Chen, Amy Hildreth, 273n4
Cheng, Vincent, 49
Children, 29n2, 173n2; homes for orphaned, 164–65; with Victoria, visit of, 162–65. *See also* Patriotic Children's Treat
Children's Day, 162–63, 165–66
Children's Tea (1900), 165–66
Chisholm, Dianne, 135
Church of England, 187
Cinematograph Volta, 105
"Circe" (Joyce, J.), 1, 42–43, 130, 171–72; criminal conversation in, 24–26; Esperanto in, 74–75; immigrants in,

50; with visit of Victoria, 6, 158–59, 162–64
Circuit Court, 139, 234, 236, 241n17
Cities, 107, 149–50, 249–50. *See also* Dublin, Ireland; Paris, France
Citizen, the, in "Cyclops," 130, 152n2, 152n8; with anti-Semitism, 94, 99–100, 143; with identity and space, 140–43; nationalism and, 39–42, 45n5, 145, 152n4; with space and culture, 144–45, 148–49; violence and, 86, 95, 147; with xenophobia, 5, 56, 84, 92–93
Citizens, Irish, 32, 116, 119n15, 163, 166; as British subject, 47, 48; with elections, 114; identity and, 94; rights for, 84–90, 96, 98
Citizenship, 5, 9, 10, 87, 96
"The City as Legal Concept" (Frug), 107
Civil Administrative Code, New York City, 249–50
Clark v. United States, 241n17
Cockburn, C. J., 241n16
Codes: intimacy with conversation in, 18–19, 25; law as social signs and, 1–2; New York City, Civil Administrative, 249–50
Coke, Edward, 125
Colles, Ramsay (Richard William), 163, 174n8; Gonne and, 162, 167; libel case and, 6, 159–61, 168–70, 172, 174n13
Collins, Michael, 89, 92, 98, 102
Colonialism, 125, 151; alcohol consumption and, 136–37, 140; as system, 136
Colonization: political recognition and, 94–98; with recognition decolonized, 98–104
Colum, Padraic, 160–61
Commercial law, 45n1
Common law, land and, 124, 125, 129
Community: identity and, 152n4; obscenity and, 235
Companies Act (1856), 32–33, 34
Company incorporation, laws for, 32–33, 34
Conley, Tim, 63–64

Connacht Tribune (newspaper), 180
Connolly, James, 119n13, 127
Contraception (Stopes), 231–33, 241n10, 241n17, 241n18, 255
Conversation, 17, 18–19, 25. *See also* Criminal conversation
Coombe, Rosemary, 198–99
Copyright, 262, 266; literary production and, 195; Spain with, 272n1
Copyright law, 273n8; criticism and, 8, 265–67; influence, 262–65; *James Joyce Archive* and, 273n5; Joyce Estate and, 262, 267–70; Random House and, 264, 268, 273n3; since 2012, 270–72
"Copyright Protectionism and Its Discontents" (Spoo), 264–65
The Copywrights: Intellectual Property and the Literary Imagination (Saint-Amour), 265, 266
Corporations, 108, 194. *See also* Dublin Corporation; Municipal corporations
Cosmic Consciousness (Bucke), 257
Cosmopolitan Style: Modernism Beyond the Nation (Walkowitz), 93–94
Cottier tenure, 124
"Counterparts" (Joyce, J.), 1, 136–38, 140
"Counterparts: *Dubliners*, Masculinity, and Temperance Nationalism" (Lloyd), 137
Creagh, John, 54–55
Criminal conversation (extramarital sexual congress): in context, 2–3, 15–17, 24; *Dubliners*, 21–24; *Exiles* and, 19–21; *Giacomo Joyce* and, 18–19; *Ulysses*, 24–29
Criminal Justice (Weis), 190n5
Crispi, Luca, 76
Criticism: copyright law and, 8, 265–67; trademark law with branding, modernism and, 193–96
Crofts, Maud I., 183, 191n9
Croke Park Massacre of 1920, 152n9
Cullen, L. M., 40–41
Cultural Capital (Guillory), 242n24

Culture, 145, 207n1, 208n7, 242n25; language and print, 84–88; public spaces with politics and, 135, 136, 140–45, 148–49; stereotype of Irish financial imprudence, 36, 45; of trademark with Joyce, J., 206–7
Cusack, Michael, 39
Cutting, Bronson, 250, 251
"Cyclops" (Joyce, J.), 1, 28, 72, 152n9; anti-Semitism in, 94, 99–100, 143; Citizen in, 5, 39–42, 45n5, 56, 84, 86, 92–95, 99–100, 130, 140–45, 147–49, 152n2, 152n4, 152n8; colonialism and alcohol consumption in, 136–37, 140; "J. J." as Cyclopean blind, 148–49, 152n8; with masculinity and alcohol, 143–44; with minority rights, 84–90; national identity and economy in, 39–40, 42; with recognition decolonized, 102–4; space in, 6, 136–38, 140–49
Czechoslovakia, 67, 73, 74

Dáil Éireann, 67, 69, 90
Daily Mail (newspaper), 55, 179, 182
Daily Sketch (newspaper), 179, 181
Daly, Mary E., 133n9
Darantiere, Maurice, 263
D'Arcy, Anne Marie, 118n1, 119n11
Davison, Neil R., 51, 86
Davitt, Michael, 52–53, 57, 126, 132
"The Dead" (Joyce, J.), 28, 126
Deaf-and-dumb language (sordomutics), 66, 77–78
Deane, Seamus, 34, 120n18
Deane, Vincent, 180, 190n8
The Decameron (Boccaccio), 237, 257
Decision. *See Ulysses* decision, Woolsey and
Dennett, Mary Ware, 224, 233–34, 241n17, 241n19
Deodand: defined, 7–8; *Ulysses* as, 248–49, 253–55
D'Esterre, John, 108–9
Dettmar, Kevin, 9

Devoy, John, 126
Dicey, A. V., 50
Digital Dubliners, 272
Digital editions: manuscripts, National Library of Ireland, 273n12; of *Ulysses*, 271–72
Digital publications, 262
Dirlik, Arif, 136
Discourse: law as source of parodic, 185–90; laws as, 1–2
Distinction: A Social Critique of the Judgement of Taste (Bourdieu), 236
Distinctiveness, trademark law with recognition and, 195
Divorce, 16–17, 24, 26–27, 29n1, 29n4
Dodd, William Huston, 167, 168
Donne, John, 230
Doyle, Bernard, 159
Dublin, Ireland: "nobody owns" in, 126–27; with Victoria, visit of, 6, 157–59, 162–65
Dublin Artisans' Dwellings Company, 43–44
Dublin Corporation, 70, 105–6, 118n1; municipal corporations and, 107–13; with tenants and landlords, 133n9
Dubliners (Joyce, J.): "After the Race," 31, 34–37, 45; "The Boarding House," 22, 28; "Counterparts," 1, 136–38, 140; "The Dead," 28, 126; Digital Dubliners, 272; editions of, 272; finance law in, 31, 36; "Ivy Day in the Committee Room," 106–7; "A Little Cloud," 21–22; with marriage, escape from, 21–24; "A Painful Case," 22–24; *Ulysses* and link to, 37
Dublin Gazette (newspaper), 175n34
Dublin's Joyce (Kenner), 126
Dunlop v. United States, 233, 241n17, 241n18
Dysart v. United States, 233, 241n18

Early Irish Laws and Institutions (MacNeill), 133n2
Earthquakes, 149–50, 152n10
Easter Rising (1916), 86, 102, 149

Index · 283

Ebury, Katherine, 10
Economy, 124; anti-Semitism and, 39–40, 42, 143; *Homo economicus*, 32, 37–45; taxes and, 42, 99
Editions, of *Dubliners*, 272
Editions, *Ulysses*: Digital, 271–72; Paris (1922), 221, 229, 247, 249, 270; Reader's Edition, 268–69
Edward VII (King), 115, 116
Egan, Annie, 171
Egan, Kevin, 128
Elections, 114, 115
Ellmann, Richard, 3, 190n8, 220
Emblems, corporate, 194
Enduring Passion (Stopes), 257
England, 150, 187, 188; Acts of Union, 157; Anglo-Irish Treaty, 67, 70, 98; anti-Semitism and, 53; with foreign investments, 33; landlords in, 122–23; Merchandise Marks Act, 194; morality influenced by, 100; national identity, 47–49; passports, 47–48; with property law in Ireland, 123–24, 129; Trade Marks Registration Act of 1875, 193–94. *See also* Finance law, British; Victoria
English language, 71
English Local Government Act (1888), 111
"The English Players Incident: What Really Happened" (Rushing), 3–4
Epstein, Edmund L., 191n17
Ernst, Morris: Tariff Act of 1930 and, 240n2, 250, 251, 253; with *Ulysses* as deodand, 254; *Ulysses* trial and, 221, 223; Woolsey, J. M., and, 231–32, 233, 235, 239, 241n13, 256, 258
Errors, typographical, 263
Escape, from marriage, 21–24, 28–29
Esperanto, 74–79, 80n10
Estate. *See* Joyce Estate, copyright law and
"Eumaeus" (Joyce, J.): economy in, 99; iconotypography and, 204; Italians in, 54; with land law, 128, 131; tenants in, 130, 131
Europe, national languages in, 67, 69–74

European Union, 58n2, 271
"Eveline" (Joyce, J.), 54, 58n3
Exiles (Joyce, J.), 19–21
Expiration, copyright, 262
Exports, 40, 42
Extramarital sexual congress. *See* Criminal conversation

Fabian Society, 119n9
Falkiner, Frederick, 163, 169
"Fallow," 175n34
"The Famine Queen" (Gonne), 6, 159, 160, 168. *See also* Libel case, media with
Fanon, Frantz, 97–98
Fenianism, 128, 132, 169
Ferrer, Daniel, 273n11
Feudalism, 128
Fiction, of trademark, 200–204, 207
Fiedler, Leslie, 243n28
Fielding, Henry, 237
Finance law, British, 4–5; *Dubliners* and, 31, 36; fraud and, 32–34; with *Homo economicus* for Ireland, 32, 37–45; Irish gambling and, 34–37; laissez-faire environment with, 32–34, 36–37; *Ulysses* and, 31
Financial being, body as, 34–35
Fink, Carole, 91
Finlason, W. F., 125, 127
Finnegans Wake (Joyce, J.), 1, 2, 30n5, 57, 191n17; Bywaters-Thompson case and, 7, 180–82, 190n5; Children's Tea and, 165–66; copyright law and, 267; Esperanto and, 78–79; in historical context, 108; iconotypography and, 204–5; language in, 63–64, 78–79; with law as source of parodic discourse, 185–90; legal inquiry and, 7, 182–85, 188–89; Maamtrasna murder trial and, 7, 183–84; national languages and neutral idioms in, 65–69; National Library of Ireland with, 273n11; note-taking for, 7, 179–84, 190n5; with Tristan and Isolde, triangle structure of, 181–82

284 · Index

The "Finnegans Wake" Notebooks at Buffalo (Joyce, J.), 68, 180. *See also* Notetaking, for *Finnegans Wake*
A First-Draft Version (Hayman), 79n1
Florilingua, 66, 77
Foley, John Henry, 163
Foreign investments, England with, 33
Forensic toxicology, 137
Forfeiture, law of: automobiles and, 248, 249–52; books and, 249–52; *in personam* and, 247, 250; *in rem* and, 247, 250, 251–52; suppression and, 7–8; with *Ulysses* as deodand, 253–55; with *Ulysses* readying to be sued, 252–53; with Woolsey, J. M., and sex instincts of average person, 255–59
Foster, R. F., 122, 123
Foucault, Michel, 30n5
France. *See* Paris, France
Fraud, 31–35, 38, 45n1
Freedom, 20, 130; with escape from marriage, 21–24, 28–29; with love and sex, 19–21, 29n4
Freeman's Journal, 17, 24, 52–53, 127, 158; libel case and, 169; on Victoria, visit of, 162
Friedman, Susan Stanford, 136
"Friends of the Emerald Island," 73
Frost, Robert, 230
Froula, Christine, 29n4
Frug, Gerald, 107, 108, 117–18
Furlong, Alice, 171

Gabler, Hans Walter, 240n3, 268, 271–72
Gaelic, 69–70, 75–76
Gaelic League, 69–70
Gale, Peter, 108, 109
Gambling, British finance law and Irish, 34–37
Gavelkind, 123
George, David Lloyd, 42
Germany, national language and, 74
Giacomo Joyce (Joyce, J.), 18–19
Gibson, Andrew, 30n7, 44, 63

Gifford, Don, 40, 114, 119n12, 202
"Gift from the Greeks" (Tenniel), 109–11, 110
Gillet, Louis, 47
Glass, Loren, 242n24
Glover, David, 50
Goldman, Jonathan, 208n13
Gombeen man, 129
Gonne, Maud: Colles on, 162, 167; libel case of, 6, 160–61, 167–70, 172, 174n13; Patriotic Children's Treat and, 162, 167, 169–71; on Taylor, 168, 175n30; with Victoria, denouncing of, 159
Government, 106–7, 111–12, 114–15, 118n1
Grady v. Grady, 26
Gray, Katharine, 163, 174n19
Grey, Edward, 39
Griffith, Arthur, 6, 42, 55, 161, 168, 174n13
Gris, Juan, 198, 208n9
Groden, Michael, 86, 271
Guide through "Finnegans Wake" (Epstein), 191n17
Guillory, John, 242n24
Gunther, Gerald, 236

"Hades" (Joyce, J.), 54, 122, 132–33
Hall, Radclyffe, 247, 257
Halsey v. New York Society for the Suppression of Vice, 241n17, 241n19
Hammer, Langdon, 243n27
Hand, Augustus, 224–25, 234, 235, 237
Hand, Learned, 7, 218, 220, 223–24, 234, 235; obscenity law and, 237; on Woolsey, J. M., 229, 236, 238
Handy, W. C., 208n10
Hardiman, Adrian, 8
Harvard Law Review, 198
Haslam, Richard, 111
Hayden, Henry, 198, 208n9
Hayman, David, 79n1
Heald, Paul J., 1
Heap, Jane, 213–14, 216, 217, 220, 229, 257
Hearst, W. R., 53

Hegel, Georg Wilhelm Friedrich, 97
Henry VIII (King of England), 150, 188
Heymoolen v. United States, 257–58
Highbrow/Lowbrow: The Emergence of Cultural Hierarchy in American (Levine), 242n25
The History of Law of Tenures of Land in England and Ireland (Finlason), 125
Holmes, Oliver Wendell, Jr., 253
Homer, 201, 217
"The Home Rule Comet" (Joyce, J.), 71
Homme moyen sensuel, 223, 235, 242n22, 243n28
Homo economicus, for Ireland, 32, 37–45
Howard, Roy, 253
Hughes, Ted, 273n4
Hyman, Louis, 51

Iconotypography, trademark law and, 204–6
Identity, 94, 99, 140–43, 152n4. *See also* National identity
Idioms, neutral: mixed and, 74–78; national languages and, 65–69
Immigration, 58n2; alien question with, 49–51; Ireland with anti-Semitism and, 51–56; Italians and, 54; Jews and, 51, 54–56; laws, 5, 48–53, 56–57; with nationality, fiction of, 56–58
Imperialism, 128
Incorporation, laws, 32–33, 34
Inebriates Act of 1898, 6, 137
Infinite Ulysses, 273n14
Inghínidhe na hÉireann, 169–72, 176n45
"The Inoperative Community" (Nancy), 152n4
In personam (against authors, publishers, or booksellers), 247, 250
Inquiry into the Ancient Corporate System of Ireland (Gale), 108
In rem (against books themselves), 247, 250, 251–52
In re Worthington Co., 237, 241n17, 241n19

Institutes of Justinian, 125
An International Language (Jespersen), 74, 77
International finance, Irish gambling and, 34–37
Intimacy, with conversation in code, 18–19, 25
Intoxicating Liquor Act of 1960, 139
Ireland: Anglo-Irish Treaty, 67, 70, 98; Dublin, 6, 126–27, 157–59, 162–65; exports and, 40; with financial imprudence stereotype, 36, 45; *Homo economicus* for, 32, 37–45; with immigration and anti-Semitism, 51–56; landlords in, 122–23; laws, 34–37, 47, 71, 109, 111–12, 114–15, 122–24, 128–29, 133n2, 150, 157; League of Nations and, 90–91, 99, 102; national identity, 39–40, 42, 47–48; nationalism, 84–88, 93–94, 118n2; national languages, 69–70; National Library of Ireland, 262, 272, 273n11, 273n12; passports, 47; role of, 108; Royal Irish Constabulary, 109. *See also* Citizens, Irish
Ireland Act (1949), 47
"Ireland at the Bar." *See* "L'Irlanda alla sbarra"
"Ireland, Island of Saints and Sages" (Joyce, J.), 56, 100, 157
Irish Citizen Army, 84
Irish Figaro (newspaper), 6, 159, 160, 168, 175n34
Irish Free State, 66–68
Irish Guards, 157–58
The Irish Landlord Since the Revolution (Lavelle), 124
Irish Republic, 86, 90–94
"The Irish Revolution of 1898" (Fabian Society), 119n9
Irish Times (newspaper), 58n3, 67–68, 74, 80n10, 158, 179–80
Irish Transvaal Committee, 161, 162
Irish Writing in the Twentieth Century (Pierce), 268

"L'Irlanda alla sbarra" ("Ireland at the Bar") (Joyce, J.), 71
Italian Università Popolare, 71
Italy, 54, 71, 74
"Ithaca" (Joyce, J.), 131
Itzkowitz, David, 33
"Ivy Day in the Committee Room" (Joyce, J.): municipal corporations and, 113–18; municipal self-government and, 106–7

Jaffe, Aaron, 207n1, 208n7
James I, 108
James Joyce (Ellmann), 3
James Joyce Archive, 271, 273n5
James Joyce Quarterly, 3–4, 196
James Merrill: Life and Art (Hammer), 243n27
Jespersen, Otto, 74, 77
Jews, 50–51, 54–56, 58n1. See also Anti-Semitism
"J. J.," as Cyclopean blind, 148–49, 152n8
Johns, Jasper, 197
Johnson, Edmond, 176n44
Jolas, Eugène, 76, 78, 122
Journal-American, 53
Journalism, with divorce and adultery, 29n4
Joyce, Giorgio (son), 29n2
Joyce, James, 29n2, 71; with culture of trademark, 206–7; on Marxist criticisms, 122; on nationality, 56; passport of, 47–48. See also specific topics
Joyce, Lucia (daughter), 29n2, 269
Joyce, Myles, 71, 183–84
Joyce, Nora Barnacle (wife), 29n2, 55, 190n8
Joyce, Stanislaus (brother), 190n8
Joyce, Stephen (grandson), 267–68, 269
"Joyce and the Law" (Spoo and Valente), 3–4
Joyce Annotated (Gifford), 114
Joyce Estate, copyright law and, 262, 267–70

JoyceWays, 272
Jurgen (Cabell), 220, 221
"Jury of matrons," 183, 191n9
Justice, freedom and, 130

Kafka, Franz, 1
Kaplan, Benjamin, 266
Keatinge, Patrick, 90
Kelly, Joseph, 3, 242n27
Kenner, Hugh, 117, 126
Kenny, Joseph Edward, 160
Kidd, John, 268
Killeen, Máire, 170–71, 175n37
Kingdom of Ireland Act (1542), 150
Kinship, culture and, 142
Klein, Naomi, 207
Konda v. United States, 241n17
"Kriegfried Ueberallgemein," 102
Krimstock, Valerie, 250, 254

Labour Electoral Association, 114, 115
Lady Chatterley's Lover (Lawrence, D. H.), 213–14
Laissez-faire environment, 32–34, 36–37, 39
Land, tanistry and, 122–23. See also Property law
Land Act (1881), 126
Landes, William M., 208n2
Land laws, 123, 131; colonialism and, 125; common and, 124, 125, 129; politics and, 125–26; property and, 126–28, 130. See also Property law
Land League, 124
Landlords: property law and interest of, 123–25; tenants and, 125–30, 133n9
Land ownership, 124, 126, 132
Land Purchase Act (1885), 126
Landry, Rodrigue, 80n5
Landuyt, Ingeborg, 79n1
Land War (1879–82), 126
Language, 5; on banknotes, 70, 71; barriers with publication, 263–64; deaf-and-dumb, 66, 77–78; Esperanto, 74–79,

80n10; in *Finnegans Wake*, 63–64, 78–79; florilingua, 66, 77; Gaelic, 69–70, 75–76; iconotypography and, 204–6; with Joyce, J., and culture of trademark, 206–7; laws, 1, 67, 71, 78–79; linguistic landscape, 69, 72, 80n5; monolingual paradigm and, 64, 67, 73, 78; Nabokov on, 214–15; nationality and, 73–74; with neutral and mixed idioms, 74–78; postal workers and, 66–68; print culture and, 84–88; of trademark law, 195–96; in *Ulysses*, 63, 85–86, 214–16, 221–22, 224–25. *See also* National languages

Language rights act, Czechoslovakia, 67
Larkin, James, 119n13
Latham, Sean, 3
Lavelle, Patrick, 124, 132
Lawrence, D. H., 213–14, 247
Laws, 3–4, 29n1, 45n1, 183, 191n9, 198; with alcohol in public spaces, 6, 136–40, 151; as discourse, social signs and codes, 1–2; immigration, 5, 48–53, 56–57; incorporation, 32–33, 34; Ireland, 34–37, 47, 50, 71, 109, 111–12, 114–15, 122–24, 128–29, 133n2, 157; language, 1, 67, 71, 78–79; Roman, 125, 185; as source of parodic discourse, 185–90. *See also* Copyright law; Finance law, British; Forfeiture, law of; Land laws; Obscenity law; Property law; Trademark law; *specific laws*
L.E.A., 115, 119n13
Leader (newspaper), 55, 179
League of Nations, 5, 74, 89, 90–91, 99, 102
Leckie, Barbara, 27, 29n4
Lee, J. J., 125
Lefebvre, Henri, 135, 136, 146, 148
Legal inquiry, *Finnegans Wake* and, 7, 182 85, 188–89
"Legal Joyce," 4
Legitimacy Act (1926), 29n2
Léon, Paul, 252

Leonard, Gary, 200
Leslie, Shane, 219
Levi, Neil, 85, 143
Levine, Lawrence, 242n25
Libel case, media with, 6, 160–61, 167–70, 172, 174n13
Librivox, 272, 273n16
Licensing, of brand names, 208n6
Licensing Act of 1902, 6, 137–39, 151
Licensing Order of 1643, 246–47
Limited Liability Act, 32, 33–34, 35
Lincoln, Abraham, 251
Lindey, Alexander, 253, 257
Linguistic landscape, 69, 72, 80n5
Literary modernism, 2, 264
Literary production, copyright and, 195
Literature, obscenity law and, 213–14, 229, 257. *See also Ulysses* trial
"A Little Cloud" (Joyce, J.), 21–22
Little Review (magazine): menstrual cycle and, 217; "Nausicaa" in, 214–15, 229; obscenity law and, 213–14, 229, 257. *See also Ulysses* trial
Littleton, Thomas de, 125
Lloyd, David, 136, 137, 140
Local Government (Ireland) Act, 111, 112, 114, 115
Lolita (Nabokov), 230
London Stock Exchange, 33, 34, 39
"Lotus Eaters" (Joyce, J.), 26, 77
Love, freedom in sex and, 19–21, 29n4
Lowe, John, 159
Lucia Joyce: To Dance at the Wake (Shloss), 269
Lyric FM, 267

Maamtrasna murder trial, 7, 183–84
Macaulay, Thomas Babington, 203
MacNeill, Eoin, 133n2
Madden, Benjamin, 243n27
Mahaffey, Vicki, 268, 271
Mallon, John, 170, 172
Manet, Edouard, 197–98
Market knowledge, financial being and, 35

Marriage, 2–3; divorce and, 16–17, 24, 26–27, 29n1, 29n4; escape from, 21–24, 28–29
Married Love (Stopes), 231, 233, 241n10, 255
Martin, Augustine, 222
Marx, Karl, 48, 147
Marxism, 122
Masculinity, alcohol and, 143–44
Materialist modernism, 8
Material Modernism (Bornstein), 264
Matrimonial Causes Act, 17, 24
Maxse, Leo, 52
McAlmon, Robert, 78
McCarthy, Mary, 230
McCarthy, Michael John Fitzgerald, 162–63
McCourt, John, 100
McCulloch, J. R., 32
McGann, Jerome, 268
McHugh, Roland, 184
Medalie, George Z., 252
Media: with libel case, 6, 160–61, 167–70, 172, 174n13; note-taking and, 179–82
Melchiori, Giorgio, 63
Melodrama, 24, 26
Men, 217; in criminal conversation cases, 16–17, 24; voices of women reported by, 19
Mendaciorum pater, 161, 174n12
Menstrual cycle, *Little Review* and, 217
Mental activity, of women, 19
Merchandise Marks Act (England), 194
Merrill, Charles E., Jr., 237–38
Merrill, James, 242n27
Mignolo, Walter D., 151
Milesi, Laurent, 63–64, 76
Mill, John Stuart, 124, 125
Miller, Arthur, 213
Milton, John, 246–47, 254, 258
Minority rights, 5; colonization and political recognition with, 94–98; decolonizing recognition and, 98–104; with global morality, 90–94; recognition of, 84–90
Mixed idioms, neutral and, 74–78
Modernism, 93–94, 118n1, 207n1, 208n13, 242n24, 243n27; literary, 2, 264; materialist, 8; trademark law with branding, criticism and, 193–96
Modernism and the Culture of Celebrity (Jaffe), 207n1
Modernism Is the Literature of Celebrity (Goldman), 208n13
Modernism/modernity (Madden), 243n27
Modernity, 135–36, 151
Monolingual paradigm, 64, 67, 73, 78
Montgomery, Robert, 159
Moore, George, 58n3
Morality, 90–94, 100
Moran, D. P., 55
Moretti, Franco, 204
The Most Dangerous Book (Birmingham), 228, 243n27
Mr. Brainwash, 197
"Mr Joyce Directs an Irish Word Ballet" (McAlmon), 78
"Multiphoniaksically spuking," 66, 77–79
Municipal Corporation Reform (Ireland) Act, 109, 114
Municipal corporations: history of, 107–13; "Ivy Day in the Committee Room" and, 113–18; laws for Irish, 109, 111–12; role of, 107
Municipal Yearbook and Public Services Directory, 112
Murphy, William, 220

Nabokov, Vladimir, 214–15, 230
Nancy, Jean-Luc, 152n4
Nash, John, 66, 79n3
National Archives Northeast Region, 252
National identity, 85; in context, 5, 47–49; Ireland and, 39–40, 42, 47–48
National Insurance Act (1911), 42
Nationalism, 137; Irish, 84–88, 93–94, 118n2; Patriotic Children's Treat and,

166–67; in *Ulysses*, 39–42, 45n5, 128–30, 132, 145, 152n4
Nationality: immigration with fiction of, 56–58; Joyce, J., on, 56; language and, 73–74; with residence, legal right of, 48, 49
National languages: in Europe, 67, 69–74; with neutral idioms in *Finnegans Wake*, 65–69
National Library of Ireland, 262, 272, 273n11, 273n12
National Women's Memorial, 173n2
Naturalization, process of, 48
"Nausicaa" (Joyce, J.), 214–16, 221–22, 229
New York City, Civil Administrative Code, 249–50
New York Society for the Suppression of Vice, 214, 241n17, 241n19
"Nobody owns": in Dublin, Ireland, 126–27; in "Hades," 132–33. *See also* Property law
Noel, Thomas, 122
Nolan, Emer, 45n5, 85–86
Note-taking, for *Finnegans Wake*: Bywaters-Thompson case and, 7, 180–82, 190n5; Maamtrasna murder trial and, 7, 183–84; media sources and, 179–82

Oath of Supremacy, 108
O'Brien, Joseph V., 43–44, 112, 119n14, 120n19
Obscenity, 3, 242n24; cases, 231–33, 237, 241n10, 256; community and, 235; Tariff Act of 1930, 229, 240n2, 248, 250, 251, 253, 255
Obscenity law: books and, 228, 230, 233, 241n10, 241n18, 249; literature and, 213–14, 229, 257; with publishers, books and authors, 247; *Regina v. Hicklin*, 216–18, 222–23, 231, 237, 241n16, 256; sex instruction and, 224, 234. *See also Ulysses* decision, Woolsey and; *Ulysses* trial
O'Connell, Daniel, 108–9, 124

O'Curry, Eugene, 123
O'Donovan, John, 123
Ó Gráda, Cormac, 51, 57
O'Hanlon, John, 190
O'Leary, John, 169
O'Leary-Curtis, May, 171
Original Memphis Five, 208n10
Osteen, Mark, 41, 43, 45n3, 200
Ottoman Empire, 38, 73
Overcrowding, 127
Ownership. *See* Land ownership; "Nobody owns"
"Oxen of the Sun" (Joyce, J.), 49, 128; branding and, 201, 204; copyright law and, 267
Oxford English Dictionary, 232, 233

"A Painful Case" (Joyce, J.), 22–24
Paris, France: peace treaties, 72, 73, 79, 86, 90, 102; with *Ulysses* publication (1922), 221, 229, 247, 249, 270
Parnell, Charles Stewart, 29n4, 40, 113, 118, 126
Parnell, Katharine O'Shea, 29n4
Passports, 47–48
Patriotic Children's Treat (1900): Gonne and, 162, 167, 169–71; nationalism and, 166–67; as political demonstration, 167, 169–70; Rooney, W., and, 167, 170, 175n37
"The Pauper's Drive" (Noel), 122
Pearse, Pádraig, 175n30
Penal Laws, land ownership and, 124
People v. Wendling, 233, 241n18
"The Perils of Literary Celebrity: The Archive Stories of Ted Hughes and Sylvia Plath" (Chen), 273n4
Picasso, Pablo, 198, 208n8
Il Piccolo della Sera (newspaper), 71, 183
Pierce, David, 268
Pile, Maud, 163
Piracy, 4, 262–63, 264
Plan of Campaign (1885), 126
Plato, 214, 217, 225

Poetry, *Ulysses* decision and, 236–40
Poetry Genius, 272
Poland, 55, 68, 73
Politics, 112, 124; city with space and, 149–50; with colonization and recognition, 94–98; land law and, 125–26; with Patriotic Children's Treat as demonstration, 167, 169–70; public spaces with culture and, 135, 136, 140–45, 148–49; with space, organization of, 140–46, 149
A Portrait of the Artist as a Young Man (Joyce, J.), 272
Posner, Richard, 15, 208n2
Postal service, of Irish Free State, 66–68
Potter, Matthew, 109, 111, 119n7
Pound, Ezra, 195, 214, 215, 217, 265
Power, Arthur, 180, 205
Prestige, *Ulysses* decision and, 236–40
Principles of Political Economy (Mill), 124
Print: culture and language, 84–88; with language on banknotes, 70, 71
"Privacy and Piracy in the Joyce Trade: James Joyce and *le droit moral*" (Shloss), 4
"Privacy and the Misuse of Copyright" (Shloss), 269
Private life, 15, 17, 28
The Production of Space (Lefebvre), 135, 136, 146
Prohibition, 252
Property law: Brehon and, 122–23, 128; Ireland with English, 123–24, 129; land and, 126–28, 130; landlord interest and, 123–25; nationalism and, 128; politics and, 125–26
Protestant Church, 109, 124, 126
Publication: digital, 262; language barriers with, 263–64; of *Little Review* with menstrual cycle, 217; of *Ulysses*, 217, 220–21, 229, 240n3, 247, 249, 259n2, 263–65, 270. *See also* Copyright
Public health, overcrowding and, 127
Public life, private and, 15

Public space: forces producing, 147–48; laws governing alcohol in, 6, 136–40, 151; modernity and, 135–36; politics and culture with, 135, 136, 140–45, 148–49. *See also* Pubs
Public Works: Infrastructure, Irish Modernism, and the Postcolonial (Rubenstein), 118n1
Publishers, 247, 250. *See also* Random House
Pubs: alcohol laws restricting clustering of, 6, 136, 138–40; as cultural and political institutions, 136, 140; political organization of space, 140–46; as urban space, 146–47
Pulbrook, Anthony, 34, 36
Punch (magazine), 109, 110

Quinn, John: with *Ulysses* trial, 7, 215, 217–22; *United States v. Kennerley* and, 220
Quinn, Máire, 175n38
Quinn, Margaret, 175n38

Rabelais, François, 237, 257
Race, national identity and, 49. *See also* Minority rights
Racism, 103. *See also* Anti-Semitism
The Rainbow (Lawrence), 247
Random House, 229, 235, 237; Cerf at, 221, 241n13, 247–49, 257, 259, 259n2; copyright law and, 264, 268, 273n3; with *Ulysses*, readying to be sued, 253; Woolsey, J. M., and, 249. *See also* Ernst, Morris
Reader's Edition, 268–69
Reader's Guide to "Finnegans Wake" (Tindall), 187
"Reasonable man," 216, 223, 235, 242n23
Recognition: colonization and political, 94–98; decolonizing, 98–104; minority rights and, 84–90; trademark law with distinctiveness and, 195; trademark law with repetition and, 198–200

"Redeeming Value: Obscenity and Anglo-American Modernism" (Glass), 242n24
Redmond, John, 119n8
Reform, municipal corporations, 109, 114
Regina v. Hicklin, 216–18, 222–23, 231, 237, 241n16, 256
Reichman, Ravit, 2, 15
Reid, B. L., 220
Repetition, trademark law with, 198–200
Residence, legal right of, 48, 49
Resistance, to marital and sexual norms, 21
Resources, control over scarce, 142
"Rethinking Colonialism: Globalization, Postcolonialism, and the Nation" (Dirlik), 136
Rice, Elmer, 229–30
Rights: for Irish citizens, 84–90, 96, 98; language, 67; municipal corporations as threat to, 107. *See also* Minority rights
Roberts, Frederick Sleigh, 158, 160, 172, 173n1
Robinson, Henry Morton, 186, 187
Rocco, John, 196
Roman Catholic Church, 108–9
Roman law, 125, 185
Rooney, Judith, 171
Rooney, William, 167, 170, 175n37
Rose, Danis, 190, 268–69
Rose, Mark, 266
Rosenbach Manuscript, 268–69, 273n10
Rosen v. United States, 241n17
Rosiers, Erika, 63, 64, 76, 80n11
Roth, Samuel, 194, 247, 252, 255, 262–64
Roth v. United States, 225
Royal Commission, on anti-Semitism, 50
Royal Irish Constabulary, 109
Rubenstein, Michael, 118n1, 119n15
Rushing, Conrad, 3–4
Russell v. Russell, 29n4
Ryan, Frederick, 55–56

"Sacred Emily" (Stein), 206
Saint-Amour, Paul K., 3, 195, 265–67
Sanitation, with overcrowding, 127
Saturday Review of Literature, 229, 237–38
Savage, Gail, 29n4
Savige, Jaya, 10, 41
Schechter, F. W., 198
Scholarship, future, 10
Scotland, 132
"Scylla and Charybdis" (Joyce, J.), 172, 204
Seagle, William, 232
Self-government, 106–7
Senn, Fritz, 6
Sex: autonomy, 19–21, 29n4; desire and conversation, 18–19, 25; instincts of average person, 223, 233, 235, 242n22, 243n28, 255–59; instruction and obscenity law, 224, 234; norms, resistance to, 21. *See also* Criminal conversation; Obscenity
The Sex Side of Life (pamphlet), 234
Shadow text, 181–82
Shakespeare, William, 237, 242n25
Sherlock, Lorcan, 127
Shloss, Carol, 4, 269–70
"Shule Aroon" ("Siúil a Rún"), 76
Sinn Fein, 39, 41, 42
"Siren" (Joyce, J.), 130, 204
"Siúil a Rún" ("Shule Aroon"), 76
Slote, Sam, 76, 263, 273n11
Slovakia, 73–74
Smyly, Ellen, 164
Social signs, law as codes and, 1–2
Society for the Preservation of the Irish Language, 69
Society of Authors, 268
Soja, Edward, 135, 136, 141–42, 144, 152n3
Sonny Bono Copyright Term Extension Act, 270, 273n8
Sophocles, 217
Sordomutics. *See* Deaf-and-dumb language
Sotomayor, Sonia, 250
Souperism, 163, 165, 166

Space, 135, 136; city as political, 149–50; in "Cyclops," 6, 136–38, 140–49; political organization of, 140–46; urban, 146–47. *See also* Public space
Spain, 272n1
Spoo, Robert, 3–4, 194–95, 262–65, 273n3; copyright law and, 269–70; on *James Joyce Archive*, 273n5; on Joyce Estate, 267–68
Stamp collecting, 68
Statutes of Kilkenny, 69
Stein, Gertrude, 206
Stereotype, of Irish financial imprudence, 36, 45
St. Hubert Guild v. Quinn, 237, 241n17, 241n19, 242n20
Still Life with Bottle of Bass (Braque), 208n9
Still-Life With a Guitar, Bottle of Bass and Fruit (Hayden), 208n9
Stopes, Marie Carmichael, 231–33, 241n10, 241n17, 241n18, 255, 257
"Stream of consciousness," 224
Streit, Wolfgang, 30n5
Style, 93–94, 208n13; literature and, 214–16, 221–22, 224–25
Sumner, John, 214
Suppression, 159, 160; of books, 246–48; with forfeiture, law of, 7–8. *See also* Libel case, media with; Obscenity law
Swain, Joseph, *110*
Swearingen v. United States, 233, 241n18
Swift, Jonathan, 125
Swifte, Ernest Godwin, 167, 168, 169
"The Synchrony and Diachrony of Texts" (Gabler), 271
System, colonialism as, 136

Tanistry, 122–23
Tariff Act of 1930, obscenity and, 229, 240n2, 248, 250, 251, 253, 255
Tariff Act of 1922, 257
Taxes, 42, 99
Taylor, John F., 167–68, 169, 175n30

Tenants: in "Eumaeus," 130, 131; landlords and, 125–30, 133n9
Tenniel, John, 109–11, *110*
Thomas, Silken, 149, 150–51
Thompson, Edith, 7, 180–82, 190n5
Thompson, Percy, 180
Thom's Directory, 174n19
Thoughts, of women, 19
Times (newspaper), 158
Tindall, William York, 187
Tort action, 3, 16–17
To the Pure . . . A Study of Obscenity and the Censor (Ernst and Seagle), 232
Trademark law: authorial branding and, 7, 195, 200–204; Bass and, 193–94, 196–99, 207, 208n5, 208n8, 208n13; with branding, modernism and criticism, 193–96; fiction of, 200–204, 207; iconotypography and, 204–6; Joyce, J., and culture of, 206–7; language of, 195–96; *Ulysses* and, 196, 197, 200–204
Trade Marks Registration Act of 1875, 193–94
transition (magazine), 76
Travers, Pauric, 117
Treaties, 67, 70, 72, 91, 98. *See also* Paris, France
Trials. *See Ulysses* trial
Triangle: Bass, 194, 196–99, 201–3; Tristan and Isolde, structure of, 181–82
Tribunals, 188
Tristan and Isolde, 181–82
"True bill," 183, 191n9
Two Worlds Monthly (magazine), 247, 262, 264
Typography, 204–6, 263

Ulysses (Joyce, J.): adultery in, 26–27; "Aeolus," 72, 204; anti-Semitism in, 51–52, 54, 86–87, 94, 99–100, 143; Bass in, 194, 197, 201–3; "Calypso," 26–27, 38–39; "Circe," 1, 24–26, 42–43, 50, 74–75, 130, 158–59, 162–64, 171–72; copyright expiration, 262; criminal conversation and, 24–29; as deodand, 248–49, 253–55; *Dubliners* and link to, 37; editions, 221, 268–72, 279; "Eumaeus," 54, 99, 128, 130, 131, 204; finance law in, 31; "Hades," 54, 122, 132–33; Italians in, 54; "Ithaca," 131; with justice, 130; language in, 63, 85–86, 214–16, 221–22, 224–25; "Lotus Eaters," 26, 77; nationalism in, 39–42, 45n5, 128–30, 132, 145, 152n4; "Nausicaa," 214–16, 221–22, 229; obscenity and, 3; "Oxen of the Sun," 49, 128, 201, 204, 267; publication of, 217, 220–21, 229, 240n3, 247, 249, 259n2, 263–65, 270; "Scylla and Charybdis," 172, 204; sexual desire in, 25; "Sirens," 130, 204; sued, readying to be, 252–53; suppression of, 247–48; trademark law and, 196, 197, 200–204; voices of women reported by men in, 19; "Wandering Rocks," 128–29. *See also* "Cyclops"

Ulysses decision, Woolsey and, 7, 240n3, 249; argument for, 232–35; legacy of, 229–30, 240n7, 257, 260n22; with obscenity cases, other, 231–33, 241n10, 256; poetry and prestige with, 236–40; with research, 228–29

Ulysses Seen, 273n14

Ulysses trial: Anderson, M., and, 213–14, 216, 217, 220, 229, 257; forfeiture law and, 252–55; Hand, A., and, 224–25; Heap and, 213–14, 216, 217, 220, 229, 257; literature with stylistic innovation and, 214–16, 221–22, 224–25; Quinn and, 7, 215, 217–22; with sex instincts of average person, 223, 233, 235, 242n22, 243n28, 255–59; Woolsey and, 7, 221–23; Yeats, J. B., and, 218–19, 222. *See also* Forfeiture, law of

An Unhurried View of Copyright (Kaplan), 266

The Union, 123–25, 157

Union with Ireland Act of 1800. *See* Acts of Union

United Irishman (newspaper), 55–56, 170; on Children's Day, 165; Inghínidhe na hÉireann in, 171; with libel case, 6, 160; suppression of, 159, 160; on Victoria, visit of, 159, 162

United Kingdom Patent Office, 194

United States, 225, 233, 241n17, 241n18, 257–58

United States of America v. One Book Called "Ulysses," 228, 230, 233, 249. *See also Ulysses* decision, Woolsey and

United States v. Approximately 126 Assorted Glasses, 252

United States v. Bennett, 223–24

United States v. Dennett, 224, 233–34, 241n17, 241n19

United States v. Kennerley, 220, 223, 234–35, 242n19

United States v. One Book Entitled "Contraception," 241n10, 241n18

United States v. One Cash Register, 252

United States v. One Ford Truck, 252

United States v. One Obscene Book Entitled "Married Love," 241n10

Urban space, 146–47

Uruguay Round Agreements Act, 270

Valente, Joseph, 3–4

Vanderham, Paul, 3, 238, 243n28

van Hulle, Dirk, 76

Van Mierlo, Wim, 63, 64, 76, 80n11

"'Vartryville': Dublin's Water Supply and Joyce's Sublation of Local Government" (D'Arcy), 118n1

Victoria (Queen of England): criticism of, 6, 159, 160, 168; with Dublin visit, 6, 157–59, 162–65; libel case and, 162, 167–68

Violence, 86, 95, 147

Virag, Rudolf, 48

Vivès, Juan Luis, 174n12

Voices, of women, 19–21

Voltaire, 237

Voting, women and, 119n10

Wale, Blanch, 164
Wales, Katie, 63
Walkowitz, Rebecca, 93–94, 98
Walpole Society, 231, 241n8
"Wandering Rocks" (Joyce, J.), 128–29
Warhol, Andy, 197
War of Independence, 149
Webb, Beatrice, 50
Weinreich, Max, 79
Weis, René, 190n5
The Well of Loneliness (Hall), 247, 257
Wendling. *See People v. Wendling*
West, Mae, 208n8
Whately, Elizabeth, 164
White, Arnold, 52
White, Sarah, 171
Wilde, Oscar, 219
Wilhelmina of the Netherlands, 175n25
Wilson, Woodrow, 90
Without Copyrights: Piracy, Publishing, and the Public Domain (Spoo), 263
Witness testimony, note-taking and, 180
Wollaeger, Mark, 9
Women, 25–26, 119n10, 173n2, 217; "jury of matrons," 183, 191n9; with marriage and tort action, 16–17; voices of, 19–21
Women under English Law (Crofts), 183, 191n9
Woolsey, John III, 228, 240
Woolsey, John Munro, 4; criticism of, 229, 236, 238; education, 230–31; legacy, 229–30, 240n7, 257, 260n22; Random House and, 249; with sex instincts of average person, 255–59; *Ulysses* trial and, 7, 221–23. *See also Ulysses* decision, Woolsey and
Wylie, J. C., 123
Wyse-Power, Jenni, 171

Xenophobia, 5, 56, 84, 92–93

Yeats, John Butler, 218–19, 222
Yeats, William Butler, 161, 171, 218
Yildiz, Yasemin, 64
Young, Filson, 181

Zamenhof, L. L., 74

The Florida James Joyce Series
EDITED BY SEBASTIAN D. G. KNOWLES

The Autobiographical Novel of Co-Consciousness: Goncharov, Woolf, and Joyce, by Galya Diment (1994)
Bloom's Old Sweet Song: Essays on Joyce and Music, by Zack Bowen (1995)
Joyce's Iritis and the Irritated Text: The Dis-lexic "Ulysses," by Roy Gottfried (1995)
Joyce, Milton, and the Theory of Influence, by Patrick Colm Hogan (1995)
Reauthorizing Joyce, by Vicki Mahaffey (paperback edition, 1995)
Shaw and Joyce: "The Last Word in Stolentelling," by Martha Fodaski Black (1995)
Bely, Joyce, and Döblin: Peripatetics in the City Novel, by Peter I. Barta (1996)
Jocoserious Joyce: The Fate of Folly in "Ulysses," by Robert H. Bell (paperback edition, 1996)
Joyce and Popular Culture, edited by R. B. Kershner (1996)
Joyce and the Jews: Culture and Texts, by Ira B. Nadel (paperback edition, 1996)
Narrative Design in "Finnegans Wake": The Wake Lock Picked, by Harry Burrell (1996)
Gender in Joyce, edited by Jolanta W. Wawrzycka and Marlena G. Corcoran (1997)
Latin and Roman Culture in Joyce, by R. J. Schork (1997)
Reading Joyce Politically, by Trevor L. Williams (1997)
Advertising and Commodity Culture in Joyce, by Garry Leonard (1998)
Greek and Hellenic Culture in Joyce, by R. J. Schork (1998)
Joyce, Joyceans, and the Rhetoric of Citation, by Eloise Knowlton (1998)
Joyce's Music and Noise: Theme and Variation in His Writings, by Jack W. Weaver (1998)
Reading Derrida Reading Joyce, by Alan Roughley (1999)
Joyce through the Ages: A Nonlinear View, edited by Michael Patrick Gillespie (1999)
Chaos Theory and James Joyce's Everyman, by Peter Francis Mackey (1999)
Joyce's Comic Portrait, by Roy Gottfried (2000)
Joyce and Hagiography: Saints Above!, by R. J. Schork (2000)
Voices and Values in Joyce's "Ulysses," by Weldon Thornton (2000)
The Dublin Helix: The Life of Language in Joyce's "Ulysses," by Sebastian D. G. Knowles (2001)
Joyce Beyond Marx: History and Desire in "Ulysses" and "Finnegans Wake," by Patrick McGee (2001)
Joyce's Metamorphosis, by Stanley Sultan (2001)
Joycean Temporalities: Debts, Promises, and Countersignatures, by Tony Thwaites (2001)
Joyce and the Victorians, by Tracey Teets Schwarze (2002)
Joyce's "Ulysses" as National Epic: Epic Mimesis and the Political History of the Nation State, by Andras Ungar (2002)
James Joyce's "Fraudstuff," by Kimberly J. Devlin (2002)
Rite of Passage in the Narratives of Dante and Joyce, by Jennifer Margaret Fraser (2002)
Joyce and the Scene of Modernity, by David Spurr (2002)
Joyce and the Early Freudians: A Synchronic Dialogue of Texts, by Jean Kimball (2003)
Twenty-First Joyce, edited by Ellen Carol Jones and Morris Beja (2004)
Joyce on the Threshold, edited by Anne Fogarty and Timothy Martin (2005)

Wake Rites: The Ancient Irish Rituals of "Finnegans Wake," by George Cinclair Gibson (2005)

"Ulysses" in Critical Perspective, edited by Michael Patrick Gillespie and A. Nicholas Fargnoli (2006)

Joyce and the Narrative Structure of Incest, by Jen Shelton (2006)

Joyce, Ireland, Britain, edited by Andrew Gibson and Len Platt (2006)

Joyce in Trieste: An Album of Risky Readings, edited by Sebastian D. G. Knowles, Geert Lernout, and John McCourt (2007)

Joyce's Rare View: The Nature of Things in "Finnegans Wake," by Richard Beckman (2007)

Joyce's Misbelief, by Roy Gottfried (2008)

James Joyce's Painful Case, by Cóilín Owens (2008; first paperback edition, 2017)

Cannibal Joyce, by Thomas Jackson Rice (2008)

Manuscript Genetics, Joyce's Know-How, Beckett's Nohow, by Dirk Van Hulle (2008)

Catholic Nostalgia in Joyce and Company, by Mary Lowe-Evans (2008)

A Guide through "Finnegans Wake," by Edmund Lloyd Epstein (2009)

Bloomsday 100: Essays on "Ulysses," edited by Morris Beja and Anne Fogarty (2009)

Joyce, Medicine, and Modernity, by Vike Martina Plock (2010; first paperback edition, 2012)

Who's Afraid of James Joyce?, by Karen R. Lawrence (2010; first paperback edition, 2012)

"Ulysses" in Focus: Genetic, Textual, and Personal Views, by Michael Groden (2010; first paperback edition, 2012)

Foundational Essays in James Joyce Studies, edited by Michael Patrick Gillespie (2011; first paperback edition, 2017)

Empire and Pilgrimage in Conrad and Joyce, by Agata Szczeszak-Brewer (2011; first paperback edition, 2017)

The Poetry of James Joyce Reconsidered, edited by Marc C. Conner (2012; first paperback edition, 2015)

The German Joyce, by Robert K. Weninger (2012; first paperback edition, 2016)

Joyce and Militarism, by Greg Winston (2012; first paperback edition, 2015)

Renascent Joyce, edited by Daniel Ferrer, Sam Slote, and André Topia (2013; first paperback edition, 2014)

Before Daybreak: "After the Race" and the Origins of Joyce's Art, by Cóilín Owens (2013; first paperback edition, 2015)

Modernists at Odds: Reconsidering Joyce and Lawrence, edited by Matthew J. Kochis and Heather L. Lusty (2015)

James Joyce and the Exilic Imagination, by Michael Patrick Gillespie (2015)

The Ecology of "Finnegans Wake," by Alison Lacivita (2015)

Joyce's Allmaziful Plurabilities: Polyvocal Explorations of "Finnegans Wake," edited by Kimberly J. Devlin and Christine Smedley (2015; first paperback edition, 2018)

Exiles: A Critical Edition, by James Joyce, edited by A. Nicholas Fargnoli and Michael Patrick Gillespie (2016; first paperback edition, 2019)

Up to Maughty London: Joyce's Cultural Capital in the Imperial Metropolis, by Eleni Loukopoulou (2017)

Joyce and the Law, edited by Jonathan Goldman (2017; first paperback edition, 2020)
At Fault: Joyce and the Crisis of the Modern University, by Sebastian D. G. Knowles (2018)
"Ulysses" Unbound: A Reader's Companion to James Joyce's "Ulysses," Third Edition, by Terence Killeen (2018)
Joyce and Geometry, by Ciaran McMorran (2020)
Panepiphanal World: James Joyce's Epiphanies, by Sangam MacDuff (2020)
Language as Prayer in "Finnegans Wake," by Colleen Jaurretche (2020)